Girls Gone Skank

Girls Gone Skank

The Sexualization of Girls in American Culture

PATRICE A. OPPLIGER

McFarland & Company, Inc., Publishers

Jefferson, North Carolina, and London

A note to the reader: the content in this book often deals with adult themes. I chose not to censor the language in order to give a true portrayal of the tone of the material.

Because of copyright laws, song lyrics are paraphrased, purely to indicate content. Exact lyrics can be found at various websites such as Lyrics on Demand (http://www.lyricsondemand.com) and Lyric Planet (http://www.lyricsplanet.com).

LIBRARY OF CONGRESS CATALOGUING-IN-PUBLICATION DATA

Oppliger, Patrice A.
    Girls gone skank : the sexualization of girls in American culture / Patrice A. Oppliger.
        p.   cm.
    Includes bibliographical references and index.

    ISBN 978-0-7864-3522-7
    softcover : 50# alkaline paper ∞

    1. Young women—United States.   2. Teenage girls—United States.   3. Girls—United States.   4. Mass media and girls. 5. Girls in popular culture.   6. Self-esteem in adolescence. 7. Self-perception in adolescence.   8. Exploitation.   I. Title.
HQ1229.O77   2008
306.4'613—dc22   2008005359

British Library cataloguing data are available

Cover photograph ©2008 Shutterstock

Manufactured in the United States of America

McFarland & Company, Inc., Publishers
  Box 611, Jefferson, North Carolina 28640
  www.mcfarlandpub.com

To my friends and family, and
to the Candy in all of us

ACKNOWLEDGMENTS

Thanks first of all to my parents, Walter and Grace, for giving me a fantastic childhood and instilling in me confidence that has allowed me to take risks and try new things.

Thanks to my siblings, Lee Ann Zach, Gail Holcomb, and Brian Oppliger, who have had a significant role in who I am through their loving and teasing. Thanks to my in-laws, Al, Gregg, and Julie, to my nieces Sarah, Alison, Hannah, and Jill and to my nephews John and Lyle for their love and support.

Thanks to my readers, Shirley Viera, Kevin Dolan, Becca Bennett, and Joe Finnerty, for their insightful feedback on earlier drafts of the book. Thanks to my graduate assistant Jenna Baran for her creative input and creating the index. Thanks to Jim Zazzera for challenging me to write this book when he accused me of being out-skanked by a 10-year-old.

Thanks to Sean Worthington and "Chuckie" for helping me with my field research at gentlemen's clubs. Thanks to the rest of the regulars at McMenamins in Mt. Airy, PA, for their opinions and contributions: Dan, Craig, Heather, Anna, Tom, Scott, Aaron, Mike, P. J., Greg, and Paul. Thanks to the students at La Salle University and Boston University for their input in the book.

Thanks to Sandy Bernt, John Sherblom, Dolf Zillmann, and Jennings Bryant, who have taught me great lessons and nurtured my academic side.

Thanks to my close friends for their support over the years: Becka Smillie, Cyndie King, Greg Pospisil, and Ernie and Joan Spence.

And finally thanks to Candy. For those of you who have not had the pleasure of meeting Candy, she is that fun, carefree side in all of us.

Contents

INTRODUCTION

I believe in putting a woman up on a pedestal ... so that you can look up her dress.

—Steve Martin

A few years ago, I saw a girl who looked to be about 9 years old in a restaurant with her parents. She was dressed in a designer sweat suit with the word "Juicy" printed across her rear end. (I didn't realize until much later that that is the brand name.) A couple days later, I drove past a Hooters Restaurant, which is known for its raunchily dressed waitresses and references to women's breasts. The sign outside promoted their "kids eat free night." I consider myself a pretty open-minded person; however, these trends, along with dozens of others I have observed, strike me as being over the top. As a researcher of popular culture, I have become increasingly disturbed at this sort of sexual climate, especially when it involves young girls. Although it was sad, I was not completely shocked when I later heard a news story about a fifteen-year-old girl who was caught by school officials giving oral sex to five hockey players in the boys' locker room at a prestigious Boston prep school.

We live in a culture where mainstream media and retail marketers sexualize girls at younger and younger ages. I have interviewed many high school and middle school teachers in the past few years and found that almost all of them are horrified at the sexual prowess of their female students. A walk through the toy aisle is like a walk through a "grown-up" world filled with makeup kits, play high heel shoes, and make-your-own nail polish kits. Clothing departments are stocked with tiny tank tops printed with such expressions as "Hottie," "Porn Star," "Wet," "Princess," "Party Girl," and "No Angel." The well known clothing manufacturer Abercrombie & Fitch produced a line of thong underwear with expressions such as "Eye Candy" and "Wink Wink." The thongs fit girls as young as seven ("Abercrombie's Sexy Undies," 2002).

The American Psychological Association (APA) released a report detailing the harmful effects of the abundance of sexualized images of girls and young women in advertising, merchandising, and media on girls' self-image and healthy development. The APA task force defined sexualization as occurring when "a person's value comes only from her/his sexual appeal or behav-

1

ior, to the exclusion of other characteristics, and when a person is sexually objectified, e.g., made into a thing for another's sexual use" ("Sexualization of Girls," 2007). Zurbriggen (cited in "Sexualization of Girls," 2007) argued that sexualization has negative effects on girls' cognitive functioning, physical and mental health, and healthy sexual development. In terms of cognitive functioning, sexual objectification can lead to shame and anxiety on the part of girls about their bodies. Research has linked eating disorders and depression to sexualization as well. Another negative effect is on girls' ability to develop healthy sexual self-images. Therefore, girls may be more likely to engage in risky behaviors in order to please males. The study covered different forms of media, including television, music videos, music lyrics, magazines, movies, video games and the Internet. The research also included analysis of advertising campaigns and merchandising of products aimed toward girls. The report acknowledged that parents and peers play some role in influencing whether or not girls adopt these sexual models; however, evidence was strong regarding the influence of media representations.

Instead of advancing women's power, popular culture trends in the United States appear to be backsliding into sexual exploitation of women. In writing this book, I examined and discussed the effects of current trends. My goal was to investigate the effects of mass marketed images of popular culture trends on the behaviors and attitudes of young girls. I also explored other cultural and parental factors that contribute to these trends. The following chapters cover the origins, causes, and consequences of current sexual representations of women and girls in American popular culture.

Trends

Media coverage of the murder of six-year-old JonBenet Ramsey in 1996 shed light on the child beauty pageant circuit. Fair or not, it heated up a debate about exploitation of little girls in pageants. In many pageants, little girls are dressed as adult women, complete with heavy makeup, teased hair, and fake tans. The term "prostitot" was coined to describe a popular style of dress combining "prostitute" and "tot." In addition to little girls' physical appearance, pageant coaches are hired to teach the little girls how to flirt with judges and strike seductive poses. Little girls paraded about in pageants quickly learn their worth in society. A significant number of parents are obsessed with making their children into stars. One of the most outrageous strategies is signing their young daughters up for child modeling websites. The sites promise parents that posting provocative photographs of their daughters on the Internet will jump-start the little girls' modeling careers. Instead, the sites are often displays available to pedophiles to view girls as young as six years old in bathing suits and skimpy outfits in provocative poses (e.g., arched backs and spread legs).

By the time little girls hit puberty, they are ready to put their training as pseudo adults into action. Following in the footsteps of Hollywood celebrities gone wild, young girls are engaging in more and more outrageous behavior for attention. Survey research shows an increase in girls giving oral sex to boys as early as middle school. Emulating the "girl-on-girl" trends in pornography, girls in their early teens are making out with other girls at parties and in school hallways to get boys' attention. More and more teenage girls are asking parents for plastic surgery, specifically breast implants. Even more disturbing, a growing number of parents are complying with these requests. It has increasingly become popular to give breast augmentations as high-school graduation and sweet-sixteen birthday presents.

By the time they reach eighteen, many of these young women are clamoring to expose themselves (and their newly enhanced breasts) on *Girls Gone Wild* videos. There has been a progression from drunken women baring their breasts for beads on Bourbon Street in New Orleans at Mardi Gras to young women strategically planning to expose themselves in hopes of appearing in the mass marketed videos. *GGW* producers no longer need to prey on the intoxicated or coerce women into removing their tops ("Girls Still Wild," 2003). "Wild Girls" are lining up to expose themselves. Women are even propositioning cameramen and getting into physical altercations with one another to get a chance to bare all on tape. In the past few years, producers have upped the ante. In the "Dorm Room Fantasies" series, the *Girls Gone Wild* producers have moved on to full nudity. Girl-on-girl oral sex and masturbation scenes in dorm shower stalls are common inclusions in the series. Another phenomenon where women exploit themselves is the "dormcam." Hundreds of young women have set up sites on the Internet to give voyeurs 24-hour access to their private lives for a small subscription fee. Female coeds set up cameras in their rooms and broadcast their everyday activities, from getting dressed and undressed to having sex.

There is little doubt that the media and saturation of advertising have powerful effects over attitudes and behaviors of consumers of that media. The average young female is dependent on the media to set standards of beauty and success. Analysis of the media requires an investigation of various media outlets and genres of programming. Popular culture portrayals of women in magazines, pop music, shock jock radio shows, television reality shows, and film play a major role in the sexualization of females. Marketers pick up on existing trends, exaggerate them, and sell them back to the audience in a slightly different form (Rushkoff, 2001). Media channels then spread trends to every part of the country regardless of geographical location. My teenage nieces (who live in a small town in Kansas—population 99) are not immune to the latest fads from Los Angeles and New York. Exposure is so pervasive that even limited media usage and home schooling are not safeguards from exposure.

In chapters 8 through 13, I explore sexual representations of females in music, print, radio, television, film, and the Internet. Women's magazines generally play into readers' insecurities in order to sell the products advertised throughout each issue. Readers are expected to compare themselves to the air-brushed models and celebrities on the covers. Articles inside reinforce anxieties that the female reader is not thin enough, her hair is not shiny enough, and her skin is not clear enough. Similarly, self-help books prey on women's insecurities about getting and keeping a man.

The music industry has been influential in trendsetting, whether it is fashion, hairstyles, or weight standards for women. Because today's music industry relies heavily on music videos, female performers need to meet beauty standards most likely established by male record producers. Without eye-catching (i.e., sexual) videos, female performers have little chance of selling records. To attract a wider audience, young performers are sexualized at an early age. Record executives promote girls barely in their teens by dressing them in provocative clothes and makeup. In addition, these "pop-tarts" dance seductively and sing about adult sexual themes before they are old enough to drive. As they get older and grow out of the "nymphet" stage, girls are pushed to change their style to appeal to a more mature audience. Artists such as Christina Aguilera and Britney Spears adopted strategies meant to express their sexual maturity once they aged out of the "teeny bopper" market. Their physical appearance and choreography became increasingly skanky. The dark makeup and stringy hair was a sharp contrast to their younger days.

Perhaps the strongest evidence of females' self-exploitation is their appearances on shock jock radio. The willingness of young women to go on radio shows such as *Howard Stern* and *Opie & Anthony* knowing they will likely be exploited and humiliated is growing. Highlights of humiliation on Stern's show include the "wheel of sex," the tickle chair, and the Sabian (a masturbation device). Stern himself has admitted that it is no fun if the women participating in these skits do not feel humiliated. Women must invent their own outrageous and humiliating stunts to get on the *Opie & Anthony* radio show. Past performances that have gotten women on the air include one woman who drank milk until she puked and another woman who urinated on herself. Women are not only volunteering in their own media exploitation, but they are also enthusiastically competing against other women to participate.

As traditional scripted television is expanding roles for women and slowly breaking some stereotypes, so-called "reality" shows are reinforcing and advancing negative images of women. Reality shows capitalize on the sexuality of women and exploit them for ratings. First, only thin, attractive women are cast on the shows. Several women appearing on reality television shows such as *Survivor* and *The Apprentice* have gone on to pose nude for *Playboy* or semi-nude for men's magazines such as *FHM* and *Maxim*. Television reality shows such as *Extreme Makeover* and *The Swan* encourage young women who are deemed unattractive to get major multiple plastic surgeries. MTV's *Real World* consistently casts females who will inevitably get drunk, dance topless on bars, and have sex with other cast members. Dating shows generally portray women as desperate, shallow, and vindictive. A promo for *The Bachelor* enticed viewers to watch by exclaiming, "Let the cat fight begin!"

Almost all media sources contribute to the increased sexualization of women. Even women who have been elevated to action adventure heroes in film and video games are highly sexualized. In the movie *Aliens*, for example, Sigourney Weaver's character is the sole survivor of her ship's crew after a fierce battle with the aliens. She then stripped off her space suit, and the camera lingered on her as she peeled down to her tiny underwear and thin camisole. As women excel athletically, they are increasingly sexualized. Top Olympic female athletes posed in provocative layouts in *Sports Illustrated* and *FHM* prior to the games in 2004. Several female athletes have posed nude for *Playboy*. Female beach volleyball players sport tinier and tinier bikinis. Danica Patrick, a groundbreaking female Indy car driver, appeared in a sexually suggestive spread in *FHM*. The expansion of the Internet is giving girls a broader audience to show off their sexuality. YouTube videos and MySpace pages posted by teens and even preteens are often outrageous attempts to get attention from total strangers.

Another important factor to consider in how young girls develop their sexuality is parents. I included an investigation into how parenting styles have allowed or even contributed to these trends. Evidence shows parents are increasingly working more hours and some are spending less time with their children. In a desperate plea to get noticed, girls, in particular, transfer the need for attention from their parents to peers, strangers on the street, and large media audiences. In addition, the guilty parents substitute material possessions for their time. Marketers can then bypass parental approval and market directly to the young girls, catering to their desire to be noticed and to grow up quickly.

In contrast to the overextended parents who spend little time with their children, other parents appear to be more overly involved now than they have ever been. Millennials (i.e., the generation born after 1982) expect constant attention and indulgence. "Helicopter parents" are ultra-involved. They allow their children to make few choices on their own regarding how they spend their time, booking every minute of the day with lessons, sports practices, and play dates. When they are allowed to make choices, Millennials can be unsure how to make healthy decisions. They may be more likely to look to others for answers, and thus are more susceptible to peer and media pressure. Parents may also indulge their children's every whim for fear their children will not like them. Some parents strive to be their children's best friend.

Purpose of the Book

When I searched for other researchers who had investigated these phenomena, I was quite disappointed. I found significant writings about individual trends such as fashion magazines' link to eating disorders and pornography's link to sexual callousness; however, there was little or no writing that adequately tied the various trends together. It is time that researchers in the academic community look critically at the emerging direction of American society and the kinds of models being offered to the coming generations of girls. The evidence of changes in sexual representation of females over the past decade is overwhelming. I found the growing numbers of individual observations were no longer a series of unrelated phenomena. In light of the advancements of women's rights and opportunities, I am amazed to see the current attention-seeking behavior of girls and young women.

The premise of this book is to investigate whether women are in control and enjoying their sexuality as promised by the sexual revolution and women's movement of the 1960s and 1970s. It is more likely that women are participating in their own exploitation in order to gain attention from men than demonstrating their empowerment. Most disturbing is that these trends are apparent in younger and younger girls. Feminists argue that while women are gaining more rights and achieving higher power positions in society there is a backlash. The number of females is surpassing the number of males in undergraduate and graduate programs. At the same time, breast enhancement surgeries increased 700 percent between 1992 and 2004 (Shaw, 2005). Popular fashions include shirts marketed to women with derogatory sayings such as "Bitch in training" and "Instant slut, just add beer." The increased insecurity from media images of "perfect" women pushes young women toward external validation and objectification.

Women are also defending the sex industry by espousing the belief that it is the women who are in control. For example, Liepe-Levinson (2001) argued that women in strip clubs are empowered. She also contends that it is the men who go to strip clubs who are suckers. Men are supposedly "surrendering to the sexual scene." Women often claim they are expressing their sexuality in the *Girls Gone Wild* videos. Producers even labeled one of these videos "Girl Power." While Joe Francis and his *Girls Gone Wild* empire have raked in more than $100 million, the women in the videos receive no compensation other than a free T-shirt.

In the following chapters, I explore a range of issues regarding females and sexuality. My investigation highlights connections between the media, marketers, and popular culture and the attitudes and behaviors of young girls in the United States. Through textual analysis, interviews, and field observations, I offer conclusions about the meaning of the trends and present suggestions about what caused them. By the end of the book, I hope the reader will have gained a better understanding of popular-culture trends, how they developed, and what needs to be done in the future to help protect young girls—particularly from themselves. This investigation is important because these cultural representations are shaping future generations of women. Increases in health issues such as eating disorders, risky sexual behavior, and vulnerability of young girls to pedophiles need to be addressed.

1. Fashion

Historically, clothing standards were established to protect women's modesty. Certain clothing styles also helped to keep women in their place. Long skirts, corsets, and layers of petticoats not only covered women but also drastically restricted their mobility. Fashion can display a woman's wealth and "privileged idleness" and serve as a status symbol for a woman's parents or husband (S. Williams, 2006). From the 1890s to the 1930s women's roles, and thus fashion, changed from "parlor ornament" to "independent working-girl." The feminist movement of the 1960s and 1970s encouraged bra burning and rejection of binding girdles. More recent fashion, however, has put women back in restrictive clothing such as tight skirts and high heels. Fashion trends are one of the major ways females express their sexuality and their class. Clothing choices and accessories function by today's standards in a variety of ways, from establishing the wearer's status (e.g., designer labels) to attracting attention from others (e.g., skank chic).

History of Women's Fashion

The story of the American woman can be told through what she wore and what she was expected to wear (S. Williams, 2006). Women's fashion trends greatly fluctuated during the past century in the United States. Society's expectations of femininity can be seen through fashion, as well as women's status and role in society. For most of the nineteenth century women were to be modest, yet they were required to show off some of their features in order to be considered feminine. For example, their hips were disguised with hoop skirts and legs were covered completely, with just a hint of ankle. At the same time, corsets pushed the breasts together and upward, showing off extensive cleavage. Tight corsets also accentuated slender waists. Corsets were laced so tightly that they cut off blood flow and resulted in some women dying because of the damage to the internal organs. The damage also made it difficult for women during childbirth.

Near the turn of the twentieth century, women began to wear a form of trousers called bloomers. Bloomers allowed women to work and play more like men. With the increased freedom of movement and the lack of form fit, the women who dared wear them were seen as "desexing" themselves (S. Williams, 2006). By dressing more like men, women were seen as daring to challenge gender roles and equality. Traditional standards dictated that feminine fashions have an element of vulnerability. In contrast to the bloomers, styles inspired by the burlesque theaters became fashionable. Trendsetters wore clothing that was considered blatantly sexual and "unchaste." Fashions featured "voluptuous projections of the bust and the hips" and "the leg ha[d] suddenly become fashionable" (S. Williams, 2006).

Times of war changed fashions dramatically, often because materials were in short supply. Steel wires used to make corsets were needed for battleship construction. After the end of World War I, happy days were celebrated by the flapper fashions of the Roaring Twenties. Shorter, loose-fitting dresses that showed off women's legs and made it easier to perform the modern carefree dance steps of the time were in vogue. Between the Great Depression and World War II, Hollywood set fashion trends. This time, styles of the independent women were replaced with "curves and curls" (S. Williams, 2006). Jean Harlow was credited with popularizing styles that "clung to the female body, outlined feminine curves, and then draped voluminously and romantically to the floor" (S. Williams, 2006).

Changes in the workplace influenced fashion. During World War II, women filled many of the jobs the men left behind when they went off to fight. Working women had money to spend on store-bought clothing. Department stores offered not only ready-to-wear clothing but also cosmetics and accessories. Manufacturers tried giving women what they wanted while being careful not to be criticized for immorality. (Today there seems to be no struggle whatsoever in regard to the latter.)

Although still rather modest, 1950s styles emphasized "well defined bosoms" and tightly belted waists (S. Williams, 2006). There is probably no more recognizable icon of the time than Marilyn Monroe's white halter dress skirt blowing up above the subway grate. The situation comedies of the 1950s campaigned to make women more feminine. June Cleaver on *Leave It to Beaver* was rarely seen without heels and pearls, even when vacuuming. The 1950s were marked with poodle skirts, bobby sox, and cashmere sweater sets. Shows such as *Happy Days* showed that much simpler, more modest time for females. Drastic changes came with the 1960s and the age of free love. Voluptuous 1950s icons such as Marilyn Monroe were replaced by waiflike models such as Twiggy. Women were much more likely to go braless in this era as a symbol of freeing themselves from the restraints of male domination. In contrast to prim and proper June Cleaver, Laura Petry, from *The Dick Van Dick Show*, was more modern, with her tight sweaters and stretch pants. Carol Brady and Shirley Partridge were more modern moms of the 1970s, with their shag haircuts and brightly colored polyester pantsuits. New materials such as spandex hit the market, offering a clinginess not seen before. The high cut or French cut swimsuits and workout leotards of the 1970s gave men a look up a woman's leg and a peak at their pubic outline. A common skank feature of the time was the "camel toe." A camel toe is formed when tight pants cling to the front of a woman's body, showing the outline of her genital region in two bumps.

The 1980s was a bit schizophrenic, split between good girls of the Reagan era and "really good" girls of the new MTV generation. On one hand, fashion took a conservative turn, reflecting the political leanings of the time. Shirts with stiff collars were accented with a ribbon tied in a bow around the neck. Skirts, often made of heavy wool plaid, were worn below the knee. Women wore shoulder pads to look more powerful. On the other hand, in sharp contrast, skirts and dresses made of lyrca were short and clingy. Kelly Bundy, on *Married with Children*, and MTV video women wore dresses so tight and short they left little to the imaginations. The women added heavy makeup and big, bleached hair.

In the 1990s, teenage girls opted for a grunge look, complete with torn flannel shirts and Dr. Martens. Goth also became popular, marked by layers of black clothing, black hair, and pale skin. Eurotrash was a common expression that referred to those who generally wore black and were quite dirty. The *Urban Dictionary* defined Eurotrash (n.d.) as "a drug addicted, skinny, pale, sarcastic, trust fund baby, clubbing every night, male/female. Eurotrash don't bathe, smile or wash their hair on a regular basis so they may reek of perfumes and colognes." Another entry described the phenomenon as "[m]ales ... characterized by a semi-slovenly appearance (including half-shaven faces), greasy hair, rib-hugging shirts, tight jeans and loafers worn without socks [and] [w]omen ... easily distinguished by anorexia, over-bleached hair, gaudy jewelry, and plastic surgery (particularly breast-enlargement)."

Today's Fashion

Current fashion trends have evolved from sexy to slutty to skanky. "Skank chic" is also known as "trailer park fashion" or "dumpster chic." Vernon (2005) described skank chic as a "trashy subversion of normal notions of glamour and civilized celebrity behavior—which embraces matted hair, a residual air of grubbiness and the kind of roller-coaster, booze-and-drug-addled passion that can inspire physical fights in speeding trains." Vernon credited Hollywood celebrities such as Lindsay Lohan, Brittany Murphy, Kelly Osbourne, and Avril Lavigne with starting the trend. These pop icons presented a sharp contrast to "the unapologetically unwashed response to the fresh-faced, perfectly manicured tradition of teen sensations" such as Hilary Duff and Jessica Simpson (Vernon, 2005). According to Quick (cited in Vernon, 2005), skank chic became popular because young girls were getting bored with mainstream fashion. They turned to something "with edge, and with dirt under its fingernails." She argued that skank chic is the ultimate in anti-glamour and anti-pretty.

Skank fashion is accented with heavy black eye makeup, especially under the eyes, and poorly bleached hair with dark roots. Skanky clothing is usually well worn, sometimes stained, and the color is faded. I would argue that the most skanky colors are white and pink, which is ironic because they generally signify purity and femininity. These colors are generally more revealing, so that others can see darker colored underwear and bras worn underneath. They show dirt more easily than darker colors.

While exposure of breast cleavage has been a significant factor in fashion, the emphasis appeared to have migrated south. One of the highlights of the 2004 Olympics television coverage was women's beach volleyball. Players are wearing tinier and tinier bikinis that cover very little of their cheeks (see chapter 14). Some of the players, particularly the Brazilian teams, had different colored patches of material (usually white) around the genital area. Not only are the bikini bottoms tiny, the color contrast really draws attention to the crotch. There is also an interesting fashion trend I witnessed on and around the beach. Girls wear bikini tops and cutoff jean shorts; however, they leave their shorts unzipped and fold down the opening on either side to expose their swimsuit bottoms. The goal, evidently, is to draw attention to their crotches. I have witnessed young girls wearing their shorts this way as they stroll along the boardwalk with their parents.

Low-rise jeans are worn so far down on the hips that "rear cleavage" is exposed when the girls are bending over or sitting down. Photographs of race-car driver Danica Patrick in *FHM* magazine showed her bent over a car with shorts so low that a significant portion of her rear cleavage was exposed. Likewise, an ad for Christopher Brian jeans featured a billboard with a topless Kim Kardashian photographed from the back as she is pulling down the waistband of her jeans, exposing her crack.

One of the biggest skank fashion items is thong underwear. Thongs hit the height of their popularity in the late 1990s. According to Kuczynki (2004), the thong moved from the world of exotic dance to the mainstream as a way to avoid visible panty lines. The thong alone is not necessarily skanky. Skanky is when it is teamed up with low-rise jeans with the thong clearly visible. When a brightly colored thong is exposed, it is called a "whale tail." Whale tails are the appearance of the top rear strap of a woman's thong, v-string or g-string underwear above the waistline of her pants, shorts, or skirt whenever she sits, bends over or squats, though some low-rise clothing is now designed to display the whale tail at all times, so-called because the strap closely resembles a whale's tail rising from the water. Kuczynki (2004) credited Britney Spears with propelling the thong into popular culture, embracing "the virgin/temptress paradox ... [a]udiences could look, but they could never touch. The thong is an invitation, not a promise" (p. 91). In the new millennium, it appears the thong is losing its novelty, not to mention that few women look good in them. Kuczynki (2004) stated that women may be tired of looking like strippers and now want to look like debutantes.

A skank look is also created when clothes fit too tightly. Today's trend of tight fitting, low-rider jeans clashed with the increase in obesity rates. Low-rider jeans that are a size too small create a muffin top. The term "muffin top" was coined specifically for females whose flesh spills out over the top of their pants. Often clothing choices are not made according to what would be most flattering or what would best hide flaws, but what attracts attention. Low riding jeans and navel piercings on more "voluptuous" females draw attention to the excessive weight in the stomach area rather than looking attractive or cool. On the other hand, perhaps it is progress that women and girls of all shapes and sizes are comfortable enough with their bodies to let it all "hang out." Another example of skanky is when older women dress too young. It is not particularly attractive when they expose stretch marks, leathery patches of skin from sun overexposure, and varicose veins.

Marketing

One factor that distinguishes today's fashion trends is the promotion of slutty and skank by manufacturers. Fashion trends in the past often symbolized a revolt against the oppressive clothing of corporate manufacturers. Girls would alter the clothing to show off their sexuality and naughty side. In the 1980s, the trend was to cut off the collars of sweatshirts, which were worn to one side to reveal a bare shoulder (think Jennifer Beal's character in the movie *Flashdance*). I remember that girls in my high school used to roll up the waistband of their Catholic school uniform skirts to make them daringly short. Now, manufacturers are setting these sexy trends. The plaid uniform skirts are made with so little material they barely cover the groin area. One day I was shopping with my sister-in-law, Julie. I pointed to some skirts displayed on the wall. At first I was not sure if they were clothing or headbands. I blurted out, "Wow, look at those hootchie skirts." A young sales associate was passing by at the time. I was afraid I had offended her. Instead she turned around, smiled wearily, and said, "I agree."

Playboy fashion is very popular, with an estimated $350 million in annual sales (Pollet & Hurwitz, 2003). The Playboy Bunny is being used for the teen market. According to Pollet and Hurwitz (2003) the bunny is getting an extreme makeover. The company is attempting to downplay the pornographic aspect and make it a playful symbol. *Playboy*'s licensing department claims to target 18–25-year-olds. Appealing to an underage market does not appear to bother *Playboy* founder Hugh Hefner. He proclaimed, "I don't care if a baby holds up a Playboy Bunny rattle" (cited in Pollet & Hurwitz, 2003). Pollet and Hurwitz (2003) reported that a tattoo artist was hired to airbrush temporary tattoos on guests at a bar mitzvah with such items as a Playboy Bunny emblem. The 2001 November issue of *CosmoGIRL!* offered free Frederick's of Hollywood underwear that had the word "Bombshell" printed under a Playboy-style silhouette (Jacobs, 2002).

"Porn Star" clothing is a very mainstream, popular clothing line with girls as young as middle school. It takes the stripper theme a step further into porn. The popularity of actual porn stars such as Jenna Jameson and Tabitha Stevens makes it more acceptable to emulate these women who have sex on camera for money. The glam of the clothing line ignores the dark, exploitative side of the porn business experience of all but the very top sex workers. The clothing is expensive enough that it says, "I am sexy enough to be a porn star, but I am not desperate enough to actually have to do it." The Porn Star Clothing website ("About Porn," 2006) described themselves as providing "alternative" clothing for a young, risk-taking generation. They claim they are just responding to market demand, characterizing their clientele as rebels who do not take life too seriously. The whole concept trivializes the worst in female exploitation. Even the most successful stars such as Jenna Jameson have led amazingly destructive lives (see chapter 3).

American Apparel's spring 2006 catalogue featured skanky photographs on skanky models wearing skanky clothing. Photos looked amateurish, with models in unflattering positions. For example, there is one in which a young woman is sitting on the floor and the camera shoots her from above as she looks up. She is positioned leaning on her arms behind her back and her legs are spread. She has a scowl on her face. So many of the models are not smiling, even the little girls. Some of the models looked strung out on heroin. The males looked unkempt, with messy, greasy hair and beard stubble. Few of the females modeling shirts were wearing bras or pants, and some showed a little bit of underwear. The fact that the females were wearing little makeup for some reason does not look natural but rather dirty. In one shot, a mesh top was shown with a close-up of one of the breasts. There were a variety of terry cloth shorts that were extremely short and cut in the 1970s style. Other styles featured a "Boy Beater Tank" and a "Baby Rib Thong." Thongs were modeled in the catalogue, generally from the front but also from the back. "Boy shorts" were shot from the back as they crept up between the model's buttocks cheeks. Amid the micro-poli short shorts were pictures of children modeling. Immediately following pictures of children was a photograph of a woman in a T-shirt and underwear, followed by a page of thongs, followed by a page of one-year-old babies. It seemed bizarre to mix clothing for children (although the children are covered) amid the adults dressed in sexual styles.

Candies shoes featured an ad with Ashlee Simpson posing seductively in a revealing outfit and high heels. Simpson was juxtaposed with a teddy bear in the picture. The blending of a sexual image with a child's teddy bear was disturbing to some critics. Candies CEO Neil Cole (cited in "Sex Sells," 2005) stated, "She's a little promiscuous, but everything's covered, and she just looks fun. She looks a little bit sexy." The company's solution to the sexual images was to manufacture a shirt that read, "Be sexy: It doesn't mean you have to have sex."

Clothing Sayings

T-shirt designs have been popular for decades. Internet sales have made it possible to push the raunch envelope, not that stores have shied from carrying such items. The Coyote Ugly website offers "Big Twins" tube tops and "No cherries allowed" tank tops ("Coyote Ugly," n.d.). During a field trip to Atlantic City in the summer of 2006, I found a store that had a variety of T-shirts displayed on the wall. Some of the more tasteless sayings included "Eatin' ain't cheatin'," "It's not easy being easy," "Let's hook up," "I'm just here to get laid," "If you're rich, I'm your bitch," "No money, no honey," and "I'm not a bitch, I'm the bitch." There were a few positive sayings such as "I'm a keeper," but the negative far outnumbered the positive. On the boardwalk of Seaside Heights, New Jersey, I saw underwear that read, "I'm not a virgin but I have the box it came in." Many of the messages girls are wearing reinforce old stereotypes about women, such as "Flirting my way to the top."

Other T-shirt gems were found on various websites. I was not sure if some of the sayings were empowering, exploitative, or just plain raunchy. Some of the shirts read "Eager Beaver U," "I [heart] Head" (with a picture of a beer mug), "Submission is a virtue" (handcuffs picture), "Boys will be toys," and "2 drinks away from girl on girl action." Thongs were emblazoned with "Porn Star 69," "Beaver," "Bunny," "Eat me," "Open," and "Welcome" (mat). T-shirt designs for males included "Does this shirt make my penis look fat?" "I [heart] lesbians," "Help wanted: many positions available, apply inside," "MILF [mothers I'd like to f*ck] hunter," and "Viagra is for pussies." Even more tasteless sayings were "I like my women like I like my coffee (ground up and in the freezer)," "I eat more pussy than cervical cancer," "Mary was only a virgin if you don't count anal," "I support single moms" (under the caption is a silhouette of a pole dancer), "Hopeless romantic seeks filthy whore," and "I only support gay marriage if both chicks are hot." Other sayings include "You f*ck it, You buy it," "Check one: straight, bi-sexual, gay, total whore, unsure lately," and "Skinny Bitch."

One sorority at a Catholic university created a T-shirt to celebrate their homecoming that had a stick figure that had obviously fallen with a drink in hand. The tagline read "Make out, black out, or get out." Another spring break T-shirt read "no rules, no parents." I saw a woman playing volleyball with "ram this" on the back of her shorts. I assume it was supporting a school mascot. Britney Spears has been photographed in T-shirts with various sayings such as "Future MILF" and "I have the golden ticket" (with arrow down).

Clothing today gives mixed messages. It blurs the line between virgin and whore. Kilbourne gave the example of a thong with the saying "Pay up, sucker!" and another thong with a picture of a padlock. She argued that the former is a better option for girls because it "smacks less of sexual Puritanism." She contrasted these trends with a culture where schools are not allowed to teach sex education, yet sexual images of girls are everywhere.

Age Compression

The most outrageous part of this trend is age compression. Marketers use "age compression," which is when they push adult products and teen attitude on younger and younger kids ("Sex Sells," 2005). Big name clothing lines are targeting younger and younger girls with adult style clothing. For example, numerous complaints were filed against Abercrombie & Fitch for allegedly targeting children 10–13 years old in a sexually explicit catalogue (McCullough, 2003). Since then the company has discontinued their catalogue. Abercrombie & Fitch was also criticized for provocative sayings on T-shirts marketed to young girls. A spokesperson for the company stated, "Our T-shirts are sometimes controversial, which we're fine with" (Lennox cited in Shapira, 2006). According to Shapira (2006), Lennox declined to elaborate.

One of the experiences I had that compelled me to write this book is when I saw very young girl wearing a Juicy Couture tracksuit. The line features the word "Juicy" written across the backside of the bottoms. I was horrified that the parents allowed this nine-year-old to wear such a blatant sexual statement in a public restaurant. Brown (2003) described the emblazoned "Juicy" as "enabling the wearer to be both a label whore and a cock tease at the same time." Brown describes the suit as tailored to fit a 14-year-old supermodel and cut so low and fitted so tight there is no room to wear anything underneath. Brown added, "Those without jutting hipbones and concave bellies need not apply."

I interviewed a number of parents who are frustrated with clothing choices available for their preteens. It is difficult for them to find clothing for their prepubescent daughters that is not revealing. Marketers appear partly to blame for pushing little girls to grow up quickly. Worn down by the demands generated by the marketing, parents often purchase more grown-up clothing for their daughters. Mugele (cited in Deveny, 2007) described sixth graders wearing short skirts or midriff shirts to fit in with other girls and for acceptance in social groups. She added girls in particular do not want to be different. Likewise, Pollet and Hurwitz (2003) found that eighth grade girls were even wearing kids' sizes to show more skin.

According to Schor (cited in Bloom, 2004), "The gender strategies of marketers are passed along as time-honored truths that reflect essential human nature. The reigning assumption about girls is that they are not interested in success and mastery. Domesticity waned as an appealing theme for girls, and the teen culture became more pornographic" (p. 210). In Bloom's (2004) article, "Sex and the 6-Year-Old Girl," she asked where our little girls have gone. She argued that marketers are pushing them to grow up quickly and be like the MTV teen icons who move like strippers. In addition to the advice "no riding with strangers," Bloom (2004) warned little girls, "no dressing like hookers" (p. 210).

"Prostitots"

The new term coined for this trend, "prostitot," blends "prostitute" and "tot." Prostitot refers to little girls who are dressed like adult women in the sex trade. Some parents justify the practice by claiming the little girls are only playing dress up; however, this style of dress clearly sexualizes little girls. Clothing departments are stocked with tiny tank tops with words and phrases such as "Hottie," "Porn Star," "Wet," "Princess," "Party Girl," and "No Angel." "Coyote in training" shirts are available in toddler sizes, 2–4 ("Coyote Ugly," n.d.). Clothing store Abercrombie & Fitch was chastised for selling thong underwear for girls that read, "Eye Candy" and "Wink Wink." Sizes were such that they could fit girls as young as seven years old. "It's cute and fun and sweet," said Hampton Carney, a spokesman for the company based in New Albany, Ohio. This comment was especially disturbing coming from an adult male. He stated, "The thongs were designed for the girls to enjoy, and no one else.... It's not appropriate for a 7-year-old, but it is appropriate for a 10-year-old. Once you get about 10, you start to care about your underwear" (Carey cited in Ortiz, 2002). Carey added, "The underwear for young girls was created with the intent to be lighthearted and cute.... Any misrepresentation of that is purely in the eye of the beholder" (cited in Ortiz, 2002). After significant bad press, Abercrombie & Fitch no longer market the thongs.

Wal-Mart (the self-proclaimed moral authority on family values—never mind that they exploit workers and destroy small towns) expanded their use of seductive names to promote Junior Intimates such as "Juniors' No Boundaries Bra and Panty Set." The panties designs include "Juniors' No Boundaries Woven Boxers" and "Ladies' Secret Treasures Boyleg Panty." The chain Miss Teen sells padded push-up bras to tweens. La Senza Girl also sells padded bras as tiny as size "30 AA." A spokesperson for La Senza claimed it is the moms who decide if it is appropriate, although they have created the demand in the first place ("Sex Sells," 2005). Swimsuits designed for little girls are a huge industry. There are two-piece swimsuits for toddlers, with swim diapers. The 2 to 4 range features two-piece suits as well as those with halter tops. Suits come in sun protection and floating suits. Tankini tops and boy cut bottoms offer more coverage than the traditional bikini tops and bottoms offered in very small sizes.

The Pimpfant website features sweet angelic faces of a blonde haired Caucasian boy and girl and a light skinned African American boy. The website describes the business this way:

About Us: "Pimpfants ... it's more than a name, it's a movement! Our clothing bridges the generation gap between parents and kids, allowing babies and tots everywhere the opportunity to hit the playground with fresh gear and street cred. Pimpfants uses only the highest quality products, so your shorties can represent in style and comfort. If you want puppy dogs, ducks and frogs, you'll have to visit a zoo. But if you are looking for children's clothing that defines a generation, look to Pimpfants!" ["Welcome Pimpfants," n.d.].

Merchandise includes "Lil' Beaters," a ribbed sleeveless shirt. Their definition of a "beater" is a reference to a small ribbed tank top similar to that known as a "wife beater." Instead of "onezees" they had "1Zs" with "Diva" and trimmed in hot pink. Shirts with "40 oz Milk" to emulate the 40 oz. malt liquor bottles. Velour tracksuits with "Baby Bling." "The Notorious K.I.D." Little girl shirts with "D' Bomb." Basketball outfits with "Jr. Pimp Squad." The company defends its use of the word "pimp" by claiming it has evolved since the 1970s into a positive statement describing a hip baby. Although they acknowledge that it may "conjure up unpleasant thoughts for some people," they claim their intent is simply a play on words (very much like the Hooters defense).

Another website, Tshirthell.com ("Baby Hell," n.d.), has the following sayings available in sizes starting at 6 months: "badass clothing for your little devils!," "I can kick your baby's ass," "They shake me," "I'm this many" (a drawing of a baby holding up of a middle finger), "Hung like a five-year-old," "Playground Pimp," "All daddy wanted was a blowjob," "I tore mommy a new one," "!#K the milk, where's the whiskey tits?!" "Are you my daddy?" and "I enjoy a good spanking."

School Fashion

High school and middle school teachers I interviewed were horrified at how the girls dress for school. Many schools are instituting dress codes that specifically address the sexuality of the girls. Shapira (2006) reported that school wear has become blatantly sexual, sometimes known as sleazy-chic culture. School officials are reporting that T-shirts are racier than ever. A decade ago, Coed Naked sporting events on shirts were popular. School officials are now finding shirts that are much more blunt (Shapira, 2006). School systems are racing to keep ahead with revisions to dress codes. Bans that have usually included clothing that promotes cigarettes, alcohol, drugs or weapons now include vulgarity and lewdness. One of the difficulties for administrators is the gray areas, or double entendre. Shapira (2006) argued that teenagers are using "attitude" shirts as an opportunity to "show some skin without showing skin." A female senior argued, "It gives me a little edge, but it's just to get a rise out of people, because people *know* me."

One high school junior (cited in Shapira, 2006) said that, although she does not want to have sex until she is married, she likes to wear the T-shirts because they are funny and they draw attention. In the next breath, however, she claimed she does not care what the boys think about her shirts. Likewise, her mother is not worried about other people getting the wrong message from the expressions on the shirts. She claimed her daughter wears them to be ironic. Shapira (2006) concluded, "In a culture that bombards teenagers with sexual imagery, the T-shirts are just another way to revel in raunchy entertainment, without necessarily getting physical." Statistics show a decline in teen sex and teen pregnancy. The same National Center for Health Statistics survey found that more than half of all teenagers engage in oral sex.

Many school systems' dress codes include restrictions on how revealing the clothes are and how much skin can show. The dress code of a day school in Georgia stated, "Girls' shirts must extend to cover the waistline at all times. Girls must refrain from wearing revealing or tight fitting garments including: low-waisted pants/skirts, stretch pants, low-cut necklines, halter tops, and bare backs. Skirts and dresses should be no shorter than three inches above the top of the knee. Dresses and blouses must have a shoulder strap width of at least two inches" ("Upper School," 2006). A middle school in Florida explained their dress code was established because of the appropriateness of the age of the student and the school setting ("Dress Code," 2005). The school was attempting to establish a learning atmosphere. Some of the restrictions were midriff tops, tank tops, strapless tops, and spaghetti straps. In addition, no undergarments may be visible. Hemlines shall be no shorter than mid-thigh. They also included restrictions for apparel with inappropriate, obscene or profane statements or illustrations.

Carty (2006) reported that girls barely out of kindergarten were wearing midriff tops and lacey thongs. Even a nursery school and infant care center posted a dress code. Administrators asked parents, "Please dress your child in comfortable play clothing of the type that encourages self-help. Party clothes are inappropriate" ("Crossroads Nursery," n.d.). Before my nephew's Christmas program, parents were reminded that, since the children would be sitting on the floor of the stage, the length of the dresses should be taken into consideration. (Evidently there were problems in the past with underwear exposure.) Administrators at one high school were so fed up with the inappropriateness of students' clothing they suspended more than 10 percent of the students on the first day of school ("You Think I'm Kidding," 2006). Some of the suspensions were for low-cut shirts and graphic T-shirts.

Nearly every educator I interviewed, from middle school teachers to college professors, expressed concern with the dress of girls and young women. Current fashions include tight, low-cut shirts that expose bras and cleavage and low-rise jeans that reveal thongs. Revealing fashion is nothing new; it is the younger and younger wearers of such clothing that is of concern. There is a disturbing trend in children's clothing, which is often indistinguishable from sexy adult clothing. One fourth-grade teacher I interviewed told a story of an extremely bright girl who came to her fifth-grade graduation in a skanky dress. Other girls were calling her "hoochie." However, she seemed to be okay with it.

Workplace Fashion

Not understanding the proper attire at school, many young women do not realize what is proper for the workplace either. Reports from the working world indicate that there is little difference between what women wear to night clubs and the beach and what they wear to work. Career centers at colleges have always instructed graduating students on how to dress for interviews. Males are pretty clear on the business suit. It is the females who need more advising, perhaps because they have more choices.

Virginia Tech University's website ("Additional Interview," 2006) advises students that many outfits they see on television are inappropriate for work and "masquerades for professional attire." Television shows often give the impression that successful business women dress as though they were going clubbing. *Ally McBeal* and *Melrose Place* were renowned for their short, short skirts worn at the office and in court. Cutty's character on *House* usually has tight skirts and lots of cleavage. As the hospital's chief administrator, she does not appear to be the top person in power. Erin Brockovich in the eponymous film was successful despite her excessive show of cleavage, but it is doubtful to work for others. Career Builders ("What Not to Wear," 2006) warned against using the dress on the show *The Apprentice* as a model. *The Apprentice* is a reality show where men and women compete to become Donald Trump's apprentice.

Career Builders ("What Not to Wear," 2006) instructed women to avoid wearing clothes that are too trendy or that are tight or revealing. Virginia Tech's website ("Additional Interview," 2006) offered specific advice for details such as skirt lengths. Women are instructed that their skirts should end at the knee when they are standing and cover their thighs when they are seated. As a test, women are told to sit in the skirt facing a mirror before buying it to make sure they are not flashing the interviewer. Even if the skirt is long enough, it should not be so narrow or so tight that the wearer cannot walk or climb stairs. High slits are also inappropriate. The goal is not to call attention to oneself (as it is in the clubs or on the street) but to look appropriate for a business environment or gathering.

The Cocktail Waitress

While most employers are struggling to get women to dress modestly, other employers require a "skanky" look. Some establishments, primarily drinking and gambling establishments, still require skanky uniforms for their female servers. Under Title VII, businesses are prohibited from hiring only women unless they can demonstrate that being a woman is a "bona fide occupational qualification" (McGinley, 2007). The Supreme Court held that hiring by sex is allowable only if "sex or the sex-differentiated job qualification relates to the 'essence' or the 'central mission' of the employer's business and is objectively and verifiably necessary to the employee's performance of job tasks and responsibilities" (cited in McGinley, 2007). Courts found that dress codes are permissible because they make a minimal incursion into a person's rights. Under these regulations, Hugh Hefner's Bunny clubs, which were established in 1960, could hire only women and require them to wear the Bunny suits. The clubs were designed to resemble a bachelor pad where female servers were subjugated to wait on the male customers. Playmates were originally going to be required to serve drinks in nighties; however, the rabbit or bunny outfit was chosen instead. The bunny design matched the magazine's logo.

In order to legally hire only female servers, the Hooters chain of restaurants must demonstrate that sexual stimulation is an essential component to their business. It is not enough that customers enjoy the sexual environment. McGinley (2007) stated that "the sexual subordination of women cannot be used simply to gain competitive advantage." Although the organization denies their logo is purely sexual, it is blatantly obvious that Hooters is not simply referring to an owl. The owl's eyes are strategically placed over the server's breasts and "hooters" is an established euphemism for breasts. The Hooters Girl uniform consists of orange shorts, pantyhose, and a white tank top, short-sleeve or long-sleeve T-shirt. The company stated that bras are required ("About Hooters," 2006). In my observations of Hooters' outfits, the T-shirts are often a few sizes too small. The neckline is low enough to see the cleavage of most of the women. Most of the women wear push-up bras to enhance the cleavage. The shorts, made of a bright orange polyester material, are generally ill fitting. On thinner women, they tend to be baggy. On the more voluptuous women, the shorts are uncomfortably tight. In addition, the women wear suntan colored nylons that give them a fake-tan look that is in stark contrast to their face and arm coloring. The outfit is completed with white slouch socks and white high-top athletic shoes. One blogger stated, "Pantyhose under shorts is just wrong. Granted, they hold in a lot of cottage cheese, but still. If you aspire to be a Hooters girl in life, then I don't think you should need spandex to help your thighs ... could you imagine outfitting your daughter in an orange Hooters shirt?" ("Things that are," 2006).

The Hooters organization often defends its controversial wardrobe choice by arguing sex appeal is legal and it sells ("About Hooters," 2006). On the other hand, they claim part of the job of Hooters Girls is to make charitable appearances. Hooters claims that 70 percent of their customers are male, most between the ages of 25 and 54, yet the restaurants offer a kids' menu. Hooters claims they are only serving their customers who chose to bring in their children. Since Hooters sells kids' T-shirts and Barbie doll outfits, it is clear they do not mind making money off of children.

Maternity Clothing

One unlikely area of fashion that has delved into the skank factor is maternity wear. The trend gained prominence when Jennifer Aniston's character, Rachel, wore extremely tight clothing that revealed several inches of her pregnant belly (in this case a prosthesis) on the television show *Friends*. Clothing manufacturers are marketing maternity clothes as "sexy," a way to show women are proud of their bodies (Gold cited in Patton, n.d.). For example, one website posted, "Maternity clothes in fitted, sexy maternity clothing styles so you can look and feel your best while pregnant." Sites even advertise sexy maternity lingerie ("About Blossom," n.d.). Some of the marketing includes "Hot Mama summer style" and "Stay Groovy While Expecting at Due! We're Keeping Expecting Moms Hot" ("Due Maternity," 2006). Isabella Oliver clothing line offered maternity hipsters, thongs, and tankinis. Patton (n.d.) described the trend: "Tired of dowdy, frumpy clothes, pregnant women have begun flaunting their changing bodies over the last decade ... form-fitting maternity clothes have become a norm." (I am not saying that pregnant women have to wear jumbo smocks and be ashamed of their bodies, but the clothes look incredibly uncomfortable.) There appears to be little "maternity" in "maternity clothes."

Conclusion

Over the past century, women's fashions have advanced from sexual objectification to independence, where women had control over their sexuality. Today's fashions, however, appear to be reverting to a time of sexual exploitation of women. Young women and girls are getting fashion tips from strippers and MTV music video vixens. Clothing manufacturers are pushing skank trends—dirty-looking clothes with derogatory sayings and very little coverage. There is little variation from store to store. Girls are being sold one look, a trend that reinforces the view that females are interchangeable sex objects. Perhaps the most disturbing trend is that the styles are being adopted by younger and younger girls. Malls carry smaller and smaller sizes of what used to be adult clothing. Prostitot fashion is the norm, not only in beauty pageants and dance recitals but also on the street and in school.

Pomerantz, a researcher studying teen fashion, stated, "I don't know what the fuss is about. It bothers me that girls are called skanky or slutty. They are taking control of their bodies" (cited in Jacobs, 2002, p. 11). Pomerantz is off base thinking girls are wearing these fashions to express their sexuality or empower themselves. Kilbourne (cited in Pollet & Hurwitz, 2003) argued that the brand of sexuality promoted by girls has nothing to do with a girl being "an agent of her own sexual desire." Rather, girls and young women are embracing sexist stereotypes of the past. These girls are convinced by stripper-obsessed marketing machines that the most important thing they can do is gain sexual attention. T-shirts with sayings such as "Instant slut, just add beer" and "Diva" are more degrading than empowering. These phrases appear to be most popular with young girls. "Porn Star" clothing reinforces women's primary worth as sexual objects. Even young women, who should know better, are buying into the "women as sex object" styles. Outrageous amounts of money are spent on designer "stripper" fashions.

Critics warn parents to work harder to protect their children against exploitation and unwanted attention and not take fashion choices lightly. It is not always so easy for parents to compete against trends. Marketers and retailers are in the business to make a profit, not necessarily acting as a social and moral conscience. In addition, children learn early how to push their parents' buttons and wear them down until parents cave into their demands (Carty, 2006). Carty argued that some parents fear they will be seen as uptight and having no sense of humor, and even that their child will no longer love them if they say "no." It is difficult for individual parents to make a difference when so many girls are dressing so inappropriately. Schools have had to step in and institute stricter and very specific codes in order to curb inappropriate clothing choices. It is difficult to keep girls away from current fashions when there is an overlap in sizes of middle school, high school, and college students in junior sections of stores. Parents are often faced with difficult choices when store after store carries nothing but low-rise jeans and low-cut tops. Growing up is painful and girls, especially, do not want to feel different from their peers. On the other hand, not addressing the problem of over-sexualized girls is far worse for society.

2. SEXUALITY

In recent decades, the trends in the United States have changed dramatically for females in terms of having sex and expressing their sexuality. There is a major difference, however, between exploring one's sexuality and being sexuality exploited. This fine line may not always be evident to outsiders or even to women themselves.

It appears that there is a disconnect between women and their bodies. Workers in the sex industry claim it is just their bodies and not their minds/souls that they are selling. Many of the young women willing to flaunt themselves on *Girls Gone Wild* videos to get attention are disconnecting as well. They are not enjoying their bodies, they are using them for others to enjoy. They settle for the fleeting moments of attention, instead of holding out for deeper appreciation. Women claim they can have uncommitted, detached sex just like men. This "freedom" is great if they are truly getting what they want. If it is a substitute for a deeper desire instead, they will likely go to extremes looking in the wrong places for what is missing. When females act crazier and crazier, it is apparent they are desperate to find more attention rather than evolving into sexually expressive, satisfied beings. Many of the men I interviewed described the wild behavior of women as "hot"—at first. They reported that the effect quickly wears off and they express a disdain for women who lower themselves to those levels. Men appear to have a sense of which women are truly happy and free with their bodies and which women are the posers who are trying too hard to look that way.

History

Throughout history, women's bodies have been treated as a commodity. They have been bought and sold for sexual pleasure. They have been negotiation tools for families to increase wealth and status and to produce heirs. In many cultures, female children are seen as a burden, worth less than male children; therefore, dowries were paid to the husbands for taking females off their fathers' hands. Many of the traditions of today's weddings still express these themes: the father giving the bride away, the man asking the woman's father for her hand, the bride wearing white (to signify to the groom and the groom's family that the bride was a virgin and therefore worth more), the bride's family paying for the wedding (similar to the dowry and getting rid of the female child), and the woman taking the man's name. For centuries women were told sex was something they needed to endure in order to have children and fulfill their duties as wives. Until the late 1970s, most states did not consider spousal rape a crime ("Spousal Rape Law," 2007). It was 1993 before North Carolina made it illegal unless the couple was legally separated or divorced.

The beginning of the Suffrage Movement officially is marked by the 1848 meeting in Seneca Falls, New York. Female abolitionists realized they had about the same lack of rights to their own bodies and destinies as the slaves they were working to free. Through a very long and painful fight, women were finally granted the right to own property, divorce physically abusive husbands, and vote. Development of feminism and the Women's Movement in the 1960s meant sexual freedom. Women were told they could enjoy their bodies; they did not have to bind them with corsets or hide them under poodle skirts. They could enjoy sex without being considered whores. The birth control pill gave women the ability to have control over reproduction. They no longer had to abstain for fear of pregnancy or rely on a man to protect them. As with most social movements, there was a backlash against these freedoms. Cultural groups, such as the Catholic Church, forbad birth control; conservative groups tried to block anything but abstinence-only sex education programs in schools; and some pharmacies refused to carry birth control pills, citing morality concerns.

Even with the advancements in women's rights, females continue to be treated as a commodity. The female body is used to sell cars, tools, and a whole range of products. Singers, with and without talent, are encouraged to use their bodies to get recording contracts and promote their music. Pageant girls parade themselves in sexy adult clothing to win prize money and college scholarships. The advancement of women appears to have made little impact in the exchange of resources for sex, evident in prostitution, stripping, and pornography (see chapters 3 and 4). One thing that has changed is that women are now defending the exploitation. Perhaps they are resigned to the inevitable: since women are going to be exploited anyway, why not make money? However, they are doing it not just for the money but also for the attention. There has been a surprising increase in unpaid sexual behaviors, ranging from *Girls Gone Wild* to amateur Internet sex videos.

Virginity

Virginity has long been a virtue reserved primarily for females. Male promiscuity has not only been tolerated as "boys will be boys" but championed. Statistically, in the United States, the average age of virginity loss leveled off around 1990, at about 16 years old. The age at which males and females lost their virginity converged as well (Carpenter, 2005). The overall teenage pregnancy rate in 2002 was down 35 percent from 1990, according to the Centers for Disease Control (Deveny, 2007).

Virginity is at a high premium for females even in pornography and prostitution. Men will often pay extra to have sex with a virgin prostitute. Many publications advertising "escort services" market new talent such as Broken Innocence and Amateur Escorts. Platinum Playmates advertise "all new girls." Amateur Escorts touts "college co-eds, receptionists, secretaries, & athletes." Covers of porn movies tout "her first time," "her gang bang," and "her first anal." The movies are extremely popular with male audiences. Actresses get substantial amounts of money for firsts; however, many of them are quickly used up and discarded once the initial appeal is gone. To pay for college, a young woman even put her virginity up for auction on eBay (McClellan, 2005). Rosie Reid offered her virginity to the highest bidder on the Internet. According to McClellan (2005), "The 18-year-old lesbian eventually had sex in a hotel in a run-down area of north London with a 44-year-old man who paid 8,400 pounds for the privilege." A vendor began selling T-shirts that read, "I sold my virginity on eBay."

Abstinence Pledges

In order to encourage teenagers to wait to have sex until marriage, many religious groups promote "abstinence pledges." Churches hold public ceremonies where daughters take the pledge and are given a virginity promise ring by their fathers. These pledges appear to be ineffective in the long run. According to Twenge's (2006) study, teens kept the pledge for about a year and a half and had fewer partners than those who did not pledge. On the other hand, statistics show that 88 percent of teens who take abstinence pledges have vaginal sexual intercourse before marriage. The gap between pledgers and non-pledgers for high-risk behavior was statistically significant (cited in "Many Teens," 2005). Boys who had pledged abstinence were four times as likely to have engaged in anal sex as those who did not pledge. Overall pledgers were reportedly six times as likely to have engaged in oral sex as teens who had not had intercourse but did not take a pledge (Bruckner cited in "Many Teens," 2005). In addition, participants in abstinence programs were less likely to use condoms (Twenge, 2006). Bearman and Bruckner (2004 cited in "Many Teens," 2005) reported that studies show that the rate of sexually transmitted diseases is relatively the same for those who have made abstinence pledges and those who have not. On the other hand, Unruh (cited in "Many Teens, 2005) called these studies bogus and argued that those teens who had reported being pledgers had not pledged true abstinence, which forbids oral and anal sex.

"Virgin" on a Technicality

While rates of teenagers having intercourse are down, there has been a dramatic increase of oral sex with girls as young as middle school. Teens, especially girls, are finding loopholes in being "technically" a virgin (Mayden, 2005). It appears that many teens do not consider oral-to-genital contact as sex (Fortenberry cited in Jayson, 2005). Even among college students, 38 percent of females and 44 percent of males reported they did not consider oral sex as sex (Sanders & Reinisch cited in Jayson, 2005). Jayson (2005) cited a study that found 13- to 17-year-olds agreed that oral sex was "casual" and "not a big deal ... it's not sex." According to a CDC report (cited in Jayson, 2005), one-quarter of teens who have not had intercourse have had oral sex. Between the late 1960s and the 1990s, the occurrence of high school- and college-age women who had engaged in oral sex rose from 42 percent to 71 percent. Of all teens from 15 to 19 years old, more than half have given or received oral sex. According to DeLamater (cited in Jayson, 2005), abstinence-only education may too narrowly focus on sexual intercourse and give the impression oral sex does not count.

Hymenoplasty, which is hymen repair or hymen reconstruction, is increasing in popularity. This surgery repairs a torn hymen due to intercourse or accidental tears. Hymen repair is usually done to restore virginity for cultural or religious reasons. An Internet search for hymenoplasty yielded a number of sites offering the procedure. For example, there is a site for the Manhattan Center for Vaginal Surgery. The website explains they "understand the discreet nature of the need for this surgery" ("Hymen Repair," n.d.).

Celebrity Virginity

Popular culture sends mixed signals regarding virginity. Britney Spears and Jessica Simpson proclaimed their Christian morals while at the same time exploiting their sexuality in their music videos and performances. Spears recanted on her pledge to maintain her virginity. Then, following her 55-hour marriage in Las Vegas, she wed again after briefly knowing Kevin Federline, whose ex-girlfriend was pregnant with their second child. Their reality show, *Britney and Kevin: Chaotic*, included crude discussions of their premarital sex. In November 2006, Spears filed for divorce a month after the birth of their second child. Jessica Simpson presents herself as a Christian who waited until marriage to have intercourse; however, her fashion choices and videos are very sexual. The contrast of their avowed virgin positions to the behaviors of these women trivializes virginity, making it appear freakish. Simpson may have "technically" waited to have sex until marriage; however, her husband disclosed in an interview on *Howard Stern* in 2004 that there was plenty of premarital oral sex. Now that Simpson's marriage has ended, celebrity media reports she had not abstained from sex until her next marriage.

Dating Trends

One way to understand trends of sexual activity is to look at the dating trends of young people. In the past, gender rules were very clear. Girls were supposed to wait at home for a boy to call. It was her responsibility to not let him go too far on a date. She was warned that if she gave away the milk, he would never buy the cow (such a flattering comparison). The best selling book, *The Rules* (Fein & Schneider, 1995), revived this advice to women. The authors presented the idea that men like the chase and women must play the game in order to keep them interested. For example, the authors recommend that females only occasionally return his calls, make him pay for dates, and dump him if he does not give romantic gifts on birthdays, etc.

Most girls and young women today have shunned "old fashioned" ideas of dating in favor of the "hookup." A 2001 study found that 60 percent of high school juniors who had had sex had done it with someone who was no more than a friend (cited in Twenge, 2006). Lavinthal and Rozler's (2005) *The Hookup Handbook* comically labeled different hookups such as "The fall-down-drunk hookup," "Oops, I did it again" ("the ex-boyfriend"), and "The Snuffleupagus" ("the hookup you deny but everyone else knows it really exists"). AdultFriendFinder.com, for example, is an "anti-dating" site. While its counterpart, FriendFinder.com, focuses on dating and marriage, the Adult site focuses on the hookup. A promo for the site stated, "You bought her dinner. You bought her flowers and chocolates. Result? Nada! Don't waste your time dating when you can cut straight to the chase. AdultFriendFinder.com is 10 million people looking for one thing" ("Adult Friend," n.d.).

One takeoff of the hookup is the "friends with benefits" phenomenon. The idea is based on both males and females getting the benefits of sex without the burden of a relationship. Denizet-Lewis (2004) reported "friends with benefits" has trickled down from college students to high school and even junior high students. He cited a Bowling Green University study that found that over half of high school juniors said that if they had already had sex, it had been with a friend. Some females relish the option of having sex without needing to be dependent on males to call and having to follow a list of rituals of dating. They may also see it as a way to get rid of the need to lie and deceive. Young women and girls are either exercising their sexual freedom by not waiting, or expecting a relationship.

On the other hand, critics argue that this is a sign that women have given up trying to find romance and are settling for strictly physical relationships. Some critics question whether "friends with benefits" is a defense mechanism used to protect females against heartache of a failed relationship. Females could also be resigning themselves to the inevitable fact that some males are only looking for sex; therefore, why get their hopes up. They could also be looking for attention and validation through physical encounters. Pinksy (cited in Denizet-Lewis, 2004) argued that girls do not actually enjoy hookups nearly as much as boys, even though they report they do. Shalit stated that "girls are being manipulated, but by a society that tries to convince them that they should act like boys, turning sexual modesty into a sign of weakness or repression" (cited in Denizet-Lewis, 2004). In other words, girls are acquiescing because they think that is what they are supposed to do to be liberated. Milburn (cited in Denizet-Lewis, 2004) stated, "Most of the time, it's the younger girl performing fellatio on the older boy, with the boy doing very little to pleasure the girl."

In response to the Denizet-Lewis (2004) article, one female wrote that the bottom line is that girls want boys to find them attractive. The sexual attention makes them feel grown up. She referenced Hollywood make-over movies where physical, and sexual, transformations change their status. She added that the problem is that girls who are looking to gain sexuality are counting on some equally confused teenage boy to affirm it. Madison (cited in Ashbrook, 2006) stated that empowerment should be about what feels good rather than being able to have sex like a guy. She tells females to "own your miniskirt." Myers (cited in Ashbrook, 2006) argued that women's option to say "yes" as well as "no" is empowering.

Trending Younger

Younger girls are doing more outrageous things, not necessarily in great numbers, but disturbing nonetheless. The movie *Thirteen*, which was cowritten by and based on real life experiences of thirteen-year-old Nikki Reed, illustrated the outrageous things and the shocking pressure girls are under to fit in with their peers. The film demonstrated scary trends of sexuality, cutting, and drug use. The motivation of these behaviors appears to come from desperation to gain acceptance by others.

A study by the National Center for Health Statistics and the Centers for Disease Control and Prevention (cited in Young, 2005) found 25 percent of 15-year-old girls and 50 percent of 17-year-olds had engaged in oral sex. An earlier study found that 4 percent of adolescents 13 to 14 years old said they have had oral sex. Other survey data showed no significant changes in reported rates of oral sex of unmarried males of similar ages (Young, 2006).

Burford (cited in Young, 2006) explained that girls are nonchalant about performing sexual acts on adult males. Girls reported having "rainbow parties" where girls would wear different colored lipstick. They would perform oral sex, leaving their individual marks on the male's penis. A tween fad is wearing colored jelly bracelets that signal sexual activity. One young girl (cited in "Buying into Sexy," 2005) described the colors: "Pink means 'kiss,' blue means 'blow job' and black means 'going all the way.'" Evidently, if a boy pulls the bracelet off, it means she has to follow through. Most girls do not do the things publicized in the media. Most of them wear the bracelets for fun; they are just playing with their sexuality. Although adults take the color scheme more seriously than the kids, it shows how sexually aware the kids are.

Sex has always sold, but now it is children who are buying. Tweens—kids aged eight to fourteen—are a hot target for companies for items such as video games with bikini-clad babes and music videos that feature plenty of sexual innuendo (Mesley, 2005). Tweens can shop at chain stores at the mall that cater to them. The stores are stocked with racy clothing, makeup, and lingerie. One 12-year-old explained that she and her peers do not want to be kids anymore (cited in "Buying into Sexy," 2005). They want all the fun with none of the responsibility that comes with being grown up. Her mother explained that although her daughter hasn't noticed boys yet, she wants to look sexy. The girls find that when they dress in sexy clothes strange males stare and approach them.

Milton Academy Incident

One specific incident in a private prep school near Boston illustrates new trends in sexual behavior and also brings up questions of consent for minors. At Milton Academy, five boys from the hockey team were caught receiving oral sex from a 15-year-old girl in the locker room. According to Slack (2005) the hockey players requested and received oral sex from the girl in a boys' locker room (Slack, 2005). Local prosecutors are trying to decide whether or not to charge the five boys with rape because the girl was underage, and the school says the girl was de facto "coerced" simply by virtue of the male/female ratio present in the locker room at the time ("Blowing It," 2005). Because the girl was 15, the boys who were 17 or 18 could have been charged with statutory rape (Levenson & Russell, 2005). Three young men charged with statutory rape in the incident at Milton Academy were sentenced to two years probation after apologizing to the victim and her family.

The commentary about the case in the media was vicious. The girl was repeatedly referred to as a "whore" in newspapers and on talk radio. The male commentators focused on her sexual appetite rather than on the boys' illegal behavior. Bloggers and postings on the *Boston Herald* bulletin board were screaming "slut" at the girl. One blogger stated, "If she's a slut I have no sympathy for her. If it turns out to be the way it appears on the surface, I have no sympathy for the boys" ("Milton Academy Sex," 2005). Another blog story was titled, "Blowing It at Milton Academy" (2005). The author argued that it was sad that only the boys were being punished. He questioned whether it could be called coercion if the girl was underage or because there were multiple boys around and only one girl involved. He argued that the boys might have been the ones coerced. "What boy is going to refuse oral sex freely offered by a girl his own age while his buddies look on? Seems to me it would take as much courage to refuse to accept as it would for the girl to refuse to oblige in the first place, right?" ("Blowing It," 2005). Finley (2005) argued that the girl had a reputation of being a "notorious slut." He referred to her as "our young nympho" and "MAS" (Milton Academy Slut). He cited a party where she allegedly answered the door topless. Most of his allegations came from rumors he had heard rather than factual evidence. That did not stop any of the bloggers from spreading incorrect facts.

This whole argument is disturbing. I was shocked at the incredible disdain for a 15-year-old girl. These men are bullies beating up on a girl who is not even old enough to drive a car. Some of these boys were 18 years old. Authorities uncovered a pattern of sexual misconduct in the girl's family (complaints her father touched one female student and masturbated in front of others and her brother who at 15 had a sexual relationship with an adult male teacher).

School Dances

Less drastic than the Milton Academy story, but still disturbing, are trends in high school and even middle school dances. Dancing has served a variety of cultural functions, from celebrations to warding off evil spirits. Even in the animal kingdom dancing is done in mating rituals. Some religious groups forbid dancing because of the sexual implication. A few decades ago, Catholic school dances often included the "flashlight test." Nuns would shine a flashlight to make sure there was enough space between the boy and the girl who were slow dancing. If no light shined through, the couple was dancing too closely. One middle school teacher (cited in Downes, 2006) stated she no longer chaperones middle school dances because of the sexualized dancing. She stated it is difficult because she has no authority to stop the behavior or send students home. In New Hampshire and California, school officials banned school dances because of the style of dance (Hernandez, 2006). According to Mehta (2006) many educators are drawing up specific rules of behavior, even changing the music format that they say encourages "freak" dancing. Specifically, freaking is when the girl is bent over in front of the boy, rubbing her rear end against his groin. According to Mehta (2006), a video of the dance showed a boy dancing behind his date, hands on her hips, thrusting his pelvis against her while she "hitches up her satiny gown and bends at the waist."

Charles Salter, principal of a California high school, banned dances after what he said looked like "simulated sex" that verged on sexual harassment. Salter explained that his responsibility as principal is to teach students "appropriateness" (Norris, 2006). Salter (cited in Hernandez, 2006) stated, "I'm still waiting for the first father to tell me he doesn't mind his daughter dancing that way." About 20 percent of students who filled out a survey reported that the type of dancing at school dances made them uncomfortable. Salter argued that parents need to step up and be parents. They need to have these discussions with their teens. Some students complained that if freaking was banned they would not attend school dances. One 15-year-old stated, "I wouldn't go.... It would be boring. How else do you dance?" (cited in Mehta, 2006).

The teens are seeing the freaking-type dancing on music videos. Recently singer Akon was criticized when he "danced" with a 14-year-old at a concert. The dance-off competition was a publicity stunt where the winner would get a trip to Africa. There was no dancing involved. He was simply humping her, or what many are calling dry railing, or even dry raping, on the stage. First, he picked her up so she was straddling him and then proceeded to simulate intercourse, driving her up and down on his groin. At one point, he had her pinned against a guardrail and humped her some more. Then he laid her onstage with her legs spread and humped her from above. What stood out on the video footage of the incident was that, when he finished with her, he did not even look at her. He walked off as one of the stage crew went to help her up. His defense was that he did not know she was only 14.

Dance Competitions

A common pastime for little girls across the United States is dance lessons. Parents and grandparents gather in an auditorium once a year to watch a dance recital. A selected group goes on to enter competitions. I interviewed my cousin Desiree, who is a dance instructor in a small town in Nebraska (personal communication, July 6, 2006). She told me that some of the competitions she has seen look like a Las Vegas show and the song choices are often disturbing. For example, she stated that girls as young as 13 were performing to the song "Hey, Big Spender" while playing up to male judges and audience members. In the song, the female voice refers to "popping" her cork. Although she claims she does not do it for every man, she offers the listener a good time (obviously in exchange for money). When asked if the younger girls understood the lyrics, she said that their facial expressions appear to be in line with the song's meaning. Generally if they use a love song, they will try to put a "Disney" frame around the romantic love rather than a lustful one. There have been significant changes in the last ten years. The age is getting lower as well. Song choices for 8-to-12-year-olds are by Metallica and "Dr. Feelgood" by Motley Crüe. Desiree remarked that the dancers are well trained and that it is a shame they have to be so sexual. Most dancers in competitions wear short skirts and bikini tops, regularly showing off their midriffs. Some 16- and 17-year-olds use lingerie as costumes.

Desiree has final approval over her dancers' outfits. The girls are allowed to select outfits from costume books. Her criteria is that they choose only outfits that are tasteful and that everyone look good in them. Many times it is the ill fit that makes the costumes inappropriate. Parents thank her for having strict standards. They tell her they cannot believe what the other girls in the competition are wearing. She argued that dance teachers need to realize that dads and grandfathers are in the audience. One drawback is that other teams are often rewarded for the sexier outfits. Her team competes against bigger towns in Omaha and Des Moines. The rules highlight that the dance moves and outfits should be appropriate for all audiences and all dancers. However, the sexier ones are the ones that win. The rules are on paper, but not enforced. Desiree described some of the dance moves as the girls spreading their legs toward the audience and including lots of hip gyrations. Judges are generally a mix of male and female, so female judges are rewarding this behavior as well. She said she met a five-year-old who demonstrated some of the dance moves she was learning from another teacher. She put her hands on her shoulders and shook her chest. She called it the "sassy walk."

Downes (2006) described a middle school talent show he attended on Long Island. For their talent, many of the girls danced to pop songs and imitated the music videos. He described the dancing: "They writhe and strut, shake their bottoms, splay their legs, thrust their chests out and in and out again. Some straddle empty chairs, like lap dancers without laps." What was most disturbing to Downes was that the parents were cheering on this spectacle. At the same time parents overprotect and overschedule their children, they "allow the culture of boy-toy sexuality to bore unchecked into their little ones' ears and eyeballs, displacing their nimble and growing brains and impoverishing the sense of wider possibilities in life" (Downes, 2006).

Cheerleading/Dance Teams

Cheerleading outfits and moves have changed dramatically in high schools and colleges over the past couple of decades. In some ways cheerleading has become more athletic. Competitions show high structures and daring throws. At the same time, it has become more sexual. Many of the dance moves emulate strippers. Even very young girl squads use these same sexual moves. Many of the uniforms are made of spandex. (I personally think about 1 percent of the female population looks attractive in spandex.) The material clings to each and every developing curve and bulge. A mother on the Bravo show *Sports Kids Moms and Dads* selected a tight fitting outfit for her eight-year-old daughter. She claimed the daughter needed to show off her athleticism for a cheerleader competition. The little girls performed sexy moves that rivaled NFL cheerleaders. According to Adams (cited in Jayson, 2005), All-Star cheerleading (fashioned after the Dallas Cowboy Cheerleaders) is the fastest growing segment of cheerleading. Adams described the change from girl next door to Las Vegas showgirl.

The Texas State House of Representatives approved a bill banning sexually suggestive cheerleading at middle and high school athletic games and events (Mack & Turner, 2005). The law would prohibit drill and cheerleading teams from performing overtly sexual routines at a school-sponsored or extracurricular event. The bill was in response to coaches and administrators who were concerned with tiny skirts, midriff tops, and "MTV-inspired" dance

moves. The arguments are extremely heated. Texas cheerleading was compared
to Internet pornography; a legislator likened it to "something you would see
at an adult club" (Edwards cited in Mack & Turner, 2005). The cheerleaders
themselves often do not think they are too provocative. Of course, these girls
have Britney Spears as a role model.

Cheerleaders and dance teams have been used for decades to enhance the
experience for men. The Dallas Cowboy Cheerleaders in the 1970s created a
huge industry of sideline shows, posters, and calendars. Dallas Cowboys owner,
Tex Schramm, decided in 1971 that he wanted to have beautiful model-like
cheerleaders that could dance the same Broadway style dances as those notable
groups from Broadway. This new breed of "cheerleader" would be the best of
the best and half-time entertainment would be the rave of the future, and so
the Dallas Cowboy Cheerleaders were born ("Dallas Cowboys," n.d.). Other
dance teams, such as the NBA's Los Angeles Laker Girls, picked up on their
popularity and the race began. Camera angles were used to accent their body
parts. (Eventually, the craze died down. Although a nice accent, male sports
fans were ultimately more interested in the game. Besides, there were plenty
of other outlets to get their dose of hoochie.)

The teams have interesting names, such as Chicago Lovabulls, New
Orleans Honeybees, and Nu Skin Jazz Dancers. The Philadelphia Eagles
Cheerleader site warns web surfers of "age appropriate" material on their site.
There is a DVD available of the making of the lingerie calendar with a warning for "mature audiences only." The Heat Dancers will even appear at business receptions, bar mitzvahs, birthday parties and more, according to their
website ("Book the Heat," n.d.). The Nu Skin Jazz Dancers, dance team for
the Utah Jazz, take part in school assemblies and various fundraising events.
One mother of two daughters tried out for a squad. She argued that she wanted
to show her daughters there was a way to entertain and be "classy and sophis-
ticated." She added that her husband is very proud.

After the Janet Jackson halftime demonstration, the NFL has made
changes to be more family friendly. During the games the cheerleaders are
much more subdued. Their moves are less sexually suggestive and their costumes provide more coverage. They are still sexual, however, in a different
context. For example, the Philadelphia Eagles cheerleaders offer a lingerie calendar for charity. The dance teams in the NBA are a bit different. Taking place
indoors, their outfit choices can be more revealing. The NBA also has a
different feel, different marketing strategies. One dance team had very short,
white flowing skirts. The purpose was to expose the white bottoms underneath. The bottoms (much like swimsuit bottoms) were sexy enough, but the
sneak peek under the skirt highlighted the titillation. It gave the illusion of
the innocence of the high school cheerleader with the pleasurable experience
of seeing under her skirt. The camera angle was shot from below so that the
peek under the skirt was maximized.

Nightclubs/Dancing

The acceptability of women dancing with each other was a breakthrough in the social scene. Females no longer have to wait for a male to ask them to dance. The ritual has shifted to where men will then go out to the dance floor by themselves, searching for an attractive woman. The men will dance up to them and gauge their reactions. If the woman is unresponsive the average man will move on to other women. On the other hand, this process allows strange men to start rubbing against women uninvited. The females' dancing is similar to an audition, not unlike a stripper, which only adds to perverted behavior of some males. Dance clubs often have a pole installed. The implication is that women are exhibitionists inside and secretly want to dance for men. The mainstream club appears to be a safe place for some women to "play" at being a stripper. Some of the women I observed would take a couple of turns at the pole and then run giggling back to their friends. They would then goad the other women in the group to try.

In the early 2000s, foam was popular at parties and in bars. Dance floors would be filled with three to six feet of soap suds. Women generally stripped down to their bra and underwear if they had not planned ahead and worn a bikini. Men wore shorts or boxers. Kardian (cited in "Steve Kardian Advice," n.d.) described the scene as venturing into a dark room filled with half naked, groping strangers. Stratton-Coulter (2006) reported even underage clubs were holding foam parties. Although there was a maximum age limit of 17, adult males had gotten into the clubs. One young male interviewed stated he knew guys who fondled unsuspecting girls. Because of the foam, it is difficult to identify the perpetrator. Even the president of a foam machine distributor agreed that the foam promotes an aggressively sexual environment (cited in Stratton-Coulter, 2006).

Women often take on a different persona at dance clubs. It appears to be an excuse to wear revealing clothing and play with their sexuality. The clubs are usually dark, and, therefore, club goers may feel anonymous. The clubs supply poles on the dance floor to allow women to "play" stripper. Alcohol fuels the fire, as well.

At one of the clubs I attended, I observed identical twin females with matching blonde hairstyles, low cut jeans, and slightly different white tops— one strapless and one halter. They were dancing together working the crowds, playing on men's fantasies of twins. They would move around to the different dance floors from one group of men to another. The guys watching them were very interesting: they were looking without seeming to look. Others watched and laughed to each other. At one point a guy joined them. The twin in the middle was back and forth with playing along and ignoring him. The other twin was pulling her closer, trying to get her away from this guy who was overstepping his boundaries. Eventually they left the dance floor since he didn't take their hints. One woman in particular was monopolizing the pole at the dance club that night. My friends and I noticed her as soon as she walked in the door with thigh-high fishnet stockings that ended just below her short denim skirt. Except for the fact that she kept her meager clothes on, she looked like a professional stripper. Again, there were few people watching her.

One popular trend on the dance floor is to act out the lyrics to a song. Some classics are "Stop in the Name of Love" and "I Will Survive." Some of the current songs played in the clubs are incredibly degrading to women, yet females are out on the dance floor singing along and acting out the lyrics. Three songs that caught my attention were "Face Down, Ass Up," "Back That Ass Up," and "Smack That." The lyrics to "Face Down" describe how the member of 2 Live Crew like to have anal sex because they are tired of doing it from the front. The male singer orders the woman to get on all fours with her ass in the air. When he gets tired, he wants her to give his friend oral sex while he is riding her. In the chorus, the singer asks the male listeners to chant that female genitalia is only "meat." "Smack That" and "Back That Ass Up" lyrics also reference submissive women bending over to expose their ass. The male voice in "Smack That" invites the woman to watch as he smacks her until she is sore.

Girls Gone Wild

Joe Francis has built his empire solely on college students flashing their breasts (Pollet & Hurwitz, 2003). His $100,000,000 company produces about 80 DVDs a year. The tradition of women exposing their breasts for beads on Bourbon Street during Mardi Gras has exploded. The practice spread to spring break, which is marketed as a wild time.

The enormous popularity of *Girls Gone Wild* videos is not significant just because of the number of males who purchase the tapes, but also because of the willingness of women to appear on them for free. Producers no longer have to use alcohol or coax women into removing their tops. Females have reportedly propositioned cameramen and physically attacked other women for a chance to get on tape. One of the *GGW* recruiters (cited on Winfrey, 2006b) stated that it was easy to persuade dozens of young women to flash their private parts and perform "lewd acts" for the cameras. The girls were looking for their 15 seconds of fame. The recruiter stated that, even though many of them were drunk at the time, very few of the participants regretted it afterwards. Francis estimated that 70 percent of women asked say yes when approached to be on the videos. He stated, "Any young woman will lift her top for the low price of guaranteed male attention" (cited in Garcia, 2003). According to Garcia (2003), *Girls Gone Wild* girls flashed as a way to become famous. Others rationalized that they might as well show it off while they are young. Francis plays off some young women's desire to be seen as "wild," taking chances, and breaking the rules.

Leahy (2003) surmised that Francis sells naughtiness. Regular pornography no longer shocks, but getting a regular girl to expose herself is titillating. According to Sauer (2004), the company has distanced itself from the pornography industry. It advertises on late night basic cable television with black bars over the naughty parts. Sauer (2004) claimed that there is added value to the videos because the women are not being paid. It relies on "spontaneous exhibitionism." Sohn (sited in Edgers, 2003) argued that the idea that women would expose themselves for free T-shirts is more disturbing than hard-core porn. The phenomenon reinforces the fantasy that women everywhere are ready to take their clothes off for the pleasure of men. In addition, since nudity is so prevalent, the assumption follows that if a woman does not want to pose nude or dares to voice opposition, she is labeled as frigid or prudish. On the other hand, supporters state that the flashing is liberating. According to Pollet and Hurwitz (2003), Francis compared women flashing their breasts at Mardi Gras to feminists burning their bras.

More recent videos show women doing much more than flashing their breasts. Young women are shown licking each other's nipples, for example. The "Dorm Room Fantasies" series has moved into full nudity, masturbation, and girl-on-girl sex acts. Video titles include: *Girls Gone Wild Extreme Orgy*, *Girls Gone Wild Sex Starved Coeds*, and *Girls Gone Wild Lipstick Lesbians*. Google search results yielded *Real Girls, Uncensored & Out of Control*, and *The Hottest Nude Videos*, which was described as "college girl co-eds in non teen tit flashing action." In one *Girls Gone Wild* promo, two girls are making out; it is clear one is nude, the other only in a thong. The nude girl is running her hand down her body. The camera cuts away just as her hand reaches her thong. There is one woman who is clearly masturbating under the tub faucet. Others are rubbing their bare breasts together. Others are dry humping, topless and wearing thongs. One is taking off the other's pants. Others are spanking. One girl is shown as she is talking on the phone saying, "Hey, Dad, I'm just about to be on *Girls Gone Wild*." The girls sort of act shy at times, giving that illusion of innocence. They close their eyes and cover their faces afterwards. The premise is that they are competing in games, obstacle courses that are incorporated with girl-on-girl action. The announcer stated that the women are young, hot, and out of control. He added, "No rules, no parents, and of course no clothes. These girls are willing to do whatever it takes to win."

There is a new version of the Gone Wild videos called *Guys Gone Wild*. The series is very similar to the female version: young males expose their private parts and are in various stages of masturbation. Unlike the female versions there appears to be no contact between the males. In some scenes it is apparent that other guys are in the background but there is a regulated distance between them and an apparent unspoken rule about looking at the other guy's exposed areas. It differs from pornography because there are nonthreatening themes such as naked pizza delivery. The tapes are plugged heavily on LOGO, the cable channel for lesbians and gay men.

According to Sauer (2004) the *Girls Gone Wild* brand is cool. Lentini (2007) reported that Francis is opening a chain of restaurants and a clothing line. As a way of expansion, the company is also featuring a search for the wildest bar in America. The *GGW* website featured photos that show a resurgence of wet T-shirt contests and girl-on-girl action on the dance floor. Many of these bars were in very small towns, such as Tahlequah, Oklahoma, and Chicopee, Massachusetts. There is an air of normalcy when dealing with the phenomenon of *GGW*. A special was aired by VH-1 featuring behind the scenes segments. According to their website,

> We will be living in the moment with him as he jets across the country, from gig to gig, on his 2003 College Tour. We'll be with him as he hosts a celeb-studded Super Bowl bash in San Diego. His cameras won't be rolling but ours will. Also, we will be tracking a group of girls who are preparing to go to their first Girls Gone Wild party. We will live in their anticipation and thrill, and ultimately their reaction when they wake up the following morning ["GGW Uncovered," 2003].

If there is any doubt that the *GGW* phenomenon is affecting popular culture, a police officer reported that a video showed a 16-year-old boy offering girls a sucker if they would lift their shirts. Three of them did, exposing their breasts. One of the girls was 14 years old (Mitchell, 2006).

Changes in Types of Sex

A common fantasy among men is seeing women together performing sexual acts. Barton (2006) described the phenomenon as the voyeuristic pleasure of male viewers. Griffin (n.d.) explained men's fascination with "lesbians," rather pseudo lesbians, by comparing them to beer: "Aren't two beers better than one?" He further distinguishes between "attractive" or "lipstick lesbians," the second tier, and the bull dykes, or man-hating lesbians. Lipstick lesbians also like men. They are often just experimenting or trying to make their men happy.

Reports show that more and more girls in high school are making out with each other, not because they are attracted to other females or exploring their sexuality. They are doing it in front of boys to get attention. One poster ("Top Ten Reasons," 2005) wrote that those young women think they are being liberated, but they are "bringing the stereotypical male porno fantasy to life." She distinguished true sexual evolution from pandering to men by asking whether the women would do the same action when no one was watching. She is surprised, actually calling it diabolical, that women offer to do it without being goaded. Warn (2003) referred to the type of woman who does this for attention as either "bi-curious" or "heteroflexible." She argued that straight women are capitalizing on this male fantasy rather than improving lesbian visibility.

According to Barton (2006), the girl-on-girl performances in media "do not reflect subjective lesbian desire but, rather, at best, a bisexual expression of lust designed to arouse and satisfy men" (p. 114). The Madonna-Britney Spears kiss during the MTV video awards was a controversial publicity stunt. The event was supposed to mark the passing of the baton from Madonna to Britney Spears and Christina Aguilera. Madonna has been known for her sexual dominance, but it looked like it was Spears who initiated the use of her tongue in the kiss. Warn (2003) described the kiss as raunchy. The musical duo t.A.T.u. regularly kiss passionately onstage and touch each other in sexual ways as part of a marketing campaign (see chapter 8).

As pornography goes mainstream, it becomes more common to believe that all women should not only engage in male fantasies but share the same fantasies. The expectation is that women want all forms of extreme sex. The standard becomes that really liberated women want to engage in threesomes and anal sex. Levy (2005b) argued that girls and young women are imitating strippers and porn stars whose job it is to fake sexual pleasure and power; therefore, our culture is getting further and further away from "authentic experience." Many women see sex as a competition for men's attention. They think that men find women most attractive when they are willing to participate in sex acts once considered deviant.

The act of anal sex can be degrading. The woman is almost completely submissive and defenseless in this position. Even porn star Jenna Jameson refuses to do anal on camera. Jameson (2004) described anal sex as an emotional component, as an exchange of power. She stated that every man she has met loves the idea of dominating women through anal sex. She claimed it would be compromising herself. The hip-hop artist Nelly used the concept of the "tip drill" in his music and videos. A tip drill is described as a situation where a woman is so unattractive to a man that he can have sex with her only from behind so he does not have to look at her face. Anal sex can also be physically dangerous if not performed the correct way. "Sexperts" from the University of California at Santa Barbara warned that the delicate tissues in the area are easily irritated or damaged. HIV and other sexually transmitted diseases are more easily transmitted in this way ("What Danger," 2007). Fecal matter, which is filled with bacteria, can cause very painful infections if transferred to the mouth, penis or vagina.

Conclusion

The women's liberation movement and the sexual revolution of the 1960s and 1970s were supposed to free women to enjoy their sexuality. Women were told they were entitled to have sexual pleasure for themselves. Instead of moving forward, it appears girls and young women today are reverting to pleasing men. They are not only being sexually exploited, they are also exploiting their own bodies to gain attention. This generation appears to see equality as the freedom for women to be as raunchy as men. Levy (2005) called this phenomenon "female chauvinism." She argued that, because we live in such a commercialized society, "[we] reduce sexuality to something that can be bought and sold like polyester underpants and implants."

Media outlets instruct women to release their inner sexpot. Perhaps there is a stripper inside every woman dying to get out. Flashing breasts and dancing at amateur night at strip clubs may be wonderful outlets for women to explore their "more playful" side. "Friends with Benefits" and other sex without commitment trends may free up women and girls from restrictive roles. However, there is little evidence that the majority of women and girls are doing these acts for themselves. There appears to be a growing disconnect between females and their bodies.

The scariest trend of all is the sexualization of little girls. Some parents are fanatical about injury-free playgrounds and antibacterial everything, yet they increasingly sexualize their daughters. Many of the same parents who preach "abstinence only" programs in school allow their teen and preteen daughters to dress provocatively. Parents put their daughters in beauty pageants and dance competitions where they are highly sexualized. Parents and other adults are making age compression marketing incredibly lucrative. They support fashion designers who are pushing little girls to show up at middle schools as young Britney Spears wannabees. As a society we need to slow down the sexualization of females and let little girls be little girls. We need to teach young women healthy and empowering ways to express their sexuality.

3. Pornography

There is little doubt that pornography is popular in the United States, although there is a dispute about how popular. Many outlets have reported that the pornography industry has grown to an $8–10 billion business (see Schlosser cited in Barton, 2006). Klatell (cited in Ackman, 2001) rejected these figures and stated the industry is as marginal as it ever was. He claimed that the $10 billion figure was from an unsourced report that was cited over and over again until it became a commonly accepted truth. Ackman (2001) noted that adult video sales and rental figures were wildly inflated ($4 billion) in an industry trade magazine. Other studies (see Adams Media Research, Forrester Research, Veronis Suhler Communications Industry Report, IVD cited in Ackman, 2001) reported the following figures in the adult entertainment industry: $500 million to $1.8 billion for adult videos; $1 billion for Internet; $128 million for pay-per-view; and $1 billion for magazines. These estimates total $2.6 billion to $3.9 billion for the industry. According to Braiker (2007), adult sales and rentals account for just 2 percent of the whole $24.3-billion DVD pie.

It is no longer seedy, backroom companies making money on porn. Mainstream businesses are raking in huge profits. Major hotels such as Marriott, Westin, and Hilton generate more money from in-room X-rated movies than from their minibars (Kirk & Boyer, 2002). Cable and satellite companies take in approximately 80 percent of the pay-per-view dollar on porn (Asher cited in Kirk & Boyer, 2002).

In what was once a taboo proposition, there is an elevated status for women posing naked or near naked in men's magazines. Women now appear in *Playboy* at the height of their careers, which once was a desperate move for struggling actresses or models. Posing nude has become the norm rather than an isolated incident. Even several Olympic gold medalists have posed nude. Porn stars are gaining more mainstream popularity, appearing in advertisements and MTV videos. No longer thought of as desperate women forced into pornography by poverty or bad men, these very beautiful, bright, articulate female porn stars chat freely about how they love sex. Jenna Jameson has made regular appearances on mainstream television shows, including E!'s *Wild On*,

The Man Show, and *Entertainment Tonight*. She has been in rock videos and done commercials for Abercrombie & Fitch and Pony sneakers. Her autobiography made the *New York Times* Best Seller list. Sex videos of celebrities such as Pamela Anderson and Paris Hilton are an extension of this acceptability of kinky sex for voyeuristic consumption.

Magazines

The most successful "adult" magazine of all time is *Playboy*, which was first published in 1953. Hugh Hefner broke new ground when he created a mainstream magazine for men. *Playboy* was seen as having style and class. Women were photographed in the nude; however, the soft lighting gave it more of an art feel. Ehrenreich (cited in "Men's Magazines," n.d.) noted that *Playboy*-type magazines emerged in the 1950s, shortly after the beginning of the baby boom era. Men were feeling constrained by marriage, fatherhood, mortgage payments, etc. *Playboy* celebrated the bachelor's lifestyle and male independence from domestic responsibilities. Hefner expanded his empire to include Bunny Clubs. Now his Grotto is world famous for parties attended by top celebrities and sports stars.

Hustler, a Larry Flynt creation, is much raunchier than *Playboy*. Flynt abandoned any pretext of "art" in his photos, which often included sex toys and penetration. According to the *Hustler* website, the company has expanded into more raunchy versions: *Hustlers Hardcore Unlimited Edition* ("bursting with explicit, uncensored images of sexual drama. This is NOT the frilly, soft-focus newsstand publication") and *Hustler Asian* ("If you love Asians, then your dreams are about to all come true! *Hustler* presents the hottest Asian girls, doing all the things that you love best! They are captured doing anal, dp, blow jobs, getting facials and more!") ("Hustler," n.d.). Flynt often got into trouble with his tasteless cartoons, such as Chester the Molester. One of the most controversial items was the woman in the meat grinder. A pair of long, lovely women's legs was shown sticking up out of a meat grinder while ground up, meat-like substance was coming out the other end.

Bob Guccione's *Penthouse* magazine was a middle ground between *Playboy* and *Hustler*. "*Penthouse Letters*" was an infamous feature of the magazine where mostly men submitted explicit descriptions of their sexual fantasies. Because of competition from Internet pornography, *Penthouse* began showing female urination, fulfilling some men's fantasy of "golden showers."

Magazine Models

The women who appear in these nudie magazines were once seen as harlots and fallen women. Most of the time, they were desperate either for money or for fame. These concepts of desperation have been replaced by women who will do it for free, or nearly free, for attention, and celebrities who already have fame but want more. *Playboy* has featured many celebrities, especially the aging actresses who want to hold on to their youth and still be considered sexy. The average model is no longer a naïve girl who gets tricked into posing by a manipulative photographer or a desperate, penniless, wannabe actress. Famous people who have appeared in *Playboy* include Farrah Fawcett, Katarina Witt, Daryl Hannah, and Rachel Hunter.

Porn magazines also feature editions of "ordinary" women in their "Women of" series. For example, "Women of Enron," "Women of Starbucks," and "Women of Wal-Mart" displayed nude photographs of actual female employees. The lower-wage employees perhaps give the viewer a superior stance or perhaps the fantasy that they will find someone in their local stores so easily willing to take their clothes off. The *Playboy* website brags, "*Playboy* has always had a knack for finding sexy women, often in unexpected places" ("Playboy," n.d.). The producers of *Playboy* tapped some of America's most well-known franchises, such as Home Depot, for models. They discovered that "sexy salesgirls" could be found right in men's neighborhoods, even behind the counter of McDonald's. Issues of college students are popular as well. Over the last decade, producers of the "Girls of ..." college sports conferences (e.g., the SEC, Big 12, Big 10, Pac 10, and ACC) issues have gone to college campuses to recruit. These issues are popular because they feature regular women rather than sex industry models. The images allow men to fantasize that the person serving them fries will be hot and strip for them. The college editions give the impression that these females are not desperate, like the stereotypical strung out crack whore, but a little naughty. They are perhaps rebelling against their parents. Speaking of parents, some of them appear to be posing as well. *Playboy*'s Hottest Housewives edition featured stay-at-home moms.

In response to the "Women of Enron Uncover Their Hidden Assets," issue of *Playboy*, Carlson (2006) stated that in other countries bankruptcy might be considered shameful, a tragedy. In the United States, however, it is a good excuse to get naked. Carlson sarcastically wrote, "This photo spread proves that Americans have not lost the spirit of can-do optimism that made this country great." One of the former Enron employees who posed (cited in Carlson, 2006) argued it was her time to "get a little bit back," meaning her 15 minutes of fame after her job and life savings was wiped out in an executive scam.

Another trend is the posing of pseudo celebrities. Runner up for *Joe Millionaire*, Sarah Kozer stated, "I wanted something good to come out of the whole *Joe Millionaire* experience. So I said yes [to posing nude for Playboy]" ("Why I Posed," p. 66). *Who Wants to Marry a Multimillionaire*'s Darva Conger; *Real World*'s and *Road Rules*' Flora, Beth S., Veronica, Jisela, Trishelle and Arissa; and *Survivor*'s Jerri, Jenna, and Heidi. *Playboy* DVD's Girls of Reality TV says: "From MTV's *Real World Las Vegas* and *Road Rules*, to *Survivor* and *Big Brother*, this *Playboy* exclusive release reveals some of the sexiest young stars on reality TV.

From MTV's *Real World Las Vegas* Trishelle Cannatella & Arissa Hill; from
MTV's *Road Rules* Katie Doyle; from NBC's *Survivor: Marquesas* Sarah Jones;
from CBS's *Big Brother 2* Shannon Michelle; from *Big Brother 3* Tonya Paoni."
There is a Women of *Fear Factor* DVD. The female contestants from *The Apprentice* turned down *Playboy* but posed in sexy underwear for *FHM* magazine.

Changes in the Industry

While pornographic magazines have been popular, technological advances
have hindered their success. With easy Internet access, traditional print magazines are having a hard time competing. Print versions also have to deal with
legal issues such as store sales and postal laws concerning the delivery of inde-
cent and obscene material. *Playboy* profits fell in the last quarter of 2006 because
of declines in publishing advertising and lower pay-per-view revenue (Spain,
2007). Second tier skin magazines such as *Screw* dropped from 140,000 copies
a week to around 30,000 ("Porn Mag Sales," 2003). *Screw* and *Penthouse*'s parent companies both filed for bankruptcy protection in 2003. Circulation had
declined by more than 40 percent in a five-year period ("Porn Mag Sales,"
2003). Flynt (cited in "Porn Mag Sales," 2003) stated that although the industry will not likely disappear, it will never have the impact it once did. In order
to stay viable, Flynt has diversified to the Internet and movies. *Playboy* has
raised revenue in its venue at the Palms Casino Resort in Las Vegas (Spain,
2007). Goldstein planned on putting out a new version of *Screw*, as he
described, "dirtier and filthier than ever" ("Porn Mag Sales,"2003).

Films

As the film industry grew, some theaters specialized in what was then
known as "XXX" films. The stereotype of the typical patron was a man in a
trench coat sneaking in to sit in a dark theater. *Deep Throat* was perhaps the
first pornographic movie to get any type of mainstream attention. The lead
character's clitoris was located in her throat. The film featured Linda Lovelace,
who lacked gag reflexes and could perform oral sex on males with extraordi-
nary skill. According to Cale (2005), both men and women formed lines around
the block to see the movie. Even well-known Hollywood celebrities showed
up at screening. It is difficult to think of other such movies appearing in mainstream theaters to date.

Affordable videocassette recorders gave viewers the option of discretely
viewing pornography in the privacy of their own home. Videos could be ordered
through the mail and sent in a plain, brown paper wrapper. Video stores had
a section with an "adults only" sign that often had a curtain partitioning it off
from the other selections of the store. Home videos, and later DVDs, created
a new market for porn. One of the themes of the current porn title was the
allusion to youth and innocence: for example, *Naughty Slumber Party, Don't Tell*

Daddy, Barely Legal, Gang Bang a Teen, Teenage Runaways, Private School Girls, and *Deep Throat Virgins.* Not only was youth celebrated, but fantasies about MILF were featured in such titles as *Mom's Anal Adventure* and *Real Amateurs* (older, married women). There is also a theme of women who really want to perform for men but are too oppressed. These titles include *I Want to Be Bad, Housewives Unleashed,* and *Dirty Debutante.* Characters such as cheerleaders, sorority girls, and nurses are also popular: *Please Help Me Pay for College, Lesbian Cheerleading Squad, Lesbian Big Boob Nurses, Night Shift Nurses,* and *Sorority Sex Kit.* There was also a sense of the peeping tom in titles such as *Real Hidden Locker Rooms.* There was an ethnic theme as well, for example, *Male Order Teens from Poland, Swedish Erotica,* and *Young Asian Cuties.* The harder core selections I found had physical brutality in the titles, such as *Throat Gaggers* and *Bondage Classics.* These titles reinforce the notion that the degradation of women and the deviance of the material is the titillating part of the industry.

Film Producers

The PBS documentary *American Porn* (Kirk & Boyer, 2002) showed behind-the-scenes footage of the pornography industry. It featured interviews with both male and female producers. Adam Glasser (cited in Kirk & Boyer, 2002), a porn producer who legally changed his name to Seymore Butts, pleaded no contest to obscenity charges in 2001 for his video *Tampa Tushy Fest.* The video was singled out for its depiction of double vaginal fisting. Glasser credited the idea to two women who started doing it in the back of his van. He stated that he filmed the act because the women were doing something they enjoyed. Glasser also argued that it was important to release the video because women wrote to him telling him that is what they want. Fisting (often called "punching"), if done forcefully, can cause bowel rupture, internal tears, urinary tract infections, and temporary fecal incontinence (Inciardi, Surratt, & Telles, 2000). Fingernails can also cause scratches or tears of mucosal tissue.

Glasser (cited in Kirk & Boyer, 2002) described his movies as educational tools, and stated it is his duty to help others. He claimed that women walk up to him to tell him he saved their marriages. He stated the money was great but claimed it was not important compared to helping men and women over their confusion regarding sex. In the Kirk and Boyer (2002) interview, Glasser admitted that women are degraded and taken advantage of in the industry. He stated that he tries to do something when it is brought to his attention but admitted that is in only 5 percent of the abuse cases. Glasser stated, "My world deals with the woman's orgasm and the woman's pleasure and her being in control. I think that's what makes my movies so attractive, not only to men but also to women, because they get that feeling."

Producer Robert Zicari (aka Rob Black) and his wife, Janet Romano (aka Lizzy Borden), were indicted for distributing obscene materials in 2003. The following is a list of the movies under investigation with descriptions provided by contributors to Wikipedia: *Extreme Teen 24* ("a scene of a naive 'pre-teen' being talked into having sex by an adult man"), *Cocktails 2* ("various scenes of women drinking vomit and other bodily fluids"), *Ass Clowns 3* ("A female journalist is being raped by a gang led by Osama bin Laden; the journalist is freed and the gang members killed. The director's cut version also contains a scene where Jesus steps off the cross and has sex with an angel"), *1001 Ways to Eat My Jizz* and *Forced Entry* ("the story of a serial rapist and killer who eventually gets killed by a mob") ("Rob Zicari," n.d.). Although Wikipedia entries may be suspect, they are still extremely disturbing. Zicari himself described the *Cocktail* series as pretty repugnant (cited in Kirk & Boyer, 2002). He explained that in one version a woman has sex with two men who spit and ejaculate in a bowl, which she then drinks. In another version a woman is giving fellatio to several men in a line. She then gags so much she vomits. Humiliation is often a significant part of the turn-on for some viewers.

As another example of the extreme things they do, Zicari described a scene where two female prison guards strap on a fake penis and rape a male inmate. In an interview (later in this chapter), Zicari's wife described another rape scene with a female actor who was not told before the scene she was going to be raped on camera (Romano cited in Kirk & Boyer, 2002). Zicari (cited in Kirk & Boyer, 2002) justified his material by comparing it to other media work such as *Banned from TV, Caught on Video*, where footage of people dying in horrible accidents are filmed and sold in video stores. He argued, "But if I want to do a scene where a guy walks into a room and has sex with a woman, and then shoots her in the head and steals her money, why not?" He further justified his work by stating it is fake; for example, when a man is choking a woman in his films it is fake.

Some feminists argue that the problem with pornography is that the industry is controlled by men. They reason that things would be better if women created the movies. In some such cases, the material is actually more degrading. Women are not automatically sensitive to other women. If they have been abused or subjugated, they may be more than willing to sell someone else out to relieve themselves. Janet Romano stated that her rationale for making hardcore pornography is that women are degraded no matter what they do, so she might as well make money doing it (cited in Kirk & Boyer, 2002). She admitted that it is normal in her world to be harassed sexually and verbally. She also stated that she uses the fact that she is a female producer to her advantage. If a male were to ask the things she does of female actors, he would be considered a pervert.

Romano produced a film where a woman's car breaks down. She is raped by two strange men who call her "a cunt, a whore, a slut, and a piece of shit." The men pretend to cut her throat, spit on her, and leave her in a pool of blood. The most troubling aspect is that the actress had no idea any of this was going to happen. Romano (cited in Kirk & Boyer, 2002) stated she just has to "let happen what's gonna happen." Romano claimed the actress who received the beating and was "put through hell" is her best friend. She nonchalantly stated before the filming she will give her friend a hug and take her out to dinner afterward. Her rationale was that she can only abuse someone she knows. She claimed she knew her friend could take it. She even stated her friends liked it rough.

In the interview with Kirk and Boyer (2002), Romano winced and put her hands over her face as she watched her friend being beaten in the scene. The PBS film crew left the scene because it was so brutal. Reportedly there was evidently nothing illegal about the act because it was all done between consenting adults. It is hard to imagine that the female actor gave her consent willingly. Romano admitted the idea for the beating and rape was her idea. She suggested that the interviewer for the PBS documentary hit his wife a little bit. She explained that hitting them makes women horny and, in her words, more "tingly down in your genital area." She wants to make "real" movies, not the "lovey dovey" pornography that other producers make. In her world, romantic sex is not real. Abusive sex is. She described it as hot steamy sex that acts like a drug. It is frightening to think that naïve viewers, both male and female, may think abuse is supposed to be part of the sexual pleasure.

Romano's callousness evidently came from her childhood. She admitted that her stepfather was an alcoholic. It is not a real stretch that he abused her as well. She also disclosed that she was exploited when she did pornography. Her rationale for abusing other women is that if someone is going to do it, it might as well be her. She admitted that she has deep issues and that abusing others is therapeutic for her. She stated, "I'm exploiting people, taking all my inner demons and aggression out on them. But it's good for me. So I guess that's all that matters" (cited in Kirk & Boyer, 2002). She often goes home and has a nice dinner after a day of abusing others. She has a very self-centered, immature view of the world. In the PBS special, she sounded absolutely demented, schizophrenic. She must have detachment issues the way she can go back and forth between feeling and not feeling. It is interesting that she is aware that her past affects her present. She got physically upset when she was watching the rape, so she also feels something. She is not totally numb to the situation. She justified her actions with the "giving the audience what it wants" theory. It is very disturbing to see a woman exploiting other women. She seems clear in her rationale of hurting others because she is damaged.

Romano likely represents a very small percentage of female producers. One of the most famous female producers is Danni Ashe, the CEO and model for Danni's Hard Drive. At one time she was the most downloaded woman on the Internet. Ashe (cited in Kirk & Boyer, 2002) claimed her work is not degrading to the female models she uses in her work. She stated her goal is to reverse some of the sexual repression in the United States about nudity and sex. Ashe's theory is that the more the culture is repressed, the more unhealthy, even violent, reactions will surface. She argued that repression will create anger, which may result in the blurring of sex and violence in violent pornography.

Changes in Porn Content

As pornography has become more prevalent and more easily available, there is an "arms race" to produce the most titillating material. Consumers get desensitized quickly and are looking for the next big thrill. In response, pornography has added everything from humiliation scenes (e.g., urination, defecation) to pseudo lesbian/girl-on-girl action. Inexperienced models and first-timers are popular in pornography. In addition to *Playboy Magazine*'s "Women of" series that has featured Wal-Mart and McDonald's workers, *Playboy* has released "Sexiest Amateur Home Videos." *Girls Gone Wild* "Dorm Fantasies" is an example of amateur fascination. Voyeurism is popular as well. There are hundreds of sites that claim they have hidden cameras and the women having sex have no idea they are being recorded. The amateur quality of the videos adds to the realism.

Another trend is material that verges on child pornography. Britney Spears' video *Baby One More Time* touched on the fantasy of the sexed up school girl (she was 16 at the time). In addition, lingerie such as "baby doll" pajamas is often made childlike with frills and ribbons. The film series *Barely Legal* features an 18-year-old's first experiences of sex for money. Other porn producers capitalize on the "firsts" on promotional materials such as box covers. For example, the cover might feature a first "boy-girl" or first on-screen anal. The porn actress has a very short shelf life. After she has performed something once or twice, the demand wanes and thus the price goes down. Once the mystery is gone, audiences move on to the next new thing. (The word "thing" is used on purpose.)

Whereas the exploitation of women in general is arousing for some men, seeing powerful women is often even more intriguing. It is often more titillating to see a rich girl exposing herself, someone who is not desperate for the money but is doing it as rebellion (e.g., the Paris Hilton sex tape). Other consumers see the opportunity to put strong women in their place. The porn industry often uses the fantasy of the uptight schoolteacher shedding her glasses, unbuttoning her stiff collared shirt, and releasing her long flowing hair from her stern bun. Underneath the prim exterior lies a sensuous woman. The Van Halen video *Hot for Teacher* featured junior high boys (young look-alikes of the group members) sitting next to a runway where their teacher stripped down to a bikini and danced for them.

There is something creepy about the men who understand that many of the women performing have been abused as children and still enjoy it.

Perhaps for some men it plays into a desire to control these women. They can more easily dominate and humiliate women who are dependent on them.

Girl-on-Girl

Girl-on-girl sex acts are incredibly popular. I hesitate calling them lesbian acts because the purpose is not for the participants' pleasure but to please the voyeuristic males. Examples of girl-on-girl can be found anywhere, from an episode of *The O.C.* to Madonna and Britney's kiss on MTV's Video Music Awards. Women kissing other women is a staple of the *Howard Stern Show*. There is even a version of *Girls Gone Wild* called *Girls Who Like Girls*. According to one posting ("Top Ten Reasons," 2005), "It's rare to see women who are genuinely hot for each other" in so-called lesbian porn. Rather, the portrayal of women is that they are just doing each other until the male watching can join in to form a threesome. Another poster noted that 99.8 percent of girl-on-girl action is fake lesbian porn sold to men ("Top Ten Reasons," 2005). Real lesbian porn, often directed by women and produced by small production companies, tends to scare many heterosexual men because of the differing standards of beauty.

One very open lesbian (D. Levits, personal communication, Jan. 13, 2007) stated she is not really upset with girl-on-girl scenes made to titillate men. She explained the scene might start with two females getting together, but "a penis always gets involved somehow." She finds "true" lesbian porn boring, describing it as a "let's be friends" story line and not enough sex. She and her friends often watch gay male porn instead because lesbian porn is boring and heterosexual porn is "questionable."

Meg (personal communication, May 1, 2006), a former dancer, did not mind performing girl-on-girl entertainment. She stated that many women in the sex industry choose to do only girl-on-girl. Perhaps there is a perception of equality that both women are peers and therefore share power. When a man enters the equation, he is naturally dominant in most cases because of his physical size and the nature of intercourse and the penis penetration.

Porn for Women

Harshman (2004) claimed that 18–34 year old women are the fastest growing Internet porn users. According to Muskoron (n.d.), the new interest in porn for women is that they are realizing they can enjoy it as much as men. She also credits the industry for tapping into the new market. Muskeron also noted that women have been reading pornography for decades. On the other hand, women are less likely to enjoy the images of pornographic film. Evidently women like to create the images of their fantasies themselves. Reading allows them to put themselves in the fantasy. Also, there are no actual women exploited in the writing of novels.

Producers of sex films for women often refer to it as erotica rather than pornography. Some critics question whether there really is a difference. For example, just because something claims to be "for women by women" it does not mean that women are less exploited. It is difficult to find an agreed upon definition of eroticism. Goldstein (cited in Slade, 2000) argued that distinctions are based on gender, class, and personal preference. He stated, "Eroticism is what turns me on. Pornography is what turns you on." Head (cited in Harshman, 2004) claimed that female film producers are making "female empowerment adult entertainment" that appeals to women's tastes. The genre combines the sex of pornography with plots, foreplay, and cuddling. Span (cited in Muskoron, n.d.) claimed that she makes films with a "genuine female-point-of-view." Included are a proper storyline and character development. She also makes sure the camera is focused on both the female and the male.

Pornography Debate Among Women

Supporters of pornography generally tout First Amendment rights. I doubt the Founding Fathers anticipated Internet pornography in their considerations. Critics argue that political expression, which is critical to a thriving democracy, is a far cry from protecting double penetration scenes and gang bang plot lines. The United States follows a Socially Responsible Model of free speech. The individual's right to expression is weighed against the good of society. For example, it is illegal to yell "fire" in a theater or to say "bomb" in an airport. Laws against copyright infringement, libel and slander, and obscenity (e.g., bestiality and child pornography) have been considered acceptable limits on free speech. The topic should remain open for discussion.

An anti-censorship organization, Feminists for Free Expression ("Feminism Free Speech," n.d.), denied any link between degrading images and violence. Their rationale is often that research results are inconsistent. The group rarely, if ever, cites findings from highly valued academic studies. They also ignore effects beyond the pornography-rapist connection. Feminists for Free Expression ("Feminism Free Speech," n.d.) claimed that since Japan has more violent pornography and fewer rapes than the U.S., pornography has no effect on rape. These arguments ignore the vast array of contributing factors. The study of human behavior is significantly more complex than a single variable correlation. In a more practical sense, it is unlikely that anyone would bother watching pornography if it had no effect.

Feminists for Free Expression ("Feminism Free Speech," n.d.) also claimed that sexual health professionals recommend pornography as information for women and men. They suggest it may help couples talk about and experiment with sex. They fail to mention what kind of porn. I am guessing they are not recommending anal gang bangs as a way to enrich a couple's level of intimacy. Wolf (cited in Winfrey, 2006) asserted that pornography gives a false sense of sex. Women can never live up to the fantasy world of pornography. Porn stars are generally thin, with breast implants. Some actresses have even had labia reconstruction and anal bleaching. Porn hurts women by portraying a standard where women have orgasms every time, are always ready for sex, and get turned on by having sex with other women. Researchers argue that not just women but also men are affected negatively by porn. Men are confused because real women do not work that way. Wolf (cited in Winfrey, 2006) made a very interesting point that pornography does not turn men into sex fiends but does just the opposite. They lose their libido for real sex with real women. Porn sets up a world of impossible standards where there is access to women all the time, with quick results, and with few boundaries. Layden (1999) also argued that the pornography industry spreads the myth that "male sexuality is viciously narcissistic, predatory and out of control."

Female actresses in the pornography industry often defend their career choice. According to Jenna Jameson, "[Women] call the shots. We say who we want to work with. In what way is that degrading? That's us taking hold of our life" ("Jenna Jameson," 2003). Porn stars have become high profile in today's celebrity obsessed culture. However, only the top women in porn land contracts. According to Taylor (2004), a contract girl gets between $75,000 to $100,000 to appear in 10 movies a year. Most stars make very little compared to the overall profits. Not everyone has the charisma or star power of Jenna Jameson. According to her own autobiography, it is shocking how dysfunctional and out of control her life has been. Jameson (2004) acknowledged the downside of the business. She warned that some women work for two weeks and then no one wants them. She will agree to do double penetration or drink sperm to keep working. Women often get very sore, physically and emotionally. Jameson (2004) stated, "It's very easy for a girl to get into the industry, but it's very hard for her to stay there" (p. 324). Directors take humiliating shots of girls. The girls may make a lot of money that first day but will be so humiliated they will regret it and not come back.

Taylor (2004) compared being degraded working in porn and working at Wal-Mart or Denny's. He noted that "while there's a good chance that getting literally screwed will be pleasurable at least some of the time, getting figuratively screwed is never any fun" (Taylor, 2004). Jameson, on the other hand, stated porn has more pitfalls than nearly any other occupation. She was mostly referring to drugs and prostitution. Men outside the industry exploit porn actresses as well as do those inside the business. Jameson described "suitcase pimps" as men who date industry girls, become their managers, take all their money, and often leave them broke, jobless, prematurely aged wrecks. She claimed that women fall for this type of guy because they think he is going to protect and take care of them. Jameson's portrayal of the business is that women are disposable and the consequences of this lifestyle can be horrific.

It is clear that not every man who sees pornography will become a rapist; however, there are substantial negative individual and cultural effects. Wolf

(2006) warned that limiting pornography is not a moral issue, but a matter of physical and emotional health. According to Paul (2005), porn can distract men from their partners and harm relationships. Layden (cited in Devine, 2005) argued that pornography helps to normalize pathological behavior, giving rise to the belief that "it is common, hurts no one, and is socially acceptable, the female body is for male entertainment, sex is not about intimacy and sex is the basis of self-esteem." She argued that even casual use of pornography causes damage to the health of intimate relationships and an increase in sexual harassment in the workplace.

Feminist groups remain deeply divided about the issue of pornography, between protecting women from the evils in the world and allowing women to make their own career choices. It is disheartening to see the cat-fighting between one group of feminists, such as Catharine MacKinnon and Andrea Dworkin, who claimed that pornography is a hate crime against women and called for censorship laws regarding pornography, and another group of feminists, such as Nadine Strossen and Camille Paglia, who rejected the assertion that pornography is exploitative and argued it can actually be liberating for women.

Conclusion

The debate over pornography is often framed in regard to whether or not watching it will cause men to rape women. Academic researchers have found more subtle effects. Zillmann and Bryant (1988) found that prolonged exposure to pornography changed people's attitudes about sex. For example, they found subjects who had viewed pornography reported greater acceptance of premarital sex and extramarital affairs and were less likely to endorse marriage. Linz and Malamuth (1993) found that consumption of pornography reinforced rape myths. In similar studies, Garcia (1986) reported that subjects who were exposed to violent sexual material tended to believe in lighter sentences for rapists and assigned more of the blame to the rape victim than those not exposed to such material.

Kipnis (1996) stated, "Whether pornography should or shouldn't exist is pretty much beside the point. It does exist, and it's not going to go away" (x–xi). However, that does not rule out taking measures to protect women from the harm of pornography. An all-censorship or no-censorship argument creates a false dichotomy. It fails to acknowledge the vast differences between violent rape pornography and erotica. Some critics argue the answer to "bad" pornography is "good" pornography, not "no" pornography. One solution, rather than censorship, is to increase education about the effects. Another positive step would be to ensure rights and protections for workers in the industry.

4. STRIPPERS

It used to be women stripped to have a chance at greatness. Now you have to do great things to strip naked.
　　　　　　　—David E. Kelley, 2001, as Ling in *Ally McBeal*

The strip show is more popular than ever (Liepe-Levinson, 2005). A Google search showed the conservative state of Texas with the most strip clubs in the United States (222), followed by New York (215) and California (212). Nevada, often seen as sinful because of Las Vegas and Reno, was in the middle of the states (67). This was interesting for the fact that, politically, Texas brags that it is very conservative, Republican, and Christian. Kansas, notorious for its Bible belt mentality, had a significant number (37), considering the population of the state. The names of strip clubs include Bare Elegance, 19th Hole, Baby Dolls, Bottoms Up, Cheerleaders, Wet Dreams, Pussycat Lounge, Heartbreakers, Lipps, Players, Titillations, Sweet Cherry, Gold Diggers, Taboo, and Temptations. Categories ranged descriptions of the dancers, such as "elegance" and "foxy." Also presented was a cruder sense of what they were selling, such as Bottoms Up. There was an interesting mix of names that described an arousal to men, such as Titillations and Temptations. Others indicate that the men would be aroused but not satisfied, such as Woody's, Heartbreakers, and Wet Dreams. Often, the feel of the clubs, much like the porn DVDs, was the selling of innocence, in words such "cherry," "baby," and "dolls."

Working Conditions

Working conditions appear to vary a great deal from club to club. Some dancers are offered more protection than others. Some workers can come and go as they please, while some bosses threaten to fire workers if they call in sick, or at least still charge them fees even if they do not work. The inconsistency of the industry makes it difficult to improve conditions for women who dance there. As long as good working conditions exist in some clubs, it is likely that nothing will be done to protect the interests of the dancers in the bad clubs. Club owners consistently report that there is an ample supply of women willing to dance. They use this leverage of "if you won't, someone else will" to justify dreadful working conditions. Owners know the dancers do not have the clout or the resources to challenge them.

A negative aspect of the club is that management often creates tension by overbooking dancers. Because most dancers work on commission rather than being paid wages, the owners have nothing to lose by over hiring. Owners make their money off of a percentage of tips plus a dancing fee paid by the women. Dancers report that women in the clubs get territorial and competitive for money. The dancers may then pull tricks on other dancers, such as hiding costumes or badmouthing others. According to Cooke (cited in Holsopple, 1998), this competition drives women to engage in more explicit activities for audiences, outside of their normal boundaries.

One of the reasons why dancers have so little protection is that clubs hire them as independent contractors. According to Fischer (1996), contractors are denied legal protections afforded to employees. They are not entitled to file discrimination claims or receive workers' compensation or unemployment benefits. Owners pay no Social Security taxes, sick pay, or health insurance. Some clubs even force dancers to wave their right to sue the club for any reason before they will be hired (Holsopple, 1998). The dancers are totally reliant on customers' tips, which may force them to put up with obscene behavior in order to support themselves and their children. Barton (2006) noted that heavily built dancers took off more clothing and performed more graphic moves in order to compete. For as much as some dancers claim they are one big happy family at the club, there are those who experience threats and hostile environments because of the fierce competition (Hageman, 2000).

Not only do the dancers not get paid a wage at most clubs, they often must pay outrageous fees for the privilege of working. Some dancers are forced to turn over 40 to 50 percent of their income for stage fees and mandatory tips out to the staff (Forsyth & Deshotels, 1997). In some clubs, dancers must pay for drinks if they do not get customers to buy them the minimum number. Because dancers are independent contractors and there are so many women willing to work as strippers, dancers are let go for minor infractions, especially as they get older (Frey, 2002). Clubs often have strict rules, from costumes to pubic hair. Dancers are fined for calling in sick, for taking off their shoes, and for being touched by a customer (Holsopple, 1998). According to club rules, dancers could be sexually assaulted and then fined for it. Club owners even regulate when and how many times a dancer can go to the bathroom. According to Barton (2006), one club removed the doors to the bathroom stalls because of a suicide attempt. Clements (2002h) defended the profession, claiming that it is only an occasional bad club or unethical manager at fault. She pointed out that in no other industry are workers blamed for their unfair treatment.

Types of Services

Generally, stage dancing alone does not pay the bills. To make real money, there are varying grades of stripping, which range from the visual to the physical. Table dancing is usually done on a low table or portable platform near the customer's seat. Holsopple (1998) described it as the dancer's breasts and crotch being at eye level. According to Barton (2006), some dancers prefer lap or couch dances to table dances because they offer greater financial rewards. Lap dancing can either occur right at the customer's seat or in a separate room in the back. The dancer straddles the man and grinds her body against his. One stripper (cited in Chase, 2000) described the lap dance as an erotic art rather than a "sex-driven frenzy." She described the lap dance as an open, romantic, and honest bond between a man and a woman. Her description of the dance is interesting, since I once witnessed a completely nude dancer place her leg behind the head of a customer and bring her genitals inches from his face. Clements (2002f) claimed that dancers are not forced to do table or lap dances, but that it is part of the job. She stated she finds it strange that a woman would go into the business of stripping and stop there. She compared it to a dentist who will not put up with saliva. Even if dancers are squeamish at first, she claimed, they get used to it.

Strip clubs generally offer private dances in back rooms with names such as the VIP or Champagne room. Couch dancing usually includes physical contact much like a lap dance, but offers more room for body to body contact than a chair does. Bed dances are offered in some clubs. The naked, or near naked, dancer actually lies on top of the clothed customer. Although generally prohibited by law, customers get to touch if they are willing to pay more. A shower dance gives customers a chance to get into a shower with one or more women (Holsopple, 1998). The customer is allowed to soap their bodies. At each new level there is more sexual contact. Barton (2006) reported on a city where the mayor proposed legislation to curtail the amount of contact between a customer and a dancer. While the intent was to protect the dancers, many of them were concerned that it would threaten their income. In addition, they felt the law would sensationalize them in the public eye.

Clubs vary on the amount of contact the customer may have. Regulations vary, as does the enforcement. Private rooms are also provided for lap dances in certain establishments. It also varies if the dancer is nude or wearing bottoms. Dancers are often coerced into acts of prostitution in these back rooms in order to earn tips (see Forsyth & Deshotels, 1997; Ronai & Ellis, 1989). While stripping is visual, the touching involved in lap dancing enters the realm of prostitution. Although the customer may be clothed, the intent is still the same. Strippers also masturbate and fondle other women on stage.

Field Trip

In order to get first-hand experience at strip clubs, I enlisted some male friends to accompany me on a field trip. I got plenty of offers, but Sean and another friend, who requested I refer to him as "Chuckie," seemed serious about teaching me the ropes. After I had established my criteria, Sean selected two clubs in the greater Philadelphia area. Delilah's, an upscale "gentleman's club," was our first stop, followed by Daydreams, a seedier establishment. The contrast was stark and quite educational. Because of zoning laws, Daydreams was an all nude club, while Delilah's performers wore G-strings. Daydreams also had no liquor license; therefore, there were few limits on what the dancers could do.

According to the Delilah's website ("About Delilah's," n.d.), "Naturally, the world's most beautiful showgirls deserve a stunning showcase...." They offer steaks, premium cigars, and an extensive wine list. Patrons with hotel keys or sports ticket stubs are not charged a cover. The club offers not only bachelor parties but also office parties. They offer stage dances, couch dances, massages, and shot girls.

In contrast, Daydreams marketed itself as the "ultimate *all nude* strip club." It is housed inside of an old warehouse. Although they did not sell alcohol, they offered free six packs of beer Sunday through Thursday. Patrons could "BYOB" on Friday and Saturday. The wwebsite gives lengthy descriptions of the feature shows: "Daydreams is like a carnival with over *50 naked girls* on six stages. Two girl shows, shower shows and feature shows are so exciting and sexy, you won't believe you're seeing them live and in person! Throughout the year we also present porn stars, live, in-person and naked!" ("Menu of Experiences," n.d.). There were descriptions of the different services. For example, there was "Naked Couch Dancing: Imagine having a beautiful, naked 'dreamgirl' privately dancing for you. Sit back, relax if you can and enjoy. If your [*sic*] up to it you can have two or three ladies at a time!"; "Dream Seats: Your [*sic*] called up onto the main stage where your [*sic*] handcuffed to a pole and a naked 'dreamgirl' performs on you in front of everyone. You also receive a souvenir picture"; "The Ultimate Dream Seat: On the main stage, you're handcuffed to a pole and *every naked dream girl* gets into line and dances for you and you get a souvenir picture and bragging rights"; "Sweetheart Lounge: Enjoy private, intimate time with your favorite 'Dream Girl.' Enjoy dances and conversation, have dinner, drink, soft music, sweet smells, hold hands and fantasize."

As I prepared for the night, I was a bit nervous about being a woman in the clubs. I anticipated being singled out by the performers and staff. I thought they might be suspicious of my presence. I was warned by others not to stare at men, as they may be there anonymously. Part of me worried that if I did not look directly at the performers, I would seem like a prude. I hypothesized there would be mixture of older men alone and younger guys in groups. I was not sure college age kids have the money to go to strip clubs. I also figured that college males have enough contact with females at parties and regular bars that they would not need to pay for company. Reports from my students verified that sometimes it only takes the promise of a free drink to get a young woman to flash her breasts. I was interested to see how my male friends would act while we were at the clubs. I wondered if they would be absorbed in the women and ignore me, really get into the analysis, or tease me and focus on my reactions.

There was a fascinating contrast between the two clubs. Delilah's was tamer than I thought it would be, while Daydreams was much, much wilder. Men paid a $15 and $20 cover charge respectively. I paid $8 at Delilah's and got in free at Daydreams. I had been to strip clubs before, but always on the spur of the moment, without time to ponder the consequences.

Delilah's

The shot girls were interesting. They had skimpy clothes, similar to what Christina Aguilera wore in her *Dirrty* video. They had holsters full of liquor bottles low on their hips. They would climb up on a man's lap and rub their breasts in his face before pouring liquor into his mouth. (In other clubs female servers will put a shot glass between their breasts and let a man drink from there. Serving tequila shots, they put the salt between their breasts so the customer could lick it off before getting the alcohol poured down his throat. The server may also put the lemon in her mouth for him to take with his mouth.) The action on the dance floor was rather dull. The only time the audience really perked up was when two women performed a simulated oral sex act. Most of the dancers looked really bored. My favorite dancer was Veronica. She had dark hair and wore interesting bookish glasses. (She reminded me a lot of commedianne Sarah Silverman.) She had great rapport with the audience. She seemed happy to be there, while most of the other dancers seemed to be checked out. One couple changed seats, following her from one part of the stage to another. It was the female customer who finally disappeared with Veronica into the couch dance room. Veronica later told me that it was the couple's first time to a strip club together and they were very shy about approaching her.

Daydreams

Daydreams is in an old warehouse in a secluded area near a bridge into New Jersey, and it is a stark contrast to the plush surroundings at Delilah's. Instead of plush carpeting, there is a cement floor. Delilah's patrons pass through a metal detector, while Daydreams' bouncers pat down male customers. Before entering, my male companions were searched and instructed not to touch the dancers. The bouncers used a friendly vocal tone, sort of a plea to make their job easier rather than any real concern for the female dancers. One of the older and more experienced dancers told me that generally two things happen when a male customer touches a dancer. A bouncer will come over and tell him not to do it again, or he will be taken outside, told not to touch the dancers, and then let back into the club.

After the tame experience of the gentleman's club earlier in the evening, I was shocked when I walked into Daydreams. There was a flurry of activity around the main stage. Crowds of men were standing around hooting. I had to look twice to be sure what I saw happening was real and not just simulated. Two women were onstage in a 69 position giving each other oral sex. They would perform for a few minutes and then move to a different part of the stage and take turns performing oral sex on each other. They even performed oral anal. The stage was littered with balled up one dollar bills. A male emcee followed the women around the stage and collected the bills in a large plastic bag. The women then played a game called coochie ball. They held a plastic cup in their private parts with their legs spread up in the air. Male and female customers threw balled-up bills into the cups. The person who made the most shots won a T-shirt.

The two dancers then picked up cans of whipped cream and a pitcher of strawberry slices. They went around the periphery of the stage and offered customers chances to lick the whipped cream and strawberry off the two of them. Licking off the breasts cost $5. Licking off the two "lower" orifices was $10 each. Female customers could lick whipped cream off the dancers' breasts or have the dancers lick the customer's breast for free. One dancer in particular tried repeatedly to persuade me to participate. I was surprised that several of the female customers sitting next to the stage voluntarily lifted their shirts so the dancers could lick their breasts. It appeared that all the participating women were there with a male companion. It was not clear if the women really wanted the experience, or if they just wanted to turn on their dates.

Later in the evening, Chuckie insisted I go with him when he got a couch dance. Club policy dictated that female companions of male customers could observe for free. The dancer asked me if I wanted to join in. She instructed Chuckie that he could touch her anywhere but her breasts and genitals. She told me women are allowed to touch the dancers' breasts, however.

I am sure there are seedier, more explicit clubs, but this was plenty for me. The acts went beyond stripping to prostitution. One of the features of the club was the "dream seat." It was primarily the groom-to-be at his bachelor party who would sit in a chair onstage while a bouncer handcuffed his hands behind his back. One of the dancers would remove his belt and semi-pretend to hit him with it. One or more of the dancers would grind against him, sometimes violently thrusting back and forth as she straddled him. Dancers would also slap his face and undo his pants and pull his underwear out to look at his private parts. I assume this was to see if he was aroused and to possibly tease him about his size. The bouncer took Polaroid photos of him with female dancers positioned on him showing their genitals.

The field trip was exhausting. I cannot imagine going back to strip clubs anytime soon. There is sort of a monotony in the presentation. Some dancers are clearly better and more experienced than others; however, there is very little variance in the motion. There is slight variation in their bodies and hair color. Looking at the difference between the clubs, it was evident that to gain attention the acts must become more and more risqué. It was interesting the emphasis on sports in many of the clubs. Websites of many of the Philadelphia clubs offer free admission with a ticket stub after home games. A regular feature in clubs is huge television screens tuned to sports channels. It is an interesting juxtaposition, giving the impression that naked women are a sport. Of course, it is not much of a sport when men can pay to get exactly what they want.

Interview with Couples

I interviewed three couples at the gentlemen's club. Two of the couples were married, Dan and Dana and Dave and Trish, and one couple was dating, Mark and Nina. Dan and Dana were very comfortable there. Dan said he enjoyed it equally with and without his wife. Dana did not seem to care if Dan was there or if he got a lap dance. Dan said it was safer if he was at a strip club than at a regular dance club. At a strip club, he reasoned, there was no chance of his going home with one of the women from the bar. At a regular dance club there is a greater chance of a women trying to pick him up. Mark and Nina were not married, just dating. They both were comfortable there as well. Mark said he would not have been there if Nina had not come with him. He said he had done the strip club thing when he was younger, but now, in his forties, he did not enjoy it as much.

Dave and Trish were the most interesting couple. Dave and Trish have been married for two years. Trish has a 15-year-old son and a 12-year-old daughter from a previous marriage. It was Dave and Trish's first time together at a strip club. She was a little worried before they got there, but found it pretty tame. She saw lap dances as a waste of money rather than an issue of infidelity. At one point two dancers came out together and looked as though they were going to do some girl-on-girl action. Trish tapped Dave's shoulder (Dave was sitting next to the stage right in front of us) and gently said, "Honey, I'm right here." This was a great line because I think it demonstrated her desire to be okay with her husband looking at topless women and the actual hesitation she felt under the circumstances.

Profiles of Strippers

There appears to be no shortage of women willing to strip. Most strip clubs report that there is a steady stream of women answering their ads, and plenty of women who participate in amateur nights. But what makes some women comfortable undressing in front of strangers? Is it a personality trait such as exhibitionism? Is it that these women are self confident and comfortable with their bodies? Is their desire for attention so much greater than other negative feelings? How powerful are past experiences?

There are a variety of reasons why women get into the sex industry. Many in the industry say they resent being asked. Porn star Jenna Jameson (2004) complained that people continuously ask her how she got into the business. She claimed she is surprised when people ask if she was abused as a child. According to Taylor (2004), Jameson lies about the abuse because she does not want to be seen as a victim. Taylor (2004) argued that Jameson had a right to be insulted by the abuse question. She added, "When was the last time you heard it asked of a comic or an actor or a musician to explain what they do?" The question of abuse is not that outrageous. It appears to be a pattern.

Also, it is difficult to understand how some women will do it and others will not. To outsiders it often seems like a bizarre world and knowing why perhaps makes them more comfortable. Often, sad cases of poverty or past sexual abuse do not receive sympathy, but rather scorn. It perhaps makes other women feel better that there is a type who will strip and they can distance themselves from such a fate. They can claim superiority over others.

Many women cite financial reasons for becoming strippers. Some women consider the profession as a last resort, especially if they have children to support. According to Barton's (2006) research, outsourcing and automation are reducing the number of opportunities for unskilled workers to make a decent living. Clements (2002h) compared stripping to jobs such as working in slaughterhouses or cleaning up crime scenes. People do those jobs for the money or because they lack the skills to do anything else. Barton (2006) cited the failure of men to pay child support as another reason. It would be interesting to find out how many men behind in child support spent money on the sex workers who were working to support their children because the fathers of their children weren't! It is sad to think the most vulnerable women, mothers of small children, are driven to stripping in our society so crazy about family values.

The dark side of the sex industry is that between 60 and 80 percent of women in the sex industry were victims of childhood sexual abuse (see Layden, 1999). Barton (2006) argued that the abuse colors their decisions to get into the sex trade and clouds their understanding of the abuse they endure on the job. (After presenting a seminar class with statistics on sex workers and abuse victims, one student came up to me after class. He did not look pleased. He grumbled, "Thanks a lot! Now you've ruined porn for me!")

There are women who strip not because they are desperate or coerced into it but because they enjoy dancing or are exhibitionists. There appear to be few reasons in between. Sometimes youthful indiscretions can be overlooked. Barton (2006) stated, "Our culture is more forgiving of young women who have had a 'stripper phase'" (p. 78). This is especially true if it is for college tuition of if the stripper does something "better" with her life afterwards. A lifestyle choice is more degrading (Barton, 2006).

Some women report that it is their rebellious nature, as Barton (2006) called the *Girls Gone Wild* phenomenon. People feel better about stripping when it appears to be a choice by crazy, fun loving girls. Thinking about desperate money situations, drug addictions, and abuse victims brings down the crowd. The other thrill is the amateur performance. Doing it for free is very naughty, rebellious, against social standards. It is not a job for the performers, but rather a favor to the audience. It reinforces the desire for all women to be sexually available for all males.

Eaves (2000) stripped for about a year and then left to go back to school and become a reporter. Mattson (1995) was a Brown University student who stripped to put herself through college. *Candy Girl* (Cody, 2006) is a true story of a Midwestern girl who enters an amateur contest and starts stripping. Hageman (2000) described her entry into stripping. As a child she enjoyed running around the house naked. To her, dancing allowed her to show off her body and satisfy her longing for attention. She compared stripping to feeling beautiful and feeling loved. Hageman (2000) stated, "Taking off your clothes may be demeaning, but it makes you feel like a queen." Clements sounded a little like Mother Teresa as she described her job as helping people to forget their troubles. She did mention that she loved the money and attention as well. She also claimed she was able to use the power of her sexuality. She stated, "Women are exquisite, rarefied vessels—vast reservoirs of a boundless sea of erotic abundance. To share it is an amazing gift. Remember that, and do your job with dignity and reverence" (Clements, 2002f). She described strippers as some of the most compelling women on earth, actual sex goddesses.

Mattson (1995) differentiated herself and others with no other career options. She stated, "The power of choice is vital.... The majority of the girls at the Foxy Lady had no choice. They were either uneducated or addicted to the unique qualities of the job—or both. The lack of options created in them a desperation, a trapped-animal mentality. They were stuck. I swore I would never be stuck" (Mattson, 1995, p. 139). Meg (personal communication, May 1, 2006) was extremely confident and unapologetic. If anything, she was almost defiant about her choice. She said that she had told her husband that she would go back to stripping if they got into financial trouble.

Getting In

In most of the literature, either written by women in the profession or interviews with strippers, there is a common theme of "getting in" and "getting out" of the business. From the stories told by the strippers, almost all of their careers started gradually. The process reminds me of getting into cold water. The body adjusts little by little until it is numb, physically and emotionally.

Some women begin as servers in the clubs. Once they see how much money dancers make, it is hard for some to resist. Because they are often dressed like the dancers and are treated similarly, like sex objects, it is not much of a stretch to "ease" into dancing. Barton (2006) reported that clubs will purposely get the servers drunk and coerce them to get onstage or threaten to lay off servers. The "shot girls" I saw at one of the clubs wore skimpy shorts that exposed their cheeks and had barely enough material to cover their breasts.

Their job was to crawl on men's laps to serve them shots of alcohol from between their breasts. It was difficult to tell the difference between the shots and the lap dances.

There appears to be a significant step between answering the ad and getting up onstage for the first time. Dancers often mention the adrenalin rush and the encouragement of the audience/management they get the first time. New dancers get tipped heavily. Wendall (cited in Barton, 2006) reported that stripping initially makes women feel better about their bodies if men are willing to pay to see it. This initial attention appears to be short lived; it evidently becomes less exciting after the woman has done it again and again. The thrill for the male audience is that she has been coaxed into the act, which gives the power to the men, yet again. It then becomes a job, never again as exciting for either party. Barton (2006) explained men get off on the new girls' innocence, after which the women are easily discarded. She found that the longer women danced, the more dissatisfied they became no matter how much they were compensated. There is a parallel in the porn industry. First times are heavily, marketed—for example, first sex scene, first girl-on-girl, first anal, first gang bang, etc. The shattering of innocence is a turn on for some viewers. The thought is that women do not naturally want to do such scenes, otherwise they would not be as titillating.

Hageman (2000) recounted the men drooling over her the first time she danced. She was surprised at how safe she felt ... at first. She reported that when she started no one tried to grab her or called her names. She wrote that she felt like a "queen on a pedestal, with control over the men." The bliss was not to last. She reported that the customers got rowdier and more offensive later that same night. She realized that they had no respect for her. Gunn described her audition as beginning in a bathroom with a filthy toilet, a swinging bare bulb, and grease stains on the walls. She performed for a "horrible man who sat there as bored and impassive as a rock." She was surprised when she got the job.

Although Jameson (2004) was frightened the first time onstage at age 17, she wrote that she loved the attention the second time. Her motto was "Fake it until you make it." This fear pattern appears in almost every stripper's recount of her experience. Jameson learned to lie to customers and become an actress. After her first dance, she opened her eyes and saw men in the audience staring at her. She said, "Yes! Power!" Clements (2002f) gave advice to would-be strippers. She explained that if the first time goes well, fear will be replaced with new freedom and self-assurance. She tells future strippers to brace themselves for things both wonderful and awful.

Getting Out

After the newness wears off, the work becomes tedious. Getting in seems easier than getting out. The money appears to become addicting, especially at the prospect for earning a great deal for unskilled workers, or at least entry level jobs. Eventually women get tired of the business, if they are not forced out by then for being too old. Many dancers find it is difficult to exit because it is difficult to start at minimum wage when they are used to tips. Lenney (n.d.) reported that all dancers talk about their work as something they enjoy. They specifically cite financial independence and their ability to hold the attention of a roomful of men. However, if this were to remain the case, why would so many women want to get out of stripping? Lenney reported that most dancers would pursue alternatives to table dancing if they could make the same money and have the same freedom as with stripping.

Cody (2006) talked about dancing as it was an obsession that she could not stop. Money did not seem to be her motivation, because she was not making much. She eventually quit her job at an advertising agency to strip full time. She stated, "Working at a nude hustle club had emboldened me. I was fearless, jaded and calloused from the waist down. My wallet was thin, my boundaries ambiguous" (Cody, 2006, p. 150). Later in the book, she described the start of her breakdown and eventually hitting the wall. She stated, "Stripping had pummeled me bloody, but it had also stroked me and spoon-fed me and twisted its tongue in my Eustachian tube" (Cody, 2006, p. 199).

Positives

Scott (2003) found that many dancers reported they were more secure about themselves and had experienced personal growth from stripping. Ronai and Ellis (1989) argued that many women enjoy the attention and are exhibitionists. St. James (2006) defended her time spent living at the Playboy Mansion. She claimed, "I am comfortable with my own sexuality, responsible for my own orgasm, and have never been sexually or emotionally abused." While some dancers feel degraded and out of control, others do not. They often compare their job to any other, although their job is extreme in its structural inequality. Clements (2002c) noted that just because she is in the business of arousal, it does not necessarily amount to abuse. She explained that, as with any job in the service industry, customers disregard her as a person.

Clements (2002h) stated she resents women who blame the industry for exploiting them, except for the few women who are forced into stripping because of desperate poverty. She argued, "Instead of being seen as a cesspool that sucks in the needy and unsuspecting, the sex industry should be seen as an oasis for some in a desert of bad circumstances and limited earning potential" (Clements, 2002h). She taunted the reader as she claimed she can say whatever she wants on her job—"Can you?" She compared her trade to that of actors, and said that they are not exploited by getting paid for displaying their emotions. She also defended the degradation of stripping to money exchanged in marriages in the past.

To Mattson (1995), stripping was easy. She described it as being like modeling or acting or advertising, but more direct and honest. She acknowledged she was a sex object but insisted she was beyond being degraded. She stated, "I had my goddess attitude switched on high, as usual. 'I deserve tons of money, I deserve adoration,' I chanted to myself.... It was a high—being loved en masse.... It was empowering, as only the strongest, highest-paying fantasy can be" (Mattson, 1995, p. 264). Ashe (cited in Crotty, 1999) explained that "the attitude and the self awareness of the power of one's sexuality" is what is empowering, not taking her clothes off in front of men. She stated she is supposed to be objectified.

One positive theme experienced by many of the interviewed strippers is that the female dancers develop close bonds. The ability to share the experience with others not in the business is rare. Most of the strippers report a stigma of their profession with outsiders.

Negatives

According to Barton (2006), "The stripper juggles a complicated set of conditions: arousing men, coping with abuse and contempt, deflecting and neutralizing potentially dangerous situations, and, meanwhile, extracting as much money from them as she possibly can" (p. 70). Women in the sex industry suffer consequences beyond physical abuse. Layden (1999) reported on a study that over half of strippers had borderline personality disorders and 60 percent suffered from depression. Many of these problems are connected with childhood abuse many of them suffered, which perhaps caused them to begin stripping in the first place. Stripping creates a cycle of victimization. Many of the women have been damaged and will continue to be damaged in this profession (Layden, 1999). There are high rates of eating disorders and many subject themselves to numerous plastic surgeries. Substance abuse is rampant as dancers numb themselves. Kehr (2002) argued that stripping has significant psychic costs. She found common themes in strippers' stories: "Almost all of them report feeling shy, unloved and desperately unattractive as children; almost all had glamorous, sexy mothers and distant fathers; almost all admit to extensive cosmetic surgery; almost all sense an estrangement from their own sexuality and a growing disgust with men" (Kehr, 2002).

Clements (2002g) cited the advantages of the lifestyle, the freedom to take time off, to either save and retire early or live off of working a few hours a week. If this were true, we would likely see more wealthy strippers and porn stars. The men giving them the money do not seem to be suffering at all, but there are numerous horror stories about sex workers who age out or get addicted to drugs. Although some women think they can dance their way through school, Holsopple (1998) reported that it is difficult to overcome the late hours and fatigue. The promise of flexibility becomes the reality that the job is all consuming.

Since dancers are most likely to be independent contractors, they are not getting Social Security wages taken out or matched by their employer, so their benefits will be little, if any, payout at retirement. One blogger ("Open Letter," 2001) wrote an editorial refuting claims made by the sex industry. Some of the arguments were that strippers were confusing revenue with profit—not taking into account expenses and slow nights. The blogger argued that no one is as sexually liberated as they claim. Most people find it difficult to save money. When women are in this wild lifestyle and often use things (alcohol, drugs, shopping) to numb themselves, it is very difficult; therefore, they cannot get out. They save little money, thinking they earned the money and can now spend it. It is also difficult to save cash tips, especially small bills. It is difficult to work so hard and not treat oneself.

Ashe (cited in Kirk & Boyer, 2002) warned of the negative feedback and discrimination strippers and porn actresses face in the world outside the club. She noted that often apartment owners will not rent to women in the sex industry. There have been no such reports of discrimination toward male club owners or patrons.

Stripping clearly blurs into prostitution with lap dancing and allowing men to touch the stripper when putting money into various parts of their bodies. Many states have banned lap dancing and have put a "safety zone," or distance, between the dancers and the clientele. There are some similarities with the backrooms and expanded definitions and lax rules regarding lap dances in strip clubs. Many of the strippers talk about boundaries they establish, guarding against temptations to turn tricks. Keeping those boundaries when a great deal of money is offered them is a different story. The more unattractive, overweight, or older a dancer is, the more likely she will have to humiliate herself to earn money. She will have to work in raunchier clubs and perform more degrading acts. Some strippers graduate to pornography, where they can often make more money. Once a woman is numb, there may be little difference between pretending to have sex with men and having sex with men. Some critics have even called stripping a gateway drug to porn and prostitution. Prostitutes are still apparently at the bottom of the hierarchy.

Abuse from Customers

Liepe-Levinson (2005) argued that most male customers behave themselves in the clubs because they are surrendering to the sexual scene. In Barton's (2006) investigation, she found that middle-class norms of social etiquette do not apply. According to a survey of dancers, about 20 percent of all customers cause some sort of problems. Layden (1999) reported that 100 percent of the strippers in a survey reported some kind of physical or verbal abuse: 91 percent were verbally abused, 85 percent were called names such as cunt, whore, or bitch, 73 percent had their breasts grabbed, 91 percent had their buttocks grabbed, 27 percent had their hair pulled, and 24 percent reported being slapped. The abuse often took place in front of bouncers or other customers. Because they spend a great deal of money, some customers feel entitled to be abusive and obnoxious. They assume they are paying for the right to treat these women any way they want.

While some supporters argue that female dancers are in charge in the clubs, others argue just the opposite. Ciriello (cited in Holsopple, 1993) stated, "Stripclubs are criticized for being environments where men exercise their social, sexual, and economic authority over women who are dependent on them and as places where women are treated as things to perform sex acts and take commands from men." Perry and Sanchez (cited in Barton, 2006) argued that dancers are really selling the possibility for men to buy positions of sexual dominance. One stripper who had been grabbed in the crotch, breasts, and behind, argued that such behavior is not part of her job. She stated, "They should have to pay me if they want to do that" (cited in Barton, 2006, p. 96). Another stripper stated customers had touched her in ways that made her feel dirty; however, she reasoned that it came with the territory. When she is touched "down south," she stated she usually kicks them out, or rather gets a bouncer to kick them out since she likely has no power. Even after the abuse, she emphasized that she still got her money (Chase, 2000).

Despite the rules established by managers regarding the customers not touching the dancers, the rules are consistently violated. Almost all of the perpetrators suffered no consequences (Holsopple, 1998). While the manager would seemingly want to protect their employees (i.e., sources of income), there appears to be enough women willing to work that they are not obligated to protect the dancers. The dancers that are treated well are likely the ones that survive to write the books. Women's complaints are almost always dismissed by club owners and managers. Layden (1999) argued that abuse women suffer at strip clubs is unparalleled in any other legitimate workplace. He named verbal harassment, physical and sexual abuse, and financial exploitation at work, and said that they are often raped once they leave work. Seventy percent of strippers have reported that they have been followed home and 42 percent have been stalked (Layden, 1999).

The strippers are selling sex, they are tapping into the dark side; therefore, it does not seem shocking that the men would stop being polite when they are taking his money. Stripping, in a way, puts up a third wall, sort of like watching something on television and yelling at the screen. There is a sense these women are not really there and negative comments do not affect them. People have no problem trashing Britney or Paris, because they are not seen as people but as icons that are there for show.

Disdain for Customers

Barton (2006) argued that women dancers often replay the abuse they have experienced. They see taking the money from men as a kind of revenge for their pain. Barton found they develop disdain for men. One recurring theme in my interview with Meg was how stupid the men were who paid so much for, in her words, "so little." She said they were going home with an erection.

In her book, Hageman (2000) recounted the times she was very disrespectful to the customers. She was surprised when men would ask her on dates. She wrote, "What did these old fat guys think? That I would want to go out to dinner with them?" Mattson (1995) mocked the men at the club who asked her out. She stated she could not believe they would think they had a chance with her. She bragged about ways she used to get more money from men without sleeping with them, such as choosing married men (Mattson, 1995).

One stripper interviewed by Chase (2000) stated she was very aggressive in her approach as a hunter; the implication is that hunters kill their prey with little thought. Overall, it appeared as though she had nothing but contempt for her customers. She referred to them as prey she circled, thinking only of their money. She commented that when men spend their money on strippers, they are showing how stupid they are. However, if she was paid enough, she stated she would tell the men anything they want to hear. She advised other women not to marry men who go to strip clubs. Liepe-Levinson (2005) called the biggest spenders the biggest suckers. Money does not wield them power in a strip club. She claimed that the patrons are part of the show. Men humiliate themselves in front of other men for entertainment. According to Jameson (2004), "It was a high to get the upper hand over a customer. They were dumb, they were drunk, and they deserved it" (p. 48). She described the often vicious mentality of strippers. They often figure if the men are going to victimize them, then they are going to victimize men in return. She pointed out that just because a woman would run a club it would not necessarily be any better.

Coping

Clements' (2002f) advice to strippers is very telling about the profession. She acknowledged that not all strip club managers are ethical; therefore, she advised dancers to not be manipulated or intimidated. She told them to charge top dollar for what they are willing to sell, but not to take money for what they are not willing to sell. She told them to learn to say "no" without embarrassment or regret. Several times she mentioned setting boundaries and protecting oneself. She claimed that secretaries are not any safer than strippers regarding stalkers and sex crimes. Although abuses happen in all industries, it would appear that the sex industry would be the hardest to prosecute. The women also appear to be blamed because they did not take care of themselves.

Mattson (1995) had an attitude that bad things can happen to other people, but she put up boundaries to protect herself. I think she was just lucky that one of these threats did not get out of hand. Her struggle with paying for an Ivy League school differed from having children to support with no family to fall back on. She went on these pop rants about feminist scholarship.

She described herself as a male in her thinking (Mattson, 1995). Mattson described another Brown graduate who was stripping as only being comfortable at the club. She put off medical school, abandoned her friends, and eventually broke down and lost her identity.

Although dancers are warned to set boundaries, it is difficult to control a situation they have little control over. The notion that the dancer does not "let" customers touch her is not assurance that they will not touch her and she is in control. She can only report it afterward. Boundaries, if they are established in the first place, often shift over time. Dancers may not even be aware of the shift. Boundaries are often broken under the influence of alcohol or are gradually tested to get more and more money. Barton (2006) found that when women are told they are low-lifes, they may think they might as well get paid for it. The more they are mistreated, the more strippers may come to think they deserve it. Collins (cited in Barton, 2006) referred to this phenomenon as the "psychological toll of oppression." Jameson (2004) advised women to set boundaries, which puts the burden on the woman. There is a struggle between a woman wanting to think she is in control and then being blamed if she is the victim of an assault when male customers get out of hand.

Instead of a tough shell and well developed defense mechanisms, Barton (2006) found that the women had fragile self-perceptions. She attributed it to the instability and unpredictability of the job, "a roller-coaster ride of male scrutiny, adoration, and rejection" (Barton, 2006, p. 42). Women get burnt out emotionally from pretending night after night. For all the talk of mainstreaming of the pornography industry, Jameson admitted that women sacrifice the chance to ever have a normal life. She wrote, "No one comes equipped—mentally, emotionally, or socially—to deal with the recognition, the pressure, or the psychological repercussions of the work itself" (Jameson, 2004, p. 364).

Layden (1999) argued that victims of abuse often have no concept of what healthy is; therefore, many strippers may think they feel better about themselves when they are stripping. Many women stay in the abusive relationships because the abuse was gradual. Management sets up a very nice, comfortable situation that appears safe and as if the women are in control. Slowly, as time passes, the women might start to notice a shift in treatment. Customers become more abusive, tips slow down, and management imposes higher stage fees. If they are numbing themselves to stripping, playing a role, what is to stop them from making even more money by finishing the act they started and crossing over into prostitution?

Outside Relationships

Mattson (1995) admitted to feeling like an outcast in her Ivy League community. The people on campus generally saw stripping as degrading and immoral. For all her glamorization of stripping, she admitted she had few friends. She did not appear to really belong in either world. She appeared rather critical of the other strippers and was picky about who she would social-ize with at work. Most strippers are numb, much the way breast implants result in lack of sensation and pleasure. It is likely the strippers would become numb in intimate relationships outside of work. Many are detached in the first place.

Many of the strippers report that it takes a very special person to have a relationship. This person must be understanding of the profession, not judge, and not get jealous. A recurring theme with dancers is their significant oth-ers dealing with their numbness and lack of sexual interest. One positive theme experienced by many of the interviewed strippers is that the women develop close bonds. The ability to share the experience with others not in the busi-ness is rare. Most of the strippers report a stigma of their profession with out-siders.

Strippers must partition their sexuality to separate their stage act from their personal relationship. Dancers often take on different personae and stage names. This way, a dancer is able to claim she is leaving her professional life at work. She fakes it onstage. Clements (2002a) argued that strippers save their intimacy for their lovers. Contemplate the difference between sexuality and intimacy and the ability to separate the two. Problems also arise when sex is tied to money. For some dancers, the art of manipulation is hard to turn on and off.

Jameson (2004) acknowledged the difficulty women in the porn industry have with their relationships. She advised against having a relationship when working, saying that having a boyfriend can be a nightmare for a career and emotional health. She warned that ultimately the man will hate the woman for acting in porn and will hold it against them even after they quit. She advised that even dating within the industry is a bad idea, because jealousy will even-tually enter into it.

Most of Barton's (2006) subjects reported profound changes in their libido. Dancers reported their jobs of pretending to cater to the customers' sexual desires were emotionally exhausting. In addition, the more they pretend, the less connected to real life they become. According to Jameson (2004), women lose respect for men and, therefore, most strippers are bisexual. Barton (2006) reported that some women in the sex industry develop sexual and romantic relationships with other women because of their shared experiences of exploita-tion and powerlessness.

Dancers reported that their partners use their dancing as a weapon dur-ing fights. Ginger (cited in Chase, 2000) stated that as soon as a man falls in love with her, he wants her to stop dancing. She pointed out this is a problem because it may be her only means of supporting herself. Overall, she found dancing to be a very isolating experience. When she gets home from work, she wants nothing to do with men, drinking, or partying. Ironically one of the advantages dancers bragged about was all the free time they have.

Conclusion

In my interviews with men, I found an interesting mix of responses. Respondents were less nonchalant about stripping than I expected. Most of the men denied thinking stripping was mainstream. They confirmed my hypothesis that if stripping did not have a taboo element, it would not be such a lucrative business. Some men enjoy the seductive strip tease while others just want women to get naked as quickly as possible. For those who thought stripping was "no big deal," I asked if they would strip for money. Almost all of them immediately said "of course." However, their answers quickly changed when I asked these heterosexual men if they would strip for other men in a gay club. Realizing they would be objectified by an audience, they quickly changed their answers. Most studies show that female dancers eventually despise their customers.

I am not advocating censorship of strip clubs. There will always be men who want to see naked women. Likewise, there will always be women who are willing to be naked for money. As employees, strippers are afforded very few protections. The general sentiment is that they choose to strip, therefore they should expect typical club behavior. Most abuse from customers happens before a bouncer can come to their aid. Dancers are often taken advantage of by club owners. Because dancers are most likely "independent contractors," they have very few rights. As long as society shuns them or elevates them to all-powerful, little will be done to improve their condition.

5. PLASTIC SURGERY

I'd love it if someone called me a bimbo.
—Extreme Makeover candidate

The increase in acceptance of plastic surgery demonstrates the importance of outward beauty in our culture. It is almost expected that if a woman wants to remain attractive she will get some sort of plastic surgery. Since the early 2000s, Tupperware parties have been replaced with Botox parties. Groups of women get together and inject muscle paralyzing poison into their faces. The money spent on looking good is exorbitant. In 2005, Americans spent over $12 billion on cosmetic procedures ("Cosmetic Plastic," 2006). Linda Schrenko, Georgia's superintendent of schools, embezzled over $500,000, money earmarked for a school for the deaf. She allegedly used part of the money for plastic surgery, an eye lift and breast implants, etc. (Hume, 2004). Pamela Wick also embezzled nearly the same amount from her employer and likewise used it for plastic surgery (Doege, 2004).

Surgery is not just for older women who want to recapture their youth. With their parents' consent, girls under 18 are getting extensive surgeries. Girls who have not even finished developing appear to want to achieve a form of perfection being presented to them in the media. Parents are indulging their children by not only giving permission, but also offering to pay for breast enlargement as "sweet 16" birthday and high school graduation presents. They either cave in to pressure from their children or buy into the notion that this surgery will make their children happy. It could also be that over-involved parents are transferring their personal insecurities to their children. They think perfect children will reflect positively on them as parents.

Many of the females getting plastic surgery say they are doing so because they think it will improve their self-esteem. Twenty years ago the trend was for girls to get nose jobs. Since it was seen as rather shameful, they would do it over the summer so others would not notice. Now plastic surgery is a badge of honor, especially in an era of immediate gratification. Young girls are not even willing to wait until they stop growing before getting work done. On an episode of *Plastic Surgery: 18 and Younger* on the Discovery Health Channel, an 18-year-old stated she wanted breast implants so she could go to a topless beach and not be embarrassed. What was striking about the episode was that it was her father who broke down crying right before the surgery, fearing complications.

Plastic surgery is popular not only in the United States. Brazil has been an international leader in cosmetic surgery. Open markets and growing prosperity have brought the plastic surgery obsession to China. China even has "Miss Artificial Beauty" and "Miss Plastic Surgery" pageants ("China Crowns," 2004). Contestants are required to have certification from a doctor to prove they have had surgery. A trend in young Asian-American women is blepharoplasty, or eyelid surgery, a process of stitching a crease into the eyelid. The procedure is often considered "an offensive alteration of ethnic identity" (Kobrin, 2004). Because it produces a look more like Caucasian eyes, it fits the standard of beauty in the United States. It is reportedly the fastest growing type of plastic surgery in California's Asian community, even for girls as young as 14 (Kobrin, 2004). It is comparable to skin lightening for African Americans and rhinoplasty for Jewish Americans.

Procedures and Costs

According to the American Society for Aesthetic Plastic Surgery ("Cosmetic Plastic," 2004), nearly 12 million surgical and nonsurgical cosmetic procedures are performed each year in America. These procedures cost just under $12.5 billion. Between 2003 and 2004, procedures increased 44 percent. Since 1997, there has been a 465 percent increase in the total number of cosmetic procedures. Surgical procedures increased by 118 percent, and nonsurgical procedures increased by 764 percent ("Cosmetic Plastic," 2004). The most popular procedure is liposuction. Almost half a million liposuctions were done, with breast augmentation a close second at over 300,000 ("Cosmetic Plastic," 2004). Nose jobs and facelifts accounted for approximately 150,000 each. Women accounted for 90 percent of the procedures. Alonso-Zaldivar and Costello (2006) reported that worldwide implant sales reached $540 million. The implant surgery costs between $6,000 and $10,000, not including follow-up care. Special cosmetic surgery loans are available. A Google search produced dozens of companies willing to loan money for plastic surgery with as little as $99 down. Several sites (e.g., http://www.doctorssayyes.com and http://www.surgeryloans.com) offer loans to anyone. They claimed that no one is turned down.

The top procedures for teenagers 18 and under were laser hair removal, chemical peel, microdermabrasion, rhinoplasty, and laser skin resurfacing ("Cosmetic Plastic," 2004). Each year the number of breast augmentations for teenagers has more than tripled in a ten-year period between 1992 and 2002 ("Teen Breast Implant," 2005). What is most disturbing of all is that many of these girls are getting breast implants as sweet 16 or high school graduation gifts (Kreimer, 2004). According to Rohrich (cited in Kreimer, 2004), many of the procedures are done around holidays and spring break so the girls have time to recover and not miss school. One of the most popular seasons is Christmas. Implants are especially popular, not only in California but in Texas, which champions conservative values. Kreimer (2004) recounted a story of a 17-year-old who received implants as a graduation present. Her mother, grandmother, two aunts, and stepmother already had implants. She was quoted by Kreimer (2004) arguing, "If my mom is offering to pay for it now, why not?" It is little wonder where she got her value system. She sounded very nonchalant, almost resigned, to undergo dangerous and painful surgery. Parents do not seem to take these additional factors into account. Their child will have to deal with additional surgeries later.

Dangers and Risks

Many critics worry that the dangers of surgery are ignored or at least downplayed by zealous surgeons and television shows. Few recipients consider that additional surgeries will be needed months or even years after breast implants. The FDA estimated that between five and ten surgeries will be needed during the life of the implants. Additional surgeries may increase the risk of complications compared to the original surgery ("Breast Implant," 2006). Implants routinely leak, rupture, or deflate. Implants also make breast cancer detection harder and mammograms less reliable, and may interfere with breastfeeding.

The FDA urges parents and teenage girls to get information about the risks before considering plastic surgery, particularly breast implants ("Teen Breast Implants," 2005). I would question whether a parent who would permit their child to get plastic surgery has the sense to investigate the risks. Physically, teens' bodies have not finished developing. Physical complications can be temporary or permanent. Teen breast implants can cause scarring, puckering, and wrinkling. More serious complications can include "pain, bleeding, bruising, swelling, delayed healing, hematomas, seromas, chest wall deformity, loss of natural breast tissue, infection, loss of breast or nipple sensation, inability to breastfeed, and more" ("Teen Breast Implants," 2005). Teens must also be psychologically ready and have realistic expectations of what breast implants will mean. More than any other age group, teenage girls also have higher rates of body image problems ("Teen Breast Implants," 2005).

While saline implants are safer, many women elect to have silicone implants because they hold their shape and reportedly look more natural. The FDA (2006) recently allowed silicone back on the market. According to Zuckerman (cited in Alonso-Zaldivar & Costello, 2006), the FDA has not concluded that the implants are safe, only offering "reasonable assurance" of safety. Wood (cited in Alonso-Zaldivar & Costello, 2006) claims that the long term safety remains unproven. Silicone implants are approved only for women 22 and older (FDA, 2006). Because it is very difficult to detect silicone leaks, routine MRI screenings are required. These tests are expensive and may not be covered by insurance. While many critics warn of the dangers, some women are adamant about being able to choose. Silverman (2005) argued that women have a right to decide what they can do with their bodies. Cummings (cited in Neergaard, 2005), who runs a pro-gel implant website, claimed that women are neither "ignorant nor shallow" and should be able to have options.

Many women who get implants think they can change their minds later. Removing implants later is not an easy procedure, however. Removal can result in loss of breast volume, distortion and wrinkling (Kreimer, 2004). It seems stunning that women would do that to their bodies for vanity reasons. It is interesting how they will take risks, yet are so obsessed with other dimensions of safety in society. Especially troublesome are the parents who allow, and pay for, their children to have plastic surgery. For years they have been rallying for injury-proof playgrounds. The website Silicone Holocaust (www.siliconeholocaust.org) urges teenagers who are contemplating implants to view the images before committing to the surgery as a way to educate themselves to the dangers. The site shows "some of the horrors of disease and disfigurement associated with toxic breast implants" ("Now You Judge," n.d.).

Reality Television

Women, and even young girls, are buying into expectations about what they think men want and what will give them worth. The fear that women will not be able to attract a man also perhaps clouds judgment. These trends ignore the danger of surgery and anesthesia and the pain of recovery. Reality shows such as *Extreme Makeover* and *The Swan* offer ordinary women happiness through extensive surgeries. These shows equate physical beauty with personal worth. *The Swan* offers to transform six women over a three-month period. The winner is put in a pageant with "beauty" women to see if they can pass. Women on other reality shows such as *Survivor* and *The Real World* get plastic surgery in order to extend their fifteen minutes of fame. *Playboy* featured a pictorial of the women from *Survivor* with post-show breast implants. These makeover shows perpetuate the thought that standard beauty equals worth. They also perpetuate the idea that there are shortcuts to getting what one wants. Rather than putting in the work to firm up or lose weight, people undergo dangerous and expensive procedures.

Dr. 90210

Dr. 90210 was a show following a group of plastic surgeons in Los Angeles. The name was a playoff of nighttime teen drama *Beverly Hills 90210*. This famous zip code symbolizes a geographical area of wealth, decadence, and vanity. The show also followed the personal lives of the surgeons. It showed not only their wealth, but also their personal problems, such as threats of divorce and problems conceiving a child. According to the show's website, "We examine the many reasons people have for getting plastic surgery, whether to enhance their career or their self-esteem" ("Dr. 90210," 2006). One of the surgeons featured on the show, Dr. Rey, considers himself "a psychiatrist with a knife."

The show was a mix of reconstructive and cosmetic surgeries. The doctors of course wanted to be seen in the best light. One doctor stated, "We examine the many reasons people have for getting plastic surgery, whether to enhance their career or their self-esteem" ("Dr. 90210," 2006). Another doctor stated, "This episode is all about breasts—how much society focuses on them and how important they can be to a woman's feeling about herself." Dr. Matlock is the pioneer, founder and president of a laser vaginal rejuvenation institute. He presented himself as a savior, someone who listens to women and gives them what they want. He stated, "It's 100 percent about the woman.... I want what she wants.... All of these procedures have been developed as a result of listening to women" ("Dr. 90210," 2006). Breasts are a major focus of the show. An entire episode was dedicated to that part of the anatomy.

Clients featured ranged from ordinary women to porn stars. These women claimed they wanted to gain more confidence, particularly moms and recent divorcées. Although some did have medical problems and injuries, most surgeries were strictly for beauty enhancement. In one episode, a mother with a heart condition came in for breast enhancement, a nose job, and "a new outlook on life." It would seem that the heart condition would put her at great risk for surgery. The descriptions of the participants are rather amusing: a working mom who wants to "bolster her bikini confidence" and a facelift on a yoga instructor who is looking to maintain both her inner and outer beauty. Another woman wants to get work done in anticipation of her promotion to police detective, which seems very counterintuitive. A hairstylist was featured who "feels her huge success should be reflected in a slightly larger cup size." Tabitha Stevens (named after the little girl on the television show *Bewitched*) is a porn star who came in to have an anal bleaching. One woman wanted to surprise her husband who is serving in Iraq. Mother-daughter boob jobs were not uncommon on the show. A mother and daughter team were described as "quite close, so much so the two are coming to get breast implants for both of them at the same time" ("Dr. 90210," 2006). To give it some credit, the show did feature breast cancer survivors getting reconstructive surgery.

One thing I noticed about the show was that it downplayed the risks of the surgery and the pain of recovery. Viewers were left with a sense that the doctors believed in what they are doing, that they are improving people's lives. They used very gentle voices and carefully chosen words to describe procedures. They described surgeries using words such as "gentle" and "physically taxing" with little or no mention of pain. One doctor announced that a vaginal lift came out as "adorable." In one episode the doctor removed five liters of fat in liposuction in one woman. They stopped only because of guidelines. Afterwards, she complained of feeling like she had been punched in the stomach. She showed some distress as she was leaving the office, but the camera did not stay on that part of it for long. Although she stated she was leery about coming back for more, her doctor told her once she sees the results, she will want to do more.

The show was quite entertaining, in a gross-out kind of way. One episode showed the doctor going up a woman's belly button to put in her breast implants. He was all the way up to his elbow inside of her. They showed pieces of skin that had been removed from a tummy tuck. It looked like bacon. The doctor ooh-ed and ah-ed about the slab of skin as he held it up. After the procedure, they showed the patient all drugged up. At that point she did not feel much pain. Even later she claimed she was just sore but that it was not that much fun. She acknowledged that recovery was hard work. One episode featured two sisters. One was getting extensive surgery because of her weight, the other for breast implants. The mother was clearly the driving force behind both surgeries. The mother had gotten breast implants herself and stated she knows how much it can boost self-esteem. She clearly had passed her shallow insecurities on to her daughters. Her daughters were undergoing life-threatening surgery and she was acting excited and happy for them. She hoped that it would make them happy. She claimed she wanted the best for her daughters. She also hoped the plastic surgery would bring them closer together, being one thing they could share.

The overweight daughter was doing drastic surgery. It did not look as though she exercised at all. Rather, it appeared she wanted a quick and easy way to look thinner without any nutritional changes or exercise. The doctor commented that because she was heavy the procedure was much more difficult and would take much more medication. Although she stated she was nervous about the pain, she said the surgery was a way to make herself happy. For her tummy tuck, the doctor cut all the way across her stomach. He then took out about six pounds of fat. After the surgery she was doubled over in pain getting into the car to go home. The doctor cheerfully commented that she would be ecstatic with the results. As a follow-up to her recovery, she was filmed as she was out socializing afterwards. Of course she was drinking beer, which has a lot of empty calories. Is the moral of the story that if she gains the weight back, she can go in for more surgery?

The younger daughter was only 17. She had just gotten a nose job three weeks before. Now she was getting breast implants so, in her mother's words, she will not look "boyish." Although she was having more surgery, the girl suggested that others her age wanting plastic surgery should not get it. She confessed that she did not really want breast implants at this time, but her mother was offering to pay for it so it seemed like "a good opportunity." Her mother was especially excited because it was the daughter's senior year. The doctor admitted that 17 is young but was obviously going to do the surgery anyway. The girl was not only being pressured by her mother but by her sister. She stated that her sister was "really excited about me getting big boobs, she's been wanting me to for a while. She wants me to get D's but I think that's too big." The doctor then casually stated, "Instead of a new car [17-year-olds] are getting a new rack." The only mature, sane person in her life appeared to be her best friend. The friend told the girl that surgery was silly, that she jumped into it. She was disappointed in her friend's decision because she was doing it for her looks. The girl getting the surgery did show some concern about how her peers would treat her after the surgery. She commented that the kids at school could be catty. Her boyfriend stated he did not think she needed the implants. However, she protested that she wanted to look cute when they go out together. The mother again stated that she hoped the surgery would give her the confidence she was looking for. After the surgery the girl stated how she now felt like a "real woman." She recommended it for girls her age as a great self esteem booster.

Another story was about Tabitha Stevens, a porn star. She reported she had undergone six breast implants, three nose jobs, fat transfer, and chin implants. She was at the doctor's office this time to have her cheek implants removed and replaced. The doctor informed her of the danger of taking them out and stated that new implants would need to be screwed on to her cheekbones. She was a 35-year-old who looked like a 55-year-old who has had extensive surgeries. She was already planning future surgeries. She was going to have surgery on the backs of her legs and her pinky toes because they are a little chubby. She stated that lines on her face are unacceptable. She admitted that because she had plastic surgery early in her life that she is addicted. At least she warned 16- and 17-year-olds not to have surgery.

MTV's I Want a Famous Face

The show *I Want a Famous Face* documented 12 people who went to extremes to look like their favorite stars. Some of the celebrities were Pamela Anderson, Elvis, Janet Jackson, Ricky Martin, Britney Spears, and Jennifer Aniston ("I Want," 2006). The show acknowledged that the procedures were painful and risky, although I suppose that added to the show's drama. MTV added a disclaimer that it was the subjects' decision to get the plastic surgery and that MTV did not pay for the procedures ("I Want," 2006). While absolving themselves of some responsibility, they were still promoting the practice by giving it exposure. It appears everything on MTV fuels obsession with celebrity; therefore, it is difficult to believe that viewers would take this show any differently. Producers also claimed that, while some of the subjects were pleased, others "provide a more cautionary tale—with some encountering disastrous results" ("I Want," 2006).

ABC's Extreme Makeover

ABC's plastic surgery show *Extreme Makeover* offered a number of "lucky" viewers an opportunity for free plastic surgery. The producers promoted the show as a "Cinderella-like" experience, "a real life fairy tale in which their wishes come true, not just by changing their looks, but their lives and destinies" ("Extreme Makeover," 2005). The show featured an Extreme Team, including top eye surgeons and cosmetic dentists, as well as hair and makeup artists, stylists, and personal trainers ("Extreme Makeover," 2005). The "extreme" part of extreme makeover comes from excessive surgery. One woman received a nose job, ear pinning, breast implants, brow lift, tummy tuck, Lasik surgery and teeth whitening and straightening. The most heart-wrenching stories won the contestants facelifts. Viewers then got to see the before and after contestant. Very little of the pain of the surgery was spotlighted. After the transformation, family and friends were invited to witness the "dramatic unveiling." Tears were inevitably shed and lives "changed," at least according to the show's publicity,

Similar to *Dr. 90210*, the show featured stories that ranged from deformity to vanity. For example, a 21-year-old mother of a child with cystic fibrosis was selected to get a "physical and emotional overhaul" ("Extreme Makeover," 2005). It seemed incredibly shallow that all these medical resources were going to cosmetic surgery and not going toward finding a cure for her child's disease. Another story featured an 11-year-old girl who wrote in to get her single mother, who worked as a waitress, a makeover. The momentary thrill of the superficial change had nothing to do with the mother's situation of working a physically taxing job and trying to support three children on her own. On the other hand, a man had his cleft palate corrected. His mother, his seven brothers and sisters, and he had been left homeless. A teenage girl also had a physical deformity corrected. The show described her overgrown lower jaw that could potentially cause tooth loss and thus choking. The average patient on the show had a combination of nose jobs, ears pinnings, breast implants, brow lifts, liposuction, tummy tucks, Lasik surgery and teeth whitened and straightened.

The Swan

Fox selected "unattractive" women to receive extensive plastic surgery and then compete against other, "naturally beautiful" women in a beauty pageant. The contestants were secluded for about three months in order to add drama to the unveiling. *The Swan* has gotten major criticism, because of its premise, first of all. The women in this situation had no say in the cosmetic changes to their bodies. There was very little time spent on the repercussions of the surgery, such as painful recovery and the reaction of spouses. The show did offer therapy treatment for the contestants, but that too has been criticized for its lack of serious effect. Melmed (cited in Kreimer, 2004) pointed to plastic surgery television shows like *The Swan* as making breast augmentation appear to be a common procedure similar to getting a new hairstyle. Frankly, most of these makeovers could have been closely achieved through a different wardrobe, hairstyle, and makeup.

Conclusion

The number of cosmetic procedures done each year in the United States and the exorbitant amount of money spent are staggering. The news is full of stories about how medicine is being rationed, that there are not enough resources to serve the poor of the country. The rise in cosmetic surgeries may take resources from those who need surgery for life-saving measures.

The pursuit of perfection is a never ending and dangerous one. Some women admit that they are addicted, each woman having dozens of procedures. Plastic surgery is yet another symptom of our high value on physical appearance, especially for women. It also shows the desire for immediate gratification. Many individuals are willing to pay a great deal of money, endure a great deal of pain, and even risk their lives for an easy fix. Surgery also appears to be an easy path to "fixing" conditions such as obesity rather than promoting the hard work it takes to maintain weight loss. Diet and exercise regimes are too slow or the results not perfect enough. Media coverage normalizes such procedures and holds them up to standards of perfection that can never be reached. Rarely do the reality television programs show the pain involved in the procedure and recovery and the let-down when the work fails to improve self-esteem. The emphasis on plastic surgery sends the message, particularly to women, that each of us is not good enough as we are.

What is particularly horrific is that girls as young as 16- and 17-year-olds are getting work done. It is hard to believe that parents would think breast augmentation is an appropriate birthday or graduation present. First, it devalues a girl's worth, sets up unrealistic expectations, and puts her in danger. Additional surgeries will need to be done to maintain implants and correct inevitable problems such as leaks. Implants can make breast cancer detection more difficult, preventing early diagnosis and life-saving treatment. Parents are supposed to be the two people in the world that accept the child for who she is. Second, it gives the sense that the parents are hedonistic, that their child is an extension of them rather than a unique individual. It is perhaps a status symbol to be able to afford cosmetic surgery for one's child. It is also a dangerous practice to give in to children's desires with such high risks. In the case of breast implants, it seems especially deviant for the father to provide the surgery. He is sexualizing his own daughter. It is particularly horrific when she is underage. If parents are so careless about their children and doctors are so willing to perform these procedures for the money, perhaps the government needs to step in and protect children from adults' stupidity. It is also teaching a horrible lesson in selfishness and self-centeredness. If an adult, after much consideration, wants the procedure, then it is up to that person. Children under 18 generally do not have the capacity to think ahead and sufficiently weigh the pros and cons.

6. BEAUTY PAGEANTS

The JonBenet Ramsey story exposed a world where little girls are made to look like adult women, complete with heavy makeup, teased hair, and fake tans. This transformation of little girls is not the "oh, isn't that cute" dress up play when little girls put on Mom's high heels, oversized dress, and long strand of pearls. Rather, the sporting of haltertops and hot pants go beyond a game of dress-up. It is often difficult to not be fascinated with the transformation until one realizes how sexual it is when these little girls at five are made to look 25. The modeling and talent portions of the competitions are filled with sexy song lyrics and erotic dance moves. Highly paid modeling coaches teach the little girls how to strike sexual poses and flirt with the judges.

Parents often rationalize entering their little girls in pageants as a way to develop their daughters' confidence and earn money for college. However, many of the families sink incredible amounts of money into it they can never hope to recover. As a "hobby," it is an incredibly expensive one, with travel, hotel rooms, entrance fees, wardrobe, professional hair and makeup sessions, voice lessons, modeling lessons, pageant coaches, etc. Pageant advocates also claim that the girls develop social skills. Instead of developing social skills, the losing contestants are told to put on phony smiles and give air kisses to the winners, while the mothers badmouth the winning girl. The ultimate lesson girls learn in the pageant world is that if you are not the one winner, you are a loser and you lost because you are not pretty enough. The pageant mothers are often the most critical of, even hostile toward, the other little girls. It is unclear whether or not they truly understand what lesson they are teaching their children.

This chapter begins with a history of Miss America and Miss USA. I then explore the world of child beauty pageants: the good, the bad, the ugly, and the uglier. I describe one pageant I attended in New Hampshire and discuss television portrayals of pageants such as MTV's *Tiara Girls*.

Miss America

The history of pageants as we know them stems from the Miss America pageant. The pageant started in 1921 as a way to keep tourists in Atlantic City past Labor Day (Ferrari, 2006). Prizes consisted of fur coats, Hollywood contracts, and chances to earn money modeling. In 1945, the Miss America Pageant became one of the first organizations in the United States to offer college scholarships to women. Slaughter, the organizer responsible for the scholarships, wrote, "I knew that the shine of a girl's hair wasn't going to make her a success in life" (cited in Ferrari, 2006). Slaughter raised the first $5,000 by personally asking businesses for money. In 2000, the Miss America Organization became the single largest contributor of scholarships to women in the United States (Ferrari, 2006).

As the women's liberation movement gained prominence in the late 1960s, the protest of the Miss America Pageants was one of first times the movement received media exposure. One protester called the pageant a "degrading mindless-boob-girlie symbol" (Morgan cited in Ferrari, 2006). As part of the protest outside the Atlantic City Convention Center, women threw false eyelashes, girdles, and bras into "The Freedom Trash Can." The symbolic gesture was supposed to mimic the burning of draft cards during the Vietnam War. (Because the organization was unable to get a fire permit, the bras were never burned—contrary to popular legend of "bra burning" [Ferrari, 2006].)

Since the inception of the Miss America Pageant in 1921, Catalina Swimwear has been a major sponsor, using the pageant to showcase their new styles. The pageant, which stressed the wholesomeness of the contestants, was temporarily shut down in 1928 because of the impropriety of the swimsuits (Ferrari, 2006). When Yolande Betbeze, winner of the 1951 pageant, refused to wear a swimsuit in public, Catalina Swimwear representatives not only withdrew their support for Miss America but founded rival pageants: Miss USA and Miss Universe. The swimsuit competition continues to be contentious between fans and feminist groups. Organizers claim they keep it because of the demands of the viewers. In a 1994 call-in vote, 73 percent voiced their support to keep it. In an online poll in 2000, half of respondents threatened to boycott the pageant if the swimsuit competition was eliminated.

The swimsuit competition is now called "Lifestyle and Fitness." (If the pageants wanted to display a lifestyle and fitness competition they would include medical workups and athletic competitions.) Contestants do not fit the model of beauty queen unless they are genetically blessed with that bone structure. Traditional standards of beauty remain consistent. In the 1960s, the average Miss America contestant was 5 feet 6 inches and 120 pounds. Comparing the 1960s to the average height and weight of the past 75 years (up to 2002), little has changed (Ferrari, 2006).

Miss USA

After Miss USA split off from the Miss America pageant because of the controversy of the swimsuit competition in 1951, the Miss America pageant emphasized poise and character, while the Miss USA pageant stayed true to beauty. Donald Trump's Miss Universe organization has run the Miss USA and Miss Teen USA pageants since 2002. Trump publicly admits they emphasize the "beauty" in beauty pageants.

In 2006, Miss USA Tara Conner was embroiled in controversy. Newspapers splashed headlines about Conner kissing Miss Teen USA in a bar and testing positive for cocaine (Davis, 2006). Conner reportedly brought home a variety of men to her Trump Place apartment. Mothers Against Drunk Driving dismissed Miss Teen USA Katie Blair from their campaign because of her own underage drinking (Finn, 2006). On Comedy Central's *Colbert Report*, host Stephen Colbert (2006) exposed the hypocrisies of the allegations against Conner. He stated, "Miss Conner, I know you've been a pageant queen since the age of four. If it were up to me, you'd be stripped of that tiara (like your childhood). For years the pageant system has given you praise, applause, and cash awards for your legs, abs, breasts, and butt. How dare you betray it by turning around and acting like a sex object!"

Conner reportedly turned down offers from *Penthouse* and *Playboy*. It appears that the magazines want a piece of what was once a wholesome icon and getting the All-American girl in a submissive position. Racy photos of Miss Nevada Katie Rees came out at about the same time. Rees was photographed flashing her breasts and making out with another girl when she was a minor (Finn, 2006). Rather than tarnish the name of Miss USA, these incidents likely make the pageant even more popular.

The Pageant Debate

The debate between pageant supporters and pageant critics has raged on for decades. Unlike child pageants, which will be discussed later in this chapter, these pageants feature adult women who are capable of consent. The focus of the argument is not so much the exploitation of individual women, but rather the greater social impact of the pageants.

When university student Andrea Baker was crowned Miss Central Pennsylvania last month she won about $2,000 in scholarships, hundreds of dollars in prizes and, in her words, the "admiration of many." Baker admitted not everyone is impressed by her title. She stated, "All some people see is the bathing suits. They see the gowns but they don't see the time and research that goes into it and the friends that are made there" (cited in Logan, 1994). Miss America 1998, Kate Shindle, claimed that she actually found the swimsuit competition empowering. She explained that if she could model a swimsuit in front of millions of people, she could do almost anything (Ferrari, 2006).

Redd (cited in Nesoff, 2003) claimed her roles as a Miss America contestant and as a women's study graduate from Harvard were not conflicting. In order to compete in the pageant, however, Redd reportedly lost one quarter of her body weight. Nesoff (2003) stated, "Perhaps what's being reclaimed by feminists who embrace beauty pageants and impractical shoes is not feminism itself but femininity.... They can strap on those Jimmy Choos and pretend that there is no glass ceiling or rape or sexual harassment." In Baker's case it would seem there are more productive areas of life to research than pageants. As far as Shindle's claim of being able to wear a swimsuit in front of a large audience, I would not consider that empowering. It is more likely that being objectified desensitized her and lowered her standards. It is almost never expected of a man to prove himself that way in society.

Johnson (cited in Logan, 1994) said the focus on issues, such as poise and interviewing skills, may just be a mask to distract people from the actual nature of beauty pageants. Although society often professes that beauty is only skin deep, pageants reinforce the notion that looks do matter. He pointed out that young women can get money for college, but only if they look good rather than if they are the most qualified. He also argued that anything that emphasizes the importance of physical appearance is harmful for women and men.

Morgan (cited in Ferrari, 2006) claimed the pageant was sending mixed messages of a Madonna-whore combination. To win approval, she argued, "women must be both sexy and wholesome, delicate but able to cope, demure yet titillatingly bitchy.... Miss America and *Playboy*'s centerfolds are sisters under the skin." One of the critics stated that it is difficult to reconcile having young women speak intelligently on social issues and later ask them to display their bodies (Ferrari, 2006). Try as they may, organizers of the pageant have failed to make the pageant about poise, talent, and intelligence— qualities they profess to support. Viewers still see beauty as the top qualification of winners. Claims of valuing individuality and diversity have little value when year after year the contestants are cookie cutters of each other, varying little in features and body types. The first documented American diet craze occurred about the same time as the founding of the Miss America pageant (Ferrari, 2006). While critics may not be able to claim a direct cause and effect, it is an interesting correlation.

Child Pageants

The idea behind adult women competing is a matter for feminist sensibilities and issues of the perpetuation of women's beauty as worth. Child beauty pageants come with an additional set of criticisms. The main criticism is the sexual exploitation of little girls. Sweeney (cited in Logan, 1994) argued that, for thousands of women, the benefits outweigh the negative attitudes they might encounter. They see it as a way to break into modeling or acting. This strategy might be fine for adults, but not two-year-olds.

Parents, particularly mothers, of pageant contestants, spend a great deal of time justifying their actions. One mother claimed it's not about the beauty;

it is about standing up there and learning how to win and lose gracefully and how to cheer on the other contestants. The mother kept claiming "It's just for fun," "Little girls get to play dress up," "It's a hobby," "We keep it in perspective" over and over. These pageants are serious business, taking into consideration the amount of money involved. It appears the little girls are learning to fake sincerity. Parents try to downplay the emphasis on beauty, instead focusing on the personality and poise aspects of the pageants. They often use discussion boards to support each other. The sites I found were very positive; however, reports described vicious sites where mothers get so competitive they trash little girls and make thinly veiled threats to other mothers (see McGraw, 2006). One mother of a pageant contestant described discussion boards, or "bash boards," where mothers viciously attack other children and mothers. She stated some postings sounded like threats to little girls, vile language was often used, and there seemed to be little or no oversight to what was posted (McGraw, 2006).

On one beauty pageant parent website, many of the postings were looking for validation for putting their daughters in pageants ("Beauty Pageants," 2004). One poster, whose screen name is "Princess Parents," wrote looking for advice. She (I assume it is a she) stated that her daughter likes to dress up, put on makeup, prance around, and look at herself in the mirror all the time. Another poster, "Butterfly Kisses 912," advised Princess Parents not to listen to negative things about pageants. Butterfly Kisses 912 also refers to her child as "my little princess." She claimed that pageants teach girls to be confident and proud of what they look like. By dressing up pretty, Butterfly Kisses 912 claimed the little girls get a sense that they are just as pretty as the next girl. I assume she means up until that little girl loses. In this world of pageants there is a very narrow standard of beauty. Even if a little girl occasionally wins because of her poise, that is not the norm. It is more likely the attention that the little girls get from their looks will improve their poise and confidence only if they keep winning. Teaching little girls to rely on their looks could make the awkward years of puberty especially painful when many of them are no longer so cute.

Like so many other parents of pageant children, Butterfly Kisses 912 ("Beauty Pageants," 2004) made the flawed comparison with children who play sports. If involvement in sports competitions gets out of hand, that is not good either. She compared children acting out during pageants with tired children misbehaving in Wal-Mart or restaurants. The difference, however, is that these pageants go on for hours and days. A vast majority of the time is spent waiting around. To really compete on the pageant circuit requires a great deal of travel and hotel stays as well. The child is away from their own bed, and often the other parent and siblings, weekend after weekend.

There are "natural" pageants where the little girls do not wear makeup or have big hair, but according to my research, these are not easy to find. They

evidently do not attract the money that the glitz pageants do. One former pageant judge (Fleishman, cited in McGraw, 2006) stated that there is very little
room for aesthetic diversity in hair color, body shape, hair length, or race. One
mother put fake hair, fake tans, and fake teeth on her eight-year-old daughter for competitions. The message is clear not only that this little girl was
being judged for her looks, but also that her looks were not good enough.

Most parents in interviews adamantly state they will quit pageants when
they are no longer fun or the child wants to stop. One mother argued, "This
is a hobby, we keep it in perspective. If she told me tomorrow she didn't want
to do it, we wouldn't do it" (cited in McGraw, 2004). It is rare, if not impossible, that a five-year-old has the capacity to make good decisions. They still
believe in Santa Clause and the Tooth Fairy. They want to eat nothing but
candy and run with scissors. These parents claim their children know the
difference between the stage and real life. Many *adults* do not realize the
difference.

Several times parents have appeared on talk shows to defend their daughters participation in pageants or involvement in the entertainment industry
(see McGraw, 2005b). The parents claimed they were doing the pageants to
fulfill the dreams of their young daughters. Many of them are facing financial
hardship and divorce because of the pageant spending. One mother stated that
she keeps going because her six-year-old daughter would get mad if they
stopped the pageants. Parents fear their children, which sounds very distorted.
Their defense is often that this is the way the pageant world is or they point
out things that are far worse. These parents claim that this is what their child
wants; however, there are almost always tears during the pageants. These children are overbooked and constantly put up for scrutiny. The "trophy wife"
phenomenon has now become "trophy kids."

Pageant Costs

Many pageant parents claim it is okay to participate in pageants as long
as it does not get too extreme. It is difficult to see how the whole pageant scene
is not extreme when looking at the costs involved for the officials pageants.
The cost of pageants can be astronomical. Very few pageant officials acknowledge the costs of entry fees, hair and makeup people, coaching, hotel stays,
travel, and outfits in comparison to the meager winnings the majority of contestants earn. A Google search of pageant coaches produced sites such as
Abbie's AcroBabes "Coaching for Glitzy Girl" (http://gracefultwo.tripod.com/)
and Amanda's Angels (http://missamandasangels.com). Coaching fees ranged
from about $350 for a half day to $2,000 for a two-day intensive session. Many
parents travel several hours to get to these coaches. One mother reported her
personal costs as follows: $260 a month on coaching, $2,400 on dress, $400
on swimwear, $1,800 sportswear, $3,000 for western wear, hair and makeup
$200–600 a month. Pageant expenses can run between $65,000 (McGraw,

2004) and $70,000 (Owen, 2001) and up per year. These trends of excessive spending are also present in sports in the form of summer camps, private coaching, and traveling teams. Some parents claim that they are in it to win scholarship money; however, many of these parents are gambling away money that could be put in a college fund.

In order to get the contestants, or rather their parents, hooked, the pageants purposely give out awards to almost every contestant at the young levels. Eventually the girls will discover that only the genetically superior girls will win, along with those able to afford the best coaching and the most expensive outfits. The prizes give them a false sense that they have a chance to win bigger prizes. Often the lure of college scholarships gets girls into pageants, forcing them to invest large amounts of money for a small chance to win. It is similar to the midway scams at a carnival. It gets the kids to beg parents to go back. Pageants have eerie similarities to gambling—once a certain amount of money is invested in a child, there is a great deal of pressure to keep going to try to get the payoff. One mother of a four-year-old rationalized that individuals need to spend money to make money (McGraw, 2004). More and more money is poured into a losing endeavor, only this time the child suffers because of the stress put on them to win and get the big return on the investment.

The Bravo network program *Showbiz Moms and Dads* followed four mothers and one father as they tried for fame and fortune for their children, "no matter the cost." The show is described as, "We'll witness the extreme measures some parents will take to make their children into stars" ("Bravo Shines," 2004). In one storyline, Debbie is the mother of the four-year-old beauty contestant Emily. They are shown rehearsing with coaches, getting fake spray-on tans, and buying $500 dresses. Debbie instructed Emily not to cry when she does not win. She then prompted her daughter to hug the winner. It was interesting that Debbie reminded the little girl that "we" enjoy them and that pageants are not about winning. Not too much time went by before Debbie stated that if Emily continues not to win, they will reevaluate competing—a sharp contrast to being in pageants because they are fun. One blogger pointed out that after the mother told the daughter that winning wasn't important, she herself was sobbing in the arms of another pageant mom when the daughter lost ("Showbiz Moms," 2004). After the airing of the show, Debbie reported receiving death threats because viewers felt strongly that she was exploiting her child (McGraw, 2004).

Other Negative Aspects

A sexual abuse prevention group, Love Our Children USA ("Sexual Abuse Prevention," 2005), included the following advice on its website: "Avoid parading your children in suggestive ways such as beauty pageants. She could get the idea that she is only worthwhile if adults reward her for her looks." At the pageant I attended, I was allowed to walk in off the street. The girls were easily accessible, running up and down the halls unsupervised for the most part.

They were identified by their full name and hometown so it would not be hard for a predator to track down where they lived and went to school. They are much more vulnerable than other children because of the exposure and the sexual vibe of the pageants. They are also exposed to the craziness of the parents (although sports' parents are likely just as bad).

Summers (cited in Ransford, 1997) argued that pageants give little girls the perception that being physically attractive is the only option for success and popularity. In addition, it could set them up for bulimia, anorexia and depression if they cannot make the transition to teen pageants. Summers also contended that problems with friends and siblings could arise because of envy, jealousy, and conceit. Children are also pressured to look and act like adults on stage. Ransford (1997) advised parents to look at their personal motivation and egos for wanting their children to be in pageants.

The emphasis on looks can create monsters. A kindergarten teacher reported that the 5-year-old pageant contestant in her class was becoming a diva (McGraw, 2005c). Reportedly the little girl said, "You can't tell me 'no.' I'm pretty, I'm a princess." One former pageant judge (Fleishman, cited in McGraw, 2005c) stated that many little girls were rude and condescending to her until they found out she was a judge. They were evidently rude to anyone that they thought was of little or no value to them.

The documentary *Living Dolls: The Making of a Child Beauty Queen* highlighted the negative social aspects of pageants ("Plot Summary," 2001). The girls were not considered beautiful based on character but on their physical conformance to social norms. For example, "The femininity of the girls is being presented for the viewing of society rather than a natural product.... The beauty pageant just reinforces female subservience to men, since the girls are presenting their beauty for a generally male oriented viewer" ("Plot Summary," 2001, ¶3).

The sexualization of children cannot be healthy for a society no matter what supporters call it. One blogger posted an article titled "Child Pageants or How to Make Your Kid Look Like a Hooker" (2004). The blogger was appalled by the latent sexuality that ran throughout the pageant. For example, it was the father who encouraged his six-year-old daughter to flirt with the judges. The blogger also noted that the little girls were "shaking it" in short shorts and halter tops, commenting further that there was nothing to shake. One dance instructor stated that most pageant entrants she deals with are older, seniors in high school at the youngest (D. Johnson, personal communication, July 6, 2006). She claimed she can tell right away when a little girl does pageants. She noted a tremendous difference in their personalities when they go from little girls in dance class into "pageant mode." One 8-year-old took dance lessons for her talent for pageants. Her mother picked out sexy clothes for her daughter and demanded Johnson choreograph more difficult and sexier moves. When Johnson refused, the mother claimed it is "only sexy to the eyes who think it is." The little girl quit soon after.

America's Yankee Miss

In November 2006, I attended the America's Yankee Miss Pageant in Nashua, New Hampshire. I think in some ways I was less horrified going to the gentlemen's club and watching the strippers than I was at this pageant. The parading of little girls across the stage reminded me of a kennel show, but instead of dogs it was little girls all groomed and trained to strike poses. The word "grooming" was actually mentioned specifically in the judging criteria. During intermission, a two-year-old was running around the stage. The Master of Ceremonies announced, "Someone put a leash on her."

The youngest contestant at the pageant was 7½ weeks old. I can't imagine how they judged her "personality." (Her drooling was adorable!) A 9-month-old contestant won in the categories glitz photo, modeling, and outfit of choice awards for the two years and under group. A 4-month-old also won photogenic and outfit of choice prizes. The pageant coordinators explained outfit of choice award was not about the outfit but how the contestant wears it. I am not sure how a 4 month old "wears" an outfit.

At the start of the pageant the little girls appeared happy and hopeful. It seems cruel to judge such little girls on their looks. It was obvious by the outcome of the pageant that any judgment of personality and poise comes only after the initial attractiveness is assessed. In contrast to other competitions, there seems to be little the girls can do to do better other than hire expensive coaches and hair and makeup professionals. Expensive costuming is a pageant staple. I counted four costume changes for one of the nine-month-old contestants. Having investigated the price of pageant wear, I am guessing the outfits cost up to $500 each. Considering the top prize was $1,000, the wardrobe cost alone (never mind the other expenses) was a terrible return on investment. Many of the parents in the audience looked dirt poor. The economic strain on the family was especially obvious in the appearance of the non-pageant siblings who were there. It was clear that the most attractive child in the family received the most attention and resources.

It was immediately clear which of the contestants were regulars on the circuit. They tended to have bigger, more adult styled hair and custom gowns rather than off the rack dresses many of the other girls were wearing. I predicted that the cutest girls, as in most natural, would not win. I was not wrong, although my "favorite" did win the talent portion. I was a little surprised, since she performed an age appropriate monologue rather than the sexual dances performed by others. Another little girl I thought was more natural giggled when she was handed the microphone, which was far more charming than the polished, mechanical delivery of some of the "seasoned" contestants.

The younger girls seemed to mix easily with each other, running back and forth during intermission in random packs. The older girls seemed to form cliques, or at least group together according to glitz level. I got the impression that if the girls don't start at a very young age they are unlikely to get very far in the pageant world. Whether through being trained in the pageant "formula" or having developed a reputation with the judges, there appears to be a definite advantage. It was almost cruel that while some contestants got lots of applause, other little girls got virtually none. At one point the Master of Ceremonies tried to encourage the audience to support all the contestants and help make them comfortable. It did little to correct the situation. Breaking my role as objective observer, I could not help but clap as loud as I could for the less popular girls. All this talk of the pageants being good for children because it teaches them to support one another was strikingly lacking in the families of the contestants.

In the modeling competition, many of the girls were mimicking their mothers, who were standing behind the judges coaching the girls through the motions. It was not a surprise that so much of what the little girls were doing was imitating adult women. The 2-year-old who got the most attention was very flirtatious. She would wiggle her hips, toss her head, and bat her eyes at the judges. Another trick some of the girls used was to blow kisses, very much in the style of bombshell Marilyn Monroe. Many of them would open their mouths in a sort of shocked look as well as put their hands on their cheeks— all very grown up, flirtatious movements. "Vogue-ing" (à la Madonna) appeared to be a hit with the crowd. Other sorts of sexual images were flipping hair and looking seductively over their shoulder.

Although this was not a highly glitz pageant, the outfits were quite interesting. A seven-month-old was dressed in leopard skin print. Four-year-olds were dressed in halter tops, with their tiny midriffs showing. One little girl had a sleeveless dress with cuffs on her wrists, very much like strippers wear. Many of the little girls would take off their jackets and sling them over their shoulders as they modeled. One eight-year-old flipped the sides of her jacket back and put her hands on her hips. The older girls pursed their lips. One very tiny 12-year-old modeled a tankini with tiny bottoms and a see-through wrap around her waist. Fringe at all ages was popular, with tummies showing on many of the younger girls. It was odd seeing very grown up hair and makeup juxtaposed with lacey anklets and Mary Jane shoes.

The talent was not as bad as I had predicted, as I had seen other pageants and clips from other pageants on television. The stripper-like, sexy dance moves were less evident in this competition; however, the choice of songs was often inappropriate for girls twelve and under. "These Boots Were Made for Walking" was a popular choice. The song is about getting revenge on a man who is cheating, lying, and having sex with another woman. The video of this song shows a very sexy Jessica Simpson. One little girl sang "Someone Say I'm in Love," which I found totally age inappropriate. Another contestant danced to a Brooks and Dunn song, "We've Got a Party Going on Here," which includes lyrics that make a reference to the bumper sticker "If this van is rockin' don't bother knockin.'"

The implication is that the occupants of the vehicle are having sex. The song replaces the word "van" with "party." The Brooks and Dunn video features sexually explicit dancing between young men and women. One six-year-old modeled to the Moulin Rouge montage of "Diamonds Are a Girl's Best Friend" and "Material Girl." At the end of the recording, Nicole Kidman, who is playing a prostitute in the movie, shouts for the boys to come and get her.

The most horrifying was that a two-year-old and a ten-year-old modeled to the song "Barbie Girl" by Aqua. The lyrics portray females as bimbos men can control. The song begins with a woman with a girlish voice describing herself as a Barbie girl who lives in a "Barbie world." She states that it is fantastic that life is in plastic. The lyrics key on the importance of partying for young women and girls. She is acquiescing to the superficial, sexist world. She identifies herself as a blond bimbo, as his dolly. She allows him the power to make her walk and talk. The lyrics are fraught with sexual references and submissive statements. For example, she invites him to touch her wherever he wants, undress her everywhere, and do whatever he pleases with her. She is even begging on her knees for him to sexually have his way with her. I admit I lost some of my composure as a researcher and could not help but sit with my hand over my mouth. It was shocking that such young girls were parading around to this song with the blessing of their parents and pageant officials.

There was a vast range in the preteen division. Some of the 12-year-olds had already developed breasts, while others were flat chested. Seeing both in adult gowns and makeup was disturbing. A ten-year-old was running around holding up her dress because the zipper on her strapless gown broke just before the awards ceremony.

As part of the introduction, either the Master of Ceremonies or the girls declared their interests, which ranged from makeup to shoes. Some of them added they enjoyed volunteering and helping others. The older girls bragged about their academic accomplishments. Many had selected modeling as their career of choice, with teacher or doctor mentioned once or twice. More than once, contestants mentioned their desire to be in television competitions such as *America's Top Model* and *American Idol*. *America's Top Model* features a very catty side of modeling, a horrible role model for young girls.

Pageant scoring was reported as follows: one-third general appearance, which included grooming and attire; one-third personality, which included enthusiasm and friendliness; and one-third stage presence, defined as poise and confidence. The two contestants who earned the most points won the grand prize of a $1,000 savings bond ("Pageant Entry," 2006). According to my calculations it cost a total of $245 to even be in the race for the grand prize: entry fee $95, photogenic $25 per photo (natural and glitz), modeling $40, talent $60 (could enter two talents). This total does not take into account costumes, travel, and hotel expenses, not to mention lessons and coaching.

While there are lots of prizes given in pageants—even trophies for just entering—it is obvious who the big winners are. There were so many categories it took over 45 minutes for the awards ceremony. Trophies were awarded for the first contestants who entered the competition, for anyone who suggested a friend, and for the little girl who brought in the most fans. Recommending a friend got the little girl a "beautiful friendship trophy," while "Miss Popularity" won a trophy, sash, and crown. This use of prizes for non-competition aspects of the pageant was an interesting marketing ploy. Contestants are lured in with cheap metal-plated trophies. A "Golden Sport" was awarded to a girl who had entered the pageant five times without ever winning, what was more accurately the "five-time loser" award. Some of the girls were getting four and five trophies while other little girls were getting none. The distribution of so many prizes seemed even crueler for those who didn't win when there were so many opportunities. Comparing pageants to athletic competition is flawed. Every game is not the championship, whereas there is an ultimate winner of the pageant who doesn't just leave with a win, but a crown, sash, trophy, etc. In sports, kids play. In pageants, the kids spend all but a few minutes of stage time waiting around.

There was an interesting juxtaposition between the pageant and the selling of raffle tickets to support St. Jude's Hospital. A competition that emphasizes outward appearance is a vast contrast to life threatening illnesses. At the same time, the pageant officials were pushing parents to see the professional photographer across the hall and purchase photos.

There seems to be a blanket rationale that the sexual behavior is okay because the girls are just having fun. There appears to be little or no thought put into what might be inappropriate. I honestly tried to go into the pageant with an open mind. I figured a small town pageant such as this would be toned way down from the glitz pageant footage I had seen on television. I couldn't help but think of the movie *Little Miss Sunshine*. [Spoiler alert if you haven't seen it yet.] What made it so funny was the innocence of Olive as she dances like a stripper. The overt dance contrasts to the subtle sexuality of the other contestants. According to Kincaid (2006), audiences may find "the lumpy little heroine of the film utterly disgusting, turning from her to feast their eyes on little vamps." I watched the movie with a group of friends. During the scenes with the pageant participants, my friend Sean muttered, "I feel really uncomfortable." A chorus of voices agreed, saying they were horrified at the presentation of the young girls. The roomful of people was yelling at the screen for Olive's family to take her home before she performed in the talent competition. They hooted and cheered as she performed. They were particularly happy when the father stood up for his daughter.

Tiara Girls

The MTV reality show *Tiara Girls* highlighted the world of pageants by following contestants before, during, and after the pageant. According to the

MTV website, "*Tiara Girls* documents the struggles of several young women and their journeys to win what they believe is the most coveted sign of success—a beauty pageant crown" ("Tiara Girls," 2006). A trademark of all reality shows, it was full of obnoxious behavior on the part of the girls and their parents.

The first contestant was Jaime, who described herself as humble and giving in a practice interview session. She attended a Christian high school, yet she came across as very snobby about her competitors. She claimed the other girls were checking her out like lesbians. She referred to the first runner-up as the first loser. The shows bleeped the very abusive language she used when she was talking to her parents. She freely used the "f" and "s" words in front of them with no repercussions. According to Jaime, her mother is her assistant and her father is the "blank check." Her mother insisted Jaime put breast enhancers in her bra before she went out to get pageant instructions. Her father was shown picking at Jaime, telling her that her arms were flabby. He described himself as very competitive and wanted her to win at any cost. Jaime screamed at her father when he announced he was going to call her principal and get her out of doing her homework for the next three days. As Jaime binged on snack cakes, she told the camera that she had given up her life for the Miss Teen Florida pageant. She stated that if she lost, she was going to die onstage. She kept saying over and over that she was busting her ass and working really hard to win. At one point she ran out on her $100 per hour coaches in a rant. She was shown memorizing a prepackaged speech while her coach yelled at her that she was not doing it sincerely.

In the pageant, Jaime did not even make the top ten. She sobbed, "I worked so hard and there's nothing wrong with me. I should have made the top ten. I was good and good girls didn't make it. This pageant sucks. It's so f—ed up. It's a toss-up. It's like a lottery.... I got D's for this stupid-ass pageant." All the talk of learning valuable lessons from pageants was not evident in this or the other episodes of the show.

The second contestant was 22-year-old Meagan, who was about to "age out" of the pageant circuit. It was not clear what Meagan did other than prepare for the pageant. The show did not mention a job or college. It appeared that she still lived at home with her father. Her dad was described as her coach and financial support. There apparently was no mother in the picture.

Meagan did not have the typical build of a pageant contestant. Her "image" coaches were bluntly honest about her weight and recommended liposuction, which left her in tears. Even her dad visibly cringed when he found out that the swimsuit portion was 20 percent of the scoring. When she modeled her pageant dress, her father pointed out her cellulite and stated it would look dynamite on a thin girl. He hounded her about the smallest details, such as trimming her nails. His comment was "terrible" as she practiced her talent, the violin. He added, "You tend to play flat because you're sloppy." She was near tears when he was pushing her for answers to his practice questions. He told her, "Don't you dare cry!" They then argued about what to do for her "platform." It was clear she was not incredibly sincere when discussing the platform she had chosen at the last minute. She had competed in the Miss Greater Des Moines competition, which was held in a school gym. She was disappointed with her first runner-up finish, as she mumbled, "This really sucks." Like Jaime, she cried and stated, "I've worked so hard, so much time and dedication."

The third contestant, Nancy, played heavily on the fact that her mother had died of liver cancer. Her father said, "She not a daddy's girl, she's her daddy's life." As was the trend of the entire show, Nancy was very catty toward the other contestants. She stated, "All the girls who don't like the queen wish she would get pregnant." When asked during the practice interview, she could not name the current vice president of the United States. The message in this episode is that it was more important to prep for pageants than for college entrance exams, and doing so certainly was more important than friendship. Nancy's biggest worry seemed to be beating her friend Justine. Although they claimed not to let it affect their friendship, it took only seven minutes into the show before Justine declared, "I hate her." Justine was shown in tears threatening to pull out of the pageant because Nancy was getting all the attention. Nancy appeared to come from a wealthier family and could afford a pageant coach. The coach remarked to Nancy, "I know Justine is your friend ... but all is fair in love and pageants." Neither of them won.

The fourth contestant, Katarina, announced such gems as, "My entire life revolves around pageants.... Now, I'm a total diva.... This is a job.... It makes my mom happy." She described her mother as "pageant coach, drill sergeant, and best friend." Katarina stated that her father sees her as an investment and expects nothing less than 100 percent. Although the mother was overweight herself, she was shown criticizing her daughter's eating habits and weight. The father further harassed her about her eating and not going to the gym. He stated, "It's a beauty pageant, not an ugly pageant." Yet, after all this, there were donuts sitting around the kitchen and the family had pizza for dinner. On top of the criticism, the mother suggested the daughter use diuretics. She told the makeup artist, "She wouldn't go for the lipo, I tried." Her mother then took 16-year-old Katarina to get lip injections at a cost of $420.

Katarina drove six hours to a different state to see a "communication consultant." She expressed her attitude as "This is a competition. I'm not here to make friends. I'm here to win the crown." She did not even place in the pageant. Both she and her mother were in tears. Her mother stated, "I should have pushed her harder or maybe I shouldn't have put her in a pageant at all." Then the mother called the other contestants, "Hollywood, anorexic, fake biotches."

The fifth contestant, Brenda, was a Latina. Brenda called her pageant coach an asshole after he told her she should try to sound "white." To support her pageant expenses such as nails, tanning, and wardrobe, her family members made and sold food. Brenda complained that she had to be up on current affairs. She, too, could not name the vice president of the United States. She was unwilling to read news sites as instructed by her coach. Although interviews were worth 30 percent of the contestants' scores, she ended up winning the Miss Val Verda pageant.

All the girls on the show got quite upset when they lost. They seemed to typify the stereotypical, catty pageant contestants. They all seemed to have potty mouths and back talk their parents, not that their parents were much better. The families nonetheless made great financial sacrifices. These were tiny pageants, yet the families spent thousands of dollars on dresses the girls would wear only once. The show did not reflect well on the parents. Most of the fathers and mothers were highly competitive and highly critical of their daughters.

Conclusion

The concept of beauty pageants is incredibly divisive. Supporters and critics are adamant that they are right. On one hand supporters argue that pageants are fun, give women and girls valuable social skills, and provide scholarships. On the other hand, critics argue pageants demean women and sexualize little girls. From my research, a couple of things are evident. First, the cost is incredibility prohibitive (where the money could be saved for college to give her a real chance at power). Second, physical appearance is at the forefront of the competition regardless of how much supporters preach that poise and personality count. The Miss USA pageant far surpasses the popularity of the Miss America pageant. According to one of its owners, Donald Trump, the Miss USA has no pretension of being anything but a *beauty* pageant.

Child pageants are particularly harmful. The flirtation of the youngest of girls with audiences and judges is disturbing. The girls are dressed and made up like grown women. They sing and dance to adult themed songs. In this game there is only one winner and everyone else is a loser because of their looks. Sometimes, dealing with the ego of a winner is as difficult as dealing with the bruised egos of all the losers. One critic advised, "Avoid parading your children in suggestive ways such as beauty pageants. She could get the idea that she is only worthwhile if adults reward her for her looks" ("Abuse," 2005). The pageants can be quite grueling, lasting hours and hours with long periods between events.

Some pageant parents see their children as trophy kids. The parents, particularly mothers, appear to be horrible and vicious when it comes to the competition. The cattiness has to affect the child. Pageant supporters try to defend the competitions by comparing the experience to sports such as soccer.

Soccer players can become too obsessive as well. Sports, if not abused, are healthy ways to get exercise. In sports, girls are more likely to be valued for their abilities rather than objectified for their physical appearance.

I have two suggestions. First, call these competitions what they are; they are beauty pageants. They are not scholarship pageants or achievement pageants. There is a certain level of attractiveness one has to achieve before judges even consider other characteristics. Second, set age limits. An 18-year-old can make informed decisions about her life. Let kids be kids. Let them perform for Grandma and Grandpa in their own living rooms, away from the eyes of strangers.

7. BAD BEHAVIOR

The news is inundated with updates about Britney's underwear status or Lindsay's relapses. (Even MSNBC, a 24-hour news cable channel, broadcast hours of uninterrupted coverage of Paris going back to jail.) The antics of the current bevy of young, "out of control" Hollywood debutantes mark an unprecedented era of bad behavior. Perhaps this behavior is a generational trend. Howe & Strauss (2000) found that the Millennial generation (i.e., children born after 1982) has been overindulged by their parents and has an incredible sense of entitlement. It appears that girls are being trained at a young age to demand compliance from others without earning or deserving it. Even the littlest girls are dressed in "diva" and "princess" outfits and indulged with designer purses and clothing. They are thrown extravagant birthday parties and proms. Even religious ceremonies such as bat mitzvahs and first communions have become excessive affairs. It only gets worse as they get older. More and more women are demanding extravagant weddings from their families or their fiancés, putting the couple in significant debt. The notion that the bride is the center of the universe can lead to reprehensible behavior toward others. In this chapter I look at a variety of scenarios of females' bad behavior, such as at spring break, bachelorette parties, and athletic team initiations. I also examine celebrity bad behavior.

Spring Break

There seems to be a lot of money (or credit) available, better marketing, or a whole bunch of parents who felt they missed out on something by not going to a warm climate or beach for spring break. The partying is apparently getting wilder while the attendees are getting younger. High school students are venturing down to the craziest spots, not only with their parents' permission but also with their credit cards. Managers of establishments such as beaches, bars, and hotels appear to look the other way for fear of losing the competitive dollars.

Spring break has the reputation of being an excuse to get wild, especially for females who have been sheltered. Gabarino (cited in Cox, 2006) argued,

"Young women today are like superheroes ... blessed with incredible powers and not yet aware of the responsibilities that come with them." Cox (2006) followed up, stating, "Freeing girls from stereotypes hasn't made them more masculine, it's made them more *more*. Unbound from cultural constraints, they don't flip to the male side of the spectrum. They just flip out." Returning from spring break, attendees are expected to have done some crazy things—over-drink, had illicit sex, etc. In the movies and on MTV, spring break looks like one big party with friends. This trust of strangers is foolish and even danger-ous. Because these overprotected children are far from home, they likely will not know where to go for help if they need it. There is also less chance that friends will be around to stop unwanted sex—or at least sex without sober con-sent. Natalee Holloway, the high school girl who disappeared in Aruba, evi-dently was drinking and left her friends to party with strange men.

Females also think the looser atmosphere gives them the opportunity to act like the boys, especially when it comes to binge drinking. Researchers have found that alcohol can disproportionately affect women compared to men, sometimes almost doubling the effect. This disparity is a factor if a female is trying to keep up with a male counterpart (Springen, 2006). Females use alco-hol to impress others and lose their inhibitions, even though those inhibitions are there as protection. According to an AMA survey, 83 percent of female college students said spring break involves "heavier-than-usual" binge drink-ing ("Girls Warned," 2006). Almost three-fourths of the female respondents stated that women use spring break drinking as an excuse to be "outrageous," e.g., public nudity ("Girls Warned," 2006). In addition, they see being promis-cuous as a way to fit in and be popular. The drinking often leads to increased sexual activity (protected and unprotected), a 74 percent increase according to the survey. Nearly three out of five women know friends who had unprotected sex during spring break. About 40 percent of the respondents reported black-ing out from drinking. Ten percent regretted having public or group sex.

The trend is also for parents to allow high school students to attend spring break. One of Barbara Walters' most "fascinating" people of 2005 was the mother of Natalee Holloway, a girl who disappeared during a high school class trip to Aruba. I am not sure why she was selected as fascinating, since she used poor judgment in letting her young daughter go to a foreign country known for its partying with little chaperone supervision. She asked tourists to boy-cott Aruba, with no mention of her responsibility in the tragic incident.

Sports/Initiations

When females started to play sports in large numbers at the varsity level, many supporters claimed it would make sports more civilized. Female athletes, however, appeared to have adopted the model set by their male peers. Accord-ing to DeFord (2006), success and increased exposure of female sports has changed, not necessarily for the better. Many supporters thought that female athletes would elevate sports. DeFord (2006) stated, "The irony of Title IX, the landmark law that brought gender equality to intercollegiate athletics, is that it shows that sometimes you achieve equality by stepping *down*." Bowen and Shulman (cited in DeFord, 2006) documented the way women athletes have begun to mimic their fellow male jocks in all the wrong ways. Their grades have declined significantly. More and more fall near the bottom of their classes. Even those who came to college with modest grades are performing worse than would be expected. Fewer of them are going on to graduate school or participating in other activities. They have hopelessly succumbed, as Bowen and Shulman described it, to the "athletic culture."

Female athletes are falling into the same behavior as males, particularly in the area of initiations. Bad Jocks (http://www.badjocks.com) is a website exposing the bad behavior of athletes. It has displayed scores of ugly photographs of hazing on female teams. The photos posted on websites of some sports teams' initiations are very sexually provocative and disturbing. Some of the hazing incidents posted online included binge drinking, hiring male strippers, and drawing male genitalia on younger players' bodies and clothing. Catholic University's women's lacrosse team had a male stripper in a thong pose intimately with some of the younger players. In some instances, players had written crude sexual messages on themselves (DeFord, 2006). One of the freshmen had a bib on that had "I do anal" written on it ("Catholic University," 2006). Another read "tw*t eater." They also showed what looked like a male stripper performing oral sex on an underclassman. One player with "I [heart] dick" written on her shirt posed as though she was giving oral to the stripper. Another photo has them in simulated sex positions, one sixty-nine and one where he is about to lick whipped cream off of her stomach.

Northwestern women's soccer players were photographed in their underwear and blindfolded, with their hands bound by athletic tape. Players were shown consuming alcohol and performing sexually suggestive acts (Morrison, 2006). Some of Wake Forest's women's volleyball players are tied up and blindfolded. One player had a penis with testicles drawn on her neck. Another player had male underwear with a bulge stuffed into it. A third player had an adult diaper over her pants. Fordham University's women's softball players are shown with their hair gelled and shaped and wrapped in the form of a condom. They also had small blue balloons attached to their groin areas. One player was rubbing the balloons on a seated male's crotch. "I [heart] penises" was written on one of her arms.

One Fairleigh Dickenson women's softball player had on a white T-shirt with black handprints near her breasts. The caption read, "Touch me, I'm your bitch." Players drew penises on one player as she was passed out on the bathroom floor. Two of UC–Santa Barbara's women's lacrosse players were photographed in thongs, bent over with "rookies" and "rule" written on their buttocks cheeks. The backs of two of their T-shirts read "Insert here" and "I like it here" with arrows down. Comparable photos of male sports team initiations more often featured players dressed in women's underwear and diapers. There were many more homosexual references. Some of the shots showed women in attendance at the hazing.

According to Lipkins (2006), these events teach young women to treat themselves and others as sex objects. It is particularly troubling that females would sexually denigrate other females after women have fought so hard against males' denigration of women. These lessons are the exact opposite of women's movement teaching that women should respect their bodies. Female athletics, particularly, should teach women and girls that they are strong and powerful. Lipkins stated these hazings put the victims in "humiliating, demeaning and degrading positions which will definitely have a psychological effect." She stated she grieves when she sees young female athletes forced to use their bodies in public, sexualized and ridiculed (cited in Schwyzer, 2006).

Greek Organizations

Sororities have been notorious for bad behavior and cruel treatment of other women. In December 2006, Delta Zeta at DePauw University in Indiana kicked out 23 members for not being attractive and popular enough (Summers, 2007). The national chapter claimed it was "reorganizing." Evidently a poll on campus had identified Delta Zeta as having the least attractive members and that supposedly hurt recruiting, which was down. Menges, the national executive director of the sorority, stated that the only factor in determining who would stay was a commitment to recruit for the chapter. Thatcher (cited in Shenfeld, 2007), a former president of the sorority who was asked to leave, stated she and others were not allowed to go downstairs during a recruiting event. The most attractive members, plus attractive members brought in from other chapters, attended the event.

There is an evident danger to women in the Greek system. According to Mohler-Kuo, Dowdall, Koss, and Wechsler (2004), living in a sorority house triples a woman's likelihood of being raped while intoxicated and doubles her chance for other types of rape. Regardless of whether or not she lives in the house, a member of a sorority has an increased chance of rape while intoxicated by almost 75 percent. The Greek system is notorious for a code of silence. The idea of loyalty at any cost, sisterhood, is reinforced by the hazing system.

An article in *Rolling Stone* magazine highlighted the behavior of the social system at Duke University (see Reitman, 2006). Duke has a reputation of taking the motto "Work Hard, Play Hard" to an extreme. The Greek system is an especially powerful entity on campus when it comes to social status. Reitman's (2006) assessment of the campus culture is that the fraternities often express sexist and misogynistic behavior. Parties hosted by Duke fraternities have included the "Playboy" party, where the women dress up in Playboy Bunny outfits and serve shots to the fraternity brothers, a "Presidents and Interns" party, a "Give It to Me, Daddy, I Want It" party, and a "Secs and Execs" party. Allegedly, Duke's Africa organization hosted a party called "Pimpin' All Over the World." All of these parties had the common theme of subservient women and dominant men. Duke University fraternities allegedly invited sorority sisters to participate in their hazing of underclassmen (Reitman, 2006). During these "World War III" parties, freshmen males are led into a room in their boxer shorts. The young women straddle the boys in a dominatrix style. They shout obscenities at the pledges and make them lick chocolate syrup and whipped cream off their chests. The women claim they felt like they were in power because they got to "dominate the boys for a change." One young woman stated that it was an honor to be chosen for the party because it meant "you're the hottest of the hot" (cited in rollingstone.com). Lisker (cited in Reitman, 2006) pointed out that this is not just a phenomenon at Duke but a fairly common experience at campuses across the country.

Lisker (cited in Reitman, 2006) argued that the problem is that women do not always recognize these behaviors as demeaning or subservient. All these activities were done at the direction of the males, for whom the party was designed. It is difficult to argue that it is the females who are primarily benefiting from the males licking sweets off their chests. She further noted that the message from the media is that modern women play with their sexuality. In other words, it is not for women to decide how to enjoy their sexuality. The standard is to use their sexuality to please others.

After a "baby-oil" wrestling party was broken up, one fraternity member stated, "The police report made it look like a big misogynistic thing" (cited in Reitman, 2006). The fraternity member dismissed the claim that the party represented a hatred of women by arguing that it could not be misogynist because the women volunteered to participate. If the females in these situations have no respect for themselves, the males do not understand why they should have respect for women. Reitman (2006) reported that an anonymous Duke student blogger posted an article entitled, "How-to Guide to Banging a Sorority Girl." He claimed that it was easy because the sororities are full of women who are insecure and need to be part of a group of attractive girls to feel good about themselves. He argued, "Of course, they don't realize that entering the sorority world is entering a world of intense scrutiny from all directions ... which compounds their already existing lack of self-worth." Whether or not this is true, it appears to be the general sentiment of males on campus.

Bridezillas

Society's notion of weddings is primarily about love and celebrating vows before God. Historically, weddings were used as an exchange of property, including the bride. Dowries were a way for fathers to unload their daughters onto other men. Men used Bible verses, such as "Women, be submissive to your husbands" (Ephesians 5:22–24), to justify their domination. Many of the traditions of today's weddings still express these themes: the father giving the bride away, asking the father for the woman's hand, the groom not seeing the bride before the wedding and the veil over the face, the bride wearing white (to notify the groom and the groom's family that the bride is a virgin and therefore worth more), the bride's family paying for the wedding (similar to the dowry and getting rid of the female child) and the woman taking the man's name.

Today's weddings are about fantasy, perfection, and wealth. The average cost of weddings in the United States is nearing $30,000 (Wong, 2005). It will likely take decades for couples and their families to pay off credit card charges, which puts stress on the couple. Money trouble is one of the top reasons for divorce. Marketers have been successful in getting society to equate spending with love. The wedding industry perpetuates the illusion of the "perfect day" with marketing and wedding planners. Diamond companies such as De Beers created a link between the size of the diamond engagement ring and love. They used Hollywood movies to promote the association and even sent representatives to high school home economics classes to teach the students about the value of diamonds. According to Edgerton (1999), the diamond went from being a status symbol to being an emotional symbol. Love could now be measured in carats.

The effect of this stress to achieve the perfect wedding often leads to bad behavior, the phenomenon of "Bridezilla." The Bridezilla, as she is now known, appears to care nothing about the sacredness of the ceremony or about the feelings of her friends, her relatives, or even her future husband. Mac Adam (n.d.) argued, "'Bridezilla' is a special kind of insult—too cute to mean anything serious, yet devastatingly demeaning. To call a woman 'Bridezilla,' even if her prima donna antics put Diana Ross to shame, categorizes her bad behavior as a comic 'syndrome.'" Traister (2004) stated that the bride has been reduced to a "caricature of spoiled urban femininity." First, impossible standards of perfection are established, specifically by the wedding industry. As prices go up, stress does as well. The standard of these things must be in demand because the prices are so high. Wedding planners are akin to drill sergeants. The underlings in the industry are also subject to abuse from these brides when things don't go perfectly.

The importance of the wedding over the marriage is an example of immediate gratification. The Bridezilla mentality that this is her day is overlooking the decades of marriage that should follow. The selfishness of many brides doesn't bode well for the subsequent marriage after the glitter and sparkle are gone. The brides also have an opportunity to boss others around and put others down. The size of the engagement ring and the extravagance of the proposal are ways some brides have of establishing themselves higher on the social scale. The fairy-tale mission and striving for perfection could be power plays rather than sincerely wanting the day to be special. It has been hypothesized that brides subconsciously (or consciously) select ugly bridesmaid dresses to make themselves look better.

The television series *Bridezilla* sets up weddings as a forum where women are seemingly rewarded for being irrational and rude and even abusive to others. The show was broadcast on WE, which stands for "Television for Women." The promo for a new season read, "They're madder, they're badder, they're back!" ("About the Show," 2007). Even with the divorce rate around 50 percent, weddings are a bigger extravagance than ever. Perhaps the divorce rate is so high because of the emphasis on the "perfect," fairy-tale wedding day rather than on preparing for a lifelong successful marriage.

Bachelorette Parties

Bachelorette parties have become a sleaze competition with the male version. Traditionally, it was the last chance for men to enjoy the single life. Generally the "best man" would hire strippers, sometimes even prostitutes, to entertain at the party. Females have taken to their own brand of debauchery. These outings occur before what is to be the "holy sacrament" of matrimony.

There is an entire bachelorette party industry. The chain restaurant Dick's Last Resort is a popular destination for bachelorette parties. They feature penis shaped glasses with whipped cream and the bride-to-be is expected to lick off the tip. They also feature "Real Women Love Dick's" T-shirts and "Blow Job Shots" where male bartenders hold a penis shaped shot glass near their crotch area and the bride-to-be drinks from it while on her knees. Websites such as bachelorette.com include lists of other games and activities. For example, in the game "suck for a buck," brides wear T-shirts covered with candy. She then offers male strangers in bars a chance to remove a piece of candy with his mouth for $1—hence the "suck" portion of the game. Some shirts include a bull's-eye drawn around the bride-to-be's nipples. It costs $5 to remove candy attached to those areas. Another option is to have her wear a white T-shirt and ask various men at the bar to decorate it with obscene words and pictures.

Another aspect of the bachelorette party is hiring a male stripper for a party or going to a strip club for women. Liepe-Levinson (2005) argued that, while male spectators take a passive role as they watch strippers, female spectators become physically aggressive. The treatment of male strippers is often more abusive than that of female strippers by the men. For example, women often shout obscenities and grab and try to kiss the dancers. HBO's *Real Sex* (2003) featured an Atlantic City club called "Déjà Vu club: Ay! Papi Chulo! Hot Latin Daddy Revue." It is a male strip club that caters to women's birthday parties and bachelorette parties. One of the Master of Ceremonies noted that in a club with female strippers, it is taboo for male patrons to touch the dancers, but in the club women say, "I'm a female so you should allow me to touch you. So it is more or less 'I can lick you, touch you, bite you, suck you, whatever, and you are going to be happy about it.'"

The master of ceremonies at the Déjà Vu club announced to the group of women, "Tonight the word for tonight is 'dick, lots of dick.' We are going from 9½ to 14½ inches." The dancers confessed to "buffing" themselves up for a performance. In other words, they gave themselves erections by looking at porn and stroking themselves before they went out to perform. One dancer stated that the female spectators "don't want no limp Willy out there." Another dancer disclosed his secret of wearing an elastic string that "goes around your balls, get your man straight out ... then you tie it in a loop and it keeps it erect." According to the dancers, sleeping with any of the patrons damages their careers because it kills the fantasy with her friends.

Out on the stage, a male dancer unsnapped a woman's dress up from the bottom, pulled her up so she was straddling him, dry humped her, spun her around so her head was down, and then simulated oral sex on her. He went from woman to woman down the row, dry humping (front and behind) and performing oral sex through their clothes. Women not only put bills into the men's thongs, but also stuck their hands inside the thongs while other women were watching and the camera crew was filming. One woman was shown giving a dancer oral sex through the thong. Another dancer pulled aside his sheer black mesh thong to expose himself to the women. One dancer was squirming on top of a woman on the floor in a 69 position. He was rubbing his genitals in her face. It looked very uncomfortable as she turned her head away and was putting her hand over her face to shield it from his penis. It looked a lot like a rape scene. I imagine in an atmosphere such as that, a woman saying no would be laughed off as just being shy or embarrassed or playing hard to get.

A birthday girl in the audience was called onstage with all the dancers, where she used a tape measure to see who had the longest penis. After the revue, a cast of other shirtless, buff men came out to dance with the women. I imagine the appeal of paying someone is that the women did not have to worry about leading the guy on; they could be naughty without the consequences of being a tease. This is perhaps the female version, much like men who don't have to worry about being rejected when paying for women to strip or have sex.

At a nightclub at the Jersey shore I witnessed a woman in a dressy dress onstage with her legs spread up in the air. I realized she was at her own bachelorette party when I noticed the veil she was wearing on her head. Later she was dry humping various men on the dance floor as her friends hooted in approval. At a modest restaurant in New York's Little Italy, I witnessed two bachelorette parties in one night. It was earlier in the evening and the restaurant had several families with their young children. The bachelorette groups were acting out, drinking and talking loudly. Both brides-to-be were wearing penis hats. Evidently equality for some women is to be as raunchy as men.

Cougars and MILFs

The expression "Cougars" describes the phenomenon of older women sexually persuing younger men. The MILF (mothers I'd like to fuck) describes the fantasy of the older, experienced woman turning a young boy into a man. There is a point, however, of an adult woman going too far, crossing the line into statutory rape. Silvia Johnson, a 41-year-old mother, was caught hosting parties for minor boys ("Cool Mom," 2005). These parties went on almost weekly for a year. She reportedly provided drugs and alcohol to eight boys and had sex with five of them. Johnson (cited in "Cool Mom," 2005) admitted she wanted to be a "cool mom." She rationalized her behavior by claiming she was never popular in her own high school days. She stated that by partying with them she was "beginning to feel like one of the group."

Headlines occasionally feature stories where teachers are caught having sex with students as young as 12 and 13 years old. Perhaps the most infamous case was Mary Kay Letourneau, who started an affair with a sixth grader, had two children with him, and then married him after she finished her prison sentence for having sex with him. Debra Lafave also made the news when she repeatedly had sex with a 14-year-old boy. A Google search of "teachers minors sex" yielded dozens of stories of female teachers having sex with students. One headline read, "Sexy Substitute Teacher Has 'Relations' with Boy." One story was of a middle-school teacher from Kentucky who got caught fleeing to Mexico to marry her 14-year-old student. Another teacher got caught having sex with a 16-year-old male student in her car while her toddler was strapped into a seat in the back. The creator of the website Bad Jocks (http://www.badjocks. com) catalogued a considerable number of cases in which female coaches seduced their players, male and female. He calls it "the *Desperate Housewives* effect."

These older women, especially teachers, who are in a position of authority, are able to prey on very young boys because of the boys' naiveté. Society often distinguishes between the abuse of boys and girls. In general, women receive lighter jail sentences than their male counterparts who have sex with young females. Sex with boys is often dismissed as a fantasy for the boys because boys demonstrate a clear sign of arousal.

Bad Celebrity Behavior

Celebrities have always misbehaved. Fame and fortune bring many temptations. With new media outlets, however, every detail is recorded and shared with a celebrity obsessed audience. Even if someone has never picked up a

People magazine or channel surfed past *Entertainment Tonight*, they will likely know Britney shaved her head or that multiple men claimed to be the father of Anna Nicole Smith's daughter. In the past it was more common to see male celebrities doing outrageous behavior such as drinking and fighting. There has been a significant rise, however, in bad behavior among female celebrities. Examples of really bad behavior are Courtney Love's drug problems, Winona Ryder's shoplifting, and Paris Hilton's drunk driving arrest. Shannen Doherty, whom some call the ultimate "bad girl," was ordered to mandatory anger management classes after she broke a car window with a beer bottle in a fight outside a club ("Actress of the Week," n.d.). The more prevalent types of bad behavior are less serious but, nonetheless, still dramatic. The most common behaviors splashed across magazines and television celebrity shows are the partying, the feuds, and the boyfriend swapping.

Recently, the most press has been about the crashing and burning of Britney Spears. She went from All-American, Mouseketeer, to a pantyless club regular. The press could not get enough of her exploits. One blogger wrote, "During a recent night out with her new best pal, Paris Hilton, Britney relied on the sticky back plastic to keep her boobs in place. Wearing another racy outfit, Brit looked like a chick on a mission in her uber low-cut green dress. In fact, the frock couldn't have been much shorter in the leg area or much lower in the chest area if it tried" ("Britney and Boobs," 2006). At the end of one night of clubbing, both Britney and Paris wore matching fishnet stockings on their right legs only ("Britney and Paris," 2006). Oliveira (2006) reported that Spears "took off her pants and danced around the club wearing just a pair of fishnet stockings and a tight white satin shirt." Stories and pictures of Spears without underwear were plastered all over the tabloids. Spears posted an apology to her fans on her website, noting, "Thank God for Victoria's Secret underwear!" (Johnson, 2006).

The public is also privy to female celebrities' feuds and catty arguments. The BFF (Best Friends Forever) breakup of Paris Hilton and Nicole Richie was very ugly and very public. BFFs seem to last about as long as the average Hollywood marriage, or four months. Shannen Doherty feuded with the cast and crew on *Beverly Hills 90210* and Alyssa Milano, her costar on the series *Charmed*. She was briefly married to Rick Salomon, who would later costar with Paris Hilton in the infamous sex tape. Lindsay Lohan's reported feud with Hilary Duff over dating Aaron Carter at the same time has been resolved, although Duff's ex-boyfriend Joel Madden began dating Paris Hilton ("Lindsay Lohan," 2007).

Often parents are not just compliant with the process, but also initiators of sexualizing their daughters for fame and fortune. Teri Shields was accused of sexualizing her daughter Brooke in the late 1970s. More recently, critics have faulted Lynne Spears, Dina Lohan, and Joe Simpson for sexualizing their daughters ("Kid Stars," 2005). In 2004, Joe Simpson commented on his daughter Jessica's breasts in an interview. The former minister stated, "She's got double Ds! You can't cover those suckers up!" (cited in Hancock, 2006). Rick and Kathy Hilton exposed their teenage daughters to adult parties and allowed them to illegally get into New York clubs.

A rash of young female stars are checking into spa-like rehab centers. According to Fisher (2007), rehab is now "as fashionable as St. Barts as a place for stars to recover, relax and hide from bad news stories." Some critics claim it is a ploy to excuse their bad behavior and give them a bump in publicity. DeGrandpre (cited in La Ferla, 2007) argued that rehab has become so fashionable it gives a person status. Doonan (cited in La Ferla, 2007) stated, "It's almost to the point where you suspect that if you're not going into rehab, maybe you're not such an interesting person." The rehab centers are more like spas, with ocean views and personal chefs. Lindsay Lohan had apparently taken her hair and makeup person and her personal massage therapist with her. Fisher (2007) reported that Lohan celebrated the end of her rehab stint by clubbing. Britney Spears was in and out of three rehab facilities in one week. Upon her release from rehab, Miss USA Tara Conner stated the experience was "a lot of fun."

Singer Pink wrote the song *Stupid Girls* in response to the bad behaviors of other young women. She blames the epidemic of mindlessness among teenagers today on America's obsession with celebrity (cited in Winfrey, 2006b). Specifically, she stated teenage girls are playing dumb in order to get attention. *Stupid Girls* mocks obsessions with beauty, shopping, and acting dumb. The video specifically targets Paris Hilton, Lindsay Lohan and Jessica Simpson. Pink stated she does not think that these starlets are actually stupid, only that this ditzy act is having a negative effect on their fans. In the lyrics, she describes stupid girls as relying on their daddies to buy their champagne. She wonders where a girl's dream of becoming president has gone. She concludes that the girl who used to have high aspirations is dancing in a 50 Cent rap video. She describes these girls as traveling in packs with their itsy bitsy dogs. Pink thinks that a girl beleives if she dresses in tight tops and push-up bras and flips her blonde hair back boys will call her, too. Pink proclaims at the end of the song that she does not want to be a stupid girl. Doyle (2006) acknowledged that Pink and artists like her are making some headway; however the numbers of female artists who are willing to "sex it up" are much greater than those refusing to conform. The idea that women can be sexy and empowered sends mixed signals to young consumers.

Divas

At one time diva referred to female opera singers. The term was used to describe a woman of rare, outstanding talent. It has been used for superstars such as Bette Midler, Diana Ross, and Barbra Streisand. Many critics believe the word is currently overused, especially in the media, to describe any female performer who has experienced even a "modicum of success." For example, Mariah Carey, Beyonce, and Christina Aguilera are considered divas. World Wrestling Entertainment markets its female wrestlers as WWE Divas. More specifically, "diva" has evolved to describe shallow, demanding women who throw fits if things do not go their way. A diva has been defined as "a bitchy woman that must have her way exactly, or no way at all. Often rude and belittles people, believes that everyone is beneath her and thinks that she is so much more loved than what she really is. Selfish, spoiled, and overly dramatic" ("Diva," n.d.). These women stereotypically throw tantrums that receive a great deal of attention from the mass media. The diva believes she is the only one who matters, and that everyone involved in a project must cater to her every whim.

The diva is glorified through VH1 specials and magazine covers. Young girls are seeing that the quickest way to get attention is to be outrageous. Diva bad behavior includes Diana Ross's arrest for assaulting a security officer at Heathrow Airport in London and Whitney Houston's drug arrests. During an interview with Diane Sawyer, Houston infamously stated, "First of all, let's get one thing straight: Crack is cheap. I make too much money to ever smoke crack.... Crack is wack." Many supermodels are also considered divas. They rely on their looks to get their way. The reality show *America's Top Model* highlights the cattiness of the fashion industry. Even before they have even worked in the industry, these young women are already assuming the attitude of the diva. The few episodes I have watched have all included a barrage of insults from contestants. There is no shortage of using the "b" word and "two-faced." Discussions almost always break down into a round of "who-said-what" behind whose back. One episode even showed a little bit of pushing and shoving in a hallway.

Spoiled Girl TV Shows

There appears to be a fascination with young women who are famous for nothing other than coming from wealthy, indulgent families. For example, the FOX television show *The Simple Life* showcased Paris Hilton and Nicole Richie's bad behavior. The premise of the show was to see if the two trust fund babies could manipulate people to do things for them. They came off as female predators, promising the local boys modeling careers. Some viewers of *The Simple Life* I interviewed thought their bad behavior stemmed from their ignorance of life outside the penthouse. I saw their actions as nothing short of cruel. They were whiny and very disrespectful to their hosts. Perhaps they have never learned to empathize with anyone.

The Simple Life

In one episode, Richie was not watching her purse as she flitted around in a local bar. When she found it was gone, she threw a fit and poured bleach on the pool table. As she was getting kicked out, the patrons were chanting, "Go home, you bitch, go home." In an interview, Richie recounted working as a maid in *The Simple Life 2*. The two were shown trying on the clothing of the people staying at the motel without their permission. Richie laughed as she told the story of how she disliked a particular dress so she cut off the sleeves and cut a new hemline. She argued that the dress's owner would appreciate her work because it looked better. She had absolutely no comprehension that she ruined someone's dress, someone who likely had little money, considering it was not an expensive motel. It is interesting how the two women talk in interviews of how kind they are. Hilton (2004) claimed to act dumb only because television is supposed to be entertaining. She claimed the only reason people they visited said bad things about them was because the tabloids paid the people money.

The premise of *The Simple Life 4* was that Hilton and Richie would take over the woman's role in a family. It was rumored that the show's producers were looking for dads who would likely make a play for Paris or Nicole—"the friskier the dad the better" ("Simple Life 4," 2005). Because the two were feuding at the time, they were filmed separately. They did some outrageous things in order to show up the other one. This version of the show also demonstrated the disregard they have for others. They had a habit of swearing in front of young children. They called the children and their parents "bitches," affectionately of course. In one episode Nicole simulated sex from behind with the "husband" while pretending to be "pregnant" in a child birthing class. In the same episode both women wore vests that had a pair of fake breasts with bottles of milk attached to simulate breast-feeding. A boy just turning two years old was shown drinking from the bottle in the fake breasts. Richie had her two dogs licking from them on either side while wearing the vest. For the two-year-old's birthday, Richie hired a rock band and go-go girls. She had the kids do milk shots. In another episode Richie was supposed to get a four-year-old ready for preschool pictures. She stuffed the little girl's top with socks. She told the girl that she needed to do this to be popular and for the other kids to like her. The girl's father was not happy with the fake breasts or the heavy use of makeup. Hilton acted outraged at Richie's behavior and hired a professional photographer to take more age appropriate shots, sans makeup and breasts.

Rich Girls

Rich Girls was a short lived MTV series featuring the charmed life of Ally Hilfiger and Jaime Gleicher. Critics described the pair as obnoxious, ditzy and snooty. Gilbert (2003) called them the "new dumb bunnies of reality TV" who scale the heights of shallowness. He noted they came across as self-involved, vain, and socially unaware. The only empowerment they demonstrated was the ability to whip out daddy's credit card. The show, thankfully, did not last long.

My Super Sweet Sixteen

The MTV series *My Super Sweet Sixteen* showed what monsters girls can become when they are given everything money can buy. The average party on the show ranged from $100,000 to $200,000. MTV's tagline for the show was "sometimes sweet 16 ain't so sweet." In nearly all the episodes I watched, the girls manipulated their parents, using threats and tantrums to get whatever they wanted for the party. One birthday girl stated, "This party has to be over the top or I won't be happy at all ... and bad things will happen." Another girl declared, "I'd better get the hot car.... I'll do anything to make sure it happens."

The girls appeared to be younger versions of their mothers, way too mature-looking for their ages. Once the girls open their mouths, however, the look of maturity vanished as they acted like spoiled five-year-olds. One girl claimed that her mother has always been her best friend; however, the daughter was upset the mother was now trying to be a parent and say no to her. One girl, Sophie, boldly stated, "I don't take sh*t from anyone, including my mother." During a fight in the dress store, Sophie screamed, "Mom, can you shut up for like ten seconds?" and "Why are you being such a bitch?" The daughter was dismissive and ordered her mother to sit down on that little stool away from her. Her mother had earlier stated that there was no budget for the party so I guess she should not be surprised when her daughter does not respect her. It is just incredible the lack of parenting and teaching the value of money and working for what you have.

What was really surprising was the fathers' role. The fathers tended to be the ones who were willing to spare no expense for the parties. If there were any cost objections, it came from the mother. The themes of many of the episodes was "daddy's girl" or "daddy to the rescue." The fathers as a whole were totally complacent, putting up with the whining and the outrageous demands of these teens. More than one girl announced, "I'm my dad's princess." When looking at a $92,000 car, one girl stated, "That's pocket change, Daddy." Although another girl failed her driving test, her father bought her a BMW convertible anyway. One of the girls said of her father, "He knows what his little girl wants, and he'll get it!" One of the girls complained to her father that she could not find her new Gucci shoes and demanded he find them for her—otherwise, she shrieked, she would have to go to her party barefooted. He retrieved them for her without question. When many of the girls interacted with their fathers, they would flirt and touch them more like a lover than a daughter. It looked almost incestuous at times.

Money has apparently become a significant part of who these girls are. Sophie, whose party cost over $180,000, stated, "Don't try saying the world doesn't revolve around me, because today it does.... The moral of the story is 'Sophie gets what Sophie wants and Sophie is always right.'" Meleny stated,

"My parents spent over $300,000 on my party, and I'm worth every single penny of it." Meleny's goal was to go over the top with the event. She stated, "This party has to be the biggest thing.... I have to show people how rich I am." She wanted a nice car so she can show it off. She wanted to show people how rich she was by adding $4,000 worth of crystals to her dress. The story of Jazmin was especially disturbing. Having been poor before she was adopted, one would think she would be more grateful and more sensitive to others. She stated that her party cost more than her parents' wedding, but, she boldly stated, "I deserve it." When she got a BMW, she screamed that it was the best moment of her life. She relished the fact that everyone would be jealous of her.

Cruel is the one word to describe much of the girls' behavior on *My Super Sweet Sixteen*. Many of the girls used the party invitations as a weapon to humiliate less popular girls at their schools. The show allows girls to play out their acts of cruelty in front of millions of viewers. Jazmin kicked one of her friends, Britney, out of the VIP group although it was apparent that Britney did nothing wrong. Jazmin talked about how fat Britney was and called her a loser to the other girls getting ready for the party. They all screamed and squealed with delight at the shunning of this former best friend. Jazmin announced that if Britney showed up at the party she was going to ignore her because she did not associate with losers. During the party, Britney was left standing pathetically by the door while Jazmin walked right by her without acknowledging her. Her voice-over said, "She probably thinks we're friends, but I don't care what she thinks." The fact that this was done in front of a camera is horrific. It just magnifies her cruelty and need for attention.

One goal of Sophie's party was to make the other kids in her new school jealous. She stated, "A lot of people don't like me because I'm a bitch, but a lot of people want to be me." She concluded that people are mean to her because she is prettier than them. Sophie arrived at school in a chauffeured white Rolls Royce and carried the invitations around on a silver tray. She ran after one girl and accused her of stealing an invitation. She approached the girl, took the invitation away, and threatened to beat her up again in front of everyone. Sophie declared, "This party has given me soooo much power." This whole series is a disturbing commentary on perceptions of worth. I can honestly say I have never seen such a disgusting show of spoiling a child. I am hoping that the young girls watching the show can understand the negative aspects and not want to emulate the behavior.

Daddy's Spoiled Little Girl

This show portrayed a father's love through material gifts. A daughter's love is apparently contingent on the lengths he will go to submit to her wishes. There is also tremendous competition with the mothers or the "new" wife or both, the Oedipal complex in reverse. Most of these fathers have recently attained wealth. Generally old money is low key, or at least not willing to be displayed on television. The mothers are either absent (having been dumped after dad got rich) or take a backseat—literally.

One episode followed 17-year-old Chelsea Chandler as she prepared for a singing competition. Her father's motto was that second place is the first loser. After her father had spent $250,000 on singing lessons, Chelsea failed to make the finals of a local talent show. He admitted he is living through his daughter. He bribed her with a new car if she won the competition. When she lost, he bought her the $80,000 car anyway. Beyond the money, he spoiled her in other ways. For example, he picked up her laundry at her dorm room and went home and washed it for her. Other people in her life all commented on how high maintenance she was and how she was not willing to work for what she wanted. Her final words were that she was not going to give up, because everything is negotiable in life. However, she was not as rude and obnoxious as other featured daughters, just whiney and spoiled. She did have unreal expectations about life beyond Daddy.

In another two-part episode, the Uratas sisters, 28 and 30, were shown trying to break up their father and his new girlfriend so they could have him all to themselves. In the first part he was still with their mother, whom he had since divorced. They were not very nice to their mother either. They literally made her sit in the backseat when they were with their father in the car. In part two, the daughters manipulated him into going on a trip. They spent the entire time purposely excluding his girlfriend. One night, when they were all out to dinner, the younger sister squeezed herself into a small space between her father and his girlfriend, practically sitting on his lap. Every time the dad said no, he eventually did what they wanted him to do. The younger sister stated that her dad is her best friend. In the same breath she said, "He'll do anything for me."

Bad Girls Club

Oxygen's *Bad Girls Club* is a bizarre reality show to have on a network that is supposedly promoting women. The premise of the show is that producers found seven women who were particularly "bad" and put them in a house together. Most of the show is vignettes of the women, with individual commentary about each other. There is constant narration about the other females in the house. Most of the dialogue is name-calling (mostly "bitch") and talking behind each other's backs. Seconds after they bad mouth each other they are hugging and air kissing. They are all drama queens who demand things go their way. They assert that they are the way they are and are not going to change. They take turns screaming at each other and telling the others what each said behind their backs.

In one episode two of the women got into a fistfight over carrying a raft back to the car from the beach. As the two were mixing it, the camera crew caught it on tape with no effort to break up the fight. The episode was titled "Smack My Beach Up." The two were defiant about other people telling them what to do. The woman who started the fight was kicked off the show. She was still insisting that she needed to be respected. The other woman involved ranted that she "wasn't afraid of nobody." During more recent episodes, one of the women cheated on her boyfriend. The guy she cheated with ended up not only dumping her, but also continuing to humiliate her in subsequent episodes. She later made out with other women while they rubbed each other's breasts. Right away things got petty when two new women joined the house. The new and the old immediately took sides. One of the original housemates said one of the new ones looked like "trash." The show is basically about cliques forming and then reforming.

Gates (2006) argued the show looks more like *Girls Gone Wild* (without the toplessness) than the mission of the Oxygen network to "superserve" women. Gates described the emotional age of the housemates as 15. Supposedly the goal of the show is for the women to give up their "evil ways." But Gates compared their actions to that of characters in a Quentin Tarantino movie or, better yet, guests on the *Jerry Springer Show*. One poster on a *Bad Girls* Club discussion board referred to the women as "my six, idiotic hyenas" and "four drunken, scantily clad idiot girls" ("On the Outs," 2007). Another poster stated, "Like the title says, this show is bad. Really bad. And yet, I'm finding myself drawn in against my better judgment."

Analysis of Spoiled Girl TV

It is stunning to see the values that some of these "spoiled rich girl" television shows are portraying. It seems impossible for these girls to ever sustain this level of decadence. These parents are raising hedonistic children whom the rest of society will have to deal with when they are unleashed on the world. A country that once prided itself on meritocracy is now low on the list of industrialized countries where rising higher than your parents is possible. Instead of all this money bringing them happiness, I would think the excess would put tremendous pressure on the girls and their friends. They are already rife with jealousy and bitter rivalry of who is better than whom. I would think money would be like a drug and there would never be enough. There will always be someone with more.

Most of the teens I talked to who watch these shows said they did not think that this "world of the rich" was the standard. They liked to watch the fantasy of someone getting whatever she wanted. I imagine there is a bit of disdain for the way these girls act on these shows, but there is a huge element of envy as well. These shows might not necessarily change the viewers' behavior, but they likely make the spoiled rants more normal and acceptable. The shows paint a picture: if one has money then one has power and therefore can treat people badly. These shows may also be pushing parents who cannot afford such extravagance to get into extreme credit card debt trying to compete so their daughters will not feel left out with their peers. Power is derived from putting others down, making oneself look better at others' expense. The lesson of the spoiled girl reality television shows is that the girls want to flaunt their wealth, or rather their family's wealth.

Conclusion

Girls and women are apparently striving for equality by trying to be as outrageous as their male counterparts. Bachelorette parties, for example, have become very over the top raunch-fests. Spring break's reputation for excesses is growing. Each year the attendees attempt to outdo past years with more drinking and more sex. Those in the hospitality industry are doing little to curtail the behavior because of the fear the spring breakers will go elsewhere. What was traditionally a time for college students has trickled down to high school students.

From young girls to adult women, the new trend of female aggressiveness puts them in competition with each other, and the competition can get ugly. Buying young girls designer fashions sets them up for the vicious cycle of superficial superiority over their less well-off peers. Activities such as beauty pageants can create little monsters of competition and pettiness. Today, women can be downright mean and nasty. They often try to gain power and attention by being "bitchy" and demanding. They continue the behavior because somewhere, somehow, it is rewarded. Recipients of the abuse may simply give in to avoid the wrath of the diva. Therefore, it is not really power that gets females what they want, but fear or annoyance.

8. MUSIC

The music industry is an important site in examining the sexualization of women in popular culture. In the last few decades, lurid images of women have been featured in male produced music videos. Women have appeared as the subjects of derogatory song lyrics. In addition, female performers have been packaged and marketed as eye candy and sexual objects. This chapter covers the history of recorded music and the representations of women's sexuality. I focused specifically on the most popular genres of music, including their lyrics and video images.

History of Female Representation in Music

Recorded music of the pre–1960s often put women on pedestals. Male artists sang their longing for the perfect woman. Crooners such as Bing Crosby and Nat King Cole used music to seduce women. The reputation of the Rat Pack was quite misogynistic. Frank Sinatra was a notorious womanizer, especially in his older, sleazier lounge singer years. He had a habit of using terms such as "dame" and "broad" to describe women. Early rock and roll music by Elvis and the Beatles was respectful to women. Their songs included "Love Me Tender" and "I Wanna Hold Your Hand." Parents were shocked when rock and roll music sent their seemingly innocent daughters in ponytails and poodle skirts into a sexual frenzy. In the next couple of decades a variety of young pop stars such as Donny Osmond, David and Shawn Cassidy, and Leif Garrett catered to young girls' crushes. They had long, feathered hair and were featured on the cover of *Tiger Beat*. Later, squeaky clean boy bands such as New Kids on the Block were manufactured and marketed to girls.

Some of the first female recording artists, such as blues artists Billie Holiday and Ella Fitzgerald, had a certain sensuality. These women were "full figured" and voluptuous, unlike the stick-thin, over-processed female performers of today. Chart toppers Peggy Lee and Lu Lu were wholesome in their lyrics and physical appearance. Women of country music, such as Loretta Lynn and Patsy Cline, were strong and endured difficult lives with their men. Tammy Wynette stood by her man. The 1960s female performers were independent and powerful. Judy Collins sang and played antiwar songs on her acoustic guitar, while Janis Joplin showed a passionate, fiery side to femininity. Pop princesses Debbie Gibson and Tiffany played sugary sweet concerts to a generation of mall-goers.

Recorded music took on a much darker, misogynistic side in the 1970s. Heavy metal music treated women as sex objects or simply ignored them. Rap music, which began as a political statement about urban life, is now under fire for misogynistic lyrics and lurid video images. As the queen of pop music, Madonna pioneered a more powerful, if crass, version of women's sexuality. Today's young bevy of "pop-tarts" represents pseudo-empowerment. They are sexualized at a young age and are taking on skankier personae as they grow out of their Mickey Mouse Club, nymphet stages.

Rock Culture

Rock and roll is often created as a celebration of testosterone, rebellion, and anger. Gone are the doo-wop groups of the 1950s and the acoustic folk melodies of the 1960s. Seventies metal music rebelled against poodle skirts and flower power. Women were not much of a factor in hard rock and heavy metal. In general, they were ignored. Reynolds (1996) stated that rebellion includes a breaking away from mother and domesticity and from women who threatened to smother or emasculate their men. He also argued that the most exhilarating rock music is fueled by misogyny. He pointed to songs written by Johnny Rotten and Kurt Cobain, which were "disturbing love-hate songs about being smothered by a woman."

As music moved to glam rock and hair metal in the 1980s, it was the sexuality of the male performers rather than female sexuality that was featured. The male rockers wore full makeup, teased their long hair, and dressed in tight spandex. To counteract their feminine appearance and avoid labels of homosexuality, the male performers touted their sexual conquests on and off stage. A woman's role was to validate the male performers' masculinity. Hordes of female groupies hung around the dressing rooms and tour buses, hoping to hook up with someone famous. Bands added "power ballads" to their song lists to attract women to their concerts. Women in the audience were hand selected by band members during the concert and brought backstage by security. According to one band member, there were hidden cameras in the back of the tour bus. When one of the band members was having sex with a groupie in the back, the action was transmitted without her knowledge to monitors in the front of the bus where the rest of the band watched and cheered ("When Metal Ruled," 2003). The female groupies were not helpless victims who were being taken advantage of by musicians; rather the women were the ones pursuing the sexual liaisons. They earned bragging rights from their exploits, which did little to gain power and respect for women in the rock and roll world.

Rocker chicks such as Pat Benatar, Joan Jett, and Nancy and Ann Wilson from the group Heart made some inroads into the rock culture in the 1970s and 1980s. They had to battle the stereotypes of femininity and avoid being objectified and put onstage as eye candy. According to Reynolds (1996), female artists have a difficult choice. Many of them are "intoxicated and inspired by male rock 'n' roll ferocity." At the same time, they are aware that rock has often put women down or put them on a pedestal, or in Reynolds' words, "mystified them out of existence." There is a group of strong female performers today, including Alanis Morissette and Sheryl Crow, who are successful without selling their bodies and souls. Empowerment appears to come when women write their own songs and play their own instruments. Over the past decade, however, many female performers have ignored the path of female empowerment laid out by their rock sisters of the 1970s and 1980s. Instead they have exploited their sexuality and have bought into the pop music machine (discussed later in this chapter).

Lyrics

Rock lyrics are often angry and rebellious. Women are generally absent from any mention in the lyrics, as if they are of no concern to real men's issues. The one exception appears to be lyrics concerning women's role in sexually pleasing men. In the song "She Goes Down," Mötley Crüe sang about a woman making a man feel good by giving oral sex. The song states she goes down on him every day, all night. The Crüe describe how she performs oral sex, licking from the bottom up to the top. Lyrics to the Mötley Crüe song "Girls Girls Girls" glorified strip clubs. They sing that the strippers are best when they are not dancing upright but lying down (inviting them for sex). They include names of real strip clubs in the song: Ft. Lauderdale's Dollhouse and Atlanta's Tattletails. Lead singer Vince Neil calls himself a good boy and claims he needs a new toy. He promises to keep the woman over-employed as she dances for him. The song lyrics not only referenced strippers but featured them in the video.

Videos

Since the introduction of MTV in 1981, the music industry has relied heavily on music videos to promote records. Women have been used as background props and shown in sexually submissive positions. One of the most infamous scenes was Tawny Kitaen famously writhing around on top of cars in Whitesnake's video *Here I Go Again*. Scantily clad women stuck their fingers in pies and licked them and straddled speakers while men sang about getting laid. They paraded down a runway in bathing suits as prepubescent boys cheered while Van Halen sang "I'm Hot for Teacher." Eminem, Kid Rock, Blink 182, Metallica, Everclear, and Bon Jovi have all used porn stars in their videos (Paul, 2005). VH1 hosted a special called *Porn to Rock and Roll* to show

how closely the two industries are aligned. The current trend is for rock stars to date (and marry) porn stars.

In the documentary *Dream Worlds II*, Jhally (1995) described males' fantasies of women in music videos in a number of ways. First, he argued that videos make women look like nymphomaniacs. The fantasy for male viewers is that women are desperate for sex and are out of control. Second, women are catty and competitive and will fight with other women to get men's attention. One example of this is mud wrestling scenes in videos. Mud wrestling is a favorite fantasy activity because it is combat but with a fun twist so that it is not taken too seriously. It also evokes the image of the "dirty girl." Another image prevalent in videos is that of strippers, prostitutes, and porn stars. These are women who are available any time for anyone in exchange for money. Jhally (1995) also highlighted voyeurism. Women in videos often look back over their shoulder, showing that they want to be looked at and objectified. Another aspect of the male fantasy world created in videos is the camera work. Scenes of men performing are sometimes shot through the legs of a woman in tight pants or a very short skirt. Women's bodies are often panned by the camera, focusing on their most sexual parts. When women's faces are not shown, Jhally (1995) argued, it is a way to deny their uniqueness, to show they are interchangeable. Several Robert Palmer videos, specifically *Simply Irresistible*, are classic examples of the interchangeable woman. Dozens of women, all with dark, pulled-back hair, identical makeup, identical clothing, are swaying back and forth in unison to Palmer's music. Pepsi adapted the female video-trons to promote their product to an even wider audience.

The mix of violence and sex in music videos is very disturbing. In some cases it represents foreplay to sex. Initial refusals of women evolve into desire if he pursues her long enough. This theme plays on the myth that women want to be taken even though they might say no at first. In this fantasy world, "no" actually means "maybe." Women appear repressed but all it takes is some convincing by a man for them to get over their inhibitions. They strip off their white shirts, which are buttoned to the collar, to reveal lacy bras. They whip off their librarian glasses and let loose their long, flowing hair from tight buns. Women continue to be objectified by the male gaze and, thus, lack of power in these relationships. Even female performers, who should have power, relinquish it by oversexualizing themselves.

Eventually the excesses of glam metal and hair bands wore thin, giving way to grunge and the angst that came with it. Women were perhaps even more insignificant in this genre of music. Gone were the male artists who wore makeup and had long hair. Female fans looked far from feminine, sporting the shapeless flannel shirts and ripped long underwear of grunge style. At the turn of the millennium, rock music has delivered relatively innocuous videos and lyrics. If there is sexism in the music, it is under the radar. The focus of misogyny has apparently diverted from rock music to rap and the world of hip-hop.

Rap/Hip-Hop Culture

Early rap was a venue of protest against racism, police brutality, and poverty. It was a way to call attention to inner city problems. Davis (cited in Weisstuch, 2005) described hip-hop as moving from political to more satirical themes. He noted that as "gangsta rap" became more popular, lyrics became more misogynistic and glorified violence. As the artists overcame poverty and left the dangerous neighborhoods of drive-by shootings and drug deals, hip hop evolved into a "bling" culture. Gold was everywhere: gold chains, gold plated cars, gold capped teeth, etc. The media focused not on urban blight and issues of racism but on the artists' personal lives rife with bad behavior, criminal activity, personal feuds, and greed. Critics claim that rap contributes to the exploitation of women, particularly black women. Some critics argue the popularity of the "bling and ho" trends can be traced to the commercialization and mainstreaming of rap and hip-hop. White corporate owners of record companies control a significant number of hip-hop artists. Although artists put out a variety of songs, executives may choose to promote the most radical singles. Producers and agents may also pressure young artists to produce the more shocking material that sells more records to a primarily white, male audience.

Lyrics

In many rap songs, the double standard, where men who have sex are heroes and women who have sex are whores, is alive and well. One image that the genre projects is that women are greedy and manipulative when it comes to sex. There appears to be a good old boys club where men must ban together to protect themselves from women out to get their money and their sperm. These "hos" work their way up the social ladder by sleeping around, hoping to achieve their ultimate goal of trapping a Sugar Daddy. Campbell (cited in "Hip Hop Videos," 2005) stated, "They're trying to hit the jackpot. Let's be realistic. This is a business. And the business is getting ahead.... They get pregnant, clearly for the money." To teach these women a lesson, some rappers have described how they have brutal sex with women and then discard them or pass them around to their entourage. Some lyrics have even suggested that they deserve corporal punishment when they "mess" with men. In the song "U and Dat," E-40 warns that if she "fucks" around with him, he will beat the "brakes" off her "pussy."

Many of the song titles and lyrics of rap songs regarding women are quite horrifying. It took less than one minute searching on the Internet to find dozens of examples. (Warning: these songs contain explicit lyrics. I chose to transcribe them "as is" so readers could get the full impact.) In the song "Homies Can't Have None," Snoop Dogg described how he had respect for a woman until she had sex with him. He states he is going to fuck her a few times until there is nothing else to do with her. Then he will pass her around to his friends so they can have sex with her too. He does not care because she means nothing to him. In B.G's "Fuck These Hoez," he calls her a ho and a bitch and states that he does not give a fuck about her because she ain't shit. Project Pat's "Fuck a Bitch" includes lyrics about creeping into a woman's house and bringing his roadies with him to all have sex with her. He stated that love is a "pimp" thing, implying men can have sex with women at any time, regardless of the women's wishes. In Kurupt's "Ho's a Housewife," he agrees with earlier rappers that women "ain't shit." They are only good for "eating dick." He claims that he cannot stand hos that cannot cook for him.

Defenders of rap often excuse the lyrics because the artists are young and do not know any better or they come from an economically disadvantaged background. Neither explanation is true in the previous cases. These are well established artists with sizable bank accounts who are making more money with lyrics meant to shock listeners.

Some female artists use similar tones in their lyrics. Lil' Kim raps about hos and refers to herself as a queen bitch. Rapper Kia put out a song called "Fuck Dem Other Hos." She calls other women big dumb hos and tells them they need to pay attention to her. Rapper Eve was criticized for appearing in Sporty Thieves' video for their song "No Pigeons." McLune (2006) referred to "No Pigeons" as "one of the most hateful misogynistic anthems in hip-hop." McLune argued that, instead of defending other women, Eve sided with the perpetrators of hatred toward women. The moral of the story is that it is difficult for women to criticize misogynistic lyrics when other women are using or endorsing them.

After the firing of radio personality Don Imus for using the phrase "nappy headed hos," hip-hop was put on the defensive by the media, politicians, and feminist groups. Comparisons were made between Imus' comments and hip-hop lyrics (Reid, 2007). Music producer Russell Simmons (cited in Reid, 2007) dismissed the comparisons of Imus' comments with that of hip-hop culture. He claimed that hip-hop artists rap about their experiences. He argued, "Sometimes their observations or the way in which they choose to express their art may be uncomfortable for some to hear, but our job is not to silence or censor that expression" (cited in Reid, 2007). In response, the Rev. Al Sharpton stated, "No one, even in the name of creativity, should enjoy a large consumer base when they denigrate people based on race and based on sex" (cited in Reid, 2007). Sharpton argued for a balance between free speech and sexist language. Chris Rock's response in his comedy act was, "It's hard to defend [Snoop Dogg's lyrics] 'I've got hoes in different area codes'" (cited in Bates, 2005).

Hip-Hop Videos

In a significant number of hip-hop videos, men in expensive tracksuits rap poolside while women in bikinis crawl over them and display their "booty" for the men's approval. Pollet and Hurwitz (2003) used examples of videos such as Wreckx'N'Effect's *Rumpshaker* to show how hip-hop videos embrace stripper culture. They describe the video as setting the stage for other videos that glorify the "*Lifestyles of the Rich and Famous*–style locales and high-heeled bikini-clad babes." Most hip-hop fans see only edited or clean versions of rap videos on MTV and BET. Uncut versions of the videos are sold on DVD or aired late at night. Critics consider the uncut videos particularly disgusting and misogynistic. Often rappers will get local strippers to do nude (and in some cases pornographic) versions of the video.

After a protest from female students at Spelman College, Nelly canceled his concert at the historic African American school. The students asked Nelly to justify his treatment of women, particularly in his video for "Tip Drill" (Weisstuch, 2005), before performing on their campus. In the lyrics Nelly states he wants women to expose and offer him their asses. He also wants to spit his "pimpjuice" in them or at them (it was not quite clear). He tells a tip drill it must be her ass that attracts men because it is not her face. The term "tip drill" refers to a woman who has a hot body but an unattractive face; therefore, she is good for sex only from behind. The term is similar to the Howard Stern expression "buttaface," meaning she would be hot "but her face" is ugly. It was very disturbing to listen as the lyrics state that it must be her ass that attracts men because it is not her face drones on over and over and over again throughout the song. Women in the video are constantly shaking their thonged rear ends in men's faces. There is also a significant amount of girl-on-girl action in the video. One woman is completely bent over while the woman behind her thrust her groin area back and forth against the first woman's behind. One camera shot shows a woman kneeling down, flicking her tongue directly in front of another woman's genital region. Near the end of the video, Nelly swiped his credit card down a woman's butt crack.

According to VH1's *Hip Hop Videos: Sexploitation on Set* (2006), the women in the videos claimed they are acting in the videos, it is not who they are. They argued they liven up the videos and make them more fun. These women are motivated by the exposure, thinking it will lead to modeling and acting careers. There is intense competition for camera time; therefore, many women are motivated to do what it takes to get attention. Asia, a hip-hop dancer, sounded resigned to the trading of sexual favors for camera time. She stated, "You gotta pay, there's nothing free these days. I don't care if they call me names as long as I'm making money" (cited in "Hip Hop Videos," 2006). There is a pecking order to women who appear in videos. The order ranges from the most prestigious "video models" to the lowest "video hos," who exchange sex for an opportunity to be in videos. While some of the women are willing to have sex with the rapper, their entourage, and the crew, other women are pressured. There are few, if any, regulations in the industry to protect legitimate dancers from sexual harassment.

In her book *Confessions of a Video Vixen,* Steffans (2005) revealed the dark side of the music video industry. She admitted to sleeping her way up the music video food chain. Men in the rap industry nicknamed her "Superhead," in reference to her talents at giving oral sex. She described her appearance in the videos as being "sprawled undressed over a luxury car while a rapper is saying lewd things about me." She claimed lack of self-esteem was the top reason women appear in rap videos. She added, "No one who values, loves, or knows herself would allow herself to be placed in such a degrading position" (Steffans, 2005). She recounted that her lack of self-esteem came from growing up in an abusive family and being raped at age 13.

Analysis

Two years before the Imus scandal, *Essence* magazine developed a campaign called "Take Back the Music" as a way to "challenge the prevalence of misogyny and sexism in hip-hop lyrics and videos" (Weisstuch, 2005). Weisstuch (2005) noted that it is significant that African American women have reached the point where they find that the degree of sexism in rap is no longer defensible. The group criticized the image of harems of women in bikinis gyrating around artists in many hip-hop videos. Davis (cited in Bates, 2005), the editor of *Essence,* recalled her breaking point was when she saw Snoop Dogg walk two women down the aisle in dog chains at an MTV music awards show. A pioneer of black feminist scholarship, hooks (1994), described the cover of Snoop Dogg's record "Doggystyle" as "complete with doghouse, beware the dog sign, with a naked black female head in a doghouse, naked butt sticking out." She pointed out that the album got positive reviews from the mainstream press with no mention of the offensive, misogynistic cover. Davis (cited in "Hip Hop Videos," 2006) argued the videos perpetuate stereotypes of women of color as oversexed and there for the taking. She stated, "Sex sells, we hear that all the time. Well, crack sells. It doesn't make it good." She noted the videos could be beautiful without the butt shaking.

A study by Keltner (2001) demonstrated that rap fans showed a disdain for songs that degraded men. On the other hand, those same fans were neutral when the songs degraded women. While female non-rap fans were offended by lyrics that degraded women, female rap fans reported liking those same lyrics, finding them funny. In another study, hip-hop fans responded to rap music's treatment of women with a range of emotions ("Negative Rap," 2001). Some fans blamed the listeners for reading too much into the lyrics. They defended the hateful expressions as just a form of entertainment. A 14-year-old boy blamed "stupid teenagers" for not knowing the lyrics are not real. Most respondents agreed that these rappers are role models and their treatment of women does influence their audience ("Negative Rap," 2001). The lyrics may not make men beat and rape women, but it seems to have a degrading effect on perceptions of women in general. A 14-year-old female reported that she has heard boys using rude and insulting words that refer to women that they learned in the latest hip-hop song. She argued that when cheating on a significant other or even beating a woman is described in songs as acceptable, it then becomes acceptable in reality. Another 15-year-old female agreed and added that artists may feel they need to use profanity such as "hos" and "bitches" to become part of the rap industry. Others linked talking this way to establishing masculinity in their urban community.

Some supporters excuse the misogyny in hip-hop because some of its participants are women. The idea is that if women rap, then the industry and culture cannot be all that sexist. An 18-year-old female respondent (cited in "Negative Rap," 2001) stated, "Women may take offense at being referred to as 'bitches' and 'hos' but it's difficult to protest when the terms are used so casually and women themselves have almost fulfilled the identity." Female hip-hop artists, while marginalized within the industry, are trotted out to defend hip-hop against critics (McLune, 2006). According to Nelson (cited in Pollet & Hurwitz, 2003), female rappers originally adopted a model of rap that used talent and power as a way to earn respect. When the hip-hop industry "embraced the pimp archetype," however, female rappers were forced to take up "hyper-feminine personas" to compete. According to Nelson, today's female hip-hop stars, like Lil' Kim and Foxy Brown, are "taking their fashion cues from the table-dancing backup dancers and extras who populate male hip-hop stars' videos" (cited in Pollet & Hurwitz, 2003). Many critics blame the women in the videos for making the exploitation of women acceptable, since they are active participants. Critics also stated that women in the industry, both dancers and artists, who buy into their own exploitation make it harder for all women to gain respect.

The Spelman protest was an example of African American women standing up against commercialized sexism. These women were criticized for their protest by a number of sources. Some male students at Morehouse, another historically black college affiliated with Spelman, put the blame on the women in the video (cited on Winfrey, 2007). They argued that because the woman in the video allowed Nelly to swipe his credit card down her rear end, it was not solely the artist's fault. Message boards after the Spelman women appeared on *Oprah* were incredibly harsh as well. (It is pretty obvious why women are reluctant to speak out against sexual exploitation.) Other postings on message boards defended rap by arguing women support that kind of rap by buying it and dancing to it at the clubs (Winfrey, 2007). Even if women are bold enough to protest against the exploitation of other women, it apparently does little or no good. Reid (2007) argued that every time there has been a protest against hip-hop, the genre has gained an even larger following.

In popular rap lyrics, "bitches" and "hos" are referenced in an effort to divide and conquer women. Occasionally there will be someone who excuses the lyrics because there are women out there who are bitches and hos. McLune

(2006) found that women who sing along to women-hating lyrics are convinced that the artists are not talking about them. But there is a sentiment in the culture that all women are hos until proven otherwise. After the Rutgers basketball/Imus incident, Snoop Dogg claimed that rappers are not talking about "no collegiate basketball girls who have made it to the next level in education and sports.... We're talking about hos that's in the 'hood that ain't doing sh—, that's trying to get a n—a for his money" (cited in Reid, 2007). His statement made a clear class distinction between the educated and the uneducated. It is ironic that the basis of rap music was initially a class issue as well as a race issue.

Pioneer hooks (1994) criticized black artists for the misogyny, but also blamed the white establishment that pushes for such materials for commercial success. She asked her readers to consider "the seduction of young black males who find that they can make more money producing lyrics that promote violence, sexism, and misogyny than with any other content." In other words, while the artists need to be held accountable for the hateful things said about women, blame also needs to be assessed to the patriarchal society and the large corporations producing the music and exploiting the artists and audience. She added, "Far from being an expression of their 'manhood,' it is an expression of their own subjugation and humiliation by more powerful, less visible forces of patriarchal gangsterism." She also called for African American women to be careful to hold their men accountable, yet recognize the forces that created the environment (hooks, 1994). African American women are torn between "standing by their men" and standing up for themselves, and hooks argued that it is a false choice, that there is an alternative to demonizing black males. The real source of the problem is the white supremacist capitalist patriarchy.

Country Music Culture

One of the most traditional roles for women in the music industry is in the country music genre. Country music is in transition, however. Today, female artists are becoming sexier, to the displeasure of country purists. In the 1990s Shania Twain sent shock waves through the world of the Grand Ole Opry when she exposed her midriff. CMT (Country Music Television) recently compiled a list of the 20 sexiest female country singers. Most of the top ten were thin, blonde, one-hit wonders. A special issue of *FHM*, "Girls of FHM of Country Music," featured the female country music artists that are seemingly trading on their looks (see chapter 7). With the conservative image of country artists shattered, many of the singers are showing cleavage and wearing bra-like tops.

One reason female country artists are exploiting their sexuality is to increase their chances of crossing over into the pop charts. *American Idol* has produced crossover country stars such as Carrie Underwood and Kelly

Pickler. The cable channel CMT (Country Music Television) made country music videos available, similar to the pop music industry. Young stars such as LeAnn Rimes have taken a path somewhat similar to pop stars. She hit the charts at age 14. As she got older and grew out of her "cute little girl" stage, she lost a great deal of weight and started exploring her sexuality. In her *Life Goes On* video, she wore a skin-tight dress made of sheer material. She struck provocative poses against walls and poles as she sang.

Unlike pop music, country music includes an appreciation for women with "redneck" sexuality. For example, the lead singer of Confederate Railroad sang that he likes his women on the trashy side. He likes them to wear tight clothes and lots of makeup. He also likes hair with bad dye jobs. In Hank Williams, Jr.'s song, "That's How They Do It in Dixie," the ideal woman has cut-off jean shorts and dark roots showing through her long blonde hair. Gretchen Wilson has personified the redneck look. She generally wears tight low-rider jeans and spaghetti-strap, midriff tops, as well as dark eyeliner. In Wilson's first single, she bragged that she is a "redneck woman." In her lyrics she brags that she is not like a Barbie doll. People perceive her as trashy and hardcore; however, she considers herself as the girl next door. She brags she is not a high class woman who uses bad grammar such as "ain't no" and refers to women, including herself, as "broads." In her song "California Girls," she criticizes Hollywood types, such as Paris Hilton, with their big fake smiles and no meat on their bones.

Lyrics

While country music generally speaks kindly of women, there are songs that describe negative female characters who cheat or are trying to get every penny they can in a divorce. Hank Williams, Sr., was rather bitter when it came to women. He sang of her "Cheatin' Heart" and her "Cold, Cold Heart." Tex Ritter hit it big with the song "You Two-Timed Me One Time Too Often." Jerry Reed recounted his divorce settlement, stating, "She Got the Gold Mine, I Got the Shaft." More recently, country music has become very feminized and radio friendly in terms of lyrics. When a woman cheats on Keith Urban, he simply tells her in a soft melodic tone to take her cat with her and leave his sweater behind.

In terms of singing about sex in country music, the songs are generally more about relationships and making love than getting laid and exploiting women. There are a few exceptions, such as Toby Keith's "As Good as I Once Was." He sang about getting lucky with twins so he takes a "little blue pill." In "The Seashores of Mexico," straight laced singer George Strait sang about having a one-night stand with a woman who ends up taking his money while he sleeps. He then has an affair with a married woman. There are some cutesy country songs that play with sexual themes. One example is Joe Nichols' "Size Matters," which refers to the size of a man's heart rather than his other anatomy of interest. I remember my nephew, who was about 8 years old at the time, giggling with his friends about another Nichols' song, "Tequila Makes Her Clothes Fall Off."

Lyrics from traditional country music female performers included old-fashioned messages, such as Tammy Wynette's "Stand by Your Man," in which she laments that while men are having good times, the women will be having bad times. She advises other women that if they love their men, they should forgive them. The meaning of the song has been hotly debated. It was said that Tammy Wynette spent two hours writing it and a lifetime defending it. Critics of the song claim it is about blind devotion of a submissive wife. Supporters claim it is about the deep devotion of a woman in love. Another female performer, Patsy Cline, was pretty clear about where she stood. Although she was queen of the "he done her wrong" songs, she rarely played the victim.

Today there are female empowerment songs in country music, such as Shania Twain's "Man, I Feel Like a Woman." (She can go crazy and forget that she is a lady. She is allowed to wear short skirts or men's shirts if she wants.) Terri Clark's song "Girls Lie Too" is a "get even" song where women are elevated to the level of men by demonstrating how they can tell lies too. Carrie Underwood sang about smashing her boyfriend's car with a baseball bat when she caught him cheating. (The song is a far cry from Underwood's song about praying to Jesus to take the wheel.) The song "Sometimes It Takes Balls to Be a Woman" by Elizabeth Cook is out of the traditional norm as well. There was a major controversy when the Dixie Chicks released their song "Goodbye Earl." Supporters claimed that the song is about a woman taking matters into her own hands when a husband is abusive and the law cannot protect her. The premise of the song is that a woman comes back to her hometown when her best friend's husband puts her friend in intensive care. After deciding they had no other choice since Earl had ignored the previous restraining order, they poisoned him and threw his body in a lake. The controversy was primarily due to the comical lyrics and the upbeat tune of the song. Rap music that talks of beating and raping women is most often done in an angry tone (which apparently is more forgivable).

Videos

There has been an increase in sexual images in country music videos. Female artists are getting thinner and wearing less clothing, following mainstream music trends. A recent video featured Faith Hill writhing around on a bed on the beach covered only by a sheet in her video for "Breathe." The white sheets, the beach, and Hill's reputation as a "good girl" perhaps make the video more sensual than sexual. In her video *Delicious Surprise*, Jo Dee Messina is quite sexualized. The video begins with her posing with her arms crossed above her head. She turns to show us the back of her jeans, which have the word "love" and a butterfly stitched over her rear end. Her shirt is riding up so the audience can also see a tattoo on the small of her back. Camera shots often focus on her exposed midriff. Throughout the video, she continues to dance in circles with her arms above her head. She is shown with various colored shirts, all tank tops that are short enough to expose a couple of inches of midriff above her low-rider jeans. In her mid-thirties, she is older than other female country stars and not as traditionally beautiful. She is very toned. At the end of the video, she again treats the audience to a shot of her backside as she walks away from the camera. In Rissi Palmer's (Palmer is one of a scant few performers of color in country music) *Country Girl* video, she danced around with her top unbuttoned so low the top of her bra and much of her cleavage was showing.

The video for Hank Williams, Jr.'s song "That's How They Do It in Dixie" starts with a pretentious fashion show. He is joined by two male duos, Big & Rich and Van Zant, and one female artist, Gretchen Wilson. Sleek models of MTV caliber stroll down the runway. They are replaced with "real" women wearing cut off jeans and cowboy boots, and whose blond hair shows dark roots. They are wearing skimpy camouflage skirts so short underwear-like shorts are visible. The shorts do not adequately cover their rear ends. The cut off jean shorts are extremely short, with ragged frayed edges and long fabric strings hanging down. The camera angles are shot from below so viewers can see up the women's skirts. There is at least one quick shot up a woman's skirt to reveal her pink panties. These ideal women have, according to the lyrics, tattoos placed about "hiney high." In addition they have dangling belly button rings and fake tans. Near the end of the video, Gretchen Wilson comes out in a cowboy hat, tight jeans, and a spaghetti-strap top, with just a hint of her midriff showing. In the song, she threatens other women that if they flirt with her man she will appear on the *Jerry Springer Show*, where cat fighting is the norm. She is portrayed as one of the guys, different from the models that appear on the runway.

Country music has primarily a female fan base. Songs about pickup trucks and rowdy friends have given way to sweet love ballads. Female stars are more popular than in the past; however, they appear younger and sexier.

Pop Music

A discussion of pop music and female representation of sexuality has to start with Madonna. Of all female artists, she is perhaps the most influential fashion icon. Not only has she been commercially successful, she has also managed to do so spanning three decades and counting. She had some innocuous dance hits in the early 1980s, including "Lucky Star" and "Borderline." Her 1984 hit "Like a Virgin" established her sexually explicit reputation. The video was pretty tame; however, her performance of the song on the MTV video awards show was legendary. She wore a bride's veil, white lace bustier, and "boy toy" belt. By the end of the song she was writhing around on the floor in a fit of lust. Although tame by today's standards, it was rather shocking considering the fact she was singing about being "like" a virgin. Pop stars at the time may have hinted about it but were not announcing the loss of their virginity. The contrast of the white wedding dress mixed with a sexual theme was distasteful to some critics, even though the concept of brides wearing white to symbolize virginity had been abandoned well over a decade or two before the song hit it big.

As Madonna matured in her music and style, she blended a powerful, sexual persona with a strong business sense. She graduated from lace tops and leggings to cone bras and grabbing her crotch. The material of the cone bras was impenetrable and the sharp points at the nipples could clearly do some damage if men got too close. That she was grabbing her own crotch symbolized the site of men's power, the phallus and testicles. She released a documentary of her tour called *Truth or Dare* in 1991. The film documented the simulated sex onstage during her concerts. One thing that stood out was that almost all the sex was initiated by Madonna or the other female dancers toward the male dancers. In her 1993 tour, "The Girlie Show World Tour," Madonna played a "whip-cracking dominatrix" (Smith, 2004). Paglia (cited in Hancock, 2006) argued that, in contrast to today's pop-tarts, "Madonna was able to flash her breasts and play peek-a-boo because she is an authentic, creative artist."

At times her antics sent mixed messages. In the lyrics of "Express Yourself," Madonna sang about women standing up for themselves. She tells women they deserve the best in life and that their men should make them feel like queens. On the other hand, the video showed Madonna crawling on the floor under a table toward a bowl where she licked up milk. A few frames later she appeared naked with a large steel collar around her neck attached to the bed with a thick chain. I remember at the time she justified the video by explaining that she chained herself to the bed and therefore it was empowering for women. It is difficult to imagine that young boys saw it that way. They likely just saw her chained naked to the bed and fantasized about having control over a defenseless woman.

Another female artist who was empowered by her sexuality was Cher. Early on in her career, she appealed to feminists, who loved her strong, independent woman persona. She also had an unusual look (before all the plastic surgery) that was different from the cookie-cutter pop queens before her. Similar to Madonna, Cher has the ability to reinvent herself. After the age of 40, Cher made a significant comeback. In the video for her hit "If I Could Turn Back Time," she performed on a U.S. aircraft carrier surrounded by young, handsome servicemen in uniform. She appeared in a tiny, tiny black outfit. Although she wore a short leather jacket that covered some of her breasts, her thong revealed most of her bottom as she spun around with her back to the camera.

The Next Generation

In 2003, Madonna performed "Like a Virgin" with Britney Spears and Christina Aguilera at the MTV music awards. The concept of the performance was that Madonna was playing the role of the groom and was passing the torch to Spears and Aguilera as the next generation of female performers. The performance became notorious when Spears slipped Madonna the tongue during a kiss. It was a poor attempt to inspire new female empowerment, especially with what Spears has done with her life since then. Aguilera has shown some class and used her voice to drive her career rather than relying exclusively on exploiting her sexuality.

Rather than being empowered by their sexuality, female performers and their record companies appear to be exploiting the young female body for fame and record sales. Instead of advancements in gender equality opening up to a variety of artists and new roles for women as performers, the music industry has become more uniform and restrictive. Consolidation of record labels has created a cookie-cutter approach to selecting the next big star. Artists are at the mercy of extensive and expensive promotions, meaning there is little time to develop new talent. Performers, particularly females, without eye-catching videos have little chance of selling records. A female artist who is not thin and beautiful has almost no chance of making it big, regardless of talent. Reality shows such as *American Idol* expose and perpetuate these standards.

One reason females are so commercially successful in the pop genre is that they can be easily packaged and sold to teen and preteen girls. (It is highly unlikely that many men who are enjoying the sexual exploits of these performers are shelling out money for the music.) Girls are looking to these pop stars as icons and trend setters. In the 1980s young girls were looking up to teen idols Debbie Gibson and Tiffany, who displayed "the girl next door" look. Today, the pop music industry takes young girls, sexualizes them, and sells them to even younger audiences. I have heard a significant number of stories of mothers taking their kindergarten-age daughters to Britney Spears concerts in the early 1990s. Marketers' strategy of age compression feeds on girls' desire to grow up quickly so that boys will notice and validate them.

As performers get older and grow out of the Lolita stage, they are pushed to change their style to appeal to a broader audience. Because they have already been sexualized, it is almost impossible to go back to relying on their talent (that is assuming they had some talent in the first place). Many of the girls packaged as "nymphets" go to extremes to renew attention to their careers as they age out of the system. Most young stars never make it out of their teens as stars; they are used and disposed of quickly. Performers such as Britney Spears and Christina Aguilera employed what I call the "skank" strategy to express their sexual maturation as they entered their 20s. The skank look includes wearing dark makeup, revealing clothing, and stringy unwashed hair.

Performers with pretty blonde hair seem to all be dyeing their hair jet black (e.g., Christina Aguilera, Ashlee Simpson, and most recently Hilary Duff) to get that "dirty" girl look.

Beyoncé was once seen as a strong female performer and a self-proclaimed devoted Christian. Doyle (2006) argued that Beyoncé, who sang about sisterhood and the dangers of unhealthy relationships, has turned into a sexier Beyoncé who has begun to dress in hot pants to show off her "bootylicious behind." Doyle argued that it sends confusing messages about empowerment and sexuality to her young female fans when the videos show Beyoncé gyrating for the camera, writhing on a bed, and watering herself down with a fire hydrant.

The image of girl-on-girl for publicity can go to the extreme. The duo t.A.T.u. is a pair of young female Russian performers who often wear plaid schoolgirl outfits with short skirts. Their manager supposedly got the idea of packaging them as lesbians from surfing underage porn websites, a particular fetish of pedophiles (Weitz, 2007). The Russian version of their website shows photos of them French kissing on stage and in their videos. In a 2003 issue of *Maxim*, one of the girls has her hand down her pants, clearly in her crotch. With her other arm she is holding the other girl, who is naked except for a thong. In other pictures they are touching each other's breasts and tugging down on each other's pants. Peisner (2007) noted that these girls are not really lesbians and that it was just "an ingenious marketing ploy to sell records to creepy old men." Their image was none other than "teenage lesbianism meant for straight male entertainment" (Weitz, 2007).

Occasionally there is a show of "girl power" in the form of girl groups. Unlike the all female bands such as the Go-Go's and The Bangles, who played their own instruments, the girl groups just sing and dance (or in some cases gyrate). The group concept supposedly signifies cooperation rather than competition. In the mid–1990s, the Spice Girls hit the music scene. Members of the "prefab" group had distinct personalities, with the cutesy names "Ginger Spice," "Baby Spice," "Scary Spice," "Sporty Spice," and "Posh Spice." The group became a symbol of "girl power." Doyle (2006) argued that female acts following the Spice Girls are a watered down version of feminism. She stated that they send confusing messages to girls and young women, such as the importance of male attention over self-esteem. Doyle (2006) argued, "This new pseudo-feminism, which has become the must-have marketing ploy for any new female artist, has flaws and contradictions." Pollet and Hurwitz (2003) had a similar critique of the groups. They saw the message as "Look sexy like this and you will be powerful."

The most famous post–Spice Girls girl group to date is the Pussycat Dolls. The Dolls were originally a group of burlesque dancers. Famous stars such as Carmen Electra, Gwen Stefani, Christina Aguilera and Charlize Theron have performed as Dolls. Doyle (2006) described the group as striptease performers in "stockings, suspenders and very little else." Similar to the Spice

Girls, they claimed to be promoting "girl power," a claim strongly protested by critics. The basis of the Pussycat Dolls' hit song "Don't Cha" is a woman trying to steal away another woman's boyfriend, luring him away with her looks. They bet these guys wish their girlfriend were "freaks" like they are. Definitions of "freak" range from a girl who acts innocent and then gets wild in bed to a person who does kinky things during sex. Doyle (2006) argued that the song's theme could not be further from the ideals of feminism. In the video for their song "Buttons," the Dolls danced in bra-tops and hot pants, asking to be undressed. The video also features the infamous Snoop Dogg. One contributor to Wikipedia ("Pussycat Dolls," 2006) described their performances as teasing and innuendo rather than raunchy sex. The television network CW aired a reality show, the premise of which was to select the next Doll. Watching the first episode, I found it difficult to distinguish the cattiness and the backbiting from the World Wresting Entertainment shows.

Lyrics

In the eighties there was a sweet side to popular music. Debbie Gibson and Tiffany were mall-performing, girl-next-door types. Along with the New Kids on the Block, they were singing about love and affection. In Debbie Gibson's lyrics of one song, she states that it was more than fate that brought them together. She feels helpless because she misses him. She refers to him as the love of her life and her best friend. Tiffany sang that she will find her way to him even though she is blind with love. She can only see herself in love with him. The lyrics are similar to the male pop lyrics of today, which are watered down for a teen and preteen female audience. Producers of pop-boys such as Aaron Carter and Jesse McCartney heavily appeal to their base of young girls. Young tweens swoon as Carter sweetly asks her not to go. He tells her he is crazy for her and will do anything for her. McCartney tells his love he cannot let her go. He laments that his world has double the stars in the sky because she lives. He wants her and her beautiful soul. While the boys of pop are held to a very high standard, it appears that female acts are hanging out in the gutter.

Sexual references are apparent in some music to show women can use their sexuality to get what they want. In the Black Eyed Peas song "My Humps," Fergie sang about using her "lovely lady lumps" to get what she wants from men. She stated she will get him "love drunk" off her hump. In response to what she is going to do with the ass inside her jeans, she answered that she is going to make him scream. She brags of driving men crazy on a daily basis so they will buy her diamonds and designer clothing. According to one critic, "Fergie's materalism [sic] and willingness to use her body for it is grating. Even worse, she's proud of degrading herself" ("My Humps," 2005). No one appears to be sure what her "London Bridge" is that keeps falling down in the song "London Bridge." Some fans claim it is her underwear. (See urbandictionary. com for further, more colorful definitions.)

There is an extreme trend toward skanky lyrics not about women but by women. Some female performers are singing about explicit sex acts, particularly those performed by males on females. While the following descriptions of the lyrics are extremely explicit, the actual lyrics are far worse. SWV's "Downtown" lyrics direct her man to turn her world inside out by going downtown (i.e., oral sex) on her to taste her sweetness. Christina Milian's "Dip It Low" lyrics instruct female listeners on how to give men oral sex. She describes "dipping it low" in great detail. She raps about picking up his penis slowly and rolling it around in her mouth. In "My Neck, My Back," Khia rapped that female listeners should "pop" their "pussies." She describes him rolling his tongue from her crack to the front. She claims that the best oral sex comes from thugs. Lil' Kim's "How Many Licks" lyrics include a description of him eating her "pussy" all night. She asks a man to imagine his tongue between her thighs. He asks how many licks it takes to get to her center, a play on the classic Tootsie Pop ad. While these lyrics are not the norm, they represent yet another example of females attempting to gain power and equality by emulating the worst qualities of masculinity.

Videos

MTV changed how the music industry operates, with the emphasis of visuals over the quality of the music. To sell the albums, performers must be thinner and more beautiful. They also have to be more and more daring in their videos to get attention. In her first video, *Baby One More Time*, a 16-year-old Britney Spears wore a school girl's outfit, with her shirt knotted just below her breasts. A few years later in the video for "Toxic," she appeared in a flesh colored leotard with strategically placed glitter over her nipples and a triangle of white fabric over her crotch. In Aguilera's "Genie in a Bottle," the then 18-year-old was singing about being sexually repressed and her body saying "let's go" to sex. During the dance scenes, she was wearing a white crop top. The camera spent a significant amount of time panning up her body, almost as if it was trying to look up her shirt. There were numerous tight shots of her midriff. Her *Dirrty* video was at the height of her skanky period. One of the dance moves she performed that was particularly skanky was where she squatted down and, with her hands on her knees, spread her legs apart facing the camera. The move highlighted her tiny red panties that rode up in the back.

Videos such as *Dirrty* fit under the category I coined as "crotch rock" (Oppliger, 2004). A variety of music videos focus on women's crotch areas. Beyoncé videos are notorious for camera shots up her short dresses, especially the *Work It Out* video. Beyoncé is putting on her "freakum dress" in her video *Freakum Dress*. An entry in Urban Dictionary described a freakum dress as sexy, showing off her goodies ("freakum," n.d.).

The music video format is a way for young stars to showcase their sexuality quickly and easily. It is a vehicle that gives permission to be as "sleazy as you wanna be." Movie actresses such as Lindsay Lohan and "famous for being famous" icons such as Paris Hilton suddenly become musical performers with a few shakes on a music video. Even goody-goody artists such as Hilary Duff flirt with sexuality on their music videos. The musical background appears to give young female performers permission to move sexually, similar to strippers.

Conclusion

Obsession with female pop stars has reached new heights. Technology has made it possible to follow their every move (see http://gawker.com/stalker). Pop stars are featured in celebrity tabloids to such an extent that their personal lives are more emphasized than their music. More people could identify Ashlee Simpson because of her nose job than could name even one song that she has recorded. Music is perhaps the most important medium of popular culture because it combines lyrical messages, video images, and fashion with lessons about female empowerment/exploitation. Lyrics have been an important message for every generation, everything from a call to arms to a call to party. Music videos have made it more of a visual medium, especially with technology making video streaming available on computers and cell phones. Consolidation of radio stations and record companies has decreased the variety of artists. Music molded the sexual image of women through male oriented music. Now, popular female artists are perhaps doing more damage in regard to sexualizing and objectifying women than male artists ever did. As long as women support misogynist music by buying the records and appearing in the videos, the cycle will continue.

Although the Don Imus statement about "nappy headed hos" brought to light the degradation of women in music, it is not likely to have a lasting effect. As long as "bitches" and "hos" lyrics sell records, the industry will continue to support and promote this genre of music. Artists such as R. Kelly, who clearly has issues with underage girls, are still part of the accepted community and still continue to collect Grammies. Because of media consolidation, the music industry will remain beholden to their stockholders. Record labels are in business to make money, not to change society. Anyone interested in change will need to look elsewhere.

9. Print

Even with the rise of technology and the popularity of the Internet, print media has remained an influential medium in popular culture. Magazines continue to set beauty standards. Fashion and beauty magazines such as *Self, Jane, Cosmo, Vogue, Elle, Marie Claire, Harper's Bazaar, InStyle, W,* and *Redbook* line the magazine racks, their covers taunting women as they go through the checkout line. Many of the most popular adult women's magazines have a counterpart for girls, starting the beauty craze early and creating a fresh group of consumers for their advertisers' beauty products. Their motto should be "Destroy her self-esteem early and have a customer for life." Books are also relevant to the discussion of women's sexuality. Self-help books, romance novels, and "chick lit" are popular genres many women use to assess and define their gender roles.

Magazines

The covers of most beauty magazines feature flawless, airbrushed models with body proportions unattainable for 99 percent of the American population. There has been a noticeable shift of covergirls from supermodels to celebrities. Television and movie actresses now have to have model looks and body types in order to gain publicity for their acting. There is very little difference between men's and women's cover girls. Men's magazines sell the fantasy of sex. Women's magazines also sell sex, but all too often include the image that female readers have to starve themselves to get noticed by men. Besides attracting attention to sell more magazines, the airbrushed photos of fabulous women are to make the average female feel inadequate. Magazines then offer tips and advertise the products that make women think they can achieve the unachievable. Advertising traditionally matches the editorial and vice versa, reinforcing the message of beauty at any cost. According to Malkin (cited in "Sex and Relationships," n.d.), messages about weight loss are often placed next to messages about men and relationships. For example, she found "Get the Body You Really Want" beside "How to Get Your Husband to Really Listen," and "Stay Skinny" paired with "What Men Really Want."

Magazine photos insinuate that females are never attractive enough, thereby producing a market for the advertised beauty and diet products. The products being peddled include wrinkle cream, cellulite remover, and dandruff shampoo. Even teen issues are filled with "you are not good enough" products. In an issue of *Teen Vogue,* I found ads for facial hair bleaching cream, hair removal wax, cosmopolitan and margarita scented shaving cream, sleek and shiny hair products, and lots and lots of ads for shoes and acne treatments. A majority of models in the ads of the girls' magazines were adult women. The females in the advertisements were very sexualized in their posture, head tilts, and "bedroom eyes." For example, a topless Gisele was featured modeling eyewear. Females in women's and girls' magazine ads were also passive, just posing as if they were nothing but objects. Most of the photos of males in men's magazine ads were in action shots. Females were also often represented as body parts, with either part or their whole head cropped out of the picture.

Headlines often tell women they are deficient in their relationships and that they need to buy the magazine to read the feature stories inside to get tips on how to fix them. Magazine stories and features mainly focus on tricks to catch a man and how to keep him once he is caught. The majority of advice centers on pleasing men in bed rather than developing healthy relationships. Men's magazines offer very active advice, such as what to do on dates and how to use pickup lines. Generally the advice centers on how to get a woman to please him sexually. Both men's and women's magazines focus on females pleasing males. Women's magazines are much more about how to change the female reader to attract the male, particularly using any tips that lead to purchases of advertised products.

Teen and Tween Versions

Women's magazines often have versions that are tailored to pre and early teen girls (e.g., *CosmoGIRL!*, *Teen Vogue*, and *Elle Girl*). *Seventeen* was the first teen publication in 1944. In 1988 *Sassy* introduced sex to the previously wholesome magazines. According to Brumberg (cited in Gibbons, 2003), "The body has become the central personal project of American girls." These magazines are capitalizing on girls' obsessions with their bodies and are selling products to make girls more attractive to the opposite sex. *CosmoGIRL!* has one million readers, followed by *Teen Vogue* with about 500,000 readers (Brown, 2001). In addition, Brown reported that the 31 million teenagers in America have $158 billion in spending power. Girls spend about 75 percent of their money on clothing. Magazine advertisers try to tap into this market, hoping that these readers will later switch to adult versions that push high end products.

Although they occasionally add inspirational stories or advice on "being yourself," most of the magazines' content is dedicated to makeup hints, weight loss strategies, and fashion trends. Most disturbing to critics is the mixed messages presented in these magazines, such as, "be an adult but remain a kid;

look sexy but stay a virgin; dress like this model but maintain your own personal style" (Brown, 2001). Often advice about how to stay true and how not to be taken advantage of sexually are next to sexual ads. Gibbons (2003) stated that the magazines feature endless tips on how to look hot, at the same time publishing articles about the dangers of sexual excess. Brown (2001) argued that teen versions of adult magazines are "breeding ground for little Lolitas, a mishmash of adult imagery and naively youthful concerns." Teen magazines feature adult themes such as "Sexy, Healthy Hair Guide," "Turn Your Guy Friend into Your Boyfriend," "Four Moves to a Sexy Butt," and "How to Kiss (the Right Way)." A 2007 issue of *Seventeen* featured tips such as wearing a ruffled dress that "highlights your butt's shape by flaring out right underneath it." Another tip was for pocket detail: "Funky embellishments and stitching draw attention to your backside." A "friends with benefits" survey included responses from a 20-year-old and a 15-year-old, a vast age difference and hopefully different standards of "hooking up."

Occasionally there are positive images of "average girls." *Seventeen*, *Teen People*, *CosmoGIRL!* and *Teen Vogue* featured "less-than-perfect" figures at least once (Tam, 2005). In one instance the goal was not to celebrate our individual bodies, it was to show how to minimize defects through clothing choices. Editors reported that models were trending toward average women and girls to help teen self-esteem about not being perfect. Other teen magazines (although very few) have published articles on confidence, healthy habits, and positive thinking (e.g., *Girls' Life*). They occasionally publish positive stories but, of course, physical beauty and the importance of male attention reappears just as quickly. A letter from the editor of *Teen Vogue* informed readers of "the real skinny," that it is a model or actress's job to be skinny. The message included such gems as "most models are born that way" and "it is readers' jobs to be healthy and fit."

Teen magazines also set the agenda for young girls. The sheer number of stories on one topic can give the impression that the topic is what is most important in girls' lives. The articles themselves might be different from the headlines. But what if the reader only reads the headline and gets the impression that these actions are acceptable? While *Seventeen*'s editors claimed that the magazine encouraged independence for girls, Phillips (1993) found that two-thirds of the magazine's editorial content covered fashion and beauty. She argued that the magazines teach girls that looks and relationships with boys are the most important things in life and that such concerns would reinforce drops in self-esteem.

Gibbons (2003) argued that articles in *YM* such as "Hallway Make-out Sessions: Dos and Don'ts" and Teen's "Flirt Your Way to a Date" make school seem like a place merely for socialization. The implication in the articles is that there is a time to make out in the hall at school. Flirting also implies that it is okay for girls to use their sexuality to attract attention. *Teen's* "301 Ways to Be the Coolest Girl in Class" reinforces the idea that life is an endless popularity contest. Gibbons stated that the magazines do little to encourage girls to excel in academics or participate in civic activities. I would add that such encouragement is not necessarily the job of the magazines; however, there are very few positive messages out there in the media.

The other dominant theme of these teen and tween magazines is the emphasis on sex. Even though it may be couched in the kissing or "making out" stage, it is still a precursor for having sex and being popular. The mixed messages are confusing. The public relations departments are playing a game of titillating young readers without being noticed or offending the mothers who give their daughters money to buy the magazines. Brown (2001) highlighted articles such as *YM*'s "Your Total Turn-Him-On Guide" and "Boy Bait: 41 Moves He Can't Resist." Of course if Mom subscribes to these types of magazines herself, she may not notice these themes. In defense of sexualizing teens and preteens, Holley (cited in Brown, 2001) stated this age group is "bombarded by sex images.... They are comfortable with that." This statement is quite a leap in logic. Perhaps numb or desensitized is a better term than comfortable. Teens may not see they have a choice. When magazines do provide health information it is generally related to beauty maintenance rather than sexual health (Gibbons, 2003).

Because magazines are such a niche industry, ads sexualizing teens can be more explicit than other forms of media that might get parental attention. The same is true for clothing catalogues. Teens are a valuable market because of this generation's spending power. Mediamark Research ("American Teenagers," 2006) reported teens have a strong sense of individualism without the fierce sense of independence of past generations, which I guess makes them a marketer's dream. Teens also trust magazine ads the most of all media outlets.

Men's Magazines

Looking at a magazine shelf, it is difficult to tell the men's and women's magazines apart. The photos on the covers are often identical, most likely a barely dressed woman. According to Media Awareness ("Men's Magazines," n.d.), men's magazines have symbolically regulated women into sex objects as a backlash to their achievements in social, political, and professional equality.

Men's magazines feature celebrities as well as models, but because of Hollywood standards of beauty, there may be little difference. The celebrities are most likely looking to spice up their image with not only revealing clothing but also more sexual poses. Popular poses include spread legs and leaning over to expose cleavage. In men's magazines, many of the shots of women are tugging down on their bottoms, as if in the act of taking them off. Another popular shot is of the bottom of the breasts.

The new breed of men's magazines, such as *FHM*, *Maxim*, and *Stuff*, blur the line between mainstream publications and pornography. There appears to be a line when it comes to reputation because many celebrities will appear in the men's magazines. Jessica Biel, who was starring in the wholesome show *7th Heaven*, posed provocatively in *Gear* magazine under the headline "Fallen Angel." Alyssa Milano changed her image of teeny bopper on *Who's the Boss* to temptress in her magazine spreads. Four women contestants from *The Apprentice* reportedly turned down $250,000 to pose nude in *Playboy* but posed for *FHM* in sexy lingerie for no money. According to Donald Trump, the women were hired because of their great intelligence, but they also turned out to be beautiful, "and that's not so bad." The June 2004 *Maxim* magazine featured an issue called "Girls of Reality TV Gone Wild" and "Drama Queens." One woman claimed she was kicked off of *America's Top Model* because she looked too "men's magazine." A female contestant from the reality show *Forever Eden* was described as, "This God-fearing Utah girl.... Due to her shyness and refusal to drink on the show, the men on Eden voted her least desirable."

FHM featured an issue called "Girls of *FHM* of Country Music." The issue featured a new generation of female country singers. Although country music has traditionally been conservative, the photos looked rather indistinguishable from those of pop stars. Featured artists were Jennifer Hanson (lying on a bed with her guitar, a black bra showing from her open top); Lauren Lucas (sporting a lacy top with her bra strap down her shoulder); Tift Merritt (crouching down in a dress showing off her cleavage); Jessi Alexander (wearing a strapless dress with her feet up and her arm resting between her legs), Kerry Harvick (wearing low-rider pants and a bra-like top); Shelly Fairchild (wearing a bikini with her guitar over it); Catherine Britt (in a white spaghetti-strap dress with one strap off her shoulder). Jamie O'Neal, likely the most successful of all of them, was featured quite modestly.

Every year there is great anticipation for *Sports Illustrated*'s swimsuit issue, although I am not sure what sport that is. Often the women aren't wearing the suits but holding them. Pop star Beyoncé was on the cover in 2007. Besides the swimsuit issue, *Sports Illustrated* rarely shows women athletes. When they do, they are often in various stages of dress, holding some tool of their sport over their private parts. One example is *SI*'s coverage—or lack there of—of Olympic athletes. For example, Jenny Thompson, Olympic swimmer, appeared in *SI* topless. According to Kane, Griffin, & Messner (2002), images of swimsuit models and softcore porn are often indistinguishable from photos of the female athletes.

FHM likewise featured five female athletes on the cover of its Sexy Olympics issue. An *FHM* issue before the last summer Olympics featured Logan Tom and another indoor USA volleyball player in some pretty provocative sans clothes poses that had absolutely nothing to do with sports. Regardless of their sport all five were wearing white bikinis. Those poses suggested submissiveness rather than the aggressive athletic personalities. Even Winter Olympics athletes, such as snowboarder Gretchen Bleiler, were photographed in ski pants and a bikini top. Amanda Beard was named FHM's 2006 world's sexiest athlete. And, of course, she was wearing a white bikini and looking very skanky. Racecar driver Danica Patrick's spread in *FHM* crashed the site there were so many hits. In one of her poses she was draped across the car with her hair splayed out over the hood. In most of her poses she had her legs spread. She was dressed in tight leather, although very little leather.

The ads in men's magazines feature a surprising number of men. The women featured are almost always underdressed and catering to males, bringing them drinks or serving them food. In one issue of *Men's Health*, I had trouble finding any women in the ads, sexualized or not.

Celebrity Magazines

A favorite of both male and female subscribers is the exposure shot. Female celebrities are often caught sunbathing topless, usually on a beach, yacht or by a pool. Paparazzi have gotten fully nude photographs of Uma Thurman, Janet Jackson and Alyssa Milano. More likely shots will be of "nipple slips" and "upskirt" shots. Nipple slips occur when a celebrity wears a low cut dress with no bra. The sleeve may fall off the shoulder or the neckline may open too far. Examples include Alyssa Milano, Tara Reid, and Paris Hilton. The upskirt is when female celebrities get caught exiting a car or encounter a gust of wind. Most are wearing underwear, but some situations actually show genitalia. Paris Hilton and Jessica Simpson have been caught, but of course the most famous was Britney Spears, who got caught more than once not wearing underwear. The public seems to enjoy the humiliation. These celebrities aren't posed and airbrushed. Paparazzi photographs in celebrity magazines often catch stars in unflattering circumstances, maybe with no makeup or in clothing that might actually show an imperfection such as cellulite. Although not often thought to be sexual in nature, celebrity magazines show women's body parts.

Self-Help Books

Self-help book publishing is a multimillion dollar industry that feeds particularly on women's feelings of inadequacy. According to Bowker (cited in McEvoy, 2005), women account for the vast majority of self-help books sales. Rather than prosocial messages about women's mental and emotional health, the industry has perpetuated the victim role for women in order to sell their books. Between 1972 and 2000, the number of self-help books more than doubled (selfhelpinc.com). Sales rose 96 percent between 1991 and 1996. Sales for 1998 exceeded $500 million. Marketdata Enterprises expects the self-improvement business to grow to $12 billion by 2008 (cited in Salerno, 2005). Book titles include *Women Who Love Too Much, Men Who Hate Women and the Women Who Love Them,* and *The Unspoken Rules of Love: What Women Don't Know and Men Don't Tell You.* Similarly, the Lifetime Network (aka "television for women") airs movies that exploit women's pain and perpetuate the view of women as victims. Movie titles include *Abandoned and Deceived, A Woman Scorned, At the Mercy of a Stranger,* and *Broken Vows.*

Salerno (2005) differentiated between empowerment and exploitation. Empowerment means individuals are responsible for all they do. On the other hand, victimization is the idea that individuals are not responsible for what they do. Salerno (2005) argued that in victimization-based formats individuals are told that they will have to invest more effort if they hope to rise above their innate handicaps. This, he argued, is where the books come into play. The self-help market highlights the misery and themes, such as "you are a victim and here's why." The lack of theoretical basis for some advice sets women up for failure. It is likely the women fall victim to self-fulfilling prophecies, much like a medical book will stimulate paranoia and overreaction. The blame game, on the other hand, focused on what women can do to "fix" men because well, boys will be boys.

Romance Novels

Romance novels generally have a remarkable number of very vivid sex scenes. The romance novel has been considered women's pornography of choice. While men are considered more visual and will watch porn movies or look at porn magazines, women tend to explore their fantasies from reading. Perhaps books allow women to imagine the experience, to put themselves in the scene. These books often use euphemisms such as "her heaving bosoms" and "his aching loins" to titillate but not embarrass the reader. Marketers refer to the sex scenes as erotica since pornography is too dirty for respectable readers.

Romance novels rely on a formula that is intended to bring women out of their everyday lives. There is often an element of danger. For example, *A Kiss in the Dark* features the tag line "To love him, she would risk everything." Although they protest at first, women in the novels want to be taken. Thus, romance novels have been accused of perpetuating the rape myth. In some cases, the hero nearly rapes the female lead but is interrupted. Another message is that even if the man is inappropriate, her love will eventually tame him. Critics coined new phrases such as "forced seduction" or "near rape." Prosser (1998) described near rape as "the heroine murmur[ing] breathlessly the telltale words 'We shouldn't!' in some form or other, only to be overcome by her own desire and her lover's persistence." Prosser (1998) argued that readers are not so much bothered by the rape as by the fact that the heroine forgives the behavior because love is stronger than all mistreatment at the hands of the beloved. Television soap operas have included storylines where women eventually fall in love with their rapist (e.g., Luke and Laura on *General Hospital* and Jen and Jack on *Days of Our Lives*). Forced seduction occurs when the hero, even in the face of the heroine's "no," continues to bombard her senses until she is acquiescent (Kapakos, 1998).

Erotica Authors Association's ("Short Story," 2006) guide for short story submissions states that, although there must be sufficient sex in the manuscript, both characters must enjoy the sex. Manuscripts are rejected if they include rape or exploitation of any kind. However, there appears to be a fine line. He can force himself on her up to the point where she gives in.

Chick Lit

A new genre of literature is replacing the traditional romance novel. Nicknamed "chick lit," the books take a more modern and, some say, realistic look at sex and the single woman. She is not married but that certainly does not stop her from having sex. Unlike romance novels, she does not stop just in time to preserve her virginity for marriage. According to Schneider (2004), the female protagonist is often unsatisfied with her life and thus goes shopping and drinks at trendy bars. The books, sometimes referred to as "trashy beach reads," are often accused of being shallow and whiny. Razdan (2004) pointed out that titles such as *Running in Heels: A Novel*, *Shopaholic Ties the Knot*, and *Thirty Nothing* "relay breezy tales of spunky professional urban women worrying about their bosses, their weight, their boyfriends, and their Jimmy Choo shoes." Ferris and Young (2006) contrasted the new heroines to the flawless women in romance novels. They describe the new heroines as making mistakes at work, drinking too much, falling for the wrong man, etc.

Weinberg (cited in Razdan, 2004) called many of the books trash and fears they flood the market, pushing out smart, postfeminist writing. In addition, she wrote that she worries that all books written by women for women will be dismissed as "mere chick lit." The "chick" in chick lit is similar to movies about women being classified as chick flicks. Once a media form has the chick label, it is considered subordinate and easily dismissed.

Supporters of chick lit argue that it is only a reflection of reality. Many women claim to be able to relate to lamenting about men they can't have and clothes they can neither fit into nor afford. Fielding (cited in Razdan, 2004) claimed that if women cannot laugh at themselves, they have not gotten very far with their equality. Ferris and Young (2006) argued that some of the heroines are plus-sized characters such as Bridget Jones. They added that the books often highlight the importance of female friendships.

What worries some critics is that these types of books are often marketed to younger readers. According to Wolf (cited in Winfrey, 2006), teens are targets of the graphic, sexually explicit materials in chick lit. She argued that the two-dimensional characters send a negative message to young girls. She stated,

"These books basically tell our daughters that their value comes from how high they are in the pecking order in their high school, whether they can afford all of the fabulous designer goods, and provide a hot sexual experience for the boys in their lives."

Conclusion

Print is still an influential medium in the sexual representation of women in popular culture. Fashion and beauty magazines often set the trends for girls and young women. Airbrushed, stick-thin models saturate the pages. They sell products designed to focus on superficial physical beauty. The articles focus on how females can please males. The teen versions of these magazines, although they are toned down, are generally adult in nature.

The book industry has been mixed when it comes to representations of women. There are a number of female empowerment books on the market. The big sellers, however, appear to portray negative images of women. The self-help industry has at times encouraged women to believe they are victims. Romance novels send mixed messages about female independence. Most disturbing are the near rape scenes in many romance novels. Supporters of chick lit claim that women need to be able to laugh about themselves. Many readers can relate to the flaws and mishaps of the main characters. However, the genre's detractors argue the books are shallow and portray two-dimensional characters.

10. Radio

Shock jock radio is clear in its exploitation of women. There is nothing hidden or even subtle in their commentary about women's body parts and sexual activities. Firing of these radio hosts gets media coverage for a while; however, outrage subsides and content reverts to the previous standard, or worse. The shift from terrestrial to satellite radio, which is out of the jurisdiction of the FCC, has also made the content more explicit. Even more outrageous than the humiliation endured by women on shock jock radio is the fact that women voluntarily participate in their own exploitation. This chapter explores the phenomenon of shock jock radio and its female guests.

Howard Stern

Audiences have a love/hate relationship with Stern. After the 9/11 attacks, Stern was seen as a hero. He stayed on the air and many listeners credit him for keeping the city calm. He also raised a huge amount of money to assist the families of the rescue workers who died. The warm, fuzzy feelings did not last long. He was criticized for offering to send strippers to entertain firefighters and police officers. He also offered to take them to Scores, an upscale strip club in Manhattan, as a way to reward them for their bravery and to take their minds off of the tragedy.

One feature of the *Howard Stern Show* is the "Wheel of Sex." Stern has bikini-clad women spin the wheel and the women have to perform the act where the wheel stops. Selections include a variety of sexual and humiliating activities, with perhaps one good prize available. Female contestants had to change diapers of grown men who soiled themselves. Others had to stand naked while members of Stern's staff circled their imperfections (e.g., small breasts, cellulite) with magic markers. In other stunts, women had to bend over and get spanked with dead fish. By the end of the skit, they were bruised and covered in fish guts. Another popular activity is for the cast to smear cream cheese on a woman's rear end and throw bagels at it to see if they can make them stick. More sexual activities include tea bagging, where the woman lies on her back and a naked male cast member sits above her face and dangles his testicles over her mouth. She may also have to endure lying down while a man flatulates inches above her face.

One of the most outrageous segments was entitled "It's Just Wrong." It's Just Wrong is a trivia game where a male contestant brings in a female partner. He must answer trivia questions correctly to win money. If he misses a question, however, his female companion has to remove a piece of clothing until she is naked. The especially "wrong" part is the version where the man has to remove her clothing and the pairs consist of brothers and sisters and supposedly fathers and daughters. Even after the woman is completely naked, Stern and his staff will try to entice the pair to do even more outrageous, incestuous activities for money.

Women also come on the show and volunteer to change into a bikini and get strapped to the spanking or tickling machine. Other women get strapped in a chair while the male cast members touch various body parts with vibrators. When one female guest asked to use the bathroom, they refused and kept her strapped in the chair while they continued to tickle her, hoping she would urinate. There are pictures on the Stern website of Jenny McCarthy after she has obviously wet herself after being tickled in the chair. Most of the posted responses from male listeners commented on how hot that was.

Another feature is women who come on to see if they are good enough to pose nude for pornographic magazines. Stern has these women strip and then they are critiqued by representatives from magazines such as *Playboy*. Supporters of the show claim he is performing a public service. Stern is quite proud of the women he has gotten into the sex industry. He also runs competitions for women to win free breast implants. The premise is that the woman with the most desperate life story wins.

Stern has also set up listeners with dates with porn stars and prostitutes. For example, he fixed up a high school student with a porn star for a prom date. School officials and the boy's parents stepped in before the date could happen ("Boy Wins Porn Star," 2004). In November 2005, the "Puking for Porn!" contest offered men an opportunity to either puke on or be puked on by a porn star.

A supposed real-life pimp, Don Magic Wand, appeared on Howard Stern to describe his life. He stated that he collects all the money and "takes care" of his women, buying all their clothes and food. He described how he can get any woman to have sex and then beg him to take their money. Audience members phoned in expressing their admiration for pimps after the interview. Wand sounded comical and harmless, sort of a crazy character that relieves people's anxiety over pimps being a threat.

Humiliation

The Howard Stern website proudly posts photos demonstrating the humiliation of the women who come on the show. The site has a complete description of each show, often with photographs. Howard Stern ran a "butter face" competition, meaning that she would be a ten, "but her" face is not attractive. Contestants appeared in thong bikinis with bags over their heads. The more homely the woman was, the more they would hoot and applaud when she took off the bag. One of the guests, Ginger, described in detail her fetish of not only having men urinate on her, but also rubbing it over her body and drinking it. In the same interview, a male guest left the studio after fighting with a cast member. Stern tried to coax him back by offering him an opportunity to urinate on Ginger. Another woman, Jodie, shaved cast member Beetlejuice's testicles and "took his tea bag," in other words let him dangle his testicles in her face. Beetlejuice is a semi-retarded dwarf who appears regularly on the show. The website also offers fans opportunities to rent Beetlejuice out for parties. Male employees of the station have lined up to squeeze women's bare breasts to try to determine if they were real or implants. Jenny McCarthy allowed the male cast members to give her a "free" breast exam—at her request.

Most of the time guests readily agree to participate in the competition and even initiate some of the most outrageous stunts. When female guests refuse a stunt, Stern likes to see if he can coerce them into it. He will often keep going if she did not say yes. He points out that they did not say no either. He keeps pursuing the issue, saying there was a chance she could be swayed. In one instance, it was clear two female guests were pushed beyond their comfort zone. Stern pushed until he got one of them to spank the other. Once she started, Stern coerced her into doing it harder. Then he talked one of them into getting into the tickle chair.

Stern often trades doing stunts for letting guests promote their current projects, movies or websites. They are often given a very short amount of time to make a decision. He is a master at creating these types of situations. He negotiates options if he is refused. He will also add incentives to entice guests to go beyond what they initially agreed to do. He does it in brilliant increments that reduce resistance. He is very good at reading people and knowing how far he can push them. When two women wanted to come in to promote their movie, Stern said they could if they made out with a third woman. Before the interview was over the women were giving each other massages in their bras and panties. When Stern moved to satellite radio, he was no longer encumbered by FCC rules. The show quickly added a device called the "Sybian." The design looks like a mechanical bull but with a sexual vibrator device on it. According to the Sybian manufacturer's website, the device "gives the ultimate in sexual stimulation and is primarily used for sexual gratification but hundreds have had their first orgasm ever when using it" ("Sybian for Women," 2007).

What is fascinating about the show is the ability of Stern to get women to publicly use a sex toy. On the terrestrial show he would have the staff use vibrators on women. The Sybian represents penetration as well as stimulation. Stern promised porn star Tera Patrick a shopping trip to Tiffany's if she would strip and get on and "get off" on the Sybian. He had another female guest give him a detailed account of what she was feeling during the experience. Stern told Valentina that there is one service men can offer that the Sybian cannot: money. The show often reinforces stereotypes of women as gold diggers. To increase the shock value and keep listeners listening, he got women to take back-to-back rides. He started out with one woman on the Sybian and quickly graduated to two women at once. He gets them to make out with each other on the device as well. The fascination with the Sybian is rather bizarre. Listeners of the show cannot see what is happening; therefore, they have to rely on the audio and use their imagination.

Stern has made some interesting assessments about pornography over the years. He often points out to women that they are too good looking or too hot to be doing porn. He suggests they should be doing more mainstream jobs such as runway modeling instead. It is interesting that his perception of porn stars is that they are desperate and that only the more unattractive women should have to do porn to get by. He also tries to get porn stars to disclose their troubled childhoods. He generally does not believe them if they say there was no abuse in the past. Stern seems convinced that this is the root of why women enter the porn profession. It obviously does not stop him from exploiting them, or rather letting them exploit themselves. These discussions are interesting in terms of using abuse victims as part of the entertainment. One woman came on to promote her next project, which was a gang bang featuring 50 men over 60 years of age. It was clear this woman was a survivor of abuse.

Interview with an Intern

Once a year, the show features an internship beauty pageant. Female interns who work for Stern are invited to compete for the title. The competition includes modeling, interviews, and performing songs—lyrics they make up and sing to popular tunes. The contestants describe their sexual history, kinky things they have done, such as any girl-on-girl action or threesomes or odd places they have had sex. One of my former students won the pageant a few years ago. The pageant was 3½ months into the internship, near the end of the internship. Some of the blogs of the male interns showed a little bitterness toward the females, who were getting a chance to make it on air instead of them. Many of the males reported they had to invent stories or do outrageous things to get noticed. Kristen stated she did not feel like she received any negative feedback during the pageant. However, she found that many men outside of the show came on to her and gave her unwanted sexual attention after her appearance in the pageant.

In an interview with Kristen, she recounted the very positive experiences she had interning at the show and how she had gained valuable connections to other jobs and opportunities. She is a thin, athletic and attractive blonde. More than that, she has a very playful personality and likes to be kidded. She said she was well respected by Stern and the crew. She said she was asked sexual questions by the Stern staff after she had been there for a time. She thought that the staff took care to test the waters to see if interns were willing to play along before they started teasing them. Those who were not willing to play were left alone. Kristen commented that the staff tries to provoke guests into saying and doing things they didn't intend to do. Stern is a master at picking up on people's hesitations and continues to pry in hopes that the guest will reveal something. He is skilled at getting around barriers. She stated her experiences in the fashion industry were much harsher than at the Stern show. She experienced sexual harassment from her boss there. He would make comments, but not in the humorous, friendly joking way used on the Stern show.

Kristen concluded that many of the guests on Stern were desperate for attention. The crew would capitalize on that desperation and see how far they could push. These women were not respected. She observed the guys on the show date very smart, attractive but not "over the top" women. The women competing for their attention seldom got noticed. The men appeared to tire of such outrageousness. It might be okay for the length of an interview, but would be exhausting for any longer than that. She said some of the women would grind up against the guys on the *E!* television crew in the hallways, they were so desperate for attention. Kristen's impression was that Stern is very upfront about his intentions; he respects women who are interesting and not easily manipulated; he pushes as far as the women let him push; and he has little patience for women who claim to be willing to do certain things on the show and then back out once they are on the air.

Opie & Anthony

Gregg "Opie" Hughes and Anthony Cumia are shock jocks probably best known for getting fired. Two highly publicized stunts got them kicked off the air, but not for long. The first incident happened when the pair was working in Boston. For a 1998 April Fools' prank, they announced that the mayor had been killed in a car accident. Their second publicized firing was in 2002 during a contest for listeners to have sex in the most unusual place. For example, couples would get 25 points for sex in St. Patrick's Cathedral, 15 points for Trump Tower, and 10 points for Central Park. The promotion was called "Sex for Sam," sponsored by Sam Adams Brewing Company. A couple trying to win the contest was caught having sex in the vestibule of St. Patrick's Cathedral in New York City. What got the radio show in trouble was that one of their producers was supposedly watching the incident and reporting back live on air on his cell phone. The couples were rewarded points for different sex acts, such as a "two-point conversion" or "balloon know," slang for anal sex.

The couple at St. Patrick's earned "25 points, a two-point conversion, and eternal damnation" ("Opie and Anthony," 2002).

After getting fired, Opie and Anthony reappeared on the radio in 2006. They are currently running dual shows. The first half airs on terrestrial radio, filling Howard Stern's vacant spot on CBS affiliates. The second half airs on XM satellite radio, where they don't have to worry about FCC censorship (Fisher, 2006). In an interview, they claimed that, although they enjoy the freedom of satellite radio, they still enjoy the terrestrial radio show. Cumia (cited in Fisher, 2006) argued, "There's something about that huge automatic audience. It's having the people that hate you calling in that makes some of the most fun radio we've done." They also stated that they enjoyed working around the rules, using veiled references and code names for obscenities. Boston's Mayor Thomas Menino objected again when the show used homeless people in one of their skits In one skit, homeless people are given money and bused to shopping in a mall. The two were suspended in 2007 by XM Radio when one of their homeless guests said he would like to have sexual intercourse with Condoleezza Rice, Laura Bush and Queen Elizabeth.

Humiliation

In order for female listeners to get on the air, Opie and Anthony required them to do outrageous things such as drink milk until they puked or apply "yellow discipline" (i.e., urinate on themselves in a handstand position). One of the recurring guests is named Stalker Patti. According to the *Opie & Anthony* website, she is supposedly a "52-year old virgin who is often subjected to degrading humiliation on the show" ("Opie & Anthony," n.d.). She has crawled blindfolded through mousetraps and had her head shaved on the show. The show's lineup for a typical day is "New Hot Chick Video, More Boobs on Rate My WOW, Boobies on Webcams" ("Opie & Anthony," n.d.). The show has a variety of names for women's breasts such as "funbags." The wiffle ball bat challenge was definitely over the top. The skit aired on terrestrial radio mid-afternoons. In a not so subtle description, women were challenged to come and see how far up one of their two orifices they could get either end of the bat. Marks were made on the bat to demonstrate how far the women got. The bat was then hung on the wall of the studio.

The show distributes "WOW" bumper stickers to its male fans. WOW, which stands for "Whip 'em Out Wednesdays," entices women on the street to whip out, or show, their breasts to men with WOW stickers on their vehicles. Photos of complying women flashing the men are then posted on the show's website. As part of the incentive to post photos on the website, women are told to take pride in their "cans" and that the posting will build their self-esteem. Supporters claimed that it is the greatest radio promotion of all time. One fan stated, "WOW is a tribute to ta-tas, an homage to hooters, a great big salute to boobies.... It has since transformed itself into Whip 'Em Out

Whenever ... because boobies are good EVERYDAY" ("Opie & Anthony," n.d.). Some of the entries to the "rate my WOW" site have women tongue kissing other women or posing completely nude with a hand over the genital region.

In 2006, Opie and Anthony sponsored a "Fatty-Pig-Fatty" contest. They wanted to see if they could get overweight women to not only come into the studio, but also to wear a string bikini, put a pig mask over their face, eat snacks, weigh in, and have their picture taken for the website. Opie and Anthony claimed they were willing to pay handsomely for what they called the "privilege" of coming in and being pointed at and laughed at. They continued to emphasize that the goal of the competition was humiliation of women. Women still came. The prize is $10 per pound for the winner. Later in the competition, they were still trying to get more women to enter. To get more contestants, Opie and Anthony offered male listeners a finder's fee for bringing in large women. The contestants were bending over so the show's producer could take photos from behind—very, very degrading. Opie and Anthony remarked that they do not dislike fat people, they just like to humiliate them. They like to humiliate everyone. The winner was Honey from Binghamton, New York, at 505 pounds. It is one thing for the show to produce the segment, another for listeners to enjoy it, but the biggest mystery is why in the world women would subject themselves to such humiliation.

Don Imus

Known for his bigoted humor, Don Imus caused a firestorm in 2007 with his rant about the Rutgers women's basketball team, calling them "nappy headed hos." The discussion took place between Imus, two of his producers, and a fourth male ("Don Imus," 2007). Imus began the conversation, "So, I watched the basketball game last night.... That's some rough girls from Rutgers. Man, they got tattoos." His producer McGuirk replied, "Some hard-core hos." Imus then added to the insult, "That's some nappy-headed hos there. I'm gonna tell you that now, man, that's some—woo." McGuirk labeled the matchup between Rutgers and Tennessee as "The Jigaboos vs. the Wannabes." Another producer, Rosenberg, stated, "It was a tough watch. The more I look at Rutgers, they look exactly like the Toronto Raptors" ("Don Imus," 2007). While Imus did not initiate the name-calling, he took it one step further to include an obvious racial slur.

The Rutgers incident was not the first time the Imus show aired derogatory remarks about black female athletes. In 2001, Rosenberg called tennis player Venus Williams an "animal" ("Racism Expected," 2007). He also remarked that the Williams sisters would more likely be featured in *National Geographic* than in *Playboy*. Rosenberg was fired for the comments, but Imus rehired him shortly after the incident. Imus has a history of such remarks. In the past, Imus called tennis player Amelie Mauresmo "a big old lesbo" ("Racism Expected," 2007). He also called Contessa Brewer, a news reader on his show, "a pig," "a skank," and "dumber than dirt" on air.

Imus's comments were not just racist and sexist, but made a poignant comment about women in sports and power. If women are going to be in power, they must remain feminine in appearance. Imus declared, "And the girls from Tennessee, they all look cute, you know, so, like—kinda like—I don't know" ("Racism Expected," 2007). Although the racial difference was pretty consistent between the two teams, he remarked on their appearance and expectations of how female athletes should appear. "The Jigaboos vs. the Wannabes" is not flattering for either group of women. Gray-Lawson (cited in Knapp, 2007) argued the Tennessee players should be offended because the comment demeans their national title. She commented that the players are not valued for their achievement, but rather for their looks. Knapp (2007) argued that the remark was made about who could "pass" as part of mainstream culture. Reportedly, Tennessee players wore "shiny pony tails." Knapp (2007) stated, "If they're competing, it's not for acceptance, and when they play basketball, they're not conducting a simultaneous beauty pageant." Knapp calls for women to not put up with being divided into two camps.

Another point of contention was that media commentators remarked on how eloquently the Rutgers players spoke in subsequent press conferences. However, some critics are concerned about what would have happened if the victims had not been so articulate. It then becomes a class issue, where some women are protected from such abuse and others who are perhaps less educated or less valued as athletes are not. Attacking women, for humor or not, is most often done through sexual promiscuity. The discussion centered around the use of expressions such as hos, used in rap music. The argument ranged from blaming African American males for degrading their female counterparts to the greedy white male executive music producers. About 70 percent of rap music is reportedly purchased by young white males.

Conclusions

Shock jock radio is an exclusive boys club. Most days there are almost no women on the air unless they are there to humiliate themselves. The women who put themselves in the position to be exploited are well aware of what will happen when they enter the studio, yet they fiercely compete to get on the air. It is apparent that women who are willing to humiliate themselves in shock jock skits are not respected by the hosts nor the men who listen to the show. One posting on the Stern website stated, "If you're a slut, he interacts with you as such. If you're not a slut, he ratchets up the respect" (Kane, n.d.).

11. TELEVISION

It takes more than balls to make breakthrough television. At Oxygen, it takes an "ample supply" of comedy all day, a "full stack" of Oxygen original hit movies, and for "bust out" hit series, we're "packing" more than what it takes. Plus, our "cup runneth over" with sexy shows that command your attention. So, who needs balls? At Oxygen, "IT TAKES BOOBS."
—Promo for the Oxygen Network, 2006

Television has always had both positive and negative portrayals of women. Early television shows were mostly variety shows, westerns, and comedies. The only 1950s top rated show with a female star was *I Love Lucy*. It is interesting that the only woman with a significant role in a western was Miss Kitty, who was a thinly veiled madam on *Gunsmoke*. Today more and more scripted programming features female detectives, doctors, and lawyers who are both smart and sexy. On the contrary, the more recent popularity of unscripted or "reality" television has actually made things worse for women. In this chapter, I address scripted and unscripted television's representations of women over time.

Comedies

The comedies of the 1950s featured the elegance of June Cleaver or Donna Reed and the wackiness of Gracie Allen and Lucille Ball. In traditional television, and vaudeville before it, less attractive women and girls had to be funny to get attention and compensate for their lack of looks. Women's sexuality was not acknowledged in early comedies, unless of course they were the secretary being chased around the desk by the boss. Couples slept in twin beds. The word "pregnant" could not be used in *I Love Lucy*.

The 1960s brought us sex symbols such as Elly May Clampett from *The Beverly Hillbillies* and the sisters of *Petticoat Junction*, who were seen skinny-dipping in the town's water tower. *Gilligan's Island* brought us the classic Ginger or Mary Ann debate. Forty years later, men are still asked if they prefer the glamorous movie star Ginger or the wholesome girl-next-door Mary Ann. The later 1960s brought us *Laugh-In*, with "sock it to me" girls. Jeannie in *I Dream of Jeannie* showed off her midriff, although her belly button was not

149

allowed to show. She was every man's dream—a thin, beautiful blonde who would grant her master's every wish.

Marlo Thomas broke new ground in the mid–1960s when she played an attractive, single woman living on her own in *That Girl*. She had a boyfriend but it was clear the relationship was chaste. *The Mary Tyler Moore Show*'s Mary Richards, who debuted in 1970, was also independent but much more savvy than Thomas's Ann Marie. In the original script, Richards was supposed to be recently divorced. The storyline was changed to a broken engagement, therefore keeping the possibility of her virginity alive.

"Jiggle" comedies such as *Three's Company* were popular in the mid to late 1970s. Suzanne Somers rarely wore a bra and spent a great deal of screen time jumping up and down. Because it was a comedy, Somers was free to exaggerate her jiggle. *Three's Company*, much like *Charlie's Angels*, had a revolving door of sex symbols. The women were interchangeable. One beautiful, cleavage-showing actress was replaced with another. Rarely were female characters both smart and sexy. One exception could be Loni Anderson's character Jennifer on *WKRP in Cincinnati*.

There was a short-lived trend of comedies in the 1980s focusing on frumpy, working-class women. The title characters in *Roseanne* and *Grace Under Fire* were not in the usual mold of skinny model types on television. Later shows featuring working-class characters teamed a fat and dumpy husband with a substantially more attractive wife, such as *King of Queens*, *According to Jim*, and *Still Standing*.

In the 1980s, Kelly Bundy on *Married ... with Children* was a caricature of a ditzy bombshell. She was very similar to the girls seen on MTV rock videos at the time. This is a sharp contrast to the Marcia Brady character, who was the epitome of the girl-next-door. Many sitcoms, such as *Eight Simple Rules*, *Twins*, and *Step by Step*, have had two daughters who were complete opposites. One sister was sexy and dumb while the other was smart and less attractive.

The 1990s were rather uneventful with the exception of HBO's *Sex and the City*. Because the show was on a premium channel, there were few restrictions on language, nudity, and of course sex. The female characters on the broadcast network show *Friends* discussed sex and had multiple partners over the years, but nothing compared to the blatant dialogue and sexual encounters of *Sex and the City*. Supporters of *Sex and the City* argued it showed audiences that women could enjoy their sexuality as much as men. Critics countered with allegations that as much as the women tried to act like men, they failed miserably because they still needed men in their lives. Some critics claimed the show was really about four gay men only cast with female characters. Critics argued that ordinary women do not talk this way, or if they did they shouldn't. Women should not be that promiscuous. They saw the character of Samantha as too crass and too heartless. The show was about the difficult balance between wanting a man but not needing a man, about getting sexual needs fulfilled without compromising oneself. At the series conclusion, two of the characters were married with children, or at least with children on the way. The other two characters got their men, with ambiguous endings about how the future would play out in terms of commitment.

Female Heroes, Crime Fighters, and Lifeguards

Something about female crime fighters and superheroes appears to be a real turn-on for men. Women wielding weapons or performing martial arts perhaps resemble dominatrixes. The emphasis on the physical is apparent in the adventure genre. The outfits can be more revealing and the action shows off physical attributes.

Popular television crime fighters in the 1970s included *The Bionic Woman* and *Wonder Woman* (see chapter 15 for more details) and *Charlie's Angels*. All these roles were cast with incredibly attractive females. *Charlie's Angels* starred a variety of sex symbols: Farrah Fawcett, Jaclyn Smith, Kate Jackson, and, later, Tanya Roberts, Shelley Hack and Cheryl Ladd. As one Angel would leave the series, another beauty would slip relatively unnoticed into place. Some critics compared Charlie to a pimp. He was never seen, his voice would just give orders to the women to perform for him. The show was an interesting blend of intelligence and beauty. The most intellectual Angel was played by Kate Jackson, who was rather androgynous (shorter hair and smaller bust) compared to her bombshell costars. Bosley was purposely cast as an unattractive actor in order to eliminate competition for the male viewers; it was clear that no romantic or sexual relationship was going to develop. Likewise, the absent and older Charlie was no threat.

Entertainment Weekly proclaimed *Baywatch* as the most popular television series in the history of the planet (cited in "Baywatch Database," n.d.). Evidently sexual images of women easily translate in any country around the globe. Although the female characters occasionally saved lives, the show was the epitome of jiggle shows. A never ending cast of beautiful buxom women were shown running in slow motion down a beach in one-piece French cut swimsuits. The women were almost always seen in just their bathing suits, while the men around them were generally in full length wind pants and jackets.

In the 2000s, Jennifer Garner played a very sexy spy on *Alias*. The show ran for four seasons. Her role as an undercover operative allowed the show's producers to dress her in hooker-like costumes from time to time. According to photos on the episode guide ("Sydney Bristow," 2006), it appeared she dressed provocatively in about a quarter of the episodes. Garner's body was very toned and had average sized breasts. A post–*Baywatch* Pamela Anderson starred in a syndicated show called *V.I.P. V.I.P.* is described as a "campy syndicated series about Vallery Irons, a girl working at a hotdog stand who accidentally saves a celebrity and is mistaken for a bodyguard. She and a team of beautiful bodyguards form a bodyguard agency called V.I.P. which stands for Vallery Irons Protection" ("Plot Summary," 1998). Internet Movie Database listed the show under the search words "bodyguard," "buxom," "martial arts," "cult TV," and "Kung Fu." Anderson wore tight outfits that highlighted her curves.

Soap Operas

One genre where beautiful women have powerful roles is the daytime soap operas. They run mega-corporations and perform brain surgeries. Early on it appeared to be the one place in television where women could be in control of their own sexuality. Busy seducing married men and then blackmailing them, women of ill-repute are great stars in soap operas. Some critics argue that these women are eventually punished for their overt sexuality. They often end up alone and childless. Of course, the journey is quite thrilling for many a female soap fan.

When it comes to soaps and sexuality there is a negative side. Soaps also portray women as tricking men into marriage by either getting pregnant or lying about being pregnant. Female characters falsely claim rape to get revenge. They drug men, making them think they had sex, and then blackmail them. Much like romance novels (see chapter 9), soaps can perpetuate the rape myth that women want to be taken. Several soap opera characters have later married their rapists, such as Laura and Luke on *General Hospital* and Jen and Jack on *Days of Our Lives*. Christine became involved with her rapist, Michael, on *The Young and the Restless* and Meg married her sister's rapist, Josh, on *As the World Turns*. These plotlines put the onus of men's behavior onto women — only the love of a good woman will turn the bad guy around. He is not held accountable for his actions. It also gives the false sense that women just need to try harder to fix their men.

Nighttime Soap Operas

In the 1980s producers such as Aaron Spelling brought the soap opera to prime time with shows such as *Dynasty, Dallas*, and *Knot's Landing*. These serial dramas showed that women could be as ruthless as men. Older actresses such as Joan Collins flaunted their sexuality. Later, Spelling would produce *Melrose Place*, which had a younger feel than its predecessors. It featured especially beautiful young women who swapped partners week to week. The addition of Heather Locklear's ruthless character and her ultra short business suit skirts brought the show to its highest ratings. *Beverly Hills 90210* (another Spelling production), *Dawson's Creek, One Tree Hill*, and *The O.C.* are among the teen dramas that are criticized for modeling sexual behaviors for young viewers. The plots often include losing virginity as part of the high school experience. There are very few ramifications that come from unprotected sex, such as sexually transmitted diseases, although pregnancy scares are common. In addition, many of the actors playing teenagers were actually in their twenties, making them appear more mature.

In 2004, the *L-Word* on Showtime portrayed the life of a group of gay and bisexual women. The challenge for producers was how to make a show about lesbians without excluding male viewers and how to debunk the dyke stereotype without replacing it with the lipstick lesbian (Stanley, 2004). Men who enjoy girl-on-girl would likely not enjoy the show because of "all the talking."

Undressed was a series featuring sexual vignettes that ran on MTV 1999–2002. The storylines included same-sex, interracial, and fetishes of high schoolers to post-college couples ("Plot Summary," 2002). Sexual activity was generally started in creative, playful ways. In one episode, "Greg" is struggling with a bucket of glue as he is hanging up flyers. When his pants "accidentally" fall to the floor, "Cleo" also undresses so he doesn't look like a fool. Another episode begins with a game of strip chess. Although there are lots of sex scenes, women appear to be in positions of power where they get to initiate the sex.

Laguna Beach (hyped as "the real Orange County") supposedly uses real characters and real storylines from Orange County, California. The characters are shallow, even more so than previously scripted teen dramas. None of them appear to work but they all drive expensive cars, wear designer clothing, and are never in need of money. There is a glaring absence of parents. The few parents that make cameo appearances are "super cool" kids'-best-friend-types and very permissive. The teens are allowed to go on coed overnight trips to ski resorts and spring break destinations unsupervised. Most of the sex scenes, such as frolicking in hot tubs, are downplayed but it is clear that it was happening.

Reality Shows

While scripted television appears to be improving in terms of roles for women, exploitation of women has seemingly become the undertaking of the reality show. Representations of women on reality shows are almost always unflattering. They are portrayed as catty, self-centered, and willing to do almost anything for attention.

The Real World

An MTV creation, *The Real World* has often been credited for starting the flood of reality shows on television. The premise of the show is to put seven strangers in a house and see how they interact. The first installment, *Real World: New York* in 1992, was relatively uneventful. Viewers can easily see a progression of the show over the years. Producers began to set up scenarios and cast members that would generate more drama. More and more alcohol, more party scenes, and more sex-inducing items such as hot tubs were added. Casting became very formulaic. Party girls were matched up with uptight virgins. Conservatives were pitted against social liberals. Religious fanatics were housed with homosexuals. One female cast member was described as "a sassy, sarcastic and sexual young woman with an appetite for parties. Much of what she calls her 'darker' side has not yet been revealed to her parents or even sorority sisters. She suffers from a poor body image and struggled with bulimia in her early college years" (cited in Ryan, 1999). Further information said, "Melissa thrives on boy drama and conflict.... With blond corkscrew curls, china-doll blue eyes and a *Baywatch* body, Tonya's Barbie doll exterior belies her intelligence, strength and complexity.... With her beautiful sandy blonde hair and bikini model's body, there is never a shortage of men flocking to her." Another cast member reportedly stated, "I need crazy, mad attention from guys."

The second season, *The Real World: Los Angeles*, proved to be more successful in creating drama. In retaliation for a previous prank, one of the male house members, David, pulled off the bedcovers of a female, Tami. Tami was left in her underwear. David was later kicked out of the house and his actions compared to rape. A male member from the Miami cast was heard having sex in the shower with a woman he brought home, with his housemates listening in outside the bathroom window. A female Miami cast member, who had worked as a phone sex operator, repeatedly flashed the camera. In Chicago, one female housemate was offended by a lesbian housemate who walked around nude.

The Hawaii cast offered perhaps one of the most outrageous cast members. Ruthie was a bisexual alcoholic who was eventually sent to rehab. In the first episode paramedics were called when she lost consciousness from overdrinking. Her bad behavior ranged from giving her boss's wife a table dance to driving drunk. She and another female cast member walked around the house topless.

According to a Wikipedia contributor ("Real World," n.d.), "The Chicago season was the highest rated up until that point, and many people believe it was because of the sex—including Cara's sex life, which has been compared to a one-woman *Sex and the City*." According to Lacey (2003), the whole cast of *The Real World: Las Vegas* developed a drinking disorder. Most cast members were involved in some sort of sexual relationship, including a threesome in the jacuzzi. There was even a pregnancy scare that season. The show produced not one but two cast members who posed for *Playboy*. The San Diego cast was full of drunken one-night stands. Two female housemates from the Austin cast made out with each other in front of the cameras. Producers even put together a DVD *Real World* hook-ups. According to the product description:

> Young people are always searching for Mr. or Ms. Right, but the search fails
> more often than it succeeds. Most people can quietly banish memories of their

failures, but cast members on *The Real World* have their romances recorded and aired for the entire world to see. This one-hour exclusive DVD will show clips of the past 12 seasons of *The Real World*; and former cast members, now older and hopefully a little wiser, will comment on what went wrong (or right), what they learned from their experiences and offer up advice on HOOKING UP! ["Product Description," 2003].

Fans apparently loved the sexual exploits of the cast. Murray (2005) published a list of his top *Real World/Road Rules* sluts of all times. The criteria for "hotness" was slutty behavior (e.g., showing boobs), ability to kick ass, and level of drunkenness.

Competitions

Something about competition apparently brings out the worst in women in the reality world. Female *Survivor* contestants span from helpless whiners to dominating hags. It apparently was only a matter of time before female contestants traded on their sexuality. Two contestants flashed their breasts for food. Season after season, *America's Top Model* portrays cattiness of the fashion industry.

In *The Apprentice*, Donald Trump set up challenges for aspiring business tycoons. The winner would be his apprentice and run one of his companies. In season one, males and females were pitted against each other. Herrera (2004) argued that the women were criticized for using their physical attractiveness to win the challenges and thus advance. Teams were reshuffled after the women won the first four challenges. After the blending of males and females, six of the next seven firings were women. Although *The Apprentice* is supposed to be a show about business savvy, producers select only very attractive female contestants. In other words, the women were chosen for their looks and then criticized when they used them. Although the women proved to be oftentimes more capable than the men, clips typically showed them being catty toward each other. Reality shows capitalize on the stereotypes of women and exploit them for ratings. Four of the women from the first *Apprentice* posed in sexy underwear for *FHM* magazine for no money after turning down *Playboy* for lots of money.

Beauty and the Geek paired up beautiful but ditzy women with unattractive, socially inept guys. The premise of the show was to test to see if living together and competing in challenges would change the contestants. According to the producers, "By the end of their six-episode journey, these diverse men and women received lessons in confidence, equality, and dignity" ("Beauty and Geek," 2006). The show gives the impression that all men need is female attention.

Dating Shows

Reality "dating" shows in particular are unflattering to women. The shows present an image of women as desperate to find a man to fulfill their lives.

Dating shows perpetuate the myth of the "soul mate," which sets up unrealistic expectations of what it takes to make a relationship work. According to Hardwick (cited in Smith, 2002), "[Dating shows] are the soap operas of our generation. There is escapism, voyeurism, and it doesn't require a ton of thought. [And] college kids have the mentality of wanting to see someone fall on their face." The humiliation factor is high on reality shows. Contestants are encouraged to berate and belittle those who do not measure up to their individual dating standards.

On *The Bachelor*, producers tried out new twists each season. One Wikipedia contributor ("The Bachelor," n.d.) described the seventh season: "The new rules were that there 'were no rules,' as women fought over group dates, Charlie was allowed to give women roses on group dates instead of waiting for the rose ceremony, and the ceremony itself became a forum for bickering and arguing between the female contestants." There is a tremendous difference in the way women are shown on *The Bachelor* versus men on *The Bachelorette*. In *The Bachelorette* with Trista, men were portrayed as getting along and being sensitive. Many of the competitors claimed they backed off when they realized that Ryan had fallen in love with Trista. Women, on the other hand, are portrayed as catty and talking behind each other's backs. A promo for *The Bachelor* touted, "Let the catfight begin!"

One of the most brazen shows to portray women as gold diggers was *Who Wants to Marry a Multi-Millionaire?* which aired on Valentine's Day in 2000. Fifty women were selected to compete to be the bride of an unknown multimillionaire. In addition to marrying the multimillionaire, winner Darva Conger received a three-carat diamond ring and $100,000. After the show, reports surfaced that Rick Rockwell, the multimillionaire, had numerous restraining orders filed against him by former girlfriends. Conger sought an annulment shortly after the honeymoon. Conger later claimed she objected to being forcibly kissed by Rockwell after being chosen as his bride. Bloggers had a field day with this complaint, seeing the whole contest as prostitution. One male blogger wrote, "Didn't he see *Pretty Woman*? If he had, he would have known that hookers hate getting kissed on the mouth. You can cover them in mayonnaise and duct tape their hair to the bed, but *kissing* is out of the question" ("Who Wants," 2000). Another blogger noted that "if anyone ever questions the societal damage done by *Pretty Woman*, let this be a lesson" (Schabe, 2000). Critics also pointed out that, although Conger seemed distraught about being kissed, she was willing to pose nude for *Playboy* later that year.

The premise of *Joe Millionaire* expanded on the gold digger theme, much like the premise of *Who Wants to Marry a Millionaire?* The show's purpose was to expose women's greed, as willing to do anything to get rich. The women on the show were told that this bachelor had inherited millions of dollars, an elaborate lie. When the winner was chosen, she had to decide whether to stay with "her true love" or take a cash prize. In season one, the winner chose the working-class construction worker, even when she found out he was poor. The couple, although they did not stay together, got to keep the cash prize anyway since she did the "right" thing. The biggest story of the show was the runner-up. Kozer (2003) claimed producers edited sound clips together to make it appear as if she was giving Marriott oral sex. To fuel the fire, information came out that Kozer had performed in bondage videos prior to the taping of the show. She later posed for *Playboy*.

The premise of *Average Joe* reinforces the standards that women have to be beautiful, but men do not. Of course, this standard is prevalent in Hollywood movie pairings of unattractive men with gorgeous women. During the third season seven attractive men are added to average looking men to test whether the contestant would be shallow and go for the good looking guys.

Celebrity Reality

In addition to dating shows, fans are fascinated with celebrity relationships. These shows allowed fans to follow couples during their early stages of marriage. In the show *Newlyweds* Jessica Simpson came off as ditsy, stupid, spoiled, and high maintenance. Her husband, Nick Lachey, was simply cruel at times as well as impatient. He was passive-aggressive and often set her up for failure. In an interview with Howard Stern, he was especially mean when he responded, "How can she embarrass me more than she already has?" While her handlers set her up as wholesome, religious, and chaste, this portrayal is closer to shallow, self-centered, and cruel and judgmental of others. On the show, she was very catty toward other women and jealous of Nick's interaction with his backup dancers. After three seasons, the show ended and their marriage ended shortly afterwards. This display of how newly married people treat each other was a horrible example to young people.

In a similar vein, the show *'Til Death Do Us Part* was followed shortly by "'til the divorce is final do us part." The show followed Carmen Elektra and Dave Navarro's brief marriage. These "soul mate" relationships are fantasy; however, they are presented as reality.

Reality shows such as the *Simple Life*, *Rich Girls*, *My Super Sweet Sixteen*, and *Daddy's Spoiled Little Girl* all demonstrate the worst qualities in girls and young women. Displaying selfish behavior on television shows such as *Bridezilla* and *My Super Sweet Sixteen* would seem to expose the bad behavior. However, to a portion of the viewers, it is glamorized and perpetuated. (Descriptions of these shows appear in chapter 7.)

The reality show *Girls Next Door* is a glamorization of Hugh Hefner's lifestyle of polygamy. The show portrays the lives of three of his girlfriends living together, sharing Hefner, and making public appearances. According to Becker (2005), producers of the E! Network wanted a show that would attract male viewers but not scare off advertisers. Not only were women not outraged by the show once it aired, women 18–34 made up the highest concentration of viewers. According to one reviewer of the show, the program, rather than being scandalous, is a "bittersweet take on how one man's dream might be an imperfect fantasy for his women" ("Hef Gets Into Bed," 2005).

The three girlfriends featured on the show moved into the mansion either soon after their first date or, in the case of 21-year-old Kendra, before their first date with Hefner. The show establishes a normalcy of this lifestyle. Many episodes have a party theme; however, most of the activity that goes on in the house is daily interactions. The show is more about how women get along as roommates and coworkers than it is a harem vying for the sexual attention of a man old enough to be their grandfather. The tone of most episodes makes viewers forget that the show itself is a form of prostitution. The only reason these women are on television is that they are having sex with Hugh Hefner.

To keep the appeal of male viewers, the scenarios do get risqué. The following is a description from the *E!* website:

> In tonight's Very Special Episode (wink, wink), Kendra becomes a Las Vegas pimp. It's her 21st birthday, and things get so wild that Holly turns into a human bowling ball, Puffin talks like a gangster, and Bridget comes *this close* to getting a tattoo and becoming a pimp herself. Things to watch for: the best pole dancing this side of Hef's house, Kendra's glistening (and disappearing!) grill and lazy girls who won't get naked and get in the pool ["Episode 10," 2006].

Plastic Surgery Shows

Plastic surgery shows range from the scripted show *Nip/Tuck* to reality shows *Dr. 90210*, *The Swan*, and *Extreme Makeover*. *Nip/Tuck* on FX is a dark fictional drama about two plastic surgeons. The show portrays the dark side of the surgeons but it also follows strange stories of people seeking plastic surgery. What is interesting is that most of the reality shows portray less realistic depictions than fictional *Nip/Tuck*. Very few of the reality shows reveal the negatives of plastic surgery. They rarely focus on the risks and the difficult recovery of the patients. Of course, seeing the downside may not be a deterrent if someone is determined to get plastic surgery. (See chapter 4 for a more detailed analysis.)

Patients on *Dr. 90210* range from a porn star to a 15-year-old who wants a smaller nose. Occasionally someone comes in to correct problems after cancer surgery, an accident, or a birth defect but more common is the cosmetic surgery. MTV's *I Want a Famous Face* follows twelve average people as they go to extreme measures to look like their celebrity idols such as Pamela Anderson, Elvis, Janet Jackson, Ricky Martin, Britney Spears, and Jennifer Aniston. The show capitalizes on the plastic surgery trends and obsession with celebrities. On ABC's *Extreme Makeover*, individuals and their family members send in stories of heartbreak vying for a spot on the show. According to their promotions, "*Extreme Makeover* follows the stories of the lucky individuals who are chosen for a once-in-a-lifetime chance to be given a truly 'Cinderella-like' experience: a real life fairy tale in which their wishes come true, not just by changing their looks, but their lives and destinies. This magic is conjured through the skills of an 'Extreme Team,' including the nation's top plastic surgeons, eye surgeons and cosmetic dentists." *The Swan* was a sort of game show on FOX where women were given extensive plastic surgery and then entered into a beauty pageant against "normal women."

Talk Shows

Many behaviors of women on talk shows are class issues, preying on poor and uneducated women. Women on *Jerry Springer* have a tendency to strip. Female guests start to take their clothes off, as if it is part of a battle against other women. Generally these guests are the least attractive and are grossly overweight, so that the spectacle is humiliation rather than titillation. Some of the show's themes include "My Dream Is to Pose Nude," "I Refuse to Wear Clothes!" and "My Daughter Dresses Like a Slut." The show offers a DVD entitled "Rude Nude Riots," which includes clips from the show, such as naked Jell-O wrestling. Other DVD titles are "Too Hot for TV" and "Naked Rumbles." *Maury Povich* and *Montel* have repeatedly had shows on paternity testing of men to see if the men are the fathers of children waiting backstage. These shows make men look like scumbags who abandon their children. On the other hand, it shows women as promiscuous sluts. In some cases the women need to have five or more men tested, and the onus is on the women for being loose and not being able to keep track of who they slept with. But it also gives the impression that women are out to trap men, making them pay child support. It is outrageous that the shows are produced, stigmatizing the children and packaging their future lives of misery as entertainment.

Conclusion

Television has always portrayed stereotypical characters, regardless of age, sex, ethnicity, etc. Women of color are still stereotyped, often cast into the role of sex maniac. Shows such as *227* in the 1980s gave us the oversexed character of Jackée and the *Parkers'* Mo'Nique in the early 2000s. Charo, the consummate hot-blood "cuchi cuchi" Latina, appeared regularly on the *Hollywood Squares* game show and guest starred on *The Love Boat*. In a few cases, older women showed sexual prowess. For example, Betty White's character, Sue Ann, on *The Mary Tyler Moore Show* in the 1970s and Rue McClanahan's character, Blanche, on *Golden Girls* in the 1980s showed they were still sexually viable after 40.

Television representations appear to vary by genre. Historically, less attractive women are generally relegated to comedy roles. Apparently, unattractive women need to be funny, because they cannot get a man's attention any other way. In the 1970s, jiggle comedies made it okay to laugh at braless, busty beautiful women being ditzy. *Sex and the City* was predicted to change women's role in comedy, although no show has appeared yet to take its place. Reality television has capitalized on presenting women in the worst light. Reality shows are based on strung together snippets of activity. Most of what happens on these shows is testimonials and catty remarks by one participant about another behind her back. Producers cast stereotypes and set up scenarios to exploit them. Casting choices are based on the most outrageous, the cruelest, and the most catty. The dating shows focus on women's greed and use of sexuality to get what they want. Plastic surgery shows glamorize the procedures, or at least focus on the shallowness of, primarily, women who have the surgery. With the multimedia consumption of this generation, briefer and more prevalent images have a significant impact.

One bright spot in the television lineup is *Ugly Betty*. Based on a Colombian telenovela, Betty is a Mexican-American character who works as an assistant to a fashion magazine editor. Surrounded by outwardly beautiful people, Betty stands out as a moral icon. Some viewers took issue with the title of the show; however, supporters argued that "ugly" plays on the shallowness of beauty standards. Sales of "Be Ugly" T-shirts go to support Girls Inc., an organization inspiring all girls to be strong, smart, and bold ("Fun Stuff," 2007). I interviewed one mother who watches the show with her five-year-old daughter as well as with her nine-year-old son. She stated she wants to teach them that women can be beautiful in different ways. It is okay for television to portray all kinds of women, just so not all the women are young, busty, and willing to sleep around for attention.

12. FILM

On screen, female empowerment is exemplified by legions of well-coiffed heroines—like Elle Woods of Legally Blonde—who save the day without breaking a nail. The new feminist role models value midriff-baring tops, ankle-twisting stiletto heels, and the whistle of male peers [Nesoff, 2003].

Women are generally window dressing in film. In most major films released to theaters, the cast includes five to seven men and one, maybe two, women. The female character is generally the love interest to one of the male leads. If there is a second female character, she will most likely be the other woman's rival, vying for the same man's affection. One woman is often good, while the other is evil. The evil woman is generally destroyed by the end of the movie. If there is a female leading role or there are three or more female characters, the films are usually labeled "chick flicks" and demeaned.

Because a female's physical appearance is so important, makeover movies are extremely popular. The premise is that by simply doing a few things to the exterior of a girl or woman, she is now suddenly worthy of love. Some of the most recent makeover movies are throwbacks to *My Fair Lady*. These films include *She's All That*, *Pretty Woman*, and *The Princess Diaries*. In the movie *Grease*, Olivia Newton-John's character, Sandy, represents a reverse Cinderella story. Sandy comes down to John Travolta's character's level, changing from a clean cut, virginal image of actress Sandra Dee (i.e., poodle skirt, ponytail, and makeup-free) to a more skanky image (i.e., tight leather pants, teased hair, and heavy makeup) and therefore more desirable.

Age in Film

Female actors in Hollywood often complain about not being able to get roles as they age. In most cases women are in film to be the love interest. Generally, the older male actors (in their 40s and 50s) get the hot young female actors (in their 20s). *Something's Gotta Give* was one of the few exceptions to the rule. Jack Nicholson's character ends up with age appropriate Diane Keaton, rather than with Amanda Peet, who is almost young enough to be his granddaughter. In the film Keaton is being pursued by a much younger Keanu

Reeves. Keaton's character willingly gave up her younger man to be with Nicholson's character, while Nicholson's character showed a sort of disdain for falling in love with a woman his own age.

Occasionally there will be a younger man with an older woman, but then the age difference becomes a major plotline in the movie. Movies such as *Animal House* and *The Graduate* show older women as desperate and lonely, using alcohol and affairs to escape their dull, married lives. *American Pie* introduced a generation to the MILF. In *Thelma & Louise*, Geena Davis's character used a young Brad Pitt as a way to break free from her abusive husband and take control of her life. Of course, Pitt's character stole their money and drove them to a crime spree from which there was no escape but death. *White Palace* differed from other movies about younger men and older women. Susan Sarandon's character was involved in an actual loving relationship with James Spader's character. (Spader is only two years younger than Sarandon's real life partner, Tim Robbins.)

Sex in Film

Past media representation of women and girls in film has often focused on their sexuality. Film actresses and the roles they play are compartmentalized as good girls or bad girls, virgins or whores. Movie studios promoted virginal movie stars, such as Sandra Dee and Doris Day. When women did express their sexuality in early film they often did so in comedic roles, such as Mae West or ditzy roles, such as Marilyn Monroe. One of the few current "good girl" actresses, Mandy Moore, was ridiculed for her virginity in the movie *Saved.*

Movies sometimes show the evils of sexual temptations. *Splendor in the Grass* came out in 1961, just before the sexual revolution. Natalie Wood's character is a young girl who is tormented with sexual thoughts that her mother has told her are sinful. She eventually has a mental breakdown because she is trapped between being the kind of girl that Warren Beatty's character would marry and losing him to the other kind of girl who would "go all the way." In 1977 women were given a stern warning about sleeping around in *Looking for Mr. Goodbar*. The mild mannered school teacher was eventually murdered by one of the many men she picked up at the bar.

Sixteen Candles is a more recent version of the evils of promiscuity. The movie featured the most popular virgin of 1980s movies, Molly Ringwald. The movie contrasted her character, Samantha, with the more popular and, therefore, slutty character Caroline. The most poignant scene in the movie that demonstrates the sexual value of females is when Jake, Caroline's boyfriend and Samantha's love interest, casually tells the geek that Caroline is passed out upstairs and that he could "violate her a dozen ways" if he wanted. He then laments that he wants a nice girl like Samantha. He then "gives" the drunken, unconscious Caroline to the geek. The two wake up the next morning in the backseat of a car in a parking lot. In true teen movie fashion of the times, Caroline admits that she actually liked sex with the geek. The casual treatment of what would now be considered date rape is quite shocking.

Whereas girls have been conditioned to hold on to their virginity, there have been dozens of movies focusing on boys' quests to lose their virginity. With whom he has sex is generally immaterial. The females involved have minor roles and are either prostitutes or loose, desperate women. An entire genre of movies, such as *Porky's, American Pie, Losing It,* and *The Last American Virgin,* features boys in search of losing their virginity as a rite of passage. Often the male characters had sex with prostitutes, or at least with very loose or older women. Very seldom are girls shown in the same context. In the 1980 film *Little Darlings,* Christy McNichol and Tatum O'Neal raced to lose their virginity. In *Fast Times at Ridgemont High,* Jennifer Jason Leigh struggled through one bad sexual experience after another. Her character had one of the few abortions in a teen movie.

Men are almost always dominant when it comes to sex scenes; however, the extent of their dominance is sometimes scary. *The Postman Always Rings Twice, Last Tango in Paris* and *9½ Weeks* showed women fighting off the man's attacks. The force suddenly turns to a sexualized frenzy as she is overcome with passion.

Action Films

Women have made great advances in the role of the heroine in action adventure movies, although the new heroine is likely braless and clad in skin-tight tank tops and short shorts. In the past women in action films were almost always the victim seen running in short, tight skirts and heels. Leading women in today's action films are powerful; however, they still have to be sexy. For example, after kicking major alien ass, Sigourney Weaver peeled down to her underwear and a camisole. As Inness (1999) argued, she became resexualized as a woman after her show of force. Throughout the movie she showed little emotion and wore no makeup, traits not normally associated with femininity. As she scrambled back into her space suit when the alien returned, the camera lingered on shots of her underwear that does not sufficiently cover her bottom cleavage. Inness (1999) described the camera work as "focusing on her skimpily clad crotch and thighs as she slowly inches into a space suit" (p. 107).

Many female video game and comic book heroines have been brought to the big screen (see chapter 15). One of the earliest and most memorable was Jane Fonda's *Barbarella* in 1968. One of the taglines for the movie was, "Who seduces an angel? Who strips in space? Who conveys love by hand? Who gives up the pill? Who takes sex to outer space? Who's the girl of the 21st century? Who nearly dies of pleasure?" ("Barbarella," n.d.). Victoria's Secret supermodel Famke Janssen was cast in *X-Men.* Angelina Jolie portrayed Lara Croft in the movie version of *Tomb Raider*. Jolie is rather well endowed, as is her video-game character. Other sexy heroine adaptations have been played by Jessica Alba and Pamela Anderson.

Women's roles in James Bond movies were both love interest and villain. It is interesting to trace the progression of the Bond girls and female villains. Women use sexuality to lure in Bond. Some of the most famous female characters are Ursula Andress' Honey, as well as Pussy Galore, Plenty O'Tool, and Octopussy. Although Bond slept with many women, he took them seriously, never letting his guard down. He wasn't afraid to fight back or even kill his female attackers.

Slasher Films

Slasher movies have been notorious for the exploitation of women within a violent context. Carroll and Ward (1994) described Hitchcock's *Psycho* (1960) as one of the first examples of the genre, with the shower scene with its slashing knife and soft-focus nudity. They pointed out that the picture behind which Norman Bates had installed his peep-hole details a scene from Daniel 13 in the Bible—of a woman raped while bathing.

In most slasher movies, male victims are killed quickly, while females die much more slowly and in more graphic detail (Clover, 1989). The "Final Girl," according to Clover, is the sole survivor. We see her "scream, stagger, fall, rise, and scream again." She is distinguished from other female characters primarily because of her lack of sexual activity. The evil male will often stalk the women as they shower, have sex, or, at a minimum, are in a state of being partially undressed. A chase often ensues, with perhaps more clothes coming off as they snag on bushes. Such content is unnecessary to the plot but producers include it to attract male consumers.

Jhally (1999) criticized the sexualized violence in slasher films because the audience is sexually turned on before murder takes place. Women are put in vulnerable positions, such as in the sex act or in some state of undress. For example, in the original *Halloween*, the villain, Michael, killed a couple of teenagers after he saw them having sex. While he strangled the girl with the phone chord, her blouse fell open exposing her breasts. As she was gasping for breath, she sounds as though she is having an orgasm. Critics argue that juxtaposing sex and violence in film is creating a dangerous link between the two in the minds of viewers.

Women of Color

A film genre emerged in the 1970s called blaxploitation, a combination of black and exploitation. The films contained a great deal of sex and violence. Black males were portrayed as pimps and living in ghettos, while black women were portrayed as strong but sexual. Many of the themes involved the female hero going undercover as a prostitute, thus presenting the opportunity to dress her provocatively. Baxter (1995) stated the new stars were "curvaceous and statuesque women who flaunted their sexuality and took shit from no one." Because they did not fear men, they represented a "beacon of protofeminism." In *Coffy*, the female lead goes undercover as a "smack ho" to exact revenge on a drug dealer. Referring to Coffy's need to use her sex appeal to be powerful, Eversley (1999) stated, "The only way she can get close to her enemy/victim is to fuck him, or almost fuck him." *Foxy Brown* has a similar revenge theme. The female lead gets kidnapped and raped before she castrates the dealer who murdered her boyfriend. She then delivers his severed penis to the dealer's girlfriend (Eversley, 1999).

Asian women are generally cast in sexually submissive minor roles in American movies. They often play prostitutes. One exception is Lucy Liu in *Charlie's Angels*, and even then she is written as sexy. Latino women do not fare much better in American cinema. They are portrayed as hot blooded and sexually aggressive. When I Googled "latino women movies" and "asian women movies" I got mostly pornography sites. Exceptions to the stereotype have been roles played by Penélope Cruz and Salma Hayek. *Real Women Have Curves* was a film to counteract the thin movement. Minority women have celebrated booty, Jennifer Lopez being an example.

Prostitutes in Film

Portrayals of prostitution have a vast range in Hollywood, from the glamour of *Pretty Woman* to the grotesque portrayals in *Leaving Las Vegas* and *Whore*. *The Girl Next Door* and *Risky Business* were comedies about teenage boys and a porn star and a prostitution ring respectively.

Risky Business

In one of Tom Cruise's first films, *Risky Business*, his character gets involved in a prostitution ring. The movie is solely from a male perspective. The only speaking roles for women are his mother (who is out of town and is clueless about the situation) and the prostitutes. Cruise's female peers in the movie are not allowed to speak, which assures there is no moral compass opposing the prostitution ring. The women are grateful to get away from "Guido the Killer Pimp" and see Joel as harmless. One reviewer referred to Rebecca De Mornay's character as "the kind hooker" ("Risky Business," n.d.). The loss of virginity for the boys is simply a right of passage, regardless of the fact that each woman has multiple partners throughout the night. Even the college recruiter from Princeton apparently sees nothing wrong with the prostitution. In fact, he indulges himself. The recruiter's assessment is that "Princeton needs a guy like Joel." He pimped his way into an Ivy League school. As a pimp, Joel claims, "I deal in Human Fulfillment."

The Girl Next Door

The Girl Next Door is a knockoff of *Risky Business*. In this version, the women are porn stars rather than prostitutes. Although it looks as though they are making a porno film to raise money to bring a Cambodian boy to the U.S. (in contrast to *Risky Business*'s whorehouse for a night when he has to pay for wrecking his dad's Porsche), they are actually making a sex education video.

Navarro (cited in Overstreet, 2004) described *The Girl Next Door* as "an adolescent male fantasy—the sexy porn star who actually has a heart of gold falls for the nerdy fellow." Overstreet (2004) added, "She pulls the uptight boy out of his shell, and he helps the fallen young woman find her innocence again." Overstreet also points out that, while the movie pretends to disapprove of the objectification of women, the movie objectifies women by showing them pole dancing and has close-ups of them wearing revealing clothing. Smithouser (cited in Overstreet, 2004) agreed that the movie exploited the very objectification of women the producers pretend to condemn.

Pretty Woman

In the original screenplay, the main character in *Pretty Woman* is a drug-addicted prostitute. When her fling with a rich man ends, she was supposed to get thrown back into the street. Disney producers and director Garry Marshall called for reworking the script to make prostitution look like a Cinderella story ("Apples and Origins," n.d.). The final version of the movie sanitizes prostitution. Julia Roberts' character, Viv, and Laura San Giacomo's character, Kit, have no pimp and apparently little fear of being raped or beaten by their johns. As Viv gets into a car with a stranger, the roommates embrace and say to each other, "Take care of you." Their "territory" was on the Hollywood Walk of Fame, a well-lit, popular tourist destination. The movie is incredibly unrealistic in a number of ways. For example, when another prostitute encroaches on their territory, there was little confrontation. The prostitute simply calls Kit a "grouch" and walks away. When a prostitute is found dead in the dumpster, Kit dismisses it as only "Skinny Marie," who was on crack and evidently not worthy of protection. When Kit suggests getting a pimp, Viv proclaims they say who, when, and how much. The tagline for the movie was "Who knew it was so much fun to be a hooker?" ("Taglines," 1990).

Whore

Whore is often referred to as the "real *Pretty Woman*" (Ulibas, 2004). The story follows the unglamorous life of a low-class prostitute. Theresa Russell's character is driven to prostitution to escape an abusive husband and support her child who is in foster care. The lesson in the movie is that men often turn to prostitution not for sexual pleasure but for anger and power. According to Ilibas (2004), "Whilst movies like *Pretty Woman* show us the bright side of prostitution, *Whore* shows us its true dark self" (¶1). Ebert (1991) described it as a movie that portrays prostitution "without adornment or sentimentalism or any of the phony romantic myths that Hollywood likes to bring to the oldest profession." Ebert made an interesting point about the difference in ratings between *Whore*'s NC-17 and *Pretty Woman*'s R rating. "*Pretty Woman* was about a character who lived in an R-rated world, and *Whore* is about a woman who lives in the real one" (Ebert, 1991). He also argued that *Pretty Woman* was rewarded for glamorizing prostitution.

Leaving Las Vegas

Another movie exposing the true side of prostitution is *Leaving Las Vegas*. Elisabeth Shue's character is an extremely disturbing portrayal of a streetwalker. The most horrifying scene is when she is ganged raped by a group of college guys. It is clear that she has no recourse against the boys who beat and raped her, since they look as though they come from higher class families. The cab driver notices that she has been raped. Instead of being sympathetic and getting her help, he demands to know if she has the money to pay for the ride. He then explains that he is just covering his ass, something he tells her she should have thought about doing. When she finally makes it home, the manager evicts her from her apartment because of the bruises and cuts on her face. It was extremely difficult to find any commentary on the rape scene. Some reviews thought the scene was gratuitous. "And how did a beautiful woman like Sera allow herself to become embroiled in the world of prostitution, a profession that nearly kills her, but she sees no way out" (Vemartin, 2005). The comment here implies that only ugly women are unfortunate or desperate enough to be prostitutes.

Sexualization of Young Girls

Movies have also featured preteen prostitutes. In *Pretty Baby* (1976), a New Orleans madame auctions off the virginity of a 12-year-old daughter of one of her prostitutes. The girl is played by Brooke Shields, who was 12, the same age as the character. In *Taxi Driver* (1976), Jodie Foster plays 12½ year-old prostitute Iris. Iris is much more street smart and hardened than Shields' character in *Pretty Baby*. The Robert De Niro character, Travis, picks up Iris in his cab as she escapes her pimp. Although Travis wants to rescue Iris, she does not want to be saved and goes back to a life of prostitution.

Sexualization of young girls in film started as far back as the early 1930s. *Baby Burlesks* was a series of short films starring preschool-aged children such as Shirley Temple. The mini-actors would reenact love scenes, wearing adult clothing from the waist up with giant diapers ("Shirley Temple," 2005). The films were satires of movies and current events. Some of the themes were very sexual. One film showed a very young Temple hugging one shirtless boy while kissing another shirtless boy full on the lips. *Polly Tix in Washington* (1933) was about a corrupt politician who sends a woman of "ill-repute" (played by 5-year-old Temple) to tarnish the reputation of a country politician. The corrupt politician told Polly, "Go over and give him the works" ("Quotes from Polly," n.d.). She approached the country politician and said, "They sent me over here to entertain you." Although he resists at first, the country politician replied, "I think you're the most beautiful woman I've ever seen! You're gorgeous, you're ravishing! I'm nuts about you." Polly retorted with, "Ah, but I'm expensive," alluding to the fact she is a prostitute.

In 1962 Stanley Kubrick caused a great deal of controversy with his movie adaptation of *Lolita*. *Lolita* is a famous novel by Vladimir Nabokov about a middle aged man, Humbert Humbert, who is obsessed with Dolores, the 12-year-old daughter of his girlfriend. "Lolita," Humbert's nickname for Dolores, has become a common expression used for a nymphet or seductive adolescent girl ("Lolita," n.d.). The movie was remade by Adrian Lyne in 1997. A 15-year-old Sue Lyon played Lolita in Kubrick's version, while Lyne's Lolita was 16-year-old Dominique Swain. Kincaid (1998) described Lyon's portrayal: "erotic play between the child and Humbert is indicated only indirectly (by such things as toenail painting)." Adams (1998) claimed that Swain's Lolita was far more sexual than that of Lyon and thus disturbing. He also stated, "She runs her tongue over Irons' lips in a way adult women couldn't get away with onscreen in 1962.... It's one thing to read about a middle-aged man having sex with a 12-year-old and quite another to see it onscreen" (Adams, 1998, ¶9).

The film *Hounddog*, which debuted at the 2007 Sundance Film Festival, created a controversy. Critics are calling it "Dakota Fanning's rape movie." In the film, Fanning plays a 12-year-old girl who is raped while the Elvis Presley song *Hound Dog* is playing in the background. Although the movie does not actually show the rape, critics claim it is still disturbing. Fanning is also shown clad only in her underwear ("Dakota 12," 2007). Fanning's agent, Cindy Osbrink, claimed, "I've been working with Dakota since she was five, and this is something we haven't seen her do. Something that really challenged her talent. *Hounddog* was one of the best experiences of her life, a story that needs to be told, and she tells it with her soul as no one else can" (Friedman, 2007).

While children are protected from seeing sexual materials in movies by the MPAA rating system, critics complain that there are few regulations protecting child actors from playing these roles. Producers justify their actions by claiming they are addressing social issues, while some scenes are titillating (Krinsky, 2006). Often the scenes are broken down and done out of order to fool the child about what is happening.

The parents of child actors ultimately have the last say in which roles their children take. Hayley Mills' parents turned down the part of *Lolita*. Mills was 14 years old at the time. She was also heavily involved in family friendly movies such as *Parent Trap* and *Pollyanna* and did not want to upset Walt Disney.

Jodie Foster was also known for G-rated movies and after-school specials before she appeared in *Taxi Driver*. Foster underwent a psychiatric evaluation before taking the part of Iris (Krinsky, 2006). Jodie Foster's older sister was used as a body-double in *Taxi Driver*. A 19-year-old body double was used for any sexual or nude scenes for Dominique Swain in *Lolita*. It was reported that Brooke Shields did her own nude scenes in *Pretty Baby*.

Brooke Shields is perhaps the best (or worst) example of sexualizing young girls. Two and three years after her appearance in *Pretty Baby* respectively, she starred in *Blue Lagoon* and *Endless Love*. In *Blue Lagoon*, a 14-year-old Shields plays an innocent girl shipwrecked with a boy near her age. The two experiment with sex, eventually having a baby. Throughout the movie she is wearing very little clothing. In *Endless Love*, Shields plays a 15-year-old in an obsessive relationship with a 17-year-old boy. Calvin Klein Jeans capitalized on her "nymphet quality" in their ad campaign. The tagline was "Nothing comes between me and my Calvins," implying virginity, yet showing her topless. I remember Shields' virginity was a big issue because of the contrast between her angelic looks and her sexual roles in movies and advertisements.

Greene (cited in Kincaid, 2006) argued that society was fascinated with underage sexuality. He stated that Shirley Temple "was able to elicit excited 'gasps' from 'her antique audience'" by twitching her "well-developed little rump" and generally exercising a "sidelong searching coquetry ... with the mature suggestiveness of a Dietrich." Schmitz (cited in Kincaid, 2006) added movies such as *Home Alone* to the list of pedophile fantasies, along with *The Good Ship Lollipop*. He pointed to Macaulay Culkin's beautiful blonde hair and his "unnatural cherry-red" lips. Kincaid (n.d.) claimed that it is not Hollywood that is necessarily to blame but that we are all responsible for the cultural phenomenon of sexualizing children. Jodie Foster was rewarded with an Academy Award for best supporting actress for her role as an underage prostitute in *Taxi Driver*.

Conclusion

Hollywood films are full of beautiful people, both male and female. A female actor, however, has a shorter shelf life. She may still be attractive but if she cannot hold the sexual fantasy of viewers she is relegated to grandmother or crazy cat lady roles. Powerful women are cast in evil roles such as home wreckers and cold-blooded killers, as in *Basic Instinct*, *Cruel Intentions*, and *Single White Female*. The screenplay for *Fatal Attraction* initially portrayed Glenn Close's character as sympathetic. The moral of the story was the pain and anguish a woman who was involved with a married man experienced. When Michael Douglas's character cheated on his wife it was Glenn Close's character that was portrayed as the villain. Producers pressured the screenwriter to rewrite the original story to make her an evil psychopath rather than make the adulterer the villain. The Michael Douglas character was then seen as sympathetic, a victim of an unbalanced single woman.

While looks appear to be important at the box office, actresses have been rewarded for changing their looks to become ugly or fatter: Nicole Kidman in *The Hours*, Charlize Theron in *Monster*, and Renée Zellweger in *Bridget Jones's Diary* all won the Academy Award for best actress. Perhaps one day the ticket receipts will reflect the quality of the acting rather than the sexuality of the star.

13. The Internet

The Internet has made transmission of information instantaneous worldwide. The lack of restrictions and absence of editors or gatekeepers has allowed individuals not only the ability to retrieve information but also to create and distribute it. Traditionally, men with power often exploited women for their own pleasure. The feminist movement claimed that if women had more control, especially in the media, then more positive images of women would be portrayed. Now that women have the capability of putting out more positive images using new technology channels, they have not. Much of the Internet content produced by women is the continuation of exploitation of women, often of themselves. For example, social sites such as MySpace (http://www.myspace.com) are filled with sexual images high school and even middle school girls have posted of themselves. YouTube (http://www.youtube.com) is likewise filled with exploitative video clips underage girls have made of themselves dancing in their underwear and making out with each other. Rather than liberating images of girls who are enjoying empowerment, these images are desperate attempts to gain male attention. In this chapter, I investigate Internet content produced by and about girls and young women.

Social Networking Sites

MySpace has become the third most popular website in the United States and the most popular social networking site in the world. It accounts for 80 percent of all visits to online social networking sites ("MySpace Gains," 2006). MySpace allows people age 16 and older to have full access to the site. If someone is younger than 16, only people in their Friend Space (i.e., people that have been given permission) can access their profile. However, children chronically lie about their age to participate. My students reported their younger brothers and sisters (as young as 11 years old) have their own pages. I found a number of pages that included one age on the basic information they used in their MySpace application and another where they then reported their real ages in their profiles. When underage users are caught and their pages deleted, they simply make up a new screen name and start all over again.

Another popular site for young people is Facebook. Facebook (http://www.

facebook.com) has the largest number of registered users among college-focused networking sites (Hanisko, 2006). The site also has listings for high school students. Schools have control over Facebook sites; therefore, there is somewhat of a decrease in abuse. Administrators are creating guidelines for students' MySpace and Facebook pages. Students are asked to sign pledges that they will not "exhibit gross misconduct or behavior/citizenship that is considered detrimental to his/her team or school" (Wang, 2006). Schools and public libraries have restricted access to MySpace because it has become "a haven for student gossip and malicious comments" ("Schools Race," 2005). Another problem is that these provocative photographs and postings can come back to haunt the subjects. Employers are more and more likely to Google applicants, as well as check MySpace and Facebook pages, to get additional information on job candidates. Often embarrassing material can come up that can hurt the applicant's chances of being hired (Hanisko, 2006).

Several articles and news stories recount anecdotes of how pedophiles have lured underage children by using their MySpace sites. A man in Connecticut was arrested for raping a 14-year-old girl he contacted on MySpace when he disguised himself as another teenager (P. Williams, 2006). A Long Island man lured a 16-year-old girl to a parking lot and sexually assaulted her. Part of the problem, according to Carlin (2006), is that the questions MySpace asks their clients when setting up their pages include specific kinds of information that may lead kids to reveal more information that could identify them than they would include on their own. Even if the child does not disclose where they go to school, pictures posted may have clues to location. What many parents focus on is pedophiles' access to information about minors. These pedophiles are often drawn in by provocative photos or other sexual messages posted on the site.

A pervasive problem that is often not discussed is the image girls present. Carlin (2006) pointed out that many of the pictures are suggestive in nature. Teens and even preteens think it is appropriate to display sexualized photographs of themselves. From their perspective, that is what gets attention from other MySpace users. Teens often have two sites: one they show their parents and a racier version they hide. The sexy photos put up for "fun" may have unintended consequences. Even if only their "friends" have access to their site, it may give the wrong impression about their willingness to have sex. I found more sexual photos of 14 and 15 year old girls than 18 year olds and older. Photos show girls in their early teens obviously drunk, in various stages of dress. Whether they see this as "playing a role" or if that is how they want to see themselves, it appears damaging to the image of females in society. It is also disturbing to realize how closely physical attributes and sexuality are tied to the self-perception and self-worth of girls barely in their teens.

When I searched for the word "skank" in MySpace, it retrieved multiple entries. Most postings were from underage girls who were quite proud of their "skankiness." Of the 22 pages found using the term "skank" in their profile, at least 19 reported their age as being under 18 years old. Seven were 15 years old and six were 14 years old. Most of them used obscene sexual language and referred to themselves as the skank. Looking at their pictures, most of those who referred to themselves as skank were rather ordinary looking. Natalie_cunt whore_dattomo is 17 years old. The 16-year-old females that come up in the search for "skank" included screen names and entries such as "Mary [fucking] Sunshine," "what a skank hoe," and "kathy [SKANK]." The 15-year-olds used, "like OMG ur a skank!," "Silly Skank," and "WoSnatch." One 15-year-old described herself as the "universe's biggest skank." "Woah x Skank" listed herself as 18 years old but put "really 14" in parentheses next to it. The other 14-year-olds were "Lucie Skank," "Whore Sanchez," "Skank ass Bitch," "Skank Muffin," and "Vanessa's skank."

Other sites such as the Hot-or-Not website are examples of physical appearance at a premium. Denizet-Lewis (2004) reported that many teens are obsessed with how strangers view them. The goal for many teenagers is to make the "top girls" or "hottest guys" sections. The focus on physical appearance in society and at online social sites is not only outwardly sexual but has inward consequences. Many of the pages are from girls who are obsessed with their looks and their weight.

Pro Ana Sites

The Internet has given voice to many before who were silent. Chat rooms can create supportive communities. However, the topics can be deadly to its target population. The number of "Pro Ana" (short for pro-anorexia) websites has decreased in the last 5 years after domains such as Yahoo! shut many of them down (Eaton, 2006). They continue to be available through sites such as MySpace. Some of the MySpace screen names I found were ANAmaniac and Underweight Goddess. (These sites are just too disturbing to be made up.) ANAmaniac's profile stated she is 19 but in the text she wrote she is only 14. She wrote, "I wish the flab on my stomache [sic] would just dissapear [sic], but it just doesn't seem to go away. So I have to keep working." She posted pictures of starving models and grossly underweight celebrities such as Mary-Kate Olsen and Nicole Richie at their lightest. The site obsesses over every calorie, every body part.

Some sites, such as Pro-Ana Nation, claim they do not endorse anorexia, only that they give support for those with the condition. The site Pro Anorexia (http://community.livejournal.com/proanorexia), which claims to be the "world's largest Pro Anorexia site," is a community message board for people with eating disorders. One posting from "Ana Princess" displayed a red ribbon with the phrase "Anorexia is a lifestyle not a disease." Other posted slogans included "Hunger is only a feeling" and "NOTHING tastes as good as being THIN feels." "Ache-to-be-thin" posted a photo with the motto "Stay strong, starve on." One poster suggested readers spray their food with Windex so they won't be tempted to eat it. "Hatemyself1989" carefully notes each calorie and each exercise. Here is a sample:

> Monday: Green Tea, Rockmelon/grapes, water, lite hot choc (42 cals), coke zero, bit of ham. Plus 1 hour and 40 mins cardio (cross trainer & elliptical), then went home and did 40 crunches, 20 sit ups and 20 push ups.
>
> Tuesday: Grapes, Coke Zero, Water, Fruit Salad, 1x apiece of ham & pineapple pizza thin (i know bad), bit of rockmelon. Plus 1 hour and 40 mins cardio again (cross trainer & elliptical), few weights, sex with my man (didnt need to know that but that's excerise, right?)
>
> Wednesday (today): Well today i decided to go to the gym in the morning, because i have pole fitness tonight, so i did 35 mins on cross trainer and 35 mins on elliptical. few bits of rockmelon for breakfast and water.
>
> So right now i am sitting at work and i am so tied [*sic*]. My legs feel like jelly, i have no energy! [Angelaussie cited in "Community Journal," n.d.].

In response to this posting, someone wrote, "maybe you should try diet iced tea, or diet pepsi, caffiene pills even. anything caffiene and no cals is sure to wake you up. good luck!" "Want2btiny" wrote that she was so proud of herself when she threw away a berry slushee her mother had bought her even though she was starving. She wrote, "I can't afford to get off track right now!" O-Lolita wrote that she was doing a water/low calorie drink fast: "I don't feel hungry at all. I can do this. I NEED to do this. Hope everyone else is having as good of a day as I am!)" ("Community Journal," n.d.).

Part of eating disorders stems from the desire to be thin. Images of über-thin celebrities fuel this desire. Even when magazines address celebrities who are too thin, they are reinforcing the trend by giving them more exposure and putting them on the cover. The ultimate message is that if a woman loses a great deal of weight, she is more famous than ever. Of course, obsessive eating disorders often go beyond wanting to be thin. Often it is about gaining control where these girls and young women are not feeling in control anywhere else in their lives. However, these images and websites appear to only make matters worse.

Video Sharing Sites

The website YouTube allows Internet users to share video clips. It offers unedited footage ranging from amateurs to professionals. It is the fastest growing site on the web and has surpassed MySpace's reach (Sweeney, 2006). There have been an estimated 100 million videos posted since its inception. Although YouTube screens for pornography, sexually explicit material gets through. Users can flag certain videos as inappropriate for children. Flagging generally means that users need to sign in and agree that they are over 18 years old to view the videos. Many of the images are disturbing because minors might view them; however, it is even more disturbing that some of the most explicit images are inappropriate videos minors have posted of themselves.

I retrieved thousands of hits when searching for "sexy" and "hot girls." There were a variety of clips, from glamorous lingerie models to ordinary girls dancing in their underwear. Two girls, who looked about 16 at the most, were dancing in various outfits, from swimsuits to slips. In one scene they were dancing in long sleeve, button down shirts and flashing their underwear. The next scene they were strip dancing on the kitchen countertop. Some of the clips included "Top ten celebrity nipslips," "top ten lady liplocks," "Watch as 2 very sexy girl [*sic*] dance there [*sic*] sexy bodys [*sic*] like never before," and "Girls dancing like Shakira." Scaramouch (2006), who is a self-proclaimed regular YouTube user, admitted he is particularly fascinated with the amateur clips. Of particular interest are "the drunken sorority girls taking their first taste of forbidden love" videos taken at parties with or without their knowledge or consent.

Amateur Pornography

There is no dispute that the pornography industry exploded with the mass adoption of the Internet. In this chapter, I wish to focus on one particular version of porn, that of amateur porn. (See chapter 3 for a discussion of professional pornography.) This amateur porn trend includes the *Girls Gone Wild* videos phenomenon as well as *Playboy Magazine*'s series that features an array of amateur models, from college campuses to McDonald's restaurant counters.

Suicide Girls

Additional websites feature sex, or at least sexual images, ordinary girls and women post of themselves. One site is altporn.net. The site is naked photographs of unconventional women—in other words, those with piercings and tattoos. Many of the women look punk or goth. The site features over a thousand Suicide Girls and receives an estimated 200 new submissions per week. The name "Suicide Girls" is not a group out to take their own lives, rather it is a play on killing their mainstream side ("Real Sex," 2003). Nakkidnerds (http://nakkidnerds.com) looks like a spinoff of Suicide Girls; however, the site is described as "women with brains." The producers of the site not only claim not to use professional models, but not to use even the "amateur" models who apparently post their photos on all sorts of sites to get maximum attention. Rather than attracting attention from men, the site is supposed to be just for fun and an ego boost for the women in the photos. Dotinga (2005) described these sites as "porn even feminists can love."

One Wikipedia poster ("Suicide Girls," n.d., ¶ 1) claimed that while full nudity is required, "spread-eagle" shots are not. In addition, penetration is strictly forbidden. Those appearing on the site claim the difference between Suicide Girls and male-targeted sites is that the models are not stereotypical bimbos with breast implants who list their hobbies and turn-ons. The photos look more like the pinups of the 1950s such as Bettie Page. The women argue they have control over the photos that get posted and how they are portrayed. They claim they do not feel exploited (Glass, 2004). The women on the site state they feel empowered and post their photos to express their sexual security. The site also allows networking, and many of the women say they have made friends on the site.

An episode of HBO's *Real Sex* (2003) featured a segment on the Suicide Girls. There was a great deal of sexual energy between the women in the segment. They had gotten together and were playing spin the bottle. In the photo shoot, many of the models were undressing each other, touching each other's breasts, and French kissing. The founder of the site said that it was very "unSuicide Girl" to put oneself in a box and therefore denied the label of lesbian activity.

Sex Tapes

Sexuality for many young women has moved from the private sphere to the public arena. Advances in technology make it possible to easily transmit sexual images, with or without the subjects' permission. Sex tapes of celebrities that "leak" out often make the featured performers more popular than ever. Famous celebrity sex tapes include Pamela Anderson and Tommy Lee, Pamela Anderson and Bret Michaels, Tonya Harding and then husband Jeff Gillooly, Paris Hilton, Colin Farrell, Chyna and X-Pac (from the WWE), and rapper Eve. In addition, Kid Rock and former Creed lead singer Scott Stapp were filmed with four fans on the tour bus. (R Kelly was videotaped having sex with a 14-year-old girl, although I don't think that is widely available.)

In a brief search on the Internet, I easily found thousands of amateur, non-celebrity sex videos available. Most of the pictures and videos are done for free, leading one to the conclusion that they were done simply for the attention. Some of the descriptions brag that the woman was unaware of the taping. Most of the footage is of couples, although group sex scenes are available.

The website "inthevip.com" is supposedly an exhibition of a traveling sex show. I am not sure if it is a real site, as it proclaims these are just party going people doing it for free. There are so many photos that it seems unlikely that they paid the dozens and dozens of actors to perform. The site claims, "Every day we travel to the hottest night clubs in the country to show you what goes down in the VIP" ("In the VIP," n.d.). The site brags that wherever they go, women love getting undressed. According to the producer of the site, "We wanted to push up that little skirt, and they did with no question." They describe another woman as not being able to keep her "big titties from bursting out.... Finally she broke down and flipped that sexy dress up, and showed the whole club what she was workin' with" ("In the VIP," n.d.).

The site is littered with pictures of women showing their breasts and thongs in what looks like a regular club. There are also behind the scene photos that are full-on sex orgies. The text on the site leads viewers to believe these women (and men) are so sexually deviant they are having sex with random people out in the open. There is one clip of two couples side by side as they are having intercourse. The guys high-five as they are thrusting in and out of the women. The description of the site reads:

> This Party Hardcore event is heaving with cute, innocent girls who are just beginning to get really excited about the idea of freely sucking dick and being felt up by total strangers. A thin blond jumps up on stage and is the first one to really go for it, and soon she's lying on her back, her shirt missing, and she's choking on a dick right in front of her friends, strangers, and our cameras. Jump on in now, this is another great start to the biggest amateur stripper party site on the WWW! ["In the VIP," n.d.].

Multiple other sites are available that offer amateur porn. Several sites claim to feature amateur girls trying out for porn movies. Apparently some viewers believe the more rural the location, the better. Nebraska Coeds (http://nebraskacoeds.com) claimed it is "The ONLY site on the net that features REAL college girls getting Drunk, Naked, and Fucked, at REAL College Parties Here in Nebraska!" ("Welcome to," n.d.).

Another phenomenon feeding the desires of peeping toms is the "dorm-cam." Hundreds of young women have set up sites on the Internet to give voyeurs 24-hour access to their private lives for a small fee. College students set up cameras in their rooms and broadcast their everyday activities, from getting dressed to getting undressed and brushing their teeth to having sex with their boyfriends. The site Incrediblecam.com claimed they have 2,543 live cameras and a total of 361,401 cameras available ("Uncensored Video," 2007). The producers of the site stated, "We are the internets [*sic*] largest collection of cam girls. With hundreds of different girls to choose from, each willing to perform specially for you. Browse through our cam category or choose a girl below to find out how you can begin chatting with her immediately!" ("Uncensored Video," 2007). One example they gave was, "I just got a WebCam and I've met a lot of people through it! Well let's see, I'm a bit of an exhibitionist, I really like having guys watch me as I finger myself. My boyfriend hates that I show so much of myself on the internet, but I can't help it" ("Uncensored Video," 2007).

Child Modeling Sites

In addition to child beauty pageants (see chapter 6), parents are signing their children with pseudo modeling agencies. Readers may be wondering why child modeling websites are included in a book on sexual representations. These sites are incredibly disturbing. Although they claim they do not post nude or sexual content, they blatantly exploit the little girls. For example, "Budding beauty" is a disgusting expression used to refer to prepubescent nymphets, some as young as eight.

The website for Child Supermodels stated, "A website to promote models 7 thru 16 and their photographers. If this is you please add your link!" ("We Keep," n.d.). Each girl's picture is accompanied by an enticing tagline such as: "Tori is a poser. SHE LOVES TO PLAY" and "3 hot teen models all on 1 site!" After clicking on the photo, the web surfer is taken to another level where more photos are available for a fee. In her photos, Laurie's (no listed age, but looks about 11) training bra strap was falling off her shoulder. Megan (13) was lying down with her hand on her lower stomach and with one leg up as if she is going to masturbate. Danika (looks 11) was photographed from below looking up her short nightgown while she is wearing doggy slippers. Daisy (looks 11) was wearing a "Get ready" T-shirt while pulling up her shirt. She was also photographed in an adult style bathing suit and tugging down the strap. Chastity (looks 14) was in an off-white silk camisole with one hand on her butt and one hand on her leg near her crotch. Many of these girls have open-mouthed, apparently orgasmic expressions on their faces. Some of these little girls are holding their hands and covering their breasts. Even though there is clothing over them it still gives the impression that they are hiding them. The older models on the site appear to get fewer hits than the younger ones.

I looked for the Child Supermodels site again in early 2007; however, the site had been taken down. I had no problem finding additional sites with a Google search. Many of the sites claimed that because there was no nude photographs they were legal and therefore acceptable. Nothing could be further from the truth. I was horrified to find some international sites such as NN-Guide (http://www.nn-guide.com). This is an absolutely disgusting website with links to 71 different preteen modeling websites ("Only 5–16," n.d.). The little girls are clothed; however, one 7-year-old is photographed up her skirt showing her thong. Some of the sites say they are from Germany and Russia. There are all kinds of little girls in their underwear in sexual poses focusing on their crotches. Many of the 6–12 year olds are on all fours with their rear ends in the air and photographed from behind as they turn their heads back to look at the camera.

I showed the Mini-Models website (http://www.mini-models.com) to focus groups made up of college students. At first, many students were defending the photographs, or were at least skeptical of my assessment. After a few pictures, even the most diehard students were agreeing that the poses were inappropriate. The pictures were relatively normal on the surface, but often there was one thing in each photo that was shocking. For example, one little girl was modeling a swimsuit. The photo was no big deal in and of itself; however, she had one leg propped up, thus exposing her crotch to the camera. Another girl—the site claimed she was 11 years old—was also modeling a bathing suit ("Photo Gallery," n.d.). The arch of her back made me wince.

These sites make money by charging visitors money to look at more pictures of the girls under the guise of attracting modeling agencies. Because the girls are shown in pornography-like poses, it is more likely to attract pedophiles with credit cards. A common theme is for preteens to be shown with their training bra's straps falling off one shoulder. Many of the models are arching their backs or tugging at their tiny bikini bottoms. These are the photos anyone can see by just logging on to the site. It is hard to imagine what the paid photos show. According to Foley (cited in McCullah, 2002), "pedophiles who pay to see photos and video clips of the children in sexually suggestive poses send the children provocative clothing and bathing suits to 'model' and talk to them via email" (¶2).

Mini-Models was less blatant than the international sites, but still disturbing. It claims that all the photos are in compliance with U.S. and international laws because of the no nudity policy. What is especially disturbing is that they claim the photographs were taken under parental supervision. The parents' approval makes the abuse that much worse. Parents have justified putting their children on these sites by saying they are providing for the child's future. They may also be living vicariously through their children, seeing the child's success as an extension of themselves. One set of parents appeared on the *Dr. Phil Show* (McGraw, 2005), vehemently defending their actions by claiming the child wants to do it. McGraw then blasted them for their ignorance. In July 2007, the Mini-Models site was temporarily shut down. According to the site the closure was due to circumstances beyond their control. They hoped to reopen the site ("Photo Gallery," n.d.).

Conclusion

One thing that makes the Internet unique is that individuals can use the technology not just as passive consumers but as producers. Much of the material available now exploits girls and women in far greater proportion than it liberates them. The Internet also offers opportunities for females to exploit themselves for attention. Some of the photographs that young girls post of themselves on social networking sites such as MySpace are particularly disturbing. It appears that the younger the girl, the more outrageously sexual the site. Although some parents try to protect their daughters, some girls have a second MySpace profile they hide from their parents. The Internet, as with traditional media, both reflects and drives the sexual exploitation of women and girls. Censorship, even if were possible, will not likely help to improve the climate. Only by educating young girls about empowerment rather than exploitation can we hope for a better future. This chapter is rather brief in comparison to other chapters in the book because of the relative newness of the Internet. Hopefully, future work will include a report on the explosion of female empowerment material.

14. SPORTS

It is well documented that girls who play sports get better grades, are more likely to graduate from high school, have lower levels of depression, have fewer eating disorders, and are half as likely to become pregnant as girls who do not play sports ("Why Sports," 2000). Yet, with all these strides toward empowerment, it is still common in popular culture to sexualize female athletes. Rosenberg (2007) stated that a woman's good looks are almost always a prerequisite for female athletes to become famous, unlike male athletes who are more likely judged by their abilities. The media reinforce stereotypes that females are sexual rather than strong and powerful athletes. According to Kane, Griffin, and Messner (2002), the media are likely to show female athletes off the field and out of uniform, in more feminine ways (e.g., with their hair down, wearing makeup, or posing with their husband and children). Sexualization of female athletes is used to sell not only the sport but also copies of men's magazines, including *Sports Illustrated*.

Critics claim that print media—sports magazines in particular—portray female athletes similar to pornography. Brandi Chastain's removal of her top when the U.S. women won the Olympic Gold was a gesture of victory, mimicking the removal of shirts in men's soccer. Instead of the gesture being a display of power, commentators gave it a sexual spin. (Personally, I cannot think of anything sexy about a sports bra. They are meant to restrict the breasts so they will not move.) When Misty May and Kerri Walsh won the gold medal in women's beach volleyball, the Olympic website chose to display a photo of them rolling around in the sand in their bikinis after their victory, closely resembling soft-core porn (Zeynep, 2004).

With few professional options, female athletes must rely on sponsorship for income. "Corporate acquiescence" is a term used to describe the phenomenon. Huge sponsorship deals can be contingent on the women wearing sexual outfits. When Olympic swimmer Amanda Beard was named *FHM*'s world's sexiest athlete in 2006, her potential earnings from endorsements shot up to an estimated $100 million by 2010 ("FHM Declares," 2006). Beard (cited in Hunt, 2004) claimed her photo spreads in a white string bikini are "just for me." She added the photos are a way for her to experience other things, "like modeling and stuff." Beard posed nude in *Playboy* a year later. According to Rosenberg (2007), even though she has won seven gold medals, Beard will always be famous for being an attractive swimmer rather than a great swimmer like her male counterparts.

Olympics Athletes

The most popular women's sports in the Olympics are figure skating and gymnastics. Although these sports take an incredible amount of strength and agility, they are often put down as "feminine" sports and taken less seriously. They also have the most revealing and clingy outfits. Figure skating outfits generally have extremely short skirts with panty-like undergarments exposed throughout their program. Skin tight leotards worn in gymnastics emphasize the bodies of girls who are either very young or physically stunted from excessive training. Sports such as women's beach volleyball, pole vaulting, and track and field events have been criticized for lack of coverage of the female body. When beach volleyball officially became an Olympic event in 1996, conservative countries, such as Islamic countries, criticized the sport for being too sexualized. According to Moos (1999), at one time the International Volleyball Federation required women's uniform bottoms to be no more than two and a half inches wide. Although the women are no longer required to wear skimpy swimsuits when they play (beachcalifornia.com), most still do.

More explicit sexual images of female athletes out of uniform are available in a variety of men's magazines. *ESPN* magazine ran the headline "Sex, Olympics Go Hand in Hand" (Merron, 2004). The corresponding article described the recent exploitation of Olympic female athletes. Men's magazines ranging from *Sports Illustrated* to *FHM* to *Playboy* have featured Olympic athletes in varying stages of nudity. Katarina Witt, the 1984 and 1988 gold medalist in figure skating, posed nude for *Playboy* in 1999. Boswell (2004) noted that, although the Witt photos received criticism, the United States Olympic Committee had little reaction to nine active athletes' nude photos in *Playboy* in 2004. *Sports Illustrated* has often featured female athletes in its Swimsuit Issue. In 2000, swimmer Jenny Thompson posed with her hands covering her bare breasts. *FHM*'s "Sexy Olympic Special" issue was one of its biggest sellers ever. Five members of the U.S. Olympic team posed on the cover in white bikinis. Swimmer Amanda Beard, swimmer Haley Cope, and volleyball player Logan Tom were photographed tugging down on their tiny bikini bottoms in a very seductive way, while high jumper Amy Acuff and track and field star Jenny Adams were touching one another. In Boswell's (2004) words, Acuff and Adams cradle "one another's taut waists and gently caress the smalls of each other's backs." Boswell also described the cover: "They crush balls ... and punish their competition.... But stand them next to one

another in white bikinis and suddenly they are tender, demure, and innocent."
Inside the issue, Olympic snowboarder Gretchen Bleiler was photographed
laughing as she was pulling off her jean skirt. In another photo, she was wearing a white bikini top with her snowboarding boots and a long coat falling off
her shoulders.

Large amounts of money to pose completely or partially nude is particularly tempting for women in amateur sports with no professional league to
support their training. Struggling to meet expenses, athletes may be tempted
to trade on their sexuality for the opportunity to compete in their sport.
Women, especially in not so popular sports, are willing to bare all. Female curl-
ing athletes put out a nude calendar to raise money for the 2006 Olympics.
Boswell (2004) stated some female Olympians go on to model to capitalize
on their athletic physiques because of the lack of opportunities to play profes-
sionally. On Amy Acuff's personal website, she displays her modeling portfo-
lio right next to her high jump stats.

Beach Volleyball

Television coverage often focuses on the barely-there bikinis of female
beach volleyball players on the AVP (Association of Volleyball Players) pro
beach tour. Camera operators tend to focus on the player names that are often
written across the backs of the bikini bottoms. According to Moos (1999),
"Beach volleyball has now joined go-go girl dancing as perhaps the only two
professions where a bikini is the required uniform." To stir excitement in
females competing, the women wear almost a g-string bottom. Many of the
corporate sponsors dictate what styles of swimsuits the female players must
wear. To get noticed and gain endorsement deals, the women may feel pressured to follow the fashion trends, such as Brazilian-cut bottoms. Watching
matches, it is distracting to see these amazing athletes tugging their tops down
and pulling out their "wedgies" between plays.

Olympic gold medal winner Kerry Walsh stated, "I love our uniforms. It
was kind of an adjustment, learning to play in a bikini, but that's what we need
on the beach" (Walsh, cited in Dure, 2004). She argued that wearing baggy
clothes would hinder their game; however, she also admitted that wearing
bikinis is part of the allure of beach volleyball. There are two points here that
need emphasizing. First, there is a drastic leap from wearing baggy clothes to
sporting a near-thong, string bikini. Second, the men seem to have no problem playing in baggy shorts. According to Walsh (cited in Dure, 2004), she
and her sponsor, Speedo, worked together to create something "functional and
sassy at the same time." For anyone who has watched Walsh play, she pulls
and tugs at her suit between most plays. Fellow Olympian Misty May has likewise bought into the tiny swimsuit trend. May (cited in Dure, 2004) argued
that players can get thumbs caught in pockets and pant legs. She claimed she

is very comfortable in bathing suits, although from the sidelines she looks very uncomfortable tugging her bottoms out of her rear cleavage between plays. A former pro player, Gabrielle Reece, stated that she preferred her lycra tights to the tiny bikinis. Reece (cited in Moos, 1999) stated, "You take one step, that bathing suit goes straight up.... You're always yanking and fiddling."

The AVP sells swimsuits for players and fans on their website. The marketing slogan for the tiny "string side tie" and "hipster" bottoms and string bikini tops is not to play better but to "get noticed." The site does offer more conservative styles such as "skipper" tops, which are advertised as a "quality performance piece." On the site they also sold Women of the AVP 2006 calendars that featured very sexy photos of the players. For example, Jen Kessy was photographed topless, with only net tape covering her nipples. In 2007, the AVP tour featured women in tiny yellow and pink bikinis warming up the audience before matches. The "entertainment" was almost indistinguishable from the female athletes.

Even indoor volleyball outfits for females have become more tight-fitting and, some say, sexual. At one time the International Volleyball Federation mandated tight swimsuit-like bottoms, often referred to as "bun huggers" for games ("Bun Huggers," n.d.). Representatives of the Women's Sports Foundation argued that uniform choices should be made on the basis of performance. For example, tighter clothing is appropriate when reduction in air or water resistance is a factor. Neither of these factors is at play in volleyball. If these were factors, the men would be wearing similar uniforms. Stubb (1999) argued that the governing body changed the uniform standards to attract more male spectators. Lapiano (cited in Stubb, 1999) pointed out that male athletes are not stuffed into uniforms that "display their genitalia" to get more women to watch. In Olympic competition men are required to wear tank tops. On the beach men generally play shirtless. Many of the men wear their shorts quite low on their hips, exposing their pelvic bones.

The focus of my concern is not whether women should or should not wear bikinis per se, but particularly how drastic the cut of the bottoms should be. One aspect of the bikini, like any other sports equipment, is that it fit correctly. For example, if athletes have to continually adjust their sunglasses because they are falling down their noses, I would think they would get better fitting sunglasses. I have been to six AVP events over the last six years and I have noticed a progression of tinier and tinier bikini bottoms. The Brazilian cut is such that half of the women's cheeks are exposed. At an AVP event in 2006, I noticed Holly McPeak's cheeks were "McPeaking" out of her bikini bottoms. Rachel Wacholder's bottoms are a few inches of material away from being a thong. Another phenomenon I, along with several men around me, noticed at a 2007 APV event was more and more back cleavage showing.

The following comments are from a discussion on the BAVP (Boston Area Volleyball Players) list serve in regard to bikini standards. Many of the comments make good points that show the nuances of the outfits. Not every-one agrees on where the line is between sexy and sexual exploitation. One female volleyball player stated, "This issue is monumental for women. It's a no-brainer for me" (M. Conway, personal communication, July 12, 2006). She argued that she felt more comfortable and more mobile wearing fewer clothes. She differentiated the bikinis the pros wear and something more skanky. "Skanky would be tacky bikinis with fringes and some inviting saying written across the butt or the chest, etc." Her main point was that women should not have to apologize for being beautiful. She stated that some people not know-ing how to "handle beautiful, strong and naturally effortlessly sexy women does not mean that it is the job of women to cover themselves up or dimin-ish their beauty or power" (M. Conway, personal communication, July 12, 2006). Another female resolved that, although the bikini is a functional uni-form, female athletes will always be seen as sexual (D. Leip, personal commu-nication, July 12, 2006). She pointed out a double standard in that "hot guys" in shorts are seen as just athletes.

One male responded that he saw the issue as a choice between beach vol-leyball becoming a commercial spectator sport or not (M. BenDaniel, personal communication, July 12, 2006). He argued that the bikinis are about ad rev-enue, selling power, and making volleyball a top-rated sport. He sounded rather complacent that we live in a culture that wants to ogle women's bodies. Another male admitted that although he thought the bikinis were degrading at first, he no longer does (B. Dias, personal communication, July 12, 2006). He sees the outfits as adding to the sport, making it unique and sexy. He added that if the women are required to wear less, the men should either wear less or be paid less. Another male admitted he liked bikinis; however, he does not want to see the "bustin' out" look either for tops or bottoms. He stated that the tug-ging is very unbecoming. He suggested women with big bottoms should not be wearing tiny bikini bottoms. He stated his basic rule: "If you see a 'fold' in the skin, you need more coverage" (D. Blickstein, personal communication, July 12, 2006). Many respondents, male and female, thought that as long as the players themselves did not have a problem then no one else should.

Tennis

Women's tennis is cashing in on its sex appeal. Representatives of women's tennis even hired an "image" consulting firm to coach its players to walk and talk and dress in a more sexually appealing fashion (Stubbs, 1999). The promo for the 2006 U.S. Open focused mostly on the female players. One spot fea-tured athletic women running and lunging for balls and making fantastic plays. The taglines read: "Play fast," "Drive hard," and "Leave a good-looking mini-skirt." The female players were shown serving with their skirts flying up reveal-ing "shorties" (a cross between panties and shorts) underneath. A majority of the camera shots were from behind. The end of the promo, a female player (can't see her face because only her midsection is visible) was shown tugging on the bottom of her skirt.

Hoerrner (2006) stated that marketers are using "sex over serves." In other words, some of the players are using their "natural appeal and charisma" to get endorsements to make up for the discrepancy in pay between women and men. Top-ranked tennis star Martina Hingis appeared on the cover of *GQ* wearing a provocative dress for a profile headlined "The Champ Is a Vamp" (Stubbs, 1999). Kessel (2006) described Maria Sharapova's outfit at the U.S. Open as a little black dress with "evening wear diamante detail." Kessel also pointed out that Mary Pierce wore a similar "feminine glamour" outfit at the 2000 French Open. When searching for articles on women's tennis, many of the headlines I found referred to the sexuality of the stars. Two examples I found were "Kournikova vs Sharapova: A Match Between Tennis Players or Sex Kitten Athletes?" and "The Era of the Sex Kitten Athletes" (Democracy, 2006). Fans can vote who they think would be left standing in a catfight between Sharapova and Kournikova ("Celebrity Catfights," n.d.).

The marketing of Anna Kournikova is notorious. Critics argue that although she has never won a major singles title she managed to earn the highest endorsement deal of any other female athlete to date. In 2004 she ranked fourth in the world in product endorsements, behind Tiger Woods, Michael Jordan, and Kobe Bryant. She was voted Sexist Woman Alive by *FHM* in 2002. On the cover she was pulling up her top, showing off tiny black bikini bottoms. Critics questioned whether she wanted to be a tennis player or a model. Few considered she could do both. She is most famous for being famous. She caused a stir on the court when she wore outfits that exposed her midriff. Because she was a minor at the time, there was a risk of marketing not a tennis player but a child as a sex symbol (Bailey, cited in Berns, 2003). She was the most searched athlete on the Internet, female and male, for a long time. Maria Sharapova is challenging Anna Kournikova's reign of blonde tennis star with the victories to back it up (Hoerrner, 2006). According to Hoerrner (2006), the Williams sisters make a combined $20 million a year, Kournikova about $12 million a year, and Sharapova will likely make $100 million in endorsements over the next ten years. Of course, Tiger Woods earns about $60 million in endorsements in just one year without revealing any skin. Sharapova's website has provocative photos and bikini shots. Other tennis stars, such as Lindsay Davenport, do not have provocative shots; instead these are mostly action shots.

There is a limit, however, to exploiting the female players' attractiveness. According to Wertheim (cited in Hoerrner, 2006), "The tour certainly hasn't shied away from playing up the glam factor. But when it starts to undercut the credibility of the product, it becomes a problem." Network television aired an ad featuring Sharapova. The camera followed her as she traveled from her hotel to the stadium. Everyone around her sang "I Feel Pretty" as she passed by. They continued singing as she arrived on the court and served the ball. As she crushed the ball, nearly taking out a line judge, the singing suddenly stopped and was followed by dead silence. The ad was a great play on the fact that although these athletes are attractive, they are physically dominant. The ad was an interesting contrast between her good looks and her superior athletic ability and power on the court.

Golf

Until recently, many golf fans joked that the *L* in LPGA stood for "lesbian." Helmbreck (cited in Bamberger, 1996) claimed that CBS golf broadcaster Ben Wright told her, "Let's face facts here. Lesbians in the sport hurt women's golf." He also reportedly said that women are handicapped because their "boobs get in the way." (While Wright denied the claim, Helmbreck stands by the story.)

Today's female golfers have become eye candy. The rise of younger players, many of whom are very attractive, has been credited for increasing viewership of the Women's U.S. Open by 68 percent (Arnett, 2005). Arnett (2005) argued that the LPGA needs to embrace, not reject, the sexy look. He compared the strategy to female figure skaters and gymnasts who wear skimpy and skin-tight outfits. Arnett (2005) admitted the women are playing phenomenal golf. He contended that the women on the tour drive a ball farther than 80 percent of male amateurs. However, to truly make front-page news, they need to do so in "alluring ensembles." I admit it was funny when he compared some of the golfers' attire to uniforms from *Prison Guard Weekly*. However, I was taken aback at some of his suggestions. He argued the women should wear "ultra-feminine attire" and market themselves to a voyeuristic public. He also suggested that if players want to increase purses, they should start carrying them. He suggested they "show some emotion, throw on some eyeliner and lipstick, and wear some camera-friendly attire." Why not nude golf to attract viewers?

Jan Stephenson, "LPGA cover girl" in the 1970s, compared the selling of female golfers' sexiness to the status of men on the tour. She stated, "Tiger Woods, Greg Norman, Fred Couples, they're all sexy. Why hide it? What's wrong with a few attractive LPGA golfers in commercials saying, 'Come see us play'?" (Stephenson, cited in Arnett, 2005). Arnett added that Jack Nicklaus gained public acceptance only after losing weight. However, there is a major difference. These men are first and foremost respected as great golfers. They were not required to change their appearance to get sexual attention as female golfers are being asked to do.

Female golf stars such as Natalie Gulbis have posed for swimsuit calendars. Carin Koch and Jill McGill were listed as the sexiest LPGA players in a Playboy.com poll. On the other hand, Nancy Lopez did not require gimmicks or stripper outfits to get people's attention. Arnett (2005) stated, "Lopez's winning recipe of a stellar game (from 1978 through the early '90s), charismatic smiles, unlimited autograph signings, and a willingness to promote the sport vaulted her into the public consciousness."

WNBA

The Women's National Basketball Association has gone through the same troubles as the LPGA. They have had to battle the stereotype of female athletes as lesbians. It has influenced the way the sport has been marketed. In a 2003 ad campaign, WNBA marquee players appeared in a "glitz-and-glam ad showing them as more than one-dimensional, pony-tailed basketballers" (Levesque, 2003). Levesque (2003) reported that the WNBA team uniforms at one time feature cropped, untucked tops so fans could get a glimpse of midriff when players shot the ball. Sports executive Jeanie Buss appeared in a magazine with nothing but basketballs covering her breasts. The feature was titled "She's Got Balls" (Stubbs, 1999). Sue Bird, a WNBA player for the Seattle Storm, appeared in an issue of *Dime* magazine. According to Levesque (2003), she looked "all sexy and come-hithery" in high heels and an Allen Iverson jersey. Bird justified the photo, arguing that it does not matter why fans come out to the games. The magazine referred to Bird as "possibly the perfect woman [looks wise] ... and the best reason we've seen for us to pay attention to women's basketball."

Auto Racing

Danica Patrick is arguably the most successful female race-car driver to date. Shortly after she reached notoriety, she appeared in *FHM* in scant clothing and sexually suggestive positions on her car. She was photographed in a tight outfit with the sides cut out, lying on her back on a car hood with her hair cascading. In another photo she was wearing a leather string bikini bottom that was so low her rear cleavage was clearly exposed. In most shots she appeared with her legs spread. Patrick explained that she just wanted to express her "femininity." She appeared on *The Today Show* after finishing 4th in the Indianapolis 500. Katie Couric awkwardly questioned her about her photos in *FHM*. Couric asked if she was worried about being compared to Anna Kournikova, that she wouldn't be taken seriously. Patrick defended herself, saying that it was "fun to be a girl." She called it a balancing act, and said that she wanted to show the other side of her personality. The moral of the story is that it is okay to be a tomboy as long as the tomboy can be cleaned up, put in a dress, made up and transformed back into a "girl."

The cover of Danica Patrick's (2006) autobiography, *Crossing the Line*, portrayed her as less than a serious competitor. She was photographed in a halter evening dress with her hair down and blowing in the wind. She was arching her back, forcing her chest out while her head was dropped submissively. She was slightly looking up at the camera. She held her driving helmet in one hand, freeing up the other to prominently display her large diamond wedding ring. She described how she hid her "girly-girl" side to fit into the racing world, but now she wants to show it off. She acknowledged that her looks helped her with sponsorships. She stated, "Some women in sports have remained reluctant to use their looks or their femininity to capitalize or exploit their roles. I say, don't be afraid. Use what God gave you—*You gotta rock what you've got* [her italics]" (Patrick, 2006, p. 178–9).

Patrick has done several television commercials. A Secret deodorant commercial showed her in an arcade beating male after male at a video racing game. The tag line read "Strong enough for Danica Patrick, strong enough for a woman." The original ads stated, "Strong enough for a man, strong enough for a woman," implying she is somewhere in between? In her latest ad for Honda, Patrick was shown using her sexuality to get out of a speeding ticket. After fixing her lipstick and hair, and making sure some cleavage was showing, she turned to the police officer only to find it was a woman.

Sports Illustrated featured Patrick on the cover in 2005. Some of the editorial content was sexually suggestive or trivializing. The articles included statements such as she "gave the boys all they could handle" (p. 54). She was called, "the 5'1", 100 pound package of marketing gold" (p. 55). Swift (2005) referred to her as "diminutive Patrick," "media darling," and a "hot pin-up and the object of marketers' affections." A couple of female race fans reported they were torn about Patrick's sexualization, but even female race fans concluded, "If you have it, flaunt it" (Lakeside & Hegeman, n.d.). Male fans were clear on how they felt about her sex appeal. Referring to a very sexy commercial Patrick did for Peak Anti-freeze, one fan said he would certainly buy Peak, being a red-blooded American male and all. Another fan added that it might not be right to use sex but it is okay, part of Americana and good solid business sense.

Women Athletes with Pictures

The online magazine *Sports Wired* features a variety of female athletes in various poses. According to its creator, "The intention of this site was to include images that were not offensive to visitors and which celebrated the beauty of the women in sports" ("Women in Sports," n.d.). The sports featuring the most athletes on the list were tennis (20), figure skating (10), swimming (10), volleyball (10 beach, 2 indoors), and, perhaps surprisingly, golf (12). Some of the unusual sports represented were billiards, boxing, and table tennis.

Some of the photos on the site are on the skanky side. Tatiana Grigorieva, pole vaulter, was pictured topless with white swimsuit bottoms. She was sitting with her knees apart, giving a clear shot to her groin area. A naked Amy Acuff, high jumper, was photographed from the back holding on to the high jump bar with her hands. In another photo Acuff was topless bending over to tie her track shoes. Jeanette Lee, billiards champion, was posed leaning seductively on the billiard table wearing a strapless tight black dress. Amanda Beard, swimmer, was shown with her top pulled up to show the bottom of her breasts as she was tugging down on her bottoms. In other photos Beard was topless with a towel around her shoulders and topless from the side with her arms wrapped around her breasts. Stacy Dragila, pole vaulter, appeared in a nude shot with strips of body paint, long black gloves, and thigh high black boots. Perhaps because of the nature of the uniforms worn in the sport, there were many sexualized photos of volleyball players. Pictures of veteran Gabrielle Reece showed her nude in silhouette. Logan Tom appeared in two photos from the back, one topless and one with the bottoms of her short shorts pulled up into a wedgie to show off her butt cheeks. Rachel Wacholder, who wears some of the tiniest bottoms on the beach, appeared in all game shot photos.

In contrast, there were some tasteful photos of the female athletes. Most of the photos of Maria Sharapova, tennis player, were very tasteful on this site. Milka Dunno, race-car driver, appeared in two photos in racing gear and two photos in elegant evening gowns. Tara Lipinski, figure skater, was photographed very tastefully in a bathing suit top and cutoffs and a very elegant strapless gown. Annie Pelletier, diver, was in pretty tasteful photos, two in evening gowns. Carlie Butler, golfer, appeared only in golf course shots. Likewise, Picabo Street, skier, was posed only in ski outfits.

Conclusion

Female athletes are getting more exposure—in more ways than one. Although it would be nice to think that women's sports are becoming more popular because women are becoming better athletes since the passage of Title IX, it is more likely that the sexualization of the female athletes is attracting more attention. Not only are sports promoters capitalizing on the sexuality of the athletes but so are the female athletes themselves. Most female athletes vehemently defend their choice to be photographed in sexual positions, saying they are just showing their feminine side. It is a legitimate argument that they are proud of their bodies and want to show off their athleticism. Boswell (2004) offered the opinion that posing for photos is a great power trip, a reward for all the hard work and sacrifice. She stated, "It's difficult to fault them for wanting to strut their stuff and say, 'Hey, check me out!'"

Dominique Dawes, a former Olympic gymnast and president of the Women's Sports Foundation, argued that female athletes have earned the right to choose where and how they appear in the media. She also said that posing for magazines was a personal choice and a celebration of their independence (Dawes, cited in Drape, 2004). Brandi Chastain justified her nude photos, arguing it was getting attention for the sport of soccer. (Since then the U.S. women's soccer league [WUSA] has disbanded.) Kerri Walsh has thus far declined magazine shoots, not because she has an issue with the exploitation of female athletes but because she thinks she just does not pose well. Walsh stated that the *FHM* sexy Olympian cover is "really positive for athletes" (Boswell, 2004). Acuff, who was one of the Olympic athletes who appeared in *Playboy*, said, "I don't see sexuality when I see a woman's body. I see strength, athleticism and beauty" (cited in Youngblood, 2006). Supporters argue that these female athletes are just comfortable with their bodies, they wear swimsuits, bikinis, and leotards to work.

When Acuff stated she sees strength and athleticism in nude photos, it is doubtful that the men buying the magazines see it the same way. O'Connor (2004) argued that Logan Tom, a graduate of Stanford University, was not helping anyone appreciate her athletic strength and beauty when she posed next to a shower head shooting water into her mouth. Kane, Griffin, and Messner (2002) argued that the bottom line is that men are consuming them, not respecting them. Boswell (2004) expressed concern that by posing nude, or nearly nude, the actions of a few could be undoing previous strides women have made in terms of earning respect as athletes. Kane (cited in Youngblood, 2006) also argued that those athletes who show off their bodies to get attention for their sport ultimately trivialize and marginalize women in sports. The rationale for many of the athletes is that it is a way to promote their sports. It does bring attention, but is it the right kind of attention? As for gaining attention for the sport, Kane responded, "I've found no statistical correlation to readers of *Playboy* increasing ticket sales for the WNBA" (cited in Youngblood, 2006). Supporters argue that once men are lured to the game they might appreciate female athletes for their talents. Menzies (cited in Stubbs, 1999) compared this rationale to men going to Hooters for the chicken wings. Rosenberg (2007) argued that athletes such as Amanda Beard are not exchanging their athletic fame for the fame of a model. Their athletic fame *is* the fame of a model.

Some female athletes are refusing to be objectified for their sport. Danielle Drady, ranked second in the world in squash, wrapped her naked body in cling wrap. She then hung a "for sale" sign around her neck and invited the media to take pictures of her (Kessel, 2006). When asked to model a revealing outfit, badminton star Gail Emms stated, "[The sponsors] are always trying to get me into ... some sort of contraption that I couldn't fit one boob into, let alone my arse" (cited in Kessel, 2006). Youngblood (2006) stated that there have been a few marketing campaigns to counteract the sexualized images of female athletes' bodies. In 2006, Nike featured an ad campaign that glorified strong, muscular women. The copy read, "My butt is big, but that's fine, those who scorn it are invited to kiss it." Youngblood (2006) noted, however, that the angle at which the photograph was taken sexualized the figure.

Boswell (2004) wrote that she wonders why more people are not more upset. In her opinion, one answer is that sex and sports have become intertwined. Kane and associates (2002) argued the situation might be different if there were lots of coverage of women's sports. But sexualized photographs are some of the only images of female athletes we see. It sets up artificial expectations of gender and sports. These images create the foundations for boys' images of women. Many of the editorials I found were resigned to the sex/sports connection. Arnett (2005) stated, "No one ever said this sex-appeal prejudice was fair. It's just reality." Following this logic, would it not be advantageous for baseball to allow steroids use? After all home runs sell. Perhaps hockey and football should have fewer rules that protect the players. After all, violence sells. It is a sad commentary on our society if female athletes have so few choices to make decent money and get attention that they feel pressured to pose nude.

O'Connor (2004) stated that when athletes allow themselves to be photographed with portions of their breasts and buttocks exposed, they are sending the message, "We are objects, not athletes. Ogle us. Desire us." Kane (cited in Huang, 2004) stated that women should be proud of their muscular, athletic bodies, but wondered to which muscle group bare breasts belong. She insisted that society at least be honest that those images are to titillate men. Kane added that thinking *Playboy* spreads show off women as competent athletes is either naïve or foolish. If nudity were a way to celebrate athletic bodies, we would see equal numbers of nude male athletes. Boswell (2004) concluded that female athletes, especially Olympians, belong on Wheaties boxes and not exposing themselves in men's magazines.

15. FANTASY

Psychiatrists and child advocates argue that age compression or KGOY (kids getting older younger), is hurting children by robbing them of their childhood. A big part of childhood is fantasy and play. Both are increasingly becoming more mature in nature. Little girls are in a hurry to grow up and become sexual beings as modeled by the dolls they play with and the female action heroes they see in the movies and on television. Age compression is shrinking the market for toys such as baby dolls, action figures and other mainstays (Shen, 2002). Toys-R-Us Inc. is closing stores and laying off workers because the peak of the toy age has fallen to age 8. Sales of Barbie dolls are down since she is now considered a babyish toy for 3-to-5-year-olds—previously she appealed to 6 to 10 year olds. Tweens (generally 8–12 years old) are abandoning toys in favor of movies, music, and microchips (e.g., Playstations, cell phones, etc.). Fisher-Price now markets a line of toys called "Pre-Cool," including laptops for 2-year-olds. According to a company spokesperson, the toys are for smaller children who want to emulate older kids. Well-meaning education-oriented electronic toys are harmful to children's creativity. Singer (cited in Shen, 2002) stated that computer games produce convergent thinking and alter children's learning styles.

Many children's fantasies are directly related to gender roles and likely influence children's expectations of what it means to be male and female. Even with so much talk about gender-neutral child rearing, toys are perhaps more sex specific than ever. Whereas "girl" toys used to center on mothers-in-training, they now feature sex-objects-in-training. Store aisles are filled with sexy dress-up costumes and makeup and nail kits. The toy aisles present boys with a double bind: they are fed the Peter Pan phenomenon of never growing up on one hand, but are encouraged to be aggressive like adult men on the other. This chapter looks at the development of fantasy in children's lives. Fantasy topics include video games, professional wrestling, comic books, and dolls.

Video Games

Sexualization of women is present in a significant number of video games. Children Now reported that 38 percent of the female characters in video games are scantily clad, 23 percent bare breasts or cleavage, 31 percent expose thighs, another 31 percent expose stomachs or midriffs, and 15 percent bare their behinds ("Sex and Relationships" n.d.). Female characters are drawn with tiny waists and exaggerated breasts. Critics claim that not only are these female characters victims of violence, but at times they are also victims of sexual violence. It was quite shocking the first time I saw a female victim explode in a bloody mess. Most of the female characters that are killed are dressed suggestively. As they are blown up or shot up, the player may get a shot of her underwear as her skirt flies up or a shot of her breasts as her blouse is torn. Video games such as *Grand Theft Auto* reward players for having sex with prostitutes and beating them up afterward to get their money back.

My senior seminar class addressed this phenomenon one day. I asked one of my students, Brian, to play the game for the rest of the class the same way his peers would play. The other students, both males and females, laughed when he picked up a hooker. After she got in the car, Brian had to circle around a few times in order to find a private place to have sex. He finally found an alley. The car then began bouncing up and down repeatedly, indicating the two characters were having sex. Immediately after the car stopped bouncing, the car door opened and the prostitute was dumped off into the street. The students continued to laugh as he beat her up to get his money back. They claimed the laughter was because of the absurdity of the actions, not because they enjoyed abuse of prostitutes. The shock factor lost its effect and after a time the students were no longer laughing, but appeared rather bored. It appeared they had become desensitized after about ten minutes.

A review of the video game *Hitman: Blood Money* stated that women are targeted in the game; however, not consistently, contrary to some opinions ("Hitman Blood," n.d.). Supporters of the game claim that the controversy mostly comes from the marketing of the game. For example, an ad in *Maxim* magazine for *Hitman: Blood Money* featured a woman in lingere on velvet sheets with a single bullet hole in her forehead. The tagline read "Beautifully Executed." Additional ads were a cellist with a slit throat with the caption "Classically Executed," a body in a freezer with the caption "Coldly Executed," and a dead naked woman in a bathtub with an electric toaster in the water with the caption "Shockingly Executed."

There is a major discrepancy between the number of males and females playing these games. According to Williams (cited in Cohen, 2006), games that portray women portrayed as "whores" may be keeping some female players away. *Dead or Alive Xtreme Beach Volleyball* features a cast of female volleyball players on an island. The attraction to the game is likely the scantily clad women with very large breasts. In *Outlaw Volleyball* as well, women are playing in thongs (not too far from the real thing). *Playboy* magazine featured nude versions of four female videogame characters in 2004 as part of an article entitled "Gaming Grows Up."

According to Herz (1997), female video game characters of the past were window dressing and incapable of any action. They were prizes to be carried off by the victor. On the other hand, there are video games marketed to girls; however, they often appear to be quite silly and the characters are passive. Games featuring Barbie and Mary-Kate and Ashley Olsen, for example, represent a significant number of "girl" video games. Over time, women have emerged as the main character of the games. Female video game characters are becoming increasingly dangerous and even lethal. Games have been developed for characters such as Buffy the Vampire Slayer and Xena Warrior Princess. Instead of just being there to look at, these characters are active in adventures. Feminine power, however, appears to come only with a tiny waist and large breasts. One would think these characters would have a difficult time performing action stunts in their tight outfits and with their enormous breasts.

Tomb Raider character Lara Croft was initially conceived as a male character, someone who was a "cold-blooded militaristic type." Instead she developed into what one Wikipedia writer ("Tomb Raider," n.d.) described as a female Indiana Jones. Croft came from a privileged upbringing. Like many female video game characters, she is out to avenge the death of her father after his murder. She wears very large guns in a holster that hangs low on her hips. Critics claim it is a replacement phallus. Although she is a killing machine, her thin waist and large breasts magnify her femininity. According to Herbst (2004), Lara reflects masculine desires in that her design exudes hypersexuality. Rumor has it that her creator accidentally "blew up" her breasts to 150 percent of normal size. The response from other designers was overwhelmingly positive and so it stuck, so the story goes.

When confronted with sexism claims about the video game industry, supporters point to Croft as an example of a strong character. Croft gains her existence only when the "user" turns on the game. One player stated, "She is so beautiful and has these incredible breasts but still she is totally under my control. Whenever does this happen in real life?" (cited in Herbst, 2004, p. 27). Any female empowerment gained through her action is negated by her subjugation as a video game character. Herbst (2004) added that women's complaints about Croft's appearance are often silenced. They are pushed to ignore that the image of Croft was created neither by them nor for them.

Similar to Croft, the main character in *Red Ninja*, Kurenai, is out to avenge her father's death, which she witnessed. The murderers hung her by a wire and left her to die as well. One reviewer described her as a "buxom, scantily robed assassin" ("Red Ninja," n.d.). Players can make Kurenai do "sexy" things to "lure guards to their doom." The reviewer stated, "Red Ninja makes you wonder why the leaders of ancient Japanese armies just didn't employ whole armies of large-breasted female ninjas with come-hither looks in their eyes" ("Red Ninja," n.d.). BloodRayne is also a very sexual character, dressed in a revealing leather corset with six inch stiletto heels. Her character is a product of a rape. She commits a series of murders while hunting down her vampire father. While she can jump long distances and is very skilled at firing a gun, she was also described by a Wikipedia contributor ("BloodRayne," n.d.) as a "classic pale beauty—blood red hair and piercing eyes—bloodthirsty American dhampir." Aeon Flux is described as a tall, scantily clad secret agent, skilled in assassination and acrobatics. She is also a model for a foot fetish magazine called *Foozwak*. One Wikipedia ("Aeon Flux," n.d.) contributor described the game: "Graphic violence and sexuality, including fetishism and domination, are frequently depicted." One of the hit women, Eve, in the *Hitman* series is described by a reviewer ("Hitman Blood," n.d.) as young and sexy; the reviewer also said Eve "mounted her victim before stabbing him with a knife."

Comic Books

Many female comic book characters have a history of being sexualized. Adult versions have been around as long as comic books. A popular form of comic book drawing is known as "Good Girl" art. "Good" does not refer to the quality of the character. "Good" refers to skill of the illustrator to create sexy female figures. The women in the drawings are often far from moral or sexually chaste. They are usually in skimpy or form-fitting clothing and designed for erotic stimulation. The Comic Book Scare of the 1950s had a chilling effect on the comic book industry. The newly formed Comics Code Authority (CCA) restricted not only graphic depictions of violence or gore in crime and horror comics, but also sexual innuendo. According to the Comic Book Code of 1954, nudity in any form was strictly prohibited ("Code of Comics," 1954). Even suggestive postures were unacceptable. Dress had to meet standards acceptable to society. Females were to be drawn realistically with no exaggeration of physical characteristics. Other restrictions ranged from "sexy, wanton comics" to depictions of "sex perversion," "sexual abnormalities," and "illicit sex relations" as well as seduction, rape, sadism, and masochism. Storylines were supposed to emphasize the "sanctity of marriage" and those portraying scenes of passion were advised to avoid stimulating "lower and baser emotions."

The number of adult comics increased in the 1960s and 1970s as the culture changed from one of repression to one of "free love." Outfits became more revealing, breasts became larger, and more sexual storylines were depicted. Some female stars of the era were Barbarella and Valentina. Often these "sex kittens" were cold-blooded killers. To some critics, Ursa, a villain featured in the Superman series, was one of the most brutal female characters in comic books ("So You'd Like," n.d.). Ursa reportedly killed men with her thigh high boots and kicked one man in the testicles until he died. Many of the female comic book characters gained more notoriety in video game and film versions.

Japanese comic books known as anime often have very sexually explicit, adult themes. *Random House Dictionary* defined anime as a Japanese style of motion-picture animation, characterized by highly stylized, colorful art, futuristic settings, violence, and sexuality ("Anime," 2007). Hentai is a type of anime that is pornographic. Hentai originated from the Japanese word "perverted" or "perversion." Both hentai and anime porn sites on the Internet include very explicit images of bondage, lesbianism, and double penetration. The female characters have extremely large breasts and "soulful, innocent eyes."

Superheroes in Film and Television

Many of the most popular female comic book characters have been made into live actor movies and television shows. The characters are usually sexualized and therefore marketable to both male and female audiences. According to one documentary, the transformation of female comic book characters was not only sexual; the characters also were given intelligence and cunning ("Ultimate Super Heroes," 2005). Characters such as Modesty Blaise and Barbarella in the 1960s and 1970s became sexier and more physically dominant than previous female heroes. Blaise was outfitted in a skin-tight black outfit with black mod boots ("So You'd Like," n.d.). *Barbarella*, played by Jane Fonda, represented the sexual revolution of the 1970s. Posters of Fonda in her Barbarella outfit graced the walls of many adolescent boys' rooms. In the 1980s, Michelle Pfeiffer made an impression with her skin-tight latex Catwoman outfit in *Batman Returns*. She has been compared to a dominatrix, with her whip and high heeled boots. Other memorable roles of sexualized comic book adaptations were Uma Thurman as Poison Ivy and Alicia Silverstone as Batgirl. African American female actors such as Eartha Kitt and Halle Berry broke new ground playing superheroes. Grace Jones was said to have been a spectacular star, with her dominant physical appearance and facial expressions ("Ultimate Super Heroes," 2005).

According to fans, few characters compare to Pamela Anderson's appearance in *Barbed Wire*. The character was described as having big guns, big hair, big heels, and big breasts ("Ultimate Super Heroes," 2005). Supporters consider her the most gorgeous Barbie doll heroine of all time. One fan ("So You'd Like," n.d.) stated, "With every indulgent curve, she towers over her enemies and is quite brutal in carrying out her brand of justice." The adult cartoon series *Stripperella* was modeled after Anderson, who was also the voice of the character. Her character, Erotica Jones, was a stripper by night and superhero by later night (Pollet & Hurwitz, 2003). Her power source appears to have resided in her enhanced breasts.

Supermodels such as Rebecca Romijn, Cindy Crawford, Elle Macpherson, and Famke Janssen have been cast in fantasy or superheroine movies. These models turned actors used their physical appearance, such as height and physical fitness, in the roles. The roles can be compared to Arnold Schwarzenegger's and Sylvester Stallone's roles in action movies. They are cast mainly because of their looks and because they have as few lines as possible.

The casting of Lynda Carter as television's *Wonder Woman* was typical. She had very narrow hips and an incredibly tiny waist that highlighted the size of her breasts, much the way the comics were being drawn. She wore a strapless bustier and tiny little shorts with high-heeled boots. The golden lasso she carried symbolized the fantasy of bondage for some male viewers. *Bionic Woman* was perhaps the exception. She was not particularly feminine in the way she dressed, although she had long flowing hair and an attractive face. She was quite serious and did not giggle or flirt her way into success. Another adapted character was *Xena the Warrior Princess*, a spin-off of *Hercules*. Lucy Lawless, who played Xena, was tall and broad shouldered, a different body type than any other female hero. Xena wore a skirt, but so did Hercules. She was described as hard but vulnerable. Her character became a lesbian icon rather than a sex goddess.

Other television characters with superpowers were Jeannie of *I Dream of Jeannie* and Samantha of *Bewitched*. These characters were safely placed in the genre of situation comedy. Although Jeannie was not allowed to show her belly button, her harem outfit was quite sexualized. She was every man's fantasy of having a blonde bombshell obeying your every command.

Adult Sexy Superhero Costumes

Halloween is a time when people pretend to be someone they are not but perhaps always wanted to be. It is a chance for even the mildest mannered female to express her bad girl side. Many of the costumes follow a pattern of making even an angel into a sex object. Many women, or at least costume manufacturers and shops, see it as an opportunity to dress sluttily, to wear lingerie in public. Especially popular in 2006 were the naughty fairy tale characters. Perhaps it is a reaction to the helpless princess waiting for Prince Charming. This time she's waiting with a garter and stockings. Skanky versions of Alice from *Alice in Wonderland*, Dorothy from the *Wizard of Oz*, and Snow White could be seen out celebrating the Halloween holiday. The outfits appear to give the wearer an excuse to not only dress but also to act in a more provocative way.

Professional Wrestling

Women's wrestling was outlawed in several states until the 1960s because it was viewed as immoral (Farrell, 1942). Thesz (cited in Albano and Sugar, 1999) argued it was a ploy to titillate the men in the audience. In the 1970s women "accompanied" male wrestlers to the ring to offer their support for their men and to serve as weapons of distraction for the opponent. Throughout the

1980s and 1990s even the women who wrestled were slowly transformed into sexual entities. At the start of the new millennium, female wrestlers adopted more muscular builds, while becoming thinner. A majority of female wrestlers at the top level have had plastic surgery, specifically breast implants. The implants seem counter intuitive to a contact entertainment. Even the daughter of the owner (Vince McMahon) of the WWE got breast implants. Part of the ringside announcer's job is to sexualize women at every opportunity. They have delivered one-liners such as, "She certainly seems comfortable with that microphone up at her mouth like that" (cited in Assael and Mooneyham, 2002, p. 221).

Female wrestlers are represented in a variety of ways that range from powerful competitors to weak sex kittens. On one hand, women have been used to titillate a male audience. On the other hand, women's inclusion in wrestling has allowed them to participate and demonstrate their athletic abilities. Female wrestlers often defend the practice in interviews, claiming that they can be sexy and strong at the same time. A muscular build is powerful; breast implants are not. Sable became "the prototype for the aerobicized temptress in ass-hugging spandex" (Assael and Mooneyham, 2002, p. 225). Sable filed a multimillion dollar lawsuit against the WWF, claiming she was pressured into doing nudity and lesbian scenes (Orecklin, 1999). Four years later she reentered the wrestling ring wearing nothing but body paint in the shape of handprints over her breasts. She apparently either exaggerated the circumstance to try to get a cash settlement or she decided to endure the humiliation for a fee.

Chyna, at 6 feet and 200 pounds, was often described as the Amazon woman or Dominatrix. She wore black leather halter tops that revealed a lot of cleavage from her breast implants. Because of her physical appearance, it was rumored that she was actually a man. She reportedly had plastic surgery on her jaw to make it more feminine. She appeared as the centerfold in *Playboy*, partly to prove she was a woman. Debra created a frenzy with audiences. She wore business suits that were so tight and the skirts so short that they conveyed sex rather than power. Her gimmick was to lean over the top rope exposing her cleavage to distract the male wrestlers. The audiences screamed "puppies," a reference to her breasts. To tease fans, she often seductively unbuttoned her suit jacket to reveal a lacey bra underneath. In a live match I attended, Torrie Wilson appeared in the ring wearing short shorts and a crop top. The live audience catcalled as she bent over, very deliberately, first to tie her shoes and then to adjust her kneepads. (The kneepads got a special cheer, a symbol for performing oral sex.)

Stephanie McMahon started off as the sweet, innocent daughter of the WWF owner. Her character, however, became skankier. She wore short skirts, tops that showed a great deal of cleavage (to show off her new implants), and "F me" boots. She wore heavy makeup, especially dark around the eyes. Over time the plotline and her character took a radical turn. In one storyline,

Stephanie resorted to using her sexuality to get a wrestler to sign with her on *SmackDown!*

One gimmick that was extremely popular with fans was The Godfather, an African American wrestler who dressed like a pimp. He was accompanied to the ring by a string of local strippers known as the "Ho Train." Young boys in the audience would hold up signs and chant his signature catchphrase, "Pimpin' ain't easy." Women's matches ranged from exploitative "evening gown" matches, where the winner is the one who can strip the evening gown off the other—leaving her in bra and panties—to radical "hardcore" matches. In the glorious tradition of jell and mud wrestling, the women wrestled in a pool of gravy for Thanksgiving. Wrestling in these substances shows the women as something to be consumed. Mud gives the illusion that the women are dirty. Female managers would escort their men into the ring and inevitably engage in catfights with each other, rolling around in the ring with their thong underwear exposed under their skirts. Jhally (2002) described wrestling as stripping women of clothes and hence any power or agency. He argued that WWE is essentially a strip show, bringing conventions of pornography into mainstream entertainment.

The concept of Diva is prevalent in World Wrestling Entertainment. The Divas are marketed through calendars, magazines, videos, and websites. Professional wrestling has accelerated the physical ability of women at the same time they have increased the emphasis on sexuality. One of the many Diva pay-per-views, "Sex on the Beach," featured female wrestlers writhing around in the sand wearing thong bikinis. The "Divas Undressed" video features the winner of the "Golden Thong" award. *Playboy* has featured a number of professional wrestlers such as Sable and Chyna. These issues have been some of the magazine's best sellers. The WWE had a competition among the Divas, the winner of which, Torrie Wilson, appeared on the cover of *Playboy*. Most recently, Ashley posed for the magazine in 2007. Not only have wrestlers posed for pornography, adult film stars such as Jenna Jameson and Jasmine St. Clair have appeared on wrestling shows.

Fringe companies, which are not associated with the WWE, are quasi-pornographic shows that tour different venues. The shows, such as *Women's Extreme Wrestling*, feature women rolling around in oil, ripping at each other's clothes and spanking each other. According to their website, fans get "adult film stars, violence, T & A, nudity and of course some wrestling" ("Women's Erotic," n.d.). Wrestling characters' names range from "G.I. Ho," "Barroom Barbie," and "Psycho Bytch," to "Missy the Schoolgirl." One line reads, "Amy [Lee] can best be described as a very large, biker bitch!"

Fairy tales/Disney

Grauerholz (cited in Patterson-Neubert, 2003) argued that fairy tales about princesses being rescued by Prince Charming are harmful to children by reinforcing gender stereotypes. She also argued that the stories tell children that unattractive people are more likely to be evil. Little girls get the message that they are special only if they are pretty. In a content analysis of 168 Brothers Grimm fairy tales, Grauerholz and Baker-Sperry (cited in Patterson-Neubert, 2003) found that evil was associated with ugly in 17 percent of the stories and physical appearance was acknowledged in 93 percent of the stories. In one story alone, they found 114 references to beauty for females compared to 35 for males. Females are often cast in only one of two roles, the princess or the evil stepmother. Although Brothers Grimm fairy tales often have dark themes, almost half have been made into children's movies, or at least reproduced in children's books.

Some critics argue that fairy tales, especially Disney's adaptation of those fairy tales into movies, are rife with sexualized female characters. Disney's female characters have been described as "full figured, big breasted, sexually charged male fantasy icons" ("More Charming Disney," n.d.). One writer for the *New York Times* commented that Pocahontas was an "animated *Playboy* Centerfold," which has no place in a children's movie (cited in "More Charming Disney," n.d.). In order to set up a romantic relationship between Pocahontas and John Smith, Disney changed her age from 12 to twenty something. According to some reports, Disney was looking to appeal to an adult male demographic. One angry blogger wrote, "Why do adult males need to be appealed to in a children's animation? Are adult males now masturbating to Disney animations?" ("More Charming Disney," n.d.).

One blogger described Esmeralda as doing a sexy pole dance in the animated Disney version of *The Hunchback of Notre Dame*. Riley (n.d.) described characters such as Pocahontas and Ariel as curvaceous, slightly fretful, but essentially innocuous heroines. My sister refused to buy her three daughters *Little Mermaid* merchandise because she thought the seashell bikini top worn by Ariel was inappropriate and sexy. One of my friends who has a daughter said it was nearly impossible to buy diapers without a Disney Princess on them. One of the few examples of a movie that breaks with traditional stereotypes of beauty is *Shrek*. In the story the main female character lives happily ever after only when she is transformed from a beautiful maiden into an ogre (Patterson-Neubert, 2003). However, valuing internal beauty is the exception rather than the rule.

Dolls

Dolls are generally passive, often just meant to be looked at rather than actually played with. Even when dolls are flexible, it is not to move them but to pose them. Action figures, on the other hand, are meant for action, emphasizing the clear gender splits between girls and boys. In some ways, dolls train girls to be dolls, quiet and objectified. Doll fashion is marketed to very young girls. Early on they learn what constitutes fashion. Toy manufacturer Hasbro planned to make Pussycat Dolls to sell to little girls. Doyle (2006) described the Pussycat Dolls as striptease performers in "stockings, suspenders and very little else." After protests by groups such as Dads & Daughters, Hasbro has canceled the line of dolls, admitting it was for a more mature audience ("Plans for Dolls," 2006).

Barbie

Ruth Handler created the Barbie doll in 1958 in order to give little girls an alternative to traditional baby dolls. She stated that it was "important to a little girl's self-esteem to play with a doll that [had] breasts" ("Barbie," 2005). Supposedly Barbie was influenced by Lilli, a "swell-chested, semi-smutty doll" that was initially marketed to adult men in bars in Germany. Many critics have pointed to Barbie's unrealistic proportions, whose equivalent to a real woman would be 39-21-33 (Barlett, Harris, & Bonds-Raacke, 2005), as a bad role model for children. Norton, Olds, Olive, and Dank (cited in Bartlett, et al., 2005) argued that she would not be able to stand in her size 3 children's shoes because she is so top-heavy. Both Handler and Mattel argued that the exaggerated proportions are necessary for the clothes to fit properly on such a small scale ("Ruth Handler," n.d.). Even though a direct link between Barbie or action figures and negative body image has not been proven, research has laid the groundwork for such studies. One study showed that people perceive Barbie as beautiful, although her measurements are unrealistic, dangerously so (Turkel cited in Bartlett, et al., 2005). The probability of a woman attaining Barbie's measurements is less than 1 in 100,000 (Bartlett, et al., 2005).

Historically Barbie was quite conservative when she was introduced in the 1950s. Over the next decades she changed in terms of her figure, fashion, and social role. Originally her eyes looked "demure" according to Barlett et al. (2005). In 1971, she began to look straight ahead, which is thought to be a more powerful gaze. Barbie received new career options in 1975: doctor, surgical nurse, ballerina and flight attendant. Black and Hispanic Barbies hit the market in 1980. "Generation Girl" Barbie sported a nose ring and an ankle tattoo in 1999. In 2000, Barbie got a belly button. By 2005, Barbie had gone "couture." Marketers offered a Diva Collection and Couture Collection, with lines from famous designers such as Juice Couture, Kate Spade, and Armani.

Barlett and associates (2005) pointed out that there are some nonsexual aspects to the dolls; for example, Barbie has no nipples and Ken has a "genital bump rather than a proper penis." However, if you twisted Grown-Up Skipper's arm, who was introduced in 1975, her breasts would expand. Muslim countries such as Saudi Arabia object to Barbie's provocative clothing.

Bratz

Bratz dolls have overtaken Barbie in many parts of the world as the number one selling fashion doll. In 2005, Barbie sales dropped by 30 percent in the United States ("Barbie," n.d.). The Bratz dolls are also known for having fun, detailed accessories and play sets that reflect their "cool" (and somewhat materialistic) lifestyle. Bratz dolls are somewhat controversial because of their heavy diva-like makeup and their "oh-I'm-so-bored heavy attitude expressions" ("Controversies About Bratz," n.d.). Bratz are marketed to girls as young as four—complete with skimpy clothes and heavy makeup. They are billed as "boy crazy fashion fiends" ("Sex Sells," 2005). Malacrida, a publicist for Bratz, argued that the dolls are about girl power, starting trends, and making fashion statements (cited in "Sex Sells," 2005). The Bratz website described its fashions as having heavy and, at times, dark makeup and henna tattoos. There are lots of short skirts and bare midriffs. Sleepwear is pretty modest but does include very short nightgowns. The site tells little girls to "flaunt it, express your Genie Style by wearing: deep colors, wavy hair partially up, gold colored jewelry, a shawl wrapped around waist, beaded slippers" ("Bratz Style," n.d.).

Most critics complain that Bratz dolls glamorize hooker chic. Crouse (2003) pointed out their glazed expressions, pumped lips and trampy clothes. Whoopi Goldberg (cited in Crouse, 2003) joked that white parents had no clue their children were being indoctrinated into "ghetto values and culture." Crouse argued that Bratz dolls look as though they get collagen lip injections instead of breast implants. The Bratz "Superstyling Funktivity Book" is like *Cosmo* for six-year-olds. It includes topics such as "Luscious lip tips," "Design your own sexy skirt," "Is your crush real?," "Tips on being an irresistible flirt," and "Are your friends jealous of the amount of attention you get from boys?" ("Bratz Style," n.d.). Graydon (2005) argued that these messages are devastating. She cited busy parents, kids with money and access to media as the culprits. The one upside according to critics is that the dolls are multicultural and multiracial.

Bratz Babyz are smaller versions of the original Bratz dolls. They have young features such as pigtails, but they also have makeup. The website states, "Please wait.... It takes time to look this good" ("Bratz Super Babyz," n.d.). Evidently it is never too early to start obsessing about one's looks. Bratz Babyz are wearing short T-shirts with what looks like little boy underpants exposed. In the movie, they enter a karaoke competition complete with sexy outfits and sexy dance routines. They are shown flirting and batting their eyes to get their way. Since their introduction in 2001, the makers of Bratz dolls have sold more than $1 billion in dolls and merchandise (Crouse, 2003). What is most troubling, according to Crouse (2003), is that mothers of preteens are buying most of them.

American Girl

American Girl dolls offer a more wholesome choice over Barbie and Bratz dolls. The dolls are dressed in modest clothing of a certain period in American history. Each doll is accompanied by a book that explains the background of the character and teaches wholesome values (Meadows, 2005). In the American Girl doll series, girls are offered outfits to match their dolls. Although the dolls and clothing are very conservative, they are prohibitively expensive for many girls. Some critics argue that these features are getting little girls set up for designer fashion and instilling values of status. There is an entire American Girl empire in New York City, Chicago, and Los Angeles. Floor after floor offer not only dolls, clothes, and accessory choices, but also hair salons and photo studios. Party packages are as much as $250 per girl. Afternoon tea is more reasonable at $19.

Club Libby Lu

There is a store in the mall called Club Libby Lu. It is awash with pink and glitter and tiaras. There are a variety of "VIP—Very Important Princess" and "mini diva" items in the store. Some of the items are very childish but others are more adult. For example, there are robes with fur around the cuffs. While I was passing by I witnessed a birthday party in progress. Six little girls dressed in Arabian outfits (low-rise flowing pants with midriff tops over one shoulder) were crowded around a table. They were leafing through a makeup book that had "rock star" styles. The store clerks were working on the girls' hair and makeup. Traditionally girls played with their mothers' makeup, being creative and playful. These girls were getting "industry" makeovers. The whole thing seemed more strippers-in-training than an innocent party activity.

According to the Libby Lu website, the makeover choices are Rocker ("You'll rock in this hot pink headband and choker"), Tween Idol ("sparkly microphone" headset), Priceless Princess ("tiara fit for a princess"), Super Star ("cool pink hair streaks"), and Royal Heiress ("Complete this royal look with fabulous sun glasses") ("Parties & Planning," n.d.). The photos are pretty tasteful—that is, if the models were adult women. Dressing up when I was a little girl was about creativity and putting together unique looks from ordinary items our mothers had laying around. The "looks" offered here are all prefab, with little or no room for deviation. The company is dictating what it means to be a "princess."

Conclusion

In the past, children used their imagination when they played and created their own fantasies. Like much of life today, fully developed fantasies are manufactured and marketed to children. Play appears to be very structured. Toys come with pages and pages of instruction on how children "should" play, rather than letting the child determine how they can play. Video games often present only limited ways to win. Halloween costumes are pre-made, cheap plastic imitations of their favorite television and movie characters. Even Big Wheels are now motorized.

An additional concern is that fantasy television shows, movies, video games, and dolls designed for very young children often have very adult themes. Even Disney movies sexualize their princesses. Parents need to be especially diligent when it comes to monitoring the types of fantasies marketers are feeding to children. Sexual images can often sneak under the radar because the video games, movies, etc., are supposedly age appropriate. At least it says so on the package.

16. EMPOWERMENT OR EXPLOITATION?

A man approaches a woman and asks if she would have sex with him
for a million dollars. She said yes. Then he asked her if she would have sex
for $10. She said "Absolutely not, what do you think I am, a prostitute?"
He responded with, "We've already established that, now we're just dicker-
ing about the price."

—W. C. Fields

The women's movement in conjunction with the sexual revolution promised women empowerment. When women symbolically burned their bras in
the 1970s, they were taking charge of their sexuality. They were casting off the
restraints of a patriarchal system that bound them in corsets. Birth control pills
gave women control over their reproduction. Instead of embracing the gains
made by their foremothers and continuing the fight for empowerment, many
females today are choosing to participate in their own sexual exploitation.
They are offering their bodies to men in exchange for attention and acceptance. They are enthusiastically competing for the opportunity to exploit themselves in front of millions of people (e.g., reality television and shock jock
radio). They are willing to endure a great deal of pain and risk of death to
have larger breasts. It is doubtful that middle school girls are giving boys oral
sex in the back of the school bus as an expression of their desires and sexuality; rather, it is a desperate attempt to get the boys' approval.

These behaviors often stem from the notion that a woman's worth is tied
to approval of others, particularly men. Negative behavior is often seen as the
quickest and easiest way to get attention. Individuals who are not brought up
to derive worth from inside themselves are susceptible to exploitation from others. Teenage girls are desperate to feel loved and are increasingly willing to
put up with bad behavior from males, including dating violence. This is especially true if their fathers have been abusive or absent.

Empowerment Debate

Traditionally, power is gained through physical superiority, wealth, and
control of resources. There has been a shift to thinking power can be achieved

through sexuality, which is temporary and superficial. Some girls and young women are trying to attain power by getting males to look at their bodies when they dress in suggestive clothing, teasing males on the dance floor by grinding their bodies against them, and showing how liberated they are by flashing their breasts and making out with other girls. This type of power, however, likely diminishes other positions of power women have achieved. Rarely do people think sexy and smart together, especially when today's role models are the current posse of young, out of control female celebrities.

Clements (2002c) argued that a big part of feminism is supporting women's choices. It is difficult to resolve the debate between whether women should be protected from exploitation or if they should be free to use whatever means they have to get what they want. Feminism is a broad umbrella housing a range of points of view. For example, Chapkis (cited in Barton, 2006) described two types of feminists, "radical feminists" and "sex-radical feminists." Radical feminists see the sex trade as exploitative. Their goal is to protect naïve and economically desperate women from being taken advantage of by a patriarchal system. Sex-radical feminists, on the other hand, view sex work as actually liberating because it goes against traditional female roles. According to the sex-radical philosophy, women can choose to be active decision makers regarding how they will use, even exploit, their own sexuality. Supporters see sexuality as empowering and reject the notion that women are victims in the sex industry. Eaves (2000), for example, stated she was irritated by the stereotypes of exotic dancers as abused, desperate, and lacking freedom to "escape."

Strippers often defend their choice of profession by claiming empowerment. The rationale they give is that sex workers control men because men have to pay for their services. Liepe-Levinson (2001) contended that it is not the women who surrender their sexuality when they strip; rather it is the men who surrender when they are at a strip club. She argued, "In the social hierarchies of the strip show, the ability to spend money does not necessarily guarantee the male customer's ability to wield power, because the biggest spenders are often labeled the 'biggest suckers' by patrons, managers, and dancers alike" (cited in "Conversation with Liepe-Levinson," 2005).

The assertion that men surrender their power in strip clubs is a farce. Granted, a male customer may temporarily and voluntarily surrender his power, but he can restore that power at any time. He can choose to withdraw his money, physically grab or assault the dancers, or hurl insults at them. It is unlikely he will experience any reprimand at most clubs. Male owners of strip clubs rarely risk losing valuable customers. The argument that women are in control is like saying a child is in control when an adult lets them win at a game. The child is not really winning, just as the women are not really in control unless men "let" them. This, of course, is not to say women are children; however, in the context of the sex industry women have little actual power.

Women in general have less physical strength and fewer economic resources, especially in the strip club environment. They also have no clothing to protect their most vulnerable body parts.

An exotic dancer is at the mercy of the male customers to tip her, the male club owner to employ her, and the male bouncers to protect her. Even if the male customers are kicked out of the club, there are plenty of other outlets for them to see naked women. For example, they can also go home and watch naked women on the Internet for free. The women in strip clubs are dependent on the men coming in and tipping for their livelihood. Men are there simply for pleasure or entertainment. The stripper is likely there to put food on the table for herself and her children. Even in the case of the Dominatrix, the man establishes and dictates the fantasy. If she were to vary from the script, imagine his outrage. At that point he would take back his power over her. He has paid her to go against social norms, but only as much as he allows.

Critics argue that it is ridiculous to equate men's loss of money with women's potential loss of dignity. The customer is giving up money he has likely earned by selling his skills at a "regular" job, whereas she is earning her money by selling herself. Another factor threatening the theory of women's empowerment is that the ownership of adult magazines, pornography studios, and strip clubs is almost exclusively male, as are pimps. Although the performers may be seeing some of the benefit, it pales in comparison to what the majority male owners are making. Since most dancers are contract workers, owners pay no salary and take a substantial cut of the tips. For the owner it is pure profit. He controls how often women work and how many women work per shift.

According to Bell, Sloan, and Strickling (1998), dancers and customers experience mutual exploitation. Strippers claim they have power over men because the men are paying them. However, does the average person feel like they have power over their boss because they are being paid? Do servers feel superior to their customers who give them tips? I have never felt power over a boss because he or she has paid me for my work. When I waited tables, I felt good when I got tips, but I figured customers could get food without me, and therefore, I had no power in the situation. There were a few times where management sided with me over abusive customers, but generally I saw the customer receiving preferential treatment no matter how horribly they treated the wait staff. It is hard to believe strip clubs are any different.

In some of the strippers' autobiographies, they claim they can decide to refuse customers' requests if they are being mistreated. If a particular stripper refuses a customer, however, there are plenty of other dancers who will cater to him. The dancer is dependent on significant numbers of men per night to make her quota. She could end up owing the club money at the end of the night after she pays stage fees, the DJ, etc. In some sense, the dancers set the rules and conditions—but of course the male customer has the final decision on how much he is going to pay her. Because they likely receive no salary from the club, dancers are totally reliant on tips, large portions of which they do not even get to keep. Being choosy is not always an option for them. Those in the sex industry who are able to pick and choose are the exception rather than the rule.

Sex industry jobs could be seen as a way for women to play a system that is already in place. It may be quite rational to think if men are going to treat women as objects, then the women might as well use their sexuality to make money. Further, men are willing to pay large amounts of money for titillation; why not exploit that for financial gain? Supporters of pornography argue that the sex industry actually empowers women. If the industry can reframe sex work as female empowerment, producers escape responsibility for exploiting and humiliating women. They do not have to defend the industry to critics if the women themselves defend it.

Barton (2006) found that over time sex workers shift from feeling empowered to feeling oppressed. Exotic dancers reported empowering can easily become exploitive. Almost all strippers' stories that have been told here either through conducting interviews or by reading autobiographies and blog entries included a description of their first time as fearful. For many it was only after desensitization, after repeated performances, that they no longer experienced anxiety.

Researchers have attempted to determine whether dancers are being exploited or empowered by observing the interaction between female strippers and male customers. Because strippers are paid to create a fantasy onstage, it may be difficult to assess the situation accurately from the outside. Asking strippers directly can also be unreliable because the women may have convinced themselves that they are empowered by stripping. By contrast, if women do not believe they are taking pleasure in dancing, they must admit they are being exploited. Experts in attitudinal research, particularly cognitive dissonance, explain that humans are uncomfortable when their behaviors are in direct contrast to their beliefs. Festinger (1957) found that individuals dislike dissonance and are motivated to relieve the discomfort. There are several ways to accomplish relief. The most obvious way is to discontinue the behavior, in this case stop dancing. Many dancers admit they are dependent on the money or addicted to the attention. If the initial motivation to strip was to demonstrate how evolved and sexually secure one is, then admitting it was a mistake and stopping is detrimental to one's self-image.

A less challenging method than changing the behavior is to change one's attitude about the behavior. One alternative is for dancers to convince themselves they do in fact enjoy the behavior. A dancer is likely to reframe the issue, shifting her belief that she is being exploited to believing she is in control of the situation. Another alternative is to diminish the negative aspects of the behavior by comparing it to another alternative that is worse. For example, she might argue that stripping is okay because at least she is not prostituting herself. Call girls will minimize what they do by arguing that at least they are not streetwalkers. Seeing few alternatives for employment, some women elevate the choice they made to strip. Many dancers argue that it is better to strip than work at Wal-Mart for minimum wage. Individuals may also rationalize the behavior because it is simply a means to an end. For example, dancers may rationalize stripping as a way to achieve a greater goal such as paying for college or saving enough money to do other things.

The dissonance created by feeling exploited is rarely addressed. It is easier to give women the illusion of choice, thus silencing critics. Mattson's (1995) recount of her experience of stripping looks fun at first read. The money allowed her to do other things, including getting an Ivy League education. But as much as she described her experience as "wonderful," she wrote how she paid a price. She was often judged by others and isolated outside the club. The few hours a week she spent at the club making money appeared to have taken a significant toll on the rest of her life.

Legal Protections and Physical Risks

Whether women should be protected from a patriarchal system of exploitation or given the right to choose their profession has long been an issue in the feminist movement. Leigh coined the term "sex worker" in 1978 in an effort to change the focus from women being seen as victims to women voluntarily working in the professions of prostitution, pornography, and stripping (Barton, 2006). Taormino (2000) defended the term sex worker because sex is work and should be treated like any other job. Therefore, some argue that sex workers should at least be protected by labor laws.

Supporters of the sex industry often claim that women are exploited and harassed in all fields of employment; therefore, abuse in stripping and pornography is a fact of life. Sex workers are perhaps the most vulnerable workforce in society, physically and emotionally. The atmosphere is conducive to harassment and assault. Not only are sex workers in danger on the job, they are often stalked and assaulted outside of work by overzealous "fans" (Layden, 1999). Sexual assault is perhaps the most degrading of all crimes and creates the most long-term damage to its victims. Although some sex industry supporters compare working at Wal-Mart to stripping, being grabbed while one is completely exposed and vulnerable is hardly comparable to being forced to wear an ugly smock and clean up aisle seven.

Clements (2002d) demanded that those who are willing to take on the risks of the sex industry have the right not to be protected from themselves. As a society, we protect people from themselves all the time. Minimum wage and labor laws are in place not because workers are stupid or helpless; we have labor laws because employers with the resources, and thus the power, are likely to exploit their workers to make a profit if given free reign. The premise that if women do not want to take on the risks of stripping they should not do it is faulty at best. Workers have always been desperate enough to work for almost no money; however, our society has minimum wage laws in place to prevent employers from taking advantage of workers. Likewise, laws regarding over-time pay (although the Bush administration made sure to reverse this protec-tion for many workers) and safety standards are implemented to protect those individuals with less power. In much the same way, society would be protect-ing women from being exploited by a patriarchal system where women have little control. When laws have been passed regulating strip clubs and partic-ularly lap dances, responses from the dancers were mixed (Lewis, 2000). The main difference between whether a dancer supported the law or not depended on how much control she thought she had over the situation (Lenney, n.d.).

Women in strip clubs are supposedly protected by the law and manage-ment; however, it is only after the abuse has occurred that the perpetrator suffers any consequences. In most clubs patrons have full access to the dancers as the women are generally trolling the audience looking for lap dance cus-tomers. The dancer is completely vulnerable once the lap dance begins. In one of the backrooms where I observed women giving lap dances, couches were surrounded on three sides with partitions. Although there was a bouncer sta-tioned at the door, almost all of the dance areas were out of his line of vision. If a patron did assault a dancer, it would be a while before help arrived.

It seems almost impossible to think a man who assaults a dancer in a strip club will be arrested. Bringing in the police would only make the club look bad and chase away other customers. The sex industry makes money from fan-tasy and escape from the real world where men are held accountable for their behavior. I was told by workers at one strip club that very little was done when male customers get out of line. According to one dancer, being grabbed is just part of the job, a trivial infraction at the most. The perpetrator will likely get a "talking to" and then let back in the club. She stated it was made clear to her that the clubs are selling sex, so what do they care if there is an incident every now and then. It is unlikely a sex worker will protest, for fear she will be labeled a troublemaker and likely fired. The women are protected in most cases only because of their worth as commodities. There may be some senti-mental feelings toward some of the women, but that sentiment is heavily out-weighed by profit margins. The common experience of the successful strippers' stories I read appeared to be that they were the "favorites" of the club owners and management, and therefore received special treatment. The other dancers were easily replaced and left to fend for themselves.

I would imagine women in the pornography industry would have even fewer protections than strippers. According to Jameson (2004), "In a worst-case scenario, a gonzo director will take a girl to a hotel room and have their friends shoot a cheap scene in which she is humiliated in every orifice possible. She walks home with three thousand dollars, bowed legs.... She'll regret it—to her dying day." Because the women voluntarily go to the room, there would be little or no recourse for any abuse that happened. Our society has demonstrated little compassion for women who seemingly "ask for it." In addition, legal pornography includes rape scenes; therefore an actual rape caught on tape could be dismissed as part of the storyline.

Workers in the sex industry are expected to take risks. They risk physical and emotional harm to provide entertainment for others. Much like an athlete who takes risks on the field or on the ice, a sex worker is not fully protected at her place of work. When a hockey player or football player takes an illegal hit that could cripple him, little happens to the offending player, in most cases. Actions that would constitute assault and battery if performed on the street are just part of the game. In a similar vein, women who are touched sexually without their consent inside a club or on a porn set are not seen as sexual assault victims as they would if this action took place on the outside to a woman not in the sex industry. Grabbing is considered a hazard of the job and rarely taken seriously. When those defending the industry say women are protected, they are only partially right. Barton (2006) argued that perhaps the best feminism can do to protect women in the sex industry is to increase their control at work and offer alternative economic options.

Some strippers graduate to prostitution as a way of earning extra money. The risk is greater because of the secluded one-on-one interaction. There may or may not be a third party there for her protection. Prostitutes are unlikely to convince police and a jury that they were raped. It is understood that she put herself in that position; therefore, what does she expect? Many people believe that if she is willing to sell herself, then her body is not worth as much as a "respectable" woman's. Our culture appears to use this reasoning only when it comes to rape. I have never heard anyone make the case that if someone rents their car to someone it is a lesser offense if that car is later stolen. Outside the sex industry, accusations of rape are often questioned, particularly if the man is a celebrity or athlete. The danger is that some individuals may see a connection between women's willingness to have sex for money and a perception that women would be willing to cry "rape" for money. In many ways, victims are both blamed and abandoned. They are faced with plenty of people who are willing to pay for their services but very few who will support a safe and fair environment.

Kipnis (cited in Kirk & Boyer, 2002) argued that pornography is a class issue rather than a morality issue. She pointed out there is often a class separation between the consumers of porn and the employees of the sex industry. The issue of class was a major element of the Duke lacrosse scandal. College athletes (privileged, white, and male) hired two strippers (poor, black, and female) to entertain them by taking off their clothes. In a book about the incident, Yaeger and Pressler (2007) attacked the woman who accused the players of rape, describing her as "a ghetto stripper, a step removed from bullet wounds, tattoos, and cuts." Littlefield (2007) commented that the description made it seem as though she deserved to get raped if she had. Littlefield called it ugly and irrelevant.

Female Customers

Clements (2002c) claimed that there are more and more couples going to strip clubs together. She acknowledged that some of the women go to keep an eye on their partners or to keep their men from cheating. Other women go to make their men happy or to look like good sports. Goldman (2006) reported that some clubs are marketing to couples, "recasting the strip club as an equal opportunity adult destination." Several questions arise with this new coed experience. What happens when women participate as consumers in the sex industry? Does it make the sex industry more mainstream and thus acceptable? Is it liberating that women go to strip clubs and watch porn? Will the influence of female consumers have a positive impact on the portrayal and treatment of the sex workers? Or will women's participation further entrench the subjugation of women and make it even harder to fight exploitation?

Clements (2002c) stated that female customers, the ones who choose to come to the clubs, often have a better time than the men. She reported women surprise their partners and themselves and become caught up in the action. She stated, "More and more women are realizing that sex play is a delicious part of life, and that the erotically charged, lively and libertine atmosphere of a topless bar can be exciting and oddly freeing and not the den of degradation they had always pictured." Of course, female customers get to go home to their safe lives, while the workers are often stuck at the club. It is important to note that the women on stage and the women in the audience are in different power structures. Goldman (2006) also reported that women tip better. She argued dancers pay more attention to the woman because she holds the power in the couple. The women in the audience perhaps can afford to spend a great deal of money on entertainment. The working women in the club are likely earning a living to simply support themselves and perhaps their children. (If strippers make so much money, why don't we see more stripper millionaires?)

The Hooters organization claimed they support feminism because they allow women to use their natural sex appeal to earn a living ("About Hooters," n.d.). A former president of a local chapter of the National Organization for Women stated, "I give those women credit for exploiting the pathetic male market. Hooters exploits them, and the women who work there know it" (Oestreich cited in Samuels, 2003). Female workers often defend Hooters. A former employee, Austin, credited her "Hootering" for her getting her a job at Playboy Bunnyland ("About Hooters," n.d.). (This is probably not what the founders of the feminist movement had in mind when they set out to gain gender equality and respect for women.)

It appears to be a daunting task for feminists to make changes to improve the lives of women when women themselves are showing their support for the exploitation of strippers and Hooters Girls. Even though some of them feel sorry for the women who have to work in these establishments, it is doubtful they are going to stand up for dancers' rights for better working conditions. They may dismiss claims that these women are being exploited, concluding that the women they just encountered seem to be treated well and make money. In my experience and through many interviews, I do not see female customers being much different than the men who leave the club and then show personal disdain for strippers. Although they had a good time, it is clear they are eager to separate themselves from the dancers.

Othering

One way for society to continue to exploit women even further is to divide and conquer, to segregate those in the sex industry from the general female population. The term "othering" is often used by members of a group who wish to distance themselves from those with less power. They claim it is the "others" who perpetuate stereotypes about the group. Hooks (1994) argued that this is common practice for members of a stigmatized group. They frequently marginalize others in the group in order to raise themselves. Oppressed groups often turn on one another as a way to elevate themselves. They single out others for ridicule to make themselves look better. The ultimate distinction of the Bible was Mary "the virgin" and Mary Magdalene "the whore." Although it was written that Jesus loved both women, rarely is anyone today so kind. Even our fairy tales and Disney movies portray women as either the good princess or the evil witch, with few characters in between. Angell (2004) stated that people are frightened of "normal" looking prostitutes. She made the case that it would be easier for society if prostitutes were more recognizable instead of looking like their neighbors or sisters. In other words, when sex workers do not fit the stereotype they are less easily othered.

Men have long distinguished between "good girls" they can take home to Mom and "not so good girls." Part of the definition of masculinity is a man's ability to protect women while at the same time desiring to exploit them. Barton (2006) argued that men distinguish between "their" women and "other" women. There seemed to be a distinction for male customers between strippers' motivations. For example, they distinguish between women stripping because they enjoy it and others stripping to support a drug habit. It appears to be much easier to compartmentalize women as desperate with a family to support, a drug habit to support, abused, exhibitionists, and college students looking for some easy money. Some men may even get off on the submissiveness and the desperation of these women. Clements (2002c) argued that men are taught that women outside of society's norms deserve no respect and may be the recipients of hostility and humiliation. For example, the current debate about the treatment of women in the hip-hop culture included a discussion of whether words such as "bitch" and "ho" should be used in the lyrics. Some supporters claim there are women who deserve the title, therefore, it is acceptable to use the terms. The female Rutgers basketball players appear to be exempt from the terms because they "represent themselves well" and are college students.

Women also participate in the good/bad distinction of other women perhaps even more than men. Instead of protecting women's respectability, they often further the stereotypes (Barton, 2006). Even among those employed in the sex industry, there is othering. Dancers blame other dancers who "do nasty things" for giving all dancers a bad reputations. Mattson (1995) stated, "I refused to be dragged down like some of the strippers" (p. 257). She specifically referred to a fellow dancer who had been abused as a child and later became addicted to drugs and alcohol. Mattson distanced herself from the other women. She made it clear to her readers that she came from a good family and had chosen to strip to put herself through an elite college. Ashe (cited in Crotty, 1999) stated, "I have a real problem with people lumping the stripping business to the sex industry. The sex industry is about pornography, prostitution and that kind of thing. Stripping is about fantasy." There appears to be a hierarchy within the sex industry, ranging from strictly topless dancers to fully nude strippers who do special favors for their clients, from porn actresses who do not do anal and dp (i.e., double penetration) to those who do, and from high priced call girls to street-walking prostitutes. The hierarchy includes those who are performing for the thrill or to put themselves through school and those who are doing it out of financial desperation or to support a drug habit. Angell (2004) admitted that she is scared of sex workers on the street even though she worked for an expensive escort service. Although they are in the same business, Angell (2004) claimed streetwalkers and call girls have nothing in common. She made sure her readers knew that she went from being an adjunct professor at an Ivy League school to being a call girl when her boyfriend left with all her money.

Modern Feminism

There was a great deal of momentum in the women's movement in the 1970s. Women were joining together to battle a common enemy of patriarchal oppression. Each victory gave a sense of satisfaction that propelled them to striving for more change. Like all great social movements, there was a backlash. Conservative organizations pitted women against each other. "Women's libbers" were labeled as troublemakers and "feminism" was demonized. Particularly conservative women were warned to stay away from feminists or suffer the consequences. The Equal Rights Amendment, which simply stated that women could not be discriminated against because of their sex, was killed when women such as Phyllis Schlafly spread fear that the ERA would result in women being drafted and same sex marriages legalized.

The feminist movement has apparently hit a place of complacency. In some ways the movement has gone backwards. Although feminists continue the cause of advancing women's equality, they are chastised and called "man-haters" by other women. The spiral of silence is alive and well; not only are women and minorities in our society oppressed, they are also vilified if they speak out, thereby being further silenced. While almost 100 percent of my students (both male and female) are in favor of equal rights for women, very few will accept the label of feminist. As I was doing research for this book, both men and women attempted to silence me for even asking the question of whether women were exploiting themselves. I have been pressured to stop "overanalyzing" and to comply with the status quo. We are living in a polarized time where few people are willing to look at the gray in life. It really upsets me that women cannot even ask questions without being harassed and their opinion devalued. Similar to a sex worker being told to just shut up and perform, feminists are told they should just let men have their fun and not question whether it has long-term repercussions.

When women spoke out against the comments made about the Rutgers basketball team, Knapp (2007) stated, "It's a relief to hear a young woman speak that way, and sad to realize that a lot of us give up on those ideals." Many women hold back because others may question their femininity or, in this specific case, loyalty to their race. It is particularly difficult for women of color to protest. There was a backlash against the women at Spelman College when they protested Nelly coming to campus because of his exploitation of women in his videos (see chapter 8). There was a backlash against DeLores Tucker when she spoke out against misogyny in rap in the 1990s. According to John-Hall (2007), Tucker was routinely dismissed as being a "turban-wearing, out-of-touch dinosaur." Tupac Shakur slurred Tucker by rhyming her surname with an obscenity on one of his CDs.

Women of color have also been ignored in the fight for equal rights in general. Rose (cited in Neal, 2005) wrote, "Feminism is the label for members of a white women's social movement, which has no concrete link to black women or the black community." The struggle in the African-American community is finding a balance between "sanitizing" images of black women and images of the "most vile notions of sex and sexuality" originating in slavery stereotypes (Neal, 2005). Pough (cited in Neal, 2005) stated that the "sexually explicit lyrics of these women rappers offer black women ... a chance to be proud of—and indeed flaunt—their sexuality." Feminism is often classist, mostly benefiting white middle-income women. Middle-class women debate about stay-at-home moms, while working-class women have always worked outside the home to support the family.

Knapp (2007) explained that women don't stand up for themselves because they are tired of fighting and want to fit into the mainstream. When women worked for equal rights in the past, the idea was that women should be given opportunities to work for success. Young women have become complacent with what they experience as equality. Now the mission of young women is apparently to gain attention at any cost. Young people have always been interested in satisfying short-term goals. This idea of having to work for long-term goals is not as attractive in a culture intent on immediate gratification. The Paris Hiltons of the world symbolize to young girls a shortcut to a glamorous life.

Neo-feminists argue that women have already achieved equality. When I talk with my female students, I find a very idealistic generation when it comes to sex equality. Colleges and universities are very controlled settings where women now outnumber and outperform men (in most majors). By accepting stripping and pornography and the sexualization of women, there is a feeling of liberation. However, at the same time females are earning college and professional degrees at a higher rate than males, eating disorders and breast implants are at an all-time high as women strive for physical perfection. Popular fashion includes shirts marketed to women with derogatory sayings such as "bitch in training" and "instant slut, just add beer." Posing nude for *Playboy* magazine has become a status symbol for women. There is no shortage of women willing to humiliate themselves on shock jock radio or reality television shows. Howard Stern admitted that the skits would not be funny if the women on his show did not feel humiliated.

Young women's reasons for rejecting feminism may be a defense mechanism of not wanting to see that they are being exploited or that they need to be protected. Society has also gotten very good at masking its prejudices. Masked sexism is worse than overt sexism because, while it has a similar effect, it is difficult to identify. There is a fine line between being objectified and being complimented or receiving positive feedback for physical appearance. The increased insecurity from media images of "perfect" women pushes young women for external validation. Women are still tempted to use their sexuality to get ahead in situations ranging from work to getting free drinks at a bar.

Conclusion

The question remains: did women gain power just to end up exploiting themselves in even more humiliating ways? As women gain more rights and higher power positions, there almost always appears to a backlash or price to pay. Strippers and porn stars are taking directions from men and then are expected to be thrilled for the opportunity to perform for them. They are told they should feel empowered by selling their bodies for a scant share of the profits. While some financially desperate women see no other way than to participate in the sex industry, the privileged have other options. The females appearing on *Girls*

Gone Wild videos rationalize they are exploring their sexuality for fun and attention, not exploiting it for profit. These acts certainly gain attention, but this kind of attention likely creates a worse climate for women in general. It perpetuates the stereotype of women as dumb bimbos. Women in the sex industry see them as stupid for giving it away for free. Shaw (2005) asked, "How is resurrecting every stereotype of female sexuality that feminism endeavored to banish good for women? Why is laboring to look like Pamela Anderson empowering? And how is imitating a stripper or porn star—a woman whose job is to imitate arousal in the first place—going to render [them] sexually liberated?" (¶11).

Supporters of exploitation rationalize all the time. I have heard arguments such as "It is okay to bring your children to Hooters because women wear less clothing on the beach"; "Beauty pageants are okay because participation in sports often takes the same amount of time"; "It is okay for female athletes to exploit their sexuality because it attracts more spectators." Various reasons to flash one's breasts include "It is spring break and the young are supposed to be wild"; "Everybody else is doing it"; and "I might as well expose myself while I am young and still attractive."

More and more young people are resigned to the practice of the media to use women's sexuality to attract consumers and sell products. Actresses and models continue to get dangerously thinner. Current stories about celebrities starving themselves pretend to be about health concerns; instead, the continued exposure likely exacerbates the problem by rewarding it with more exposure. These women are getting even more attention by starving themselves than they did at healthy weights. The music industry appears to be backsliding as well. "Bitches and ho's" lyrics are more explicit and more prevalent than ever. The exposure the Don Imus scandal gave to this type of music has only proved to make it more popular. Protesters are silenced, called names, and told they are too sensitive or they are infringing on other's freedom of speech. The explosion of the pornography industry is undeniably aided by the Internet. Porn stars such as Jenna Jameson speak out about how empowered they are because of the money they earn. They ignore the vast majority of the women who are violated and abused by the industry. Titillation is clearly equated with the degradation of women. If it were not taboo, it is unlikely pornography would be as popular and as thrilling to the viewer.

This topic is important because our culture is shaping future generations of women. Young women and girls have not had a chance to explore their own sexuality before someone is there telling them how it should be done, in magazines and entertainment shows. It appears there is an arms race of sorts, where women need to push the sexual envelope in order to keep getting attention. Health concerns also are a factor, with the media being influential in the body image of young women. Also, men must be aware of factors that influence their perception of women and their perceived entitlement to dominate and demand sex from women.

What are we doing to make things better? Dove developed a campaign to counteract the emphasis on impossible physical beauty standards. Their 2006 Super Bowl commercial featured the song "True Colors." The message Dove presented was that little girls worry about being pretty and thin enough. Dove's answer was "Let's change their minds.... We've created the Dove self-esteem fund because every girl deserves to feel good about herself and see how beautiful she really is." This is part of their "campaign for real beauty." Every once in a while there is a television show or movie that values inner beauty and unique characteristics, such as *Little Miss Sunshine* and *Ugly Betty*. The audience loved the boldness of Olive and her "inappropriate" talent. Betty is a champion for all the not so outwardly beautiful people. But that sentiment is not coming across with enough force in popular culture.

17. CONCLUSIONS

There are few young female role models in the media other than actresses, fashion models, and daughters of the rich. Although there is a great deal of criticism about the "pop-tart" phenomenon, records sales and demand for celebrity photos of young female performers, with little or no talent, show no signs of slowing down. *FOX News Online* even has a "Pop Tarts" section that is dedicated solely to spotlighting the bad behaviors of young female celebrities. One *FOX News Online* headline read, "Jessica Simpson's Breasts Aren't Bogus" (McKay, 2007). Instead of making progress, celebrity females' images are backsliding. Paglia (cited in Hancock, 2006) stated, "These girls are lowering themselves to the level of backstreet floozies.... This is degrading the entire pro-sex wing of feminism.... They are cheapening their own image and obliterating all sexual mystery and glamour." She explained that in the past, sexual allure in Hollywood was dealt out in small doses, unlike today's deluge of sexuality, even from the youngest female celebrities.

Even when women do accomplish outstanding feats in sports, academics, or business, media coverage still emphasizes their sexuality. For example, our culture values Amanda Beard's naked body in *Playboy* far more than her five Olympic gold medals. Rushkoff (2001) argued that young female celebrities such as Britney Spears send these messages to girls: "I am a sexual object, but I'm proud of it," "Your body is your best asset," and "Flaunt your sexuality, even if you don't understand it." Girls and young women are learning that the easiest way to get attention is to use their sexuality. Fergie's lyrics describing how she can be a lady and at the same time dance like a whore sum up a great deal of the sentiment of this generation.

The roles and expectations of today's generation of young females do not appear to be one of sexual liberation but rather that of self-exploitation. In this chapter, I explore the motivation for girls to go over the line and exploit their own bodies. Environmental factors such as commercialization of our culture are pushing age compression and all but eliminating the childhood of girls. There has been a gradual shift in the mainstreaming and normalization of taboo behavior. Parents have a significant role in the evolution and can do a great deal to reverse the trends, or at least slow them down.

Motivation

Young girls have a dismal crop of role models in popular culture. With widespread media coverage, bad behavior is more glamorous and mainstream than ever. Cameras are ubiquitous, always ready to transmit the images of outrageous stunts by movie stars and professional athletes to the youth of America. Entire segments of the media are fixated on superficial fame and the phenomenon of the young, rich, and spoiled. Television shows such as *Rich Girls, Sorority Life*, and *The Simple Life* glorify the shallow and fleeting fame. Cable channels VH-1 and E! produce programs that feast on the lives of heiresses, highlighting their outrageous and spoiled behavior (e.g., *Trust Fund Babies, Bad Girls of Reality TV, Young Divas*). Today's celebrity, which takes little or no effort or talent, represents a shortcut to attention. In spite of all the "bad behavior" coverage of Paris, Lindsay, and Britney, rates of teen pregnancy, drinking and drug use have not increased. In some cases, overall rates have even decreased (Deveny, 2007). Girls may not be imitating these exact celebrity bad behaviors, but the effects are more subtle. Deveny (2007) argued that these out-of-control celebrities give a sense of normalcy to drinking, casual sex, and relationship hopping. A more cumulative effect is likely to express itself. The most obvious effect is that childhood is shortened. Girls are more sexualized at younger ages. They appear to be acting out and dressing as though they are looking for sex, even if they are too young to really understand what that means. Some high school and even middle school hallways and dance floors resemble soft porn videos.

Need for Attention

The primary issue that emerged from my research is an almost compulsive need for attention that has prompted subsequent outrageous behavior by girls and young women. Overindulged children live in a world where they are the center of their parents' universe. Many of them believe they are entitled to material wealth and attention. Similar to get-rich-quick schemes, girls are buying into get-noticed-quick schemes by altering their appearance and behavior. Negative attention is just as, if not more, powerful than recognition for positive achievements. Promotion for *Girls Gone Wild* videos include only the most beautiful and popular women. The party atmosphere and positive attention given to these women is a key strategy. The videos also incorporate male celebrities such as Snoop Dogg to help promote sales. Whereas most women in the sex industry are desperate for the money, privileged college students are flashing for the *Girls Gone Wild* cameras just for the attention and maybe a T-shirt. Girls as young as middle school are making out with each other and giving boys oral sex. Rather than expressions of sexual liberation, these acts are more likely just desperate ploys for attention. As they get older, young women appear to be turning to larger audiences to gain attention. Millions of people are privy to their bad behavior when they appear on reality television shows and post their sexualized photos and videos on MySpace and YouTube sites.

Rushkoff (2001) labeled the new trend of young female prototypes as "Midriffs." He described them as prematurely adult and consumed by appearances, while boys that age are arrested in adolescence. In one scene from the documentary *Merchants of Cool*, Rushkoff (2001) included a scene where hundreds of parents paid up to $4,000 to get their preteen and teen daughters in the International Models and Talent Association convention. It was obvious these midriffs had already been schooled in the art of self-exploitation. Girls in their early teens skillfully flirted with the adult judges. Most of the girls interviewed were already self-absorbed. One thirteen-year-old girl stated, "I want people to notice me, and to say like wow, she is pretty. I have to look good for people. I need to look good. If I don't look good, I get really upset and it ruins my day" (Rushkoff, 2001).

Lisker (cited in Reitman, 2006) found that women in college feel tremendous pressure to do well in school and get the right internships. However, at the same time, many of them feel the need to have perfect hair, skin, clothes, makeup and a size-four body. Lisker stated that she is worried that women who are smart and driven are still letting men set the social rules. Being accepted by their peers is so important to women that they dumb it down. According to the high school girls Rimer (2007) interviewed, it is cool to be smart, but being smart is not enough. The girls reported they also have to be pretty, thin, and "effortlessly hot." One girl stated, "If you are free to be everything, you are also expected to be everything."

Pressure to Be Cool

Women in this younger generation are expected to be okay with the exploitation of women's sexuality, even their own. On shock jock radio, the general sentiment is that if women are not willing to pose nude, then they somehow have "hang-ups" about it. Wolf (2003) argued that young women and girls are being taught that to be cool they have to go to strip clubs with the guys and ask for lap dances. Pollet and Hurwitz (2003) reported that one young woman stated, "We all want to be the girl who's comfortable going with her boyfriend to a strip club.... You want to be the girl who isn't fazed by going to Hooters.... No one wants to look repressed." Paul (2005) argued women are caught under new forms of social pressure from men and other women to not disdain porn. Paul stated that females have bought into, or at least pretend to buy into, the argument that pornography is just part of women's sexual self-expression. On one hand, it could be that women have become more comfortable with their sexuality and perhaps more accepting of women's right to use their bodies to make a living. On the other hand, there is a stigma of not supporting men's enjoyment of the sex industry. Women who object (whether for feminist reasons of protecting women or religious reasons of seeing the practice as immoral) are told they have "hang-ups." Feminists for Free Expression ("Feminism Free Speech," n.d.) claimed that half the adult videos in the U.S. are bought or rented by women alone or women in couples. It is unclear whether the women are doing it for their own pleasure or if they are pressured to be cool with pornography to please their men.

Pollet and Hurwitz (2003) argued that the mentality of trying to be cool and sexually free is what is contributing to *Girls Gone Wild* behavior. One Long Island high school confiscated string bikinis on a class trip. The girls argued their rights had been violated. One girl stated, "I'm not such a naïve little girl that I'm unaware of my own body, my own sexuality.... What exactly was it that they were protecting me from?" (cited in Pollet & Hurwitz, 2003). Girls and young women in particular are pressured early. Media portrayals dictate that they need to make out with other girls to show how liberated they are. Otherwise, they are ridiculed for being uptight or angry feminists.

Parents

According to Deveny (2007), attentive parents and strong teachers help counterbalance the bombardment of oversexed, underdressed celebrity images in the media. Over the past 30 years, time spent at the office has increased by 10 hours a week for most parents (Bryner, 2007). Parents are increasingly working more hours, yet, at the same time, studies show they are spending more "quality" time with their children than in the past few decades. St. George (2007) cited a study that showed married mothers and fathers are spending more focused time on their children than they did 40 years ago. Single parents' time, however, has slipped. Bianchi (cited in St. George, 2007) stated that today's parents are feeling they are not spending enough time with their children no matter how much they do. Some speculate that the guilt of working longer hours increases not only the intensity of parental involvement but also the desire to make the child happy regardless of the consequences to that child's healthy development. Parents who fear they will displease their children contribute to the problem by giving in to their children's every wish. Individuals who feel they did not receive their every desire when they were growing up are now bestowing them on their children. Too many parents want to be their children's best friends and therefore overlook bad behavior while supplying limitless material possessions. In cases of divorce, there is even more guilt and competition between the parents. Children often learn to play one parent off the other for more things and leniency toward bad behavior.

Parents are supposed to love their children unconditionally; however, it does not mean they should like unconditionally what their children do, especially if the children are doing harm to themselves. Interviews with porn stars on Howard Stern's show showed how proud and supportive the parents were of their daughters. The lack of boundaries and the acceptance of all decisions regardless of their consequences are astounding. It is an enabling kind of love. They are solely concerned with their children's happiness rather than their long-term mental and emotional health. The child's short-term happiness and immediate gratification is put ahead of raising a productive adult. Parents often side with their children against teachers who attempt to discipline students and threaten lawsuits if punishments for bad behavior are not revoked and failing grades are not changed to passing grades. Surveys of teachers who quit in the first five years often cite parents' interference as a major reason why they quit. In 2003, a group of senior girls tortured a group of juniors in a suburb in Chicago. They doused their victims with feces, urine, toxic paint, and blood after they punched and kicked them (Winfrey, 2003). Instead of making their daughters take responsibility for the acts, some of the parents hired attorneys and sued school officials for taking action against the perpetrators. These parents also threw an alternative prom when the school prohibited the girls from attending their prom.

Sometimes it is the mothers who are poor role models to their daughters. One father (cited in "The Parent Trap," 2005) stated that some of the clothes his eleven-year-old daughter wears make her look "trashy" and her shoes make her look like a stripper. The mother justified allowing her daughter to wear sexy clothing because she herself was not allowed to go out or wear makeup when she was young. She stated, "I promised myself that if I ever had a daughter, I wouldn't let her suffer, because I really resent them for it. I think if Alexia didn't fit in, I'd be extremely crushed, devastated" (cited in "The Parent Trap," 2005). She also claimed that she does not say "no" because she also wears the sexy clothes and high heels. In a youth-obsessed culture, mothers may themselves act and dress inappropriately. There appears to be a lack of clear boundaries of what is appropriate for adults and what is appropriate for little girls. Fashion designers use age compression to sell more clothing to girls who want to look older and women who want to look younger.

Another mother, who admitted that she allows her young daughter to wear sexy clothing, stated she has not had the sex talk because she thinks her daughter is far too young ("The Parent Trap," 2005). In this case, it seems incredibly irresponsible to let a child look sexual but not explain the ramifications. The daughter claimed, "Being sexy is, like, I guess you have to follow trends.... You're more popular if you're sexy. Do you know what I mean? Because nobody wants to be, like, a loner." The little girl also admitted to threatening to never talk to her parents again if they do not buy her the clothes she wants. Some parents want their children to be happy in the moment so they can feel better about themselves. A 10-year-old girl (cited in "The Parent Trap," 2005) described tight-fitting clothes as making her look cooler. She stated she loves her "sexy" clothes and that "They're clothes that could be really tight that show off your body, you're sort of half naked in it. You feel, I guess, sexy a bit." Although the mother made her change, I am curious where the 10-year-old got the sexy clothes in the first place.

Some parents also seem to be living vicariously through their children, pushing them into every activity available. Interviews with parents clearly demonstrate the pressure they put on their children, sometimes unconsciously. Deveny (2007) questioned parents' own obsession with celebrities. If children see their parents obsessing over *People* magazine and *Entertainment Tonight*, it gives them a measure of what is important. Parents are often complicit when it comes to middle school girls dressing like hookers and underage girls getting breast implants. Deveny argued that many of these problems could be solved if parents just refused to pay. Parents have a role and they need help to combat all the other messages their children are getting from peers and in the media. The parents' job is to help their children feel good about themselves on the inside and to resist outside pressure. Buying the clothing and financing cosmetic surgery is reinforcing our culture's obsession with physical appearance.

The Millennial Generation

Each generation has its own particular culture characteristics. Children born in or after 1982 have been labeled "Gen Y" or "Millennials." This era is marked by car seats and biking helmets. New fertility treatment gave couples the chance to have children, which translated into a significant increase in their obsession with children. According to Howe and Strauss (2000), "Starting as babies, kids were now to be desperately desired, to be in need of endless love and sacrifice and care—and to be regarded by parents as the highest form of self-discovery" (p. vii). They concluded that the Millennial Generation is an interesting mix of entitlement and pressure to succeed (Howe & Strauss, 2000). Twenge (2006) reported that Millennials have the highest self-esteem, but also the highest incidents of depression. She argued, "Instead of creating well-adjusted, happy children, the self-esteem movement has created an army of little narcissists" (p. 223). Critics explain that it is characteristics of this generation that made *Girls Gone Wild* videos possible.

Many parents of Millennials are described as helicopter parents (always hovering), while extreme parents are known as "Black Hawks." These are parents who obsess about which preschool their toddler attends and later use "Track My Teen" GPS devices to never let their children out of their sight. They reportedly write their children's college application essays and threaten professors about their children's grades. The trend has extended through college and now even into the workplace. According to Shellenbarger (2006), parents are tagging along on job interviews and calling workplaces trying to renegotiate their child's pay packages. Some companies have given up and are marketing jobs to parents since the children (and they do consider them children) look to parents for decisions even after they graduate from college. These parents are often so involved in their children's lives there is no room for their sons and daughters to make errors and thus be disappointed. Critics argue that while sheltering children from potential harm, parents are also depriving them of valuable decision making and self-sufficiency skills.

There has been an explosion of "recreational" lessons (e.g., music, dance) and athletic teams for children as young as 3 (St. George, 2007). I interviewed a woman whose 15-month-old niece is involved in four classes each week: swimming, music, baby yoga, and Gymboree (C. Dupree, personal communication, March 1, 2007). She described Gymboree as a way for her niece to sample a variety of things to see what she likes. The activity in and of itself may be enjoyable and beneficial; however, the price may be paid in the loss of family time and interaction with the parents—other than the child watching the back of Mom or Dad's head from the car seat in the back of the minivan. (Many vehicles now have video screens in the back, so the parent and child have no interaction at all.) These activities, while seemly harmless, set up a lifestyle of structured play and stress as the parents are running ragged to get their kids to their various activities. Little girls could get the idea that the only way to get their parent's and others' attention is through activity such as dance, cheerleading, and beauty pageants.

Our society is also producing a generation of "Daddy's girls." The bonding between a daughter and her father is endearing and essential for a female's development, but, as Freud noted, it can go too far. I wonder about females over the age of 10 who still call their fathers "Daddy." There is an indication of arrested development, of an immaturity that fathers may try to perpetuate with their daughters to keep them dependent. This dependency could lead to the daughters' having trouble with adult relationships later. On the other hand, too little attention from Dad is a recipe for producing strippers and sex workers. Nowak (2003) reported that girls become sexually active earlier and are more likely to get pregnant in their teens if their fathers were absent from the home when they were young. Girls who were raised by stepfathers engaged in sex even earlier, possibly because they learned dating behavior from their mothers. Skipper and McCaghy (1970) found that many girls who disrobe in public do so out of an unrequited need for fatherly love.

Commercialism

As a consequence of parents spending significant amounts of money on their children, manufacturers and marketers are catering to very young girls. Eight to 14 year olds spend $1.7 billion of their own cash each year ("Sex Sells," 2005). The products the market is promoting range from sophisticated toys to designer fashion and beauty products, often before girls are ready to understand the implications. The industry calls it "age compression." Parents give in because they think it is cute to dress their children like adults or they want to spoil their daughters with "fun" things. Many of the mothers perhaps feel deprived from their own childhood and vow to indulge their daughters with superficial items such as clothes and makeup. Fathers may also indulge their sons, but usually it is with items that promote activity, such as sports equipment. The problem is that many parents are going into extreme credit card debt and raising spoiled children who have no sense of delayed gratification. They are bankrupting their child's future and instilling a high priority for material goods.

One divorced mother admitted she was giving her four-year-old daughter everything she wanted in order to compensate for working full time and for her daughter not having a father in the home (see Winfrey, 2006). One example she gave of her overindulgence was that the little girl had over 50 Barbie dolls. In the video clip, it was evident the little girl did not particularly appreciate any of them. The mother's behavior is setting her daughter up to be insatiable. She also took her daughter to get manicures and pedicures every two weeks, as though they were best friends. There appears to be little for the daughter to look forward to when she gets older. It is also selfish because of other little girls who will wonder why they do not have all the things her daughter has. Other mothers will have to deal with the ramifications.

Parents are not only consumed with pleasing their children, but are also competing with other parents. This phenomenon is often manifested through consumption. Parents seem to be in a race to provide their children with designer clothing, extravagant cars and expensive colleges. The new trend is to spend exorbitant amounts of money on themed birthday parties (Quart, 2003). Birthday parties in general resemble an arms race, with parents trying to outdo each other. It is a marketer's dream to get children to associate expensive birthday parties and presents with the love of their parents. The extravagant parties are more often about the parents one-upping other each other than the celebration of an event. This escalation breeds competition between young girls, perhaps singling out the haves from the have-nots. The excessive parties and gifts demonstrate the parents' lack of establishing boundaries. MTV's *My Super Sweet 16* features extravagant parties that wealthy parents throw for their daughters (see chapter 7). Wealthy girls are shown shopping for designer dresses to wear to their 700+ guest parties. The parents are shown indulging their daughters with no boundaries. Mothers are shown as "best friends" rather than as parents. Fathers are shown as "daddies" who will deny their "little girls" nothing. In almost every episode, the birthday girl flies into a fit of rage when things do not go her way.

From interviews with parents, it appears they are conscious of the unreasonableness of the parties; however, they feel they are unable to say "no" and put a stop to the acceleration. Once again, consumerism is linked to love. These parties set a dangerous precedent about what is expected of parents. They demonstrate the escalation of party-mania. This behavior is also pushing parents who cannot afford such extravagance into extreme credit card debt trying to compete so their daughters do not feel less loved. The excess puts tremendous pressure on the girls and their friends. It creates a climate rife with jealousy and bitter rivalries of who is better than whom. Money is like a drug, and, for most girls, there will never be enough. Someone will always have more.

The religious factor for first communions is becoming secondary to the little girls feeling like princesses and pre-divas. There has been an interesting shift from veils to tiaras. Almost all of the websites are focused on little girls. There is no mention of boys' outfits on most of the sites. There are a few sites that offer suits for boys, but most of the emphasis is put on girls' dresses, accessories, and gifts. For example, one site stated, "Her holy first communion is a day she will always cherish" ("First Communion," n.d.). A balloon artist marketed himself on his website as "first communion entertainment" (Obrochta, n.d.). He also gave suggestions about party themes, such as a carnival or even Harry Potter. (First of all, if I am not mistaken, First Communion is the theme. Secondly, it is ironic because some religious groups have criticized Harry Potter for Satan worship. I am just curious about whether he makes a balloon Jesus.)

In some communities the pageantry of the Jewish ceremony of bat mitzvahs is out of control. According to Quart (2003), the religious rite of passage of bar at bat mitzvah has become an extravaganza averaging about $15,000 in some areas of the country. These once religious ceremonies are extremely commercialized. The extravagant parties appear to accentuate the most superficial, if not evil, side of adulthood, such as greed and self-centeredness. A Google search revealed many party planning sites and an offer of planning software. Marketers appeal to parents' guilt. One site offering special software to organize mitzvahs stated, "Trust me, you and your child REALLY don't want to be embarrassed in front of all your fellow family and friends during this significant religious event and then live the rest of your life in regret. Don't you want to do everything you can to make the best possible impression and show your child how special this religious ceremony truly is?" ("My Bar/Bat Mitzvah," n.d., ¶5). An over-the-top example was David H. Brooks, who allegedly spent $10 million on his daughter's bat mitzvah party. He hired musical performers such as 50 Cent, Tom Petty, and Aerosmith to perform. According to the report, "The 50-year-old Brooks changed from a black-leather, metal-studded suit—accessorized with biker-chic necklace chains and diamonds from Chrome Hearts jewelers—into a hot-pink suede version of the same lovely outfit" (Grove, 2005). The 150 kids who attended went home with $1000 gift bags.

Normalizing Bad Behavior

A 2004 article in *The Nation* (cited in Barton, 2006) identified a trend of stripper-inspired consumer habits that women have adopted, such as stripper workout videos, thongs, and stripper poles in teenage girls' bedrooms. Burana (cited in Frey, 2002) stated, "As dancing becomes less stigmatized—cool, even, among pockets of young, middle-class women—and as the media smack us daily with advertisements featuring ecstatic, next-to-naked models peddling perfume, the demand for *more* only grows." Women often "play" stripper, in exercise classes, on Halloween, or perhaps even trying out at amateur night at a strip club. They emulate strippers and rap video vixens, on the dance floor, and their wardrobes (aka stripper chic). They toy with porn star behavior on spring break and in *Girls Gone Wild* videos. Exercise classes have adopted erotic dance moves. Carmen Electra has put out an exercise striptease DVD (Stein, 2003). One instructor stated that the purpose was to get women to be more comfortable with their bodies as they shed pounds (Chaney cited in Santich, 2004). Cody (2006) listed cardio strip classes and stripper-chic fashions worn by teenage girls as signs of mainstreaming.

Mainstreaming Strippers

The influence stripping has had on women's dress and behavior in dance clubs is clear. Some clubs even have poles to make it possible for women to emulate strippers. The difference between a dance club and a strip club is the removal of clothing (although many clubbing outfits leave little to the imagination) and the distribution of dollar bills (perhaps that comes in the form of free drinks). Many of the dance moves between couples would be sex if not for thin layers of clothing. One example is "freaking," where the female bends over at the waist facing away from her partner and he grinds his crotch into her. Another example is when the man picks her up as she straddles him with her legs and he jostles her up and down crotch-to-crotch simulating sex. One stripper (cited in Barton, 2006) commented that she has seen half-naked girls in nightclubs bumping and grinding with guys they just met—for free.

Not only professional but also amateur dance teams incorporate stripper moves. Even the littlest girls' dance teams and beauty contestants perform sexualized routines. Parents, dance teachers, cheer coaches, and pageant officials all seem rather oblivious to the raunchy nature of the moves, particularly with the youngest girls. The adults brush it off as "pretending" and claim that the little girls do not realize what they are doing. Children are sponges and even at a young age remember the positive reinforcement they received for these sexual simulations.

Pollet and Hurwitz (2003) described the striptease as "rebellious, transformative and empowering, a paradigm replicated in many a girl-centric coming-of-age flick in its wake." They referenced the video for Aerosmith's song "Crazy." In the video, Liv Tyler and Alicia Silverstone sneak out of high school and ditch their Catholic school uniforms for a sexier look. To make some money, Tyler enters a contest at a strip club and wins. Pollet and Hurwitz (2003) also pointed out how Oprah Winfrey devoted an hour to "releasing your inner sexpot." The show was described as "overworked moms get stripper makeovers complete with pole-dancing lessons and new lingerie."

Fuse Network premiered a show called *Pants-Off Dance-Off* in 2006. The description of the show on their website read, "The only naked dancing show on TV" ("Pants Off," n.d.). This show was billed as a competition of striptease of "average" people. Contestants stripped completely nude, although the nudity was blocked out and the dancing stops. Viewers were then invited to log on to the website to see the contestants dance nude. Viewers were encouraged to vote via text message for the winner. The dancers include an assortment of goofy guys, hot bodies, and fat women. As the contestants danced, the other contestants trashed them, calling them names and criticizing their appearance and dancing.

Bartenders and servers in many venues flirt and dress provocatively to get tips (e.g., Hooters). Gimmicks such as "Coyote Ugly" hint at stripping but stop short of removing too much clothing. The women dance on the bar and use their sexuality to sell drinks and get tips. They wet each other down so their clothes cling and they offer body shots to the male customers. Coyote Ugly founder Liliana Lovell (n.d.) described her business plan as "beautiful girls + booze = money." She stated, "I hired beautiful girls, trained them to sell and, most of all, how to appreciate the country music in the jukebox. I began training my girls to perform my shtick. Some were good dancers, some were good singers, and others could yell at the crowd and entice them to drink." Country Music Television (CMT) ran a reality series featuring a nationwide search for a new Coyote Ugly bartender. CMT's website described the show: "Witness the tantrums, the triumphs and the tears.... The drama intensifies as the bus gets crowded and the girls face grueling auditions and emotional cuts in their quest for stardom" ("Ultimate Coyote," n.d.). Country music as a genre is very conservative. (The Dixie Chicks were crucified by the country music community for speaking out against Bush's war policy, yet it appears that sexual exploitation of women is to be celebrated.)

Mainstreaming of Pornography

Some aspects of pornography are also becoming mainstream. "Erotica" events are held in regular convention centers, featuring demonstrations of sex toys and personal appearances by porn stars. Many of the fans, both male and female, proudly get their pictures taken with the stars (Kirk & Boyer, 2002). Glasser (cited in Kirk & Boyer, 2002) argued that Hollywood is responsible for mainstreaming pornography. He noted that Howard Stern got listeners to tune in by bringing in porn stars and getting women naked in the studio. Glasser claimed that the discussions of female ejaculation and analingus on *Sex and the City* were extreme—although he specializes in anal sex pornography. It is popular for mainstream stars to pose nude in men's magazines and for porn stars to appear in mainstream media. Porn stars get endorsement deals and appear on MTV videos. Men's magazine such as *FHM*, *Stuff*, and *Maxim* have brought soft core porn to the mainstream magazine racks with just enough clothing so they can be kept in front of the counter and plain-paper-wrapper free. Video games went from rewarding smiley faces eating dots to first person shooters having sex with prostitutes (see chapter 12). One episode of *The Girls Next Door* featured an Easter Egg hunt on the grounds of the Playboy Estate. The episode was entitled "Easter Bunnies."

Aucoin (2006) argued that pornography is coming out of the shadows into the limelight, claiming "porn sensibility" now influences mainstream movies, music videos, fashion, magazines and celebrity culture. Paul (cited in Aucoin, 2006) noted, "It's not just that the culture has gotten sexier. It's that the culture is directly referencing pornography." For example, 12- and 13-year-old girls see Jenna Jameson as their role model and Brazilian bikini waxes often used in porn are now the trend. Paul also argued that perhaps pop music is where the line blurs between music and pornography the most. Dance moves and fashion can be traced directly to strippers and porn stars. Even the Food Network programming has distinct parallels to porn in terms of the cinematography, food presentation, dialogue, and body language (Aucoin, 2006).

Mainstreaming of Prostitution

Prostitutes appeared even in early television westerns. Amanda Blake played Miss Kitty on the western television show *Gunsmoke* from 1955 to 1975. In the earlier radio version of the series, Miss Kitty was just a saloon girl. It was often hinted that she did more than serve customers drinks. On the television series, if the Long Branch did house prostitutes, the show made Miss Kitty warmhearted. According to TV Land's description of the show, Miss Kitty employed a variety of young women to "make pleasant conversation and look pretty for the male customers" ("Kitty Russell," n.d.). Historically, westerns all portrayed brothels. The "feel good" Broadway show *Best Little Whorehouse in Texas* starred a wholesome Dolly Parton as the madam in the movie version. Sappy ballads told of the prostitutes' hopes for the future, not the degrading reality of the present.

Hollywood movies such as *Pretty Woman* glamorized, or at least sanitized, prostitution (see chapter 10). Audiences laughed at the portrayal of male prostitutes such as Dan Aykroyd's Fred Gervin, Male Prostitute on *Saturday Night Live* and Rob Schneider's *Deuce Bigalow, Male Gigolo*. The dark side is portrayed in films such as *Midnight Cowboy* and *Boogie Nights*. In the teen movie *Less Than Zero*, Robert Downey, Jr., paid off a drug debt by having sex with another man.

Our society glorifies the pimp. Audiences evidently see something attractive about the profession, such as having power over women and getting them to sell their bodies for a miniscule percentage of the take. The word "pimp" is used to describe everything from car remodeling to an infant clothing line.

One Wikipedia poster defined the new definition of pimp as "an American slang term for being unique, 'cool,' or socially desirable, in much the same way as the term 'ghetto fabulous.'" Expressions such as "Pimp my ride" have expanded to "Pimp my baby." There is even a line of infants' clothing called "Pimpfants" (see chapter 1). At Britney Spears' wedding reception, the males were given "Pimp" sweats to wear, while the females wore "Maids" on their outfits. According to Pimpfants' marketing material, parents can give their kids "street cred." Pimp is seen as an acceptable word referring to the changing of something. Critics are outraged that merchandisers are using this term to sell baby clothing. The word should prompt people to be outraged at the physical, mental, and emotional abuse the ownership of women creates.

In the 1970s television show, and more recently the movie version of *Starsky & Hutch*, "Huggy Bear" was a pimp who worked as an informant. The character was decked out in stereotypical black pimp fashion. Snoop Dogg played Huggy Bear in the movie version. Dogg has a reputation of glorifying pimps in his songs and his appearances in *Girls Gone Wild* video promotions. Eddie Murphy played a pimp called Velvet Jones when he was on *Saturday Night Live*. Numerous hip-hop songs use the pimp theme, complete with bling and hordes of nearly nude women. The Godfather character in the WWE made "pimpin' ain't easy" a recognizable expression on playgrounds across America. He would enter the ring with a trail of prostitutes following him. There are theme parties, such as Vicar and Tarts parties, where men dress as priests and women as hookers.

The movie *Hustle & Flow* was about a small-time pimp who plots to get the attention of a rap superstar in order to get his first record made. Popkin (2006) described the main character as "a poor and desperate Memphis pimp in midlife crisis and his attempt to break free by becoming a successful rap artist." What attracted the most attention to the movie was the 2005 Oscar for best original song for "It's Hard Out Here for a Pimp." The song references prostitutes, but mostly in passing. The main emphasis is on making money and the dangers of the business. The main character in the song is not worried about rent or groceries but rather his ability to pay for his Cadillacs. He worries about death threats from rivals but there is little or no mention about any suffering by their prostitutes. He does show some concern about taking advantage of some prostitutes. He stated, "Like takin' from a ho don't know no better, I know that ain't right." He then complained that his hos are starting to cause trouble for him. In the middle of lamenting his troubles, the pimp tries to make a deal for a threesome with a man passing by him.

One seven-year-old boy I was tutoring asked me if I knew what a "p-i-m" was. He had meant to spell the word "pimp" from the song *P-I-M-P* by 50 Cent. When I asked him if he knew what it meant, he timidly answered it was someone who beats up women. In some aspects I was horrified that he knew the word. On the other hand, at least he understood the violent nature of the pimp and did not see him as the glorified character often portrayed in the media.

Sexualization of Children

According to Kincaid (1998), children serve as erotic objects to a culture that denies it sexualizes children. For example, he argued that it is no accident that child stars are often photographed wide-eyed and opened-mouthed. One supporter of Kincaid's theory stated, "One need only look at prepubescent Britney Spears fans to find young girls who are far more overtly sexualized than 12-year-old Brooke Shields is [in the movie *Pretty Baby*], even if today's girls are just as naive as Shields' coquettish Violet" (Johanson, 2004). Kincaid (2006) noted that ten years after her death news stations are still showing footage of six-year-old JonBenet Ramsey in her pageant dress and full makeup. He argued that this footage allows society to act as though they are disgusted, while watching the footage over and over. He argued, "We are able to use the half-clothed bodies of children as centerfolds while professing shock that anyone would so display them." Kincaid (2006) reasoned that, while we are obsessed with sexual stories of children, we pay little attention to millions of children who are abused in other ways. These obsessions allow society to "ignore the poverty, neglect, malnutrition, and poor education that constitute true child abuse."

Medved (cited in Kincaid, n.d.) suggested that popular culture aids in robbing children of all shreds of innocence. A first-grade teacher (cited in Deveny, 2007) stated she sees 7-year-old girls using words like "sexy," singing suggestive song lyrics and flirting with boys. Whitehead (cited in Aucoin, 2006) drew a comparison between aging society and an adolescent culture. For example, advertisers are trying to titillate men in their 50s in beer advertisements featuring barely legal models. Critics also argue that it is disturbing that parents would give their daughters breast implants for 16th birthday and high school graduation presents. Girls have not even finished growing to see how their breasts will look. They will also need more than one operation to maintain the enlargements. Parents are subjecting their children to danger on a whim. There are few reasons to have large breasts other than to attract male attention. They make a statement about the sexual willingness of someone who would go through such a drastic procedure.

The changes in fashions to reveal more and more of little girls' bodies happened gradually, thus perhaps escaping under the radar of parents. Parents who object to slight variations of styles worry that they will be perceived as prudish, a quality they rebelled against with their own parents. Some parents, particularly mothers, push their daughters to grow up quickly by buying them mature toys, designer clothes, makeup, and jewelry. A very popular birthday party for very young girls is the "makeover" party. Instead of girls playing with makeup, the makeup is elevated to the level of professional makeup artists.

Oprah Winfrey (2006a) featured a show with a 3-year-old girl who obsesses over her appearance. She begs for makeup and tells her mother she hates her because she will not let her wear it. One of her favorite magazines is the Victoria's Secret catalogue. The message the little girl is getting is that this is her worth and if she does not wear makeup like the models she sees in magazines, she is not good enough. This is a very powerful message to get at age three. I noticed in the tape that her pillowcase had "princess" written on it. It also showed the little girl putting on nail polish and lipstick. Beckham (2005) asked, "How did we go from I-am-what-I-am feminism to a geisha-like sexism that has trickled all the way down to grammar school?" (p. 9). She noted that seven-year-olds have birthday parties at beauty salons and commented on the marketing of Bratz dolls and Bratz Babyz. She wrote, "How is it that parents go from Baby Einstein and Fisher Price toys, from monitoring everything children are exposed to, to allowing everything?" (p. 9).

In addition to sexualizing their children, parents sometimes simply expose their children to sexual images at an early age. One mother was indicted by a grand jury on charges of contributing to the delinquency of a minor and involving a minor in obscene acts because she hired a stripper for her sixteen-year-old son's birthday party ("Mom Indicted," 2005). About 10 people under the age of 18 were at the birthday party. After the initial entertainment, the stripper collected extra money from the underage boys and went fully nude. Apparently the fourteen-year-old brother of the birthday boy took pictures. The mother was caught when she had the pictures developed at a local drug store. Drug store employees notified authorities ("Mom Indicted," 2005). In an interview (Winfrey, 2006), the mother acknowledged that she asked for the pictures to be sent out and not developed in-house where the employees knew her. It was evident she knew it was inappropriate.

The mother was rather unapologetic about the situation, other than her getting caught and having a felony conviction on her record. She stated, "I tried to do something special for my son.... It didn't harm him.... Who are they to tell me what I can and can't show to my own children?" (cited in "Mom Indicted," 2005). She used the defense that "they are going to do it anyway" so it might as well be under her control. She explained that she saw it as a rite of passage. Because it was the mother introducing her son to strippers, it seems especially wrong. Even the father had initially told the mother not to hire a stripper. Once the stripper was there, however, the father did little to stop it.

The marketers of the Hooters Restaurant chain seem to want it both ways—they want men to come in to ogle the wait staff but they want to be looked at as just another restaurant where people can bring their kids. Management stated the restaurant chain is "in the business of providing vicarious sexual recreation" (cited in Samuels, 2003). They hold Hooters bikini contests and sell calendars and DVDs of Hooter Girls, yet they offer a children's menu and a "kids eat free" night. One dad interviewed brought his kids to Hooters. He adamantly defended his position, claiming kids don't see the waitresses as sexual at that age. Hooters reported three-fourths of their customers are adult males. They defer responsibility for having a children's menu to demands of the clientele. However, that does not explain the promotional "Children Eat Free" nights they offer. One blogger reported that a friend took his children to Hooters at least once a week. He suggested that the man might be using his kids as "slut-magnets" (Samuels, 2006). The number of families that go to Hooters suggests the parents see nothing wrong with taking their children there. Legere argued, "The women aren't flirting, they're friendly. There's a difference" (cited in Samuels, 2003). On the other hand, nothing says friendly like cleavage.

Conclusion

The debate continues over whether current trends of female behavior are expressions of empowerment or self-exploitation. With each step forward of the women's movement and sexual liberation for women, there appears to be one step backwards. One problem is that young women and girls appear to have a distorted sense of equality, that to be equal they must emulate males' worst attributes. Levy (2005a) referred to this trend as "raunch" culture. She stated, "If male chauvinist pigs of years past treated women like pieces of meat, now we're doing it all by ourselves." Female fashion trends expose butt cracks, drunken women grab male strippers at bachelorette parties, and women grind their genitals on strange men in dance clubs. Instead of women exploring their inner erotic fantasies, they seek approval for participating in male fantasies. Women are instructed to get in touch with their sexuality by copying strippers. Exercise classes, women's magazines, and even advice from *The Oprah Winfrey Show* highlighted the mimicking of stripper moves and dress. Most females want male attention, but it is disturbing the extent to which women are willing to compromise themselves. The sexual revolution was supposed to give women the right to enjoy their sexuality, not be further exploited. The advances of the women's movement are often trivialized by the skankiness creeping into fashion and behaviors. In the past, women's voices were ignored, now only women's voices of agreement are heard. Negative commentary is silenced. Only women who play along and act like one of the boys are acceptable.

Women are subjugated in many areas of popular culture. Aucoin (2006) stated that pornography and other sexual images of women have become so pervasive that people do not even notice it anymore. To get attention, more and more sex is added. Aucoin (2006) argued that critics are silenced and young women and girls are fooled into thinking that what they are experiencing is female empowerment rather than objectification. Rushkoff (2001) argued that marketers use a collection of the same old sexual clichés, repackaged as female empowerment. Generally, I find young women are simply unaware of the extent to which women are exploited, either by themselves or by others. They get a distorted view of pornography if all they know of the industry is Jenna Jameson bragging about how much money she makes and how much control she has. They have a *Pretty Woman* sanitized view of prostitution. They have never seen the girl-on-girl sex scenes featured on the most recent *Girls Gone Wild* videos. It is my experience that this generation overwhelmingly refuses to question the sexualization of females. In their minds sex sells; therefore, it can and should be used. Restrictions are seen as prudish or violating the First Amendment.

It would be one thing if adult women were using these behaviors to explore and exploit their sexuality, but our society allows and even encourages younger and younger girls to mimic these trends. Marketers are boldly and unapologetically selling products that sexualize little girls. Outrageous T-shirt sayings are hugely popular, such as "Future Porn Star" and "Bitch in Training" for girls. It is not just parents who allow and encourage little girls to dress in sexualized ways; it is friends of the family and "cool aunts" who buy these clothes for them. Because so many girls today are victims of age compression, they appear to be grown women although they are still little girls. Media's fascination with stars such as Paris Hilton and Britney Spears (post K Fed and sans underwear) signals to little girls what it takes to get noticed. Check little girls' iPods for songs by Fergie where she insists that men give her gifts when she shows off her body parts.

We need to be honest about the exploiting of female sexuality. I am not suggesting a boycott but asking that consumers use common sense. If people just stopped buying the hypersexual clothes for little girls and stopped obsessing about celebrity skank culture, the trends would move on to something else (hopefully something more tasteful and empowering). If parents would refuse to enter their daughters in beauty pageants and dance competitions that sexualize little girls, standards would quickly change. Again, I am not suggesting censorship; censoring often makes the trends more attractive. I am not calling for a ban on strip clubs and pornography; but pretending there are no victims is harmful. Proclaiming that women are in power in these situations only makes it easier for male owners and producers to exploit women further. The few accounts of glamorous strippers and porn stars overshadow the numerous stories of the many young women abused and discarded by a ruthless, moneymaking system. Many of the women in the sex industry do not have the opportunities or resources to make other choices. Adult women who truly choose professions in the sex industry should at least have labor protection. They should neither be despised nor glamorized. Women should be allowed to set their own boundaries without being called prudes. Shallit's (2000) work regarding women's return to modesty presents an argument for women to be empowered by remaining chaste. I doubt we need to swing the pendulum that far backwards; however, it should be an option for girls and young women.

I believe education and an honest assessment of the culture is the answer. The APA report referenced suggests schools teach media literacy skills to all students, educating them about the negative effects ("Sexualization of Girls," 2007). The writers call on parents to play a protective and educative role with their daughters. Lastly, they suggest sexualized images be replaced with positive images of girls' competence and uniqueness. We need to educate little girls that it may look fun to dress sexy but there are social and personal consequences, such as not being taken seriously and inviting unwanted sexual advances, to consider. If we are afraid to teach girls about their sexuality, they will learn it from very unhealthy sources, which are abundant in popular culture.

REFERENCES

Abercrombie's sexy undies 'slip.' (2002, May 28). *CNN Money*. Retrieved September 22, 2006, from http://money.cnn.com/2002/05/22/news/companies/ambercombie.

About Blossom Maternity. (n.d.). Retrieved July 14, 2007, from http://blossommaternity.com/about_blossom.htm

About Deliliah's. (n.d.). Retrieved June 22, 2006, from http://www.delilahs.com/about.html

About Hooters. (n.d.). Retrieved July 14, 2007, from http://www.hooters.com/company/about_hooters/

About Porn Star clothing. (n.d.). Retrieved July 12, 2007, from http://www.pornstarclothing.com/about.php

About the show. (2007). Retrieved July 12, 2007, from http://www.we.tv/shows/bridezillas/

Ackman, D. (2001, May 25). How big is porn? *Forbes*. Retrieved September 15, 2006, from http://www.forbes.com/2001/05/25/0524porn.html

Actress of the week. (n.d.). Retrieved February 12, 2007, from http://www.askmen.com/women/actress_60/89b_shannen_doherty.html

Adams, S. (1998, August 6). Girl trouble. Citypaper. Retrieved July 14, 2007, from http://www.citypaper.net/articles/073098/movies.lolita.shtml

Additional interview attire specifics for women." (2006). Virginia Tech University. Retrieved August 31, 2006, from http://www.career.vt.edu/JOBSEARC/interview/APPEARNC.html#WOMEN

Adult friend finders guide. (n.d.). Retrieved August 8, 2006, from http://www.adult-friend-finders-guide.com/doing.htm

Aeon Flux. (n.d.). Retrieved June 22, 2006, from http://en.wikipedia.org/wiki/%C3%86on_Flux

Albano, C. L., & Sugar, B. R. (1999). *The complete idiot's guide to professional wrestling*. New York: Alpha Books.

Alonso-Zaldivar, R., & Costello, D. (2006, November 18). FDA ends ban on silicone breast implants. *Los Angeles Times*. Retrieved July 12, 2007, from http://www.topix.net/content/trb/2447873129321776343403443932183126926421

American teenagers (2006). Mediamark Research. Retrieved July 12, 2007, from http://216.239.51.104/search?q=cache:JO5d4ssPg3AJ:www.magazine.org/content/files/teenprofile04.pdf+mediamark+teens+have+a+strong+sense+individualism&hl=en&ct=clnk&cd=1&gl=us

Angell, J. (2004). *Callgirl: Confessions of an ivy league lady of pleasure*. New York: Harper-Collins.

Anime. (n.d.). *Dictionary.com*. Retrieved July 19, 2007, from http://dictionary.reference.com/browse/anime

Apples and origins. (n.d.). Retrieved July 14, 2007, from http://www.ew.com/ew/report/0,6115,296556_2%7C19231%7C%7C0_0_,00.html

Arnett, R. (2005, June 30). Magnetic attraction: The LPGA needs to embrace, not reject, the sexy look. *Sports Illustrated.* Retrieved May 8, 2006, from http://sports illustrated.cnn.com/2005/writers/rick_arnett/06/30/inside.golf/index.html

Ashbrook, T. (2006, September 29). Hooking up on campus. *On Point.* [audio]

Assael, S., & Mooneyham, M. (2002). *Sex, lies, and headlocks: The real story of Vince McMahon and the World Wrestling Federation.* New York: Crown Publishers

Aucoin, D. (2006, March 19). Porn gaining exposure in American culture. *Boston Globe.* Retrieved March 30, 2006, from http://www.signonsandiego.com/union-trib/20060319/news_1c19porn.html

Baby hell. (n.d.). Retrieved July 14, 2007, from http://www.tshirthell.com/babyhell.shtml

Bachelor. (n.d.). Retrieved May 8, 2006, from http://en.wikipedia.org/wiki/The_Bachelor

Bamberger, M. (1996, January 14). Living with a lie: When CBS decided to defend announcer Ben Wright, it attacked the truth. Sports Ilustrated. Retrieved July 11, 2007 from http://sportsillustrated.cnn.com/augusta/news/wright.html

Barbarella: tagline. (n.d.). Retrieved July 14, 2007, from http://www.imdb.com/title/tt0062711/

Barbie. (2005, March 9). *Britannica concise encyclopedia.* Retrieved May 8, 2005, from http://www.answers.com/topic/barbie

Barlett, C., Harris, H., Smith, S., & Bonds-Raacke, J. (2005). Action figures and men. *Sex Roles: A Journal of Research.*

Barton, B. (2006). *Stripped: Inside the lives of exotic dancers.* New York: New York University Press.

Bates, K. G. (2005, January 31). 'Essence' campaign to clean up rap lyrics. *NPR.* Retrieved September 8, from http://www.npr.org/templates/story/story.php?storyId=4472386.

Baxter, N. (1995, November 9). Sweet's back again: In the early '70s, blaxploitation upended Hollywood stereotypes. *Metro Active.* Retrieved March 4, 2006, from http://www.metroactive.com/papers/metro/11.09.95/blax-9545.html

Baywatch database (n.d.). Retrieved July 12, 2007, from http://baywatchun.tripod.com/actors/hasselhoff_david.html

Beauty and the geek. (2006). Retrieved August 8, 2006, from http://www.tv.com/beauty-and-the-geek/show/32037/summary.html?full_summary=1&tag=show space_links;full_summary

Beauty pageants. (2004). Retrieved April 23, 2004, from http://forums.ebay.com/db2/thread.jsp?forum=105&thread=410074911&modifed=20040403084440

Becker, A. (2005, September 16). Hef's half-season gets full Mont-E! *Broadcasting & Cable.* Retrieved September 4, 2006, from http://www.tv.com/tracking/viewer.html?tid=16914&ref_id=39406&ref_type=101&tag=story_list;title;1

Beckham, B. (2005, November 13). When pop culture bursts childhood's bubble. *Boston Globe*, Globe South 9.

Bell, H., Sloan, L., & Strickling, C. (1998). Exploiter or exploited: Topless dancers reflect on their experiences. *Affilia, 13* (1998) 352–368.

Berns, Y. (2003). E! true Hollywood story Anna Kournikova [Television broadcast].

BloodRayne. (n.d.). Retrieved June 22, 2006, from http://en.wikipedia.org/wiki/Blood-Rayne

Bloom, A. (2004, September). Sex and the 6-year-old. *O, The Oprah Magazine.*

Blowing it at Milton Academy. (2005). Retrieved August 8, 2006, from http://www.insomnomaniac.com/weblog/archives/2005/03/blowing_it_at_m.html

Book the Heat dancers. (n.d.). Retrieved July 24, 2007, from http://www.nba.com/heat/dance/dance_appearance.html

Boswell, L. (2004, October 13). Olympians posing nude poses questions. *ESPN.*

Retrieved September 15, 2006, from http://sports.espn.go.com/espn/page3/story?page=boswell/040823

Boy wins porn star for prom date on Howard Stern's radio show. (2004, June 8). Retrieved May 8, 2006, from http://radio.about.com/b/a/090902.htm

Braiker, B. (2007, February 8). Hard times. *Newsweek*. Retrieved September 15, 2006, from http://www.msnbc.msn.com/id/17033892/site/newsweek/page/2/

Bratz style. (n.d.). Retrieved May 8, 2005, from http://www.bratz.com/

Bratz super babyz. (n.d.). Retrieved May 8, 2005, http://www.bratz.com/

Bravo shines the spotlight on the real lives of parents and their would-be child stars in the new original weekly series *Showbiz Moms & Dads*. (2004, April 19). Retrieved April 23, 2004 from http://www.elitestv.com/discus/messages/4/14340.html?1081435218

Breast implant questions and answers. (2006, November 17). FDA. Retrieved July 12, 2007, from http://www.fda.gov/cdrh/breastimplants/qa2006.html

Britney and boobs party. (2006). Retrieved July 12, 2007, from http://showbiz.sky.com/showbiz/article/0,,50001-1242074,00.html

Britney and Paris: Hollywood's Newest Best Friends? (2006, November 27). Retrieved, December 10, 2006, from http://extratv.warnerbros.com/v2/news/1106/27/3/text.html

Brown, J. (2001). Trash mags with training wheels: Teen glossies walk a fine line between beauty myth and teen reality—and they stumble often. Retrieved September 8, from http://www.media-awareness.ca/english/issues/stereotyping/women_and_girls/women_girls.cfm

Bryner, J. (2007, January, 23). Kids to parents: Leave the stress at work. *FOX News*. Retrieved July 10, 2007, from http://www.foxnews.com/story/0,2933,245938,00.html

Bun huggers: To wear or not to wear. (n.d.). Retrieved August 8, 2006, from http://www.womenssportsfoundation.org/cgi-bin/iowa/issues/body/article.html?record=877

Buying into sexy: The sexing up of tweens. (2005, January 9). Retrieved March 15, 2007, from http://www.cbc.ca/consumers/market/files/money/sexy/

Cale, M. (2005). [Review of the movie *Inside Deep Throat*.] Retrieved June 22, 2006, from http://www.ruthlessreviews.com/movies/i/insidedeepthroat.html

Carlin, J. (2006, February 28). MySpace: Predator's paradise. *WSLS NewsChannel 10*. Retrieved April 17, 2007, from http://www.wsls.com/servlet/Satellite?pagename=WSLS/MGArticle/SLS_BasicArticle&c=MGArticle&cid=1137834396486&path=

Carlson, P. (2002, July 16). *Playboy*'s "Women of Enron": Cashing in on the bare market. *The Washington Post*, p. C. 8.

Carmichael, M. (2007, July 24). Reality cuts. *Newsweek Health*. Retrieved July 25, 2007, from http://www.msnbc.msn.com/id/19938037/site/newsweek/

Carpenter, L. M. (2005). *Virginity lost*. New York: New York University Press.

Carroll, D. & Ward, K. (1994). Zex und zex und zex. Retrieved May 4, 2006, from http://www.tabula-rasa.info/Horror/ZexZexZex.html

Carty, M. (2006, August 25). Teed off—Parents urged to "just say no" to offensive clothing messages. *Catholic Online*. Retrieved March 17, 2007, from http://www.catholic.org/hf/parenting/story.php?id=21019

Catholic University women's lacrosse team initiation party. (2006). Retrieved August 8, 2006, from http://badjocks.com/archive/2006/catholic-university-womens-lacrosse.htm

Celebrity catfights. (n.d.). Retrieved July 13, 2007, from http://celebritycatfights.blogspot.com/2007/03/todays-catfight-maria-sharapova-vs-anna.html

Chase, M. (2000). The Art of seduction, the art of business: Interview with a g-string diva. *Verge Magazine*. Retrieved August 8, 2006, from http://www.vergemag.com/1000/feat/diva.html

Child pageants, or how to make your kid look like a hooker. (2004). Retrieved April 23, 2004, from http://www.neuroticfishbowl.com/archives/000146.html

China crowns Miss Plastic Surgery. (2004, December 18). *BBC*. Retrieved May 12, 2006, from http://news.bbc.co.uk/2/hi/asia-pacific/4107857.stm

Clements, A. (2002a). Baring our bodies, Protecting our souls. Retrieved July 22, 2006, from http://www.geocities.com/alysabethc/bodies.html

Clements, A. (2002b). From the peanut gallery: Strippers and social responsibility. Retrieved July 22, 2006, from http://www.geocities.com/alysabethc/responsibility.html

Clements, A. (2002c). Ladies' night: Civilian women in strip clubs. Retrieved July 22, 2006, from http://www.geocities.com/alysabethc/ladiesnight.html

Clements, A. (2002d). The pitfalls of the profession: A stripper's guide to survival. Retrieved July 22, 2006, from http://www.geocities.com/alysabethc/pitfalls.html

Clements, A. (2002e). Sex work isn't a euphemism: Don't patronize me. Retrieved July 22, 2006, from http://www.geocities.com/alysabethc/quotes.html

Clements, A. (2002f). So you want to be a stripper. Retrieved July 22, 2006, from http://www.geocities.com/alysabethc/beginners.html

Clements, A. (2002g). Thank god I'm a stripper. Retrieved July 22, 2006, from http://www.geocities.com/alysabethc/thanksgiving2002.html

Clements, A. (2002h). Why would a woman want to become a stripper? Retrieved July 22, 2006, from http://www.geocities.com/alysabethc/why.html

Clover, C. J. (1989). Her body, himself: Gender in the slasher film. In G. Dines & J. M. Humez (Eds.), *Gender, race, and class in the media* (pp. 169–181). Newbury Park, CA: Sage.

Code of the comics magazine association of America, Inc. (1954, October 26). Retrieved July 19, 2007, from http://historymatters.gmu.edu/d/6543/

Cody, D. (2006). *Candy girl: A year in the life of an unlikely stripper*. New York: Gotham Books.

Cohen, S. (2006, May 29). "Women gain prominence in video game world." *USA Today*. Retrieved September 12, 2006, from http://www.usatoday.com/tech/gaming/2006-05-29-female-videogamers_x.htm

Colbert, S. (2006, December 19). *Colbert Report* [Television broadcast], Comedy Central.

Community journal live. (n.d.). Retrieved June 22, 2006, from http://community.livejournal.com/proanorexia/

Controversies about Bratz Dolls. (n.d.). Retrieved September 7, 2006, from http://collectdolls.about.com/od/dollprofiles/p/bratzdolls.htm

Conversation with Katherine Liepe-Levinson, author of *Strip Show*. (2005). Retrieved August 8, 2006, from http://www.routledge-ny.com/util/resources.asp?filename=llevinsoniv.htm

Cool mom sentenced to 30 years for sex parties. (2005, November 15). *USA Today*. Retrieved February 22, 2006, from http://www.usatoday.com/news/nation/2005-11-15-momsentenced_x.htm

Cosmetic plastic surgery research. (2006). Retrieved July 12, 2007, from http://www.cosmeticplasticsurgerystatistics.com/statistics.html

Cox, A. M. (2006, March 23). The myth about girls going wild: Why alcohol has become just a handy excuse. *The Nation*. Retrieved September 12, 2006, from http://www.time.com/time/nation/article/0,8599,1176483,00.html

Coyote Ugly Saloon Shopping (n.d.). Retrieved July 19, 2007, from http://www.coyoteuglysaloon.com/shopping/baby.html

Crossroads Nursery School and Infant Center. (n.d.). Retrieved July 14, 2007, from http://www.admin.ias.edu/crossroads/parent_information.php

Crotty, J. (1999, March 31). Deborah Rowe: Stripper with a thousand faces. *Monk Magazine.* Retrieved July 16, 2007, from http://www.monk.com/display.php?p=People& id=23

Crouse, J. S. (2003, October 27). Bratz against beauty. Retrieved May 23, 2005, from http://www.cwfa.org/articles/4790/BLI/dotcommentary/

Dakota, 12, to star in "disturbing paedophile film" (2007, January 4). *Daily Mail.* Retrieved July 5, 2007, from www.dailymail.co.uk/pages/live/articles/showbiz/showbiznews.html

Dallas cowboy cheerleaders history. (n.d.). Retrieved July 16, 2007, from http://www.dallascowboys.com/cheerleaders/history.cfm

Davis, B. (2006). Miss USA Tara Conner lesbian kissing Miss Teen USA causes eviction. *National Ledger.* Retrieved January 3, 2007, from http://www.nationalledger.com/artman/publish/article_272610490.shtml

Deford, F. (2006, May 24). Women behaving badly: Sadly, the ladies have followed men's lead in sports. *Sports Illustrated.* Retrieved August 8, 2006, from http://sportsillustrated.cnn.com/2006/writers/frank_deford/05/23/womens.sports/index.html

Democracy, J. (2006, August 29). Kournikova vs. Sharapova. Retrieved July 13, 2007, from http://www.associatedcontent.com/article/55292/kournikova_vs_sharapova_a_match_between.html

Denizet-Lewis, B. (2004, May 30). Friends, friends with benefits and the benefits of the local mall. *New York Times.* Retrieved August 19, 2006, from http://www.nytimes.com/2004/05/30/magazine/30NONDATING.html?ei=5007&en=b8ab7c02ae2d206b&ex=1401249600&pagewanted=all&position=

Deveny, K. (2007, July 3). Paris, Britney, Lindsay and Nicole. *The Bulletin.* Retrieved July 12, 2007 from http://bulletin.ninemsn.com.au/article.aspx?id=225480

Devine, M. (2005, August 14). Online porn addiction turns our kids into victims and predators. *The Sun-Herald.* Retrieved September 22, 2006, from http://www.smh.com.au/news/miranda-devine/the-problem-with-pornography/2005/08/13/1123353539758.html

Diva. (n.d.). Retrieved April 4, 2005, from http://www.urbandictionary.com

Dr. 90210. (2006). Retrieved August 8, 2006, from http://www.eonline.com/on/shows/dr90210/index.jsp

Doege, D. (2004, November 30). Woman who embezzled $524,000 gets prison. *Milwaukee Journal Sentinel.* Retrieved September 22, 2006, from http://findarticles.com/p/articles/mi_qn4196/is_20041130/ai_n10997953

Don Imus to appear on Al Sharpton's radio show. (2007, April 8). *FOX* News. Retrieved July 12, 2007, from http://www.foxnews.com/story/0,2933,264859,00.html

Dotinga, R. (2005, September 28). Suicide Girls gone AWOL. *Wired.* Retrieved March 3, 2006, from http://www.wired.com/news/culture/0,1284,69006,00.html

Doyle, K. L. (2006). Don't cha wish pop was more empowering? Retrieved March 3, 2006, from http://www.thefword.org.uk/features/2006/07/dont_cha_wish_pop_was_more_empowering

Downes, L. (2006, December 29). Middle school girls gone wild. *New York Times.* Retrieved June 22, 2006, from http://www.nytimes.com/2006/12/29/opinion/29fri4.html?ex=1325048400&en=705773ca836fc865&ei=5088&partner=rssnyt&emc=rss

Drape, J. (2004, August 12). Olympians strike pinup pose, and avoid setting off a fuss. *New York Times.* Retrieved August 8, 2006, from http://www.nytimes.com/2004/08/12/sports/olympics/12women.html

Dress code. (2005, September 2). Retrieved July 14, 2007, from http://www.gotha.ocps.net/info07_dresscode.shtml 9/2/05

Due maternity. (2006). Retrieved August 8, 2006, from http://www.duematernity.com

Dure, B. (2004, March 4). Icy ad has sun shining on beach volleyball stars. *USA Today*. Retrieved August 8, 2006, from http://www.usatoday.com/sports/olympics/summer/2004-03-04-may-walsh-10_x.htm

Eaton, K. (2006). The skinny of pro-ana. *Current Magazine*. Retrieved August 19, 2006, from http://www.msnbc.msn.com/id/15734955/site/newsweek

Eaves, E. (2002). *Bare: The naked truth about stripping*. New York: Random House.

Ebert, R. (1991, October 18). "Whore." *Sun Times*. Retrieved September 22, 2006, from http://rogerebert.suntimes.com/apps/pbcs.dll/article?AID=/19911018/REVIEWS/110180307/1023

Edgers, G. (2003, January 26). Flash news! Call them reality videos. They show young women willing to lift their shirts. *Boston Globe*, p. N1.

Edgerton, R. (1999). Engagement, Inc.: The marketing of diamonds. *Stay Free Magazine*. Retrieved June 12, 2005, from http://www.stayfreemagazine.org/archives/16/diamonds.html

Ellis, N. (2005). Plot summary for *Hustle & Flow* (2005). Retrieved August 19, 2006, from http://www.imdb.com/title/tt0410097/plotsummary

Episode 10: The 21 club. (2006). Retrieved February 4, 2007, from http://www.eonline.com/On/GirlsNextDoor2/Episodes/episode10.html

Eurotrash. (n.d.). Urban Dictionary. Retrieved August 8, 2006, from http://www.urban-dictionary.com/define.php?term=eurotrash

Eversley, S. (1999). Women in blaxploitation. Retrieved August 19, 2006, from http://www.blaxploitation.com/a_12.html

Extreme makeover. (2005). ABC. Retrieved August 8, 2006, from http://abc.go.com/primetime/extrememakeover/index.html

Farrell, E. (1942). Lady wrestlers. *The American Mercury, 55*, pp. 674–680.

Fein, E. & Schneider, S. (1995). *The rules*. New York: Warner Books.

Ferrari, M. (2006). Miss America. (2006). WGBH Educational Foundation. Retrieved February 22, 2007, from http://www.pbs.org/wgbh/amex/missamerica/

Ferris, S. & Young, M. (2006, May 26). A generational divide over chick lit. *Chronicle of Higher Education*.

Festinger, L. (1957). *A theory of cognitive dissonance*. Stanford, CA: Stanford University Press.

FHM declares Amanda Beard the world's sexiest athlete. (2006, July 1). *Forbes*. Retrieved August 8, 2006, from http://www.forbes.com/feeds/businesswire/2006/07/01/businesswire20060701005006r1.html

Finley, A. (2005). Easy like Milton Academy. Retrieved August 8, 2006, from http://aidanfinley.blogspot.com/2005/03/easy-like-milton-academy-sophomore.html

Finn, N. (2006, December 20). MADD dumps Miss Teen USA. *E! Online*. Retrieved January 14, 2007, from http://www.eonline.com/news/article/index.jsp?uuid=aca93654-475c-4880-80ed-48f2686d1319&page=2

First communion dresses. (n.d.). Retrieved July 16, 2007, from http://www.1stcommunions.com

Fischer, C. B. (1996). Employee rights in sex work: The struggle for dancers' rights as employees. *Law & Inequality: A Journal of Theory and Practice*, 14: 521–554.

Fisher, A. (2007, March 11). Exotic locales are out: the hottest A-list holiday break is a stint in rehab. *The Guardian*. Retrieved March 15, 2007, from http://observer.guardian.co.uk/magazine/story/0,,2027819,00.html

Fisher, M. (2006, July 23). *Opie & Anthony*: Down to earth but also turning the air blue. *Washington Post*, p. N07. Retrieved August 8, 2006, from http://www.washingtonpost.com/wp-dyn/content/article/2006/07/21/AR2006072100291.htm

Forsyth, C., & Deshotels, T. (1997). The occupational milieu of the nude dancer. *Deviant Behavior, 18*, 125–142.

Freakum. (n.d.). *Urban dictionary*. Retrieved July 24, 2007, from http://www.urban
dictionary.com/define.php?term=freakum

Frey, H. (2002, November 7). The naked truth. *The Nation*. Retrieved July 15, 2007,
from http://www.thenation.com/doc.mhtml?i=20021125&c=2&s=frey

Friedman, R. (2007, January 3). Dakota Fanning "rape" film heads to Sundance. *Fox
News*. Retrieved April 2, 2007, from http://www.foxnews.com/story/0,2933,
240618,00.html

Fun stuff ... be ugly 07. (n.d.). Retrieved July 14, 2007, from www.girlsinc.org/gc/

Garcia, C. (2003, February 7). The naked truth about GGW. *Austin American-Stan-
dard*, p. E1

Garcia. L. T. (1986). Exposure to pornography and attitudes about women and rape:
A correlative study. *AG* 22 (1986), 382–83.

Gates, A. (2006, December 5). Graduating from bad to worse as an adventure in self-
help. *New York Times*. Retrieved December 12, 2006, from http://www.nytimes.
com/2006/12/05/arts/television/05gate.html?ex=1322974800&en=fda9970dd3c0047
2&ei=5088&partner=rssnyt&emc=rss

Gibbons, S. (2003, November 4). Wanted: Sexy virgins. *Women's eNews*. Retrieved
November 14, 2005, from http://www.alternet.org/story/17124/

Gilbert, M. (2003, November 11). Reality shows highlight the ritzy, glitzy, and comically ditzy, clueless, wealthy young women emerge as new prime-time stars. *Boston
Globe*. Retrieved September 12, 2005, from http://www.boston.com/ae/tv/
articles/2003/11/30/reality_shows_highlight_the_ritzy_glitzy_and_comically_
ditzy/

Girls Gone Wild uncovered. (2003). Retrieved August 8, 2006 from http://www.
vh1.com/shows/dyn/vh1_news_special/65188/episode_about.jhtml

Girls still going wild. (2003, October 2). *Consumer Affairs*. Retrieved September 22,
2006, from http://consumeraffairs.com/news03/girls_gone_wild_02.html

Girls warned not to "go wild" on spring break. (2006, March 17). *MSNBC*. Retrieved
August 8, 2006, from http://www.msnbc.msn.com/id/11726292/

Glass, E. (2004, May 20). Internet darlings a far cry from the meek bunnies of *Playboy* fame. *University Wire*. Retrieved July 12, from http://dailybruin.com/archives/
id/28669/

Goldman, A. (2006, July 3). Strip clubs begin to see other benefits of women. Retrieved
August 8, 2006, from http://www.lasvegassun.com/sunbin/stories/consumer/2006/
jul/03/566615631.html

Graydon, S. (2005, January 9). *CBC*. Retrieved August 12, 2005, from http://www.cbc.
ca/consumers/market/files/money/sexy/graydon.html

Griffin, S. (n.d.). Retrieved July 16, 2007, from http://www.bullz-eye.com/opposite_sex/
lesbians.htm

Grove, L. (2005, November 29). Not-so-petty cash to rock bat mitzvah. *New York Daily
News*. Retrieved October 7, 2006, from http://www.nydailynews.com/front/story/
369994p-314735c.html

Hageman, S. (2000, August 9). How I became an exotic dancer: My exhibitionist streak
saved me from slinging doughnuts. Retrieved July 8, 2006, from http://dir.
salon.com/sex/feature/2000/08/09/dancer_1/index.html?pn=1

Hancock, N. (2006, December 8). CrotchGate Part II: Camille Paglia says Madonna
gave Britney the "kiss of death." *U.S. Magazine*. Retrieved July 18, 2007, from
http://www.usmagazine.com/crotchgate_week_two_camille_paglia_says_madonna_g
ave_britney_the_kiss_of_death

Hanisko, H. (2006, July 26). MySpace is public space when it comes to job search.
Retrieved July 12, 2007, from http://www.collegegrad.com/press/myspace.shtml

Harshman, R. (2004, April 2). Porn for women, by women? *The Observer*. Retrieved

August 19, 2006, from http://www.cwru.edu/orgs/observer/archive/04-02-27/
    stories/Edit03.html
Hef gets into bed with reality TV: *Playboy* founder stars in *Girls Next Door*. (2005,
    August, 10). Retrieved August 8, 2006, from http://www.tv.com/tracking/viewer.
    html?tid=14253&ref_id=39406&ref_type=101&tag=story_list;title;5
Herbst, C. (2004). Lara's lethal and loaded mission: transposing reproduction and
    destruction. In S. A. Inness (Ed.) *Action Chicks: New Images of Tough Women in Pop-
    ular Culture*. New York: Palgrave Macmillian.
Hernandez, S. (2006, September 24). "'Freaking' packs gym with parents." *The Orange
    County Register*. Retrieved October 12, 2006, from http://www.ocregister.com/
    ocregister/homepage/abox/article_1285925.php
Herrera, I. D. (2004, April 4). *The Apprentice* exposes reality of glass ceiling. *USA Today*.
    Retrieved August 19, 2006, from http://www.usatoday.com/news/opinion/editorials/
    2004-04-04-herrera_x.htm
Herz, J. C. (1997). *Joystick nation: How videogames ate our quarters, won our hearts, and
    rewired our minds*. New York: Little Brown.
Hilton, P. (2004). *Confessions of an heiress: A tongue-in-chic peek behind the pose*. New
    York: Simon & Schuster.
Hip-hop videos: Sexploitation on set. (2005). *VH1* [video].
Hitman. (n.d.). Retrieved June 22, 2006, from http://www.softpedia.com/reviews/
    games/pc/Hitman-Blood-Money-Review-26258.shtml
Hoerrner, M. (2006, August 29). Women's tennis cashing in on sex appeal. Retrieved
    July 13, 2007, from http://www.buzzle.com/editorials/8-29-2006-106944.asp
Holsopple, K. (1998). Stripclubs according to strippers: exposing workplace sexual vio-
    lence. In D. Roche & C. Roche. Hughes (Eds.) *Making the harm visible: Global sex-
    ual exploitation of women and girls, speaking out and providing services* (pp. 252–276).
    Kingston: Coalition Against Trafficking in Women.
hooks, b. (1994, February). Sexism and misogyny: Who takes the rap? Misogyny, gangsta
    rap, and the piano. *END ZMAGAZINE*. Retrieved September 27, 2005, from http://
    race.eserver.org/misogyny.html
Howe, N., & Strauss, W. (2000). *Millennials rising: The next great generation*. New
    York: Vintage.
Huang, T. (2004, August 22). August 2004 Olympian too sexy for their own good?
    Dallas Morning Star. Retrieved July 19, 2007, from http://www.womenssports
    foundation.org/cgi-bin/iowa/issues/media/article.html?record=1064
Hume, B. (2004). Down and dirty. *ABC News*, Nov. 12.
Hunt, M. (2004, August 25). Life's great on the beach. *Milwaukee Journal Sentinel*.
    Retrieved July 12, 2007, from http://findarticles.com/p/articles/mi_qn4196/is_
    20040825/ai_n10981344
Hustler. (n.d.). Retrieved May 4, 2006, from http://www.hustler.com
Hymen repair. (n.d.). Retrieved July 22, 2006, from http://www.vaginalsurgerynyc.com/
    nyclabiaplasty/hymenrepairnyc.htm
Inciardi, J. A., Surratt, H. L., & Telles, P. R. (2000). *Sex, drugs, and HIV/AIDS in
    Brazil*. Jackson, TN: Westview Press.
Inness, S. A. (1999). *Tough girls: Women warriors and wonder women in popular culture*.
    Philadelphia: University of Pennsylvania Press.
In the VIP Room (n.d.). Retrieved June 22, 2006, from http://www.inthevip.com/main.
    htm
I want a famous face (2006). MTV. Retrieved August 8, 2006, from http://www.mtv.
    com/ontv/dyn/i_want_a_famous_face-2/series.jhtml
Jacobs, M. (2002, October 15). Looking like a skank turns tweens' crank. *Winnipeg Sun*,
    p. 11.

Jameson, J. (2004). *How to make love like a porn star: A cautionary tale.* New York: HarperCollins.

Jayson, S. (2005, October 19). "Technical virginity" becomes part of teens' equation. *USA Today.* Retrieved September 22, 2006, from http://www.usatoday.com/news/health/2005-10-19-teens-technical-virginity_x.htm

Jenna Jameson. (2003). *E!* True Hollywood Story [Television broadcast].

Jhally, S. (1995). *Dream worlds II* [video]. Northampton, MA: Media Education Foundation.

Jhally, S. (1999). *Tough guise* [video]. Northampton, MA: Media Education Foundation.

Jhally, S. (2002). *Wrestling with manhood* [video]. Northampton, MA: Media Education Foundation.

Johanson, M., (2004, August 8). Short cuts. Retrieved August 20, 2005, from http://www.flickfilosopher.com/flickfilos/shortcuts/shortcuts30.shtml#baby

John-Hall, A. (2007, April 17). Tucker called for reckoning on ugly rap: Let's have it. *Philadephia Inquirer.* Retrieved April 17, 2007, from http://www.philly.com/philly/news/columnists/20070417_Annette_John-Hall___Tucker_called_for_reckoning_on_ugly_rap__Lets_have_it.html

Johnson, R. (2006, December 14). Party's over Jones. *New York Post.*

Kane, D. (n.d.). 25 Greatest moments from the *Howard Stern Show.* Retrieved August 19, 2006, from http://www.cracked.com/index.php?name=News&sid=193

Kane, M. J., Griffin, P., & Messner, M. (2002). *Playing Unfair: The media image of the female athlete* [video]. Media Education Foundation.

Kapakos, S. (1998, August 15). New reader rifs on political correctness. Retrieved May 8, 2006, from http://www.likesbooks.com/readrif3.html

Kaplan, D. (2006, June 15). The cast and crew of *The Real World: Denver* are already stirring up trouble with the locals. *New York Post.* Retrieved August 8, 2006, from http://www.nypost.com/entertainment/real_world_gets_off_to_rockies_start_entertainment_don_kaplan.htm.

Kehr, D. (2002, August 9). Film review of *Stripped. New York Times,* Section E, p. 25. Retrieved July 8, 2004, from http://query.nytimes.com/gst/fullpage.html?res=9C00E5D7163AF93AA3575BC0A9649C8B63

Keltner, D. (2001). Maintaining the status quo: Rap music preferences. Retrieved August 8, 2006, from http://www-mcnair.berkeley.edu/2001journal/SStrings.html

Kincaid, J. R. (1998). *Erotic innocence: The culture of child molesting.* Durham, NC: Duke University Press.

Kincaid, J. R. (n.d.). Four questions and answers. Retrieved March 3, 2007, from http://www.ipce.info/ipceweb/Library/four_questions.htm

Kincaid, J. R. (2006, August 21). Little Miss Sunshine: America's obsession with Jon-Benet Ramsey. *Slate.* Retrieved March 3, 2007, from http://www.slate.com/id/2148089

Kipnis, L. (1996). *Bound and gagged: Pornography and the politics of fantasy in America.* Durham, NC: Duke University Press.

Kirk, M., & Boyer, P. J. (2002). *American porn* [video]. WGBH Educational Foundation.

Kitty Russell. (n.d.). Retrieved August 20, 2006, from http://www.tvland.com/shows/gunsmoke/character2.jhtml

Knapp, G. (2007, April 10). Women need to raise voices on Imus insult. Retrieved April 17, 2007, from http://www.sfgate.com/cgi-bin/article.cgi?f=/chronicle/archive/2007/04/10/SPGMDP5OAQ1.DTL

Kobrin, S. (2004, August 15). Asian-Americans criticize eyelid surgery craze. Retrieved August 19, 2006, from http://www.womensenews.org/article.cfm/dyn/aid/1950/context/cover

Kozer, S. (2003, May 12). Why I posed for *Playboy*. *U.S. Weekly*, p. 66.

Kreimer, S. (2004, June 6). Teens getting breast implants for graduation. Retrieved August 8, 2006, from http://www.womensenews.org/article.cfm/dyn/aid/1861/context/archive

Krinsky, B. (2006). Child Star Confidential [video]. *E! Entertainment Television*.

Kuczynki, A. (2004, September 12). Now you see it, now you don't. *New York Times*, p. 9.1.

Lacey, G. (2003, May 26). *Real World, The*—Season 12: Las Vegas Review: The best season ever! Retrieved September 22, 2006, from http://www.tvshowsondvd.com/sitereviews.cfm?ReleaseID=2340.

La Ferla, R. (2007, March 29). Having a great detox. *New York Times*. Retrieved April 15, 2007, from http://www.nytimes.com/2007/03/29/fashion/29rehab.html?ei=5088&en=c7ce3f5be4ed6583&ex=1332820800&partner=rssnyt&emc=rss&pagewanted=all

Lavinthal, J., & Rozler, A. (2005). *The hookup handbook*. New York: Simon Spotlight Entertainment.

Layden, M. A. (1999). If pornography made us healthy, we would be healthy by now. Retrieved August 19, 2006, from http://www.moralityinmedia.org/index.htm?pornsEffects/laydenhealthy.htm

Leahy, M. (2003, November 2). I see naked people. *The Washington Post*, p. W16.

Lenney, R. (n.d.). Stripping: Empowerment or objectification. *George Washington University, The Laughing Medusa*. Retrieved June 8, 2006, from http://www.gwu.edu/~medusa/stripping.html

Lentini, N. M. (2007, April 2). Girls Gone Wild branching into restaurants, clothing line. *Media Post*. Retrieved June 22, 2007, from http://publications.mediapost.com/index.cfm?fuseaction=Articles.showArticle&art_aid=58014&art_type=17

Levenson, M., & Russell, J. (2005, February 20). Milton Academy rocked by expulsions. *Boston Globe*. Retrieved March 3, 2006, from http://www.boston.com/news/education/k_12/articles/2005/02/20/milton_academy_rocked_by_expulsions/

Levesque, J. (2003, May 28). WNBA needs post-ups, not pinups: "There's no reason to hide it." *Seattle Post Intelligencer*. Retrieved August 8, 2006, from seattlepi.nwsource.com/levesque/123932_leve28.html

Levy, A. (2005a). *Female chauvinist pigs: Women and the rise of raunch culture*. New York: Free Press.

Levy, A. (2005b, September 18). Raunchiness is powerful? C'mon, girls. *Washington Post*, p. B05. Retrieved August 8, 2006, from http://www.washingtonpost.com/wp-dyn/content/article/2005/09/17/AR2005091700044.html?sub=AR

Lewis, J. (2000). Controlling lap dancing: Law, morality, and sex work. In R. Weitzer (Ed.), *Sex for sale: Prostitution, pornography, and the sex industry*. New York: Routledge.

Liepe-Levinson, K. (2001). *Strip show: Performances of gender and desire*. New York: Routledge.

Lindsay Lohan, Hilary Duff end feud, become friends. (2007, April 5). Retrieved March 8, 2007, from http://www.actressarchives.com/news.php?id=4921

Linz, D, & Malamuth, N. (1993). *Communication concepts 5: Pornography*. Newbury Park, CA: Sage.

Lipkins, S. (2006). Catholic University women's lacrosse team initiation party 2006. Retrieved September 13, 2006, from http://badjocks.com/archive/2006/catholic-university-womens-lacrosse.htm

Littlefield, B. (2007). *Only a game*. Boston: WBUR. [Radio broadcast].

Logan, R. (1994, March 3). Contestants: Pageants focus on brains, ability over beauty, bathing suits. *Collegian* (Penn State). Retrieved September 22, 2006, from http://www.collegian.psu.edu/archive/1994/03/03-16-94tdc/03-16-94dnews-2.asp

Lolita (n.d.). Dictionary.com. Retrieved July 19, 2007, from http://dictionary.reference.com/browse/lolita

Lovell, L. (n.d.). How did all of this get started? Retrieved August 8, 2006, from http://www.coyoteuglysaloon.com/spill/story.html

MacAdam, E. (n. d.). The B-word: People toss around the term "Bridezilla" and think it's cute. I'd argue it's demeaning. Retrieved August 19, 2006, from http://www.indiebride.com/essays/macadam/index.html

Mack, K., & Turner, A. (2005, May 4). House to cheerleaders: Hooray, but no hip-hips. *Houston Chronicle*. Retrieved July 16, 2007, from http://seattletimes.nwsource.com/html/nationworld/2002269204_rah10.html

Many teens who take "virginity pledges" substitute other high-risk behavior for inter-course, study says. (2005, March 21). *Medical News Today*. Retrieved June 22, 2006, from "http://www.medicalnewstoday.com/medicalnews.php?newsid=21606

Mattson, H. (1995). *Ivy league stripper*. New York: Arcade.

Mayden, B. (2005). Milton Academy scandal. *Here and now*. Boston: WBUR [Radio broadcast].

McClellan, K. (2005, May 26). Film documents sale of virginity on eBay auction. *The New Record*. Retrieved February 4, 2007 from http://www.newsrecord.org/media/storage/paper693/news/2005/05/26/ArtsEntertainment/Column.Film.Documents.Sale.Of.Virginity.On.Ebay.Auction-954133.shtml?norewrite200611241144&sourcedomain=www.newsrecord.org

McCullah, D. (2002, May 9). Too broad a ban on child models? *Wired*. Retrieved July 12, 2007, from http://www.wired.com/politics/law/news/2002/05/52379

McCullough, K. (2003, November 14). Abercrombie & Fitch to your kids: Group sex now! *World Net Daily*. Retrieved August 8, 2006, from http://www.worldnetdaily.com/news/article.asp%3FARTICLE%5FID=35579

McEnoy, S. (2005, September/October). Books with backbone: Self-help gets on the offensive. Retrieved June 27, 2006, from http://www.forewordmagazine.com/articles/printarticles.aspx?articleid=115

McGinley, A. C. (2006). Babes and beefcake: Exclusive hiring arrangements and sexy dress codes. *Duke J. Gender L. & Policy, 14, p. 257*.

McGraw, P. (2004, November 22). *Stage Parents*. Paramount [Television broadcast]

McGraw, P. (2005, April 26). *Act Your Age*. Paramount [Television broadcast]

McGraw, P. (2006, February 16). *Trouble in the Spotlight*. Paramount [Television broadcast]

McKay, H. (2007, July 16). Pop tarts: Jessica Simpson's breasts aren't bogus. *FOX News*. Retrieved July 21, 2007, from http://www.foxnews.com/story/0,2933,288655,00.html

McLune, J. (2006). Celie's revenge: Hip-hop's betrayal of black women. *Said It, 4*(1). Retrieved April 17, 2007, from http://www.saidit.org/archives/jan06/article4.html

Mehta, S. (2006, October 17). Teens' dancing is freaking out the adults. *Los Angeles Times*. Retrieved February 4, 2007, from http://www.latimes.com/news/local/la-me-freaking17oct17,1,1229173.story?coll=la-headlines-california

Men's magazines and the construction of masculinity. (n.d.). Retrieved May 29, 2006, from http://www.media-awareness.ca/english/issues/stereotyping/men_and_masculinity/masculinity_magazines.cfm?RenderForPrint=1

Menu of experiences. (n.d.). Retrieved July 12, 2007, from http://www.daydreams.us/test4_000013.htm

Merron, J. (2004, August 11). Sex, Olympics go hand in hand. *ESPN*. Retrieved August 8, 2006, from http://proxy.espn.go.com/espn/page2/story?page=merron/040811

Mesley, W. (2005, January 9). Interview with an expert: Shari Graydon on the sexing up of pre-teens. Retrieved August 19, 2006, from http://www.cbc.ca/consumers/market/files/money/sexy/graydon.html

Milton Academy sex scandal. (2005). Retrieved June 2, 2006, from http://board.uscho.com/archive/index.php/t-49986.html

Mitchell, T. (2006). 3 girls at school expose themselves for candy, police say. *The Times-*

Union. Retrieved September 22, 2006. http://www.sternfannetwork.com/forum/showthread.php?threadid=24108

Mohler-Kuo, M., Dowdall, G. W., Koss, M. P., & Wechsler, H. (2004). Correlates of rape while intoxicated in a national sample of college women. *Journal of studies on alcohol, 65,* pp. 37–45.

Mom indicted for hiring stripper for son. (2005, May 29). *MSNBC.* Retrieved September 14, 2005, from http://www.msnbc.msn.com/id/8022400/

Moos, J. (1999, January 13). Bikini blues: Beach volleyball makes the swimsuit standard. CNN. Retrieved August 8, 2006, from http://www.cnn.com/STYLE/9901/13/vollyball.bikini/

More charming Disney innocence. (n.d.). Retrieved August 19, 2006, from http://www.anomalies-unlimited.com/Disney/Disbits.html

Morrison, D. (2006, May 22). Women's soccer team releases apology for negative attention. *Daily Northwestern.* Retrieved August 8, 2006, from http://www.dailynorthwestern.com/media/storage/paper853/news/2006/05/22/Campus/Womens.Soccer.Team.

Murray, J. (2005, April 15). "The top *Real World/Road Rules* sluts of all-time!" *Dlisted.* Retrieved August 19, 2006, from http://dlisted.blogspot.com/2005/04/top-real-worldroad-rules-sluts-of-all.html

Muskeron, C. (n.d.). "Porn for girls." *Handbag.* Retrieved November 1, 2006, from http://www.handbag.com/relationships/sex/pornforgirls/

My bar/bat mitzvah companion. (n.d.). Retrieved June 22, 2006, from http://www.fivestarsoftware.com/mitzvah/).

"My Hump" is trash (2005, November 11). Retrieved July 15, 2007, from http://blogcritics.org/archives/2005/11/01/075225.php

MySpace gains top ranking of U.S. websites. (2006, July 11). *USA Today.* Retrieved August 8, 2006, from http://www.usatoday.com/tech/news/2006-07-11-myspace-tops_x.htm.

Neal, M. A. (2005, April, 6). Critical noir: Can hip-hop be feminist? *AOL Black Voices.* Retrieved April 17, 2007, from http://bv.channel.aol.com/entmain/music/critno10604/20050406

Neergaard, L. (2005, April 5). Women speak at FDA breast-implant hearing. Retrieved August 19, 2006, from http://www.mindfully.org/Health/2005/Breast-Implant-FDA-Hearing11apr05.htm

Negative rap lyrics. (2001). Retrieved May 8, 2006 from http://www.childrens-express.org/dynamic/public/Teen_talk_rap_lyrics_210501.htm

Nesoff, E. (2003, August 26). In search of feminists. *Christian Science Monitor,* p. 20.

Norris, M. (2006, November 15). A visit to the principal's office. NPR's *All Things Considered* [Radio broadcast]. http://www.npr.org/templates/story/story.php?storyId=6493089

Nowak, R. (2003, May 15). Absent fathers linked to teenage pregnancies. *New Scientist.* Retrieved June 7, 2006, from http://www.newscientist.com/article.ns?id=dn3724

Now you be the judge. (n.d.). Retrieved July 12, 2007, from www.siliconeholocaust.org

Obrochta (n.d.). First communion entertainment. Retrieved June 22, 2006, from http://www.mbd2.com/Tradeshow/first-communion.htm

O'Connor, I. (2004, August 13). Posing for magazines: Athlete or sexual plaything? *USA Today.* Retrieved July 13, 2007, from http://www.usatoday.com/sports/columnist/oconnor/2004-08-13-oconnor_x.htm

Oliveira, M. (2006, Nov. 21). Britney Spears and Paris Hilton party in Las Vegas. *All Headline News.* Retrieved January 3, 2007, from http://www.allheadlinenews.com/articles/7005587662

Only 5–16 y.o. beautiful babygirls. (n.d.). Retrieved July 12, 2007, from http://www.nn-guide.com

On the outs, Zara pouts. (2007, April 20). Retrieved May 29, 2007, from http://www.tvgasm.com/shows/bad-girls-club/

Opie and Anthony. (2002, August 23). Retrieved August 8, 2006, from http://www.thesmokinggun.com/archive/opieanthony1.html

Opie & Anthony show. (n.d.). Retrieved August 8, 2006, from http://www.opieandanthony.com/

Open letter to a stripper. (2001, July 16). Retrieved July 15, 2007, from http://www.adequacy.org/public/stories/2001.7.16.003.73487.html

Oppliger, P. A. (2004). *Wrestling and hypermasculinity.* Jefferson, NC: McFarland & Company.

Ortiz, V. (2002, May 17). Parents say kid's thong is just plain wrong. *Journal Sentinel* (Wisconsin). Retrieved August 15, 2005, from http://www.jsonline.com/news/gen/may02/43941.asp

Overstreet, J. (2004, April 15). Film forum: *Passion,* a teen porn star, and a period piece. *Christianity Today.* Retrieved August 19, 2006, from http://www.christianitytoday.com/movies/filmforum/040415.html.

Owen, R. (2001, May 13). Watching *Living Dolls: The making of a child beauty queen* is surely one of the creepiest ways to spend Mother's Day. *Post-Gazette.* Retrieved August 19, 2006, from http://www.post-gazette.com/tv/20010513owen.asp

Pageant entry information. Retrieved November 15, 2006, from http://www.coutopageants.com/yankeemiss.html

Pants off dance off. (n.d.). Retrieved August 22, 2006, from http://fuse.tv/tv/pantsoff/

The parent trap: Divide and conquer. (2005, January 9). *CBC.* Retrieved August 19, 2006, from http://www.cbc.ca/consumers/market/files/money/sexy/parents.html

Parties & Planning. (n.d.). Retrieved July 14, 2007, from http://www.clublibbylu.com

Patrick, D. (2006). *Danica: Crossing the line.* New York: Simon & Schuster.

Patterson-Neubert, (2003). Experts say fairy tales not so happy ever after. Retrieved September 22, 2006, from http://www.purdue.edu/UNS/html4ever/031111.Grauerholz.tales.html

Patton, R. (n.d.) Maternity style. *San Antonio Express-News.*

Paul, P. (2005). *Pornified: How pornography is transforming our lives, our relationships, and our families.* New York: Owl Books.

Peisner, D. (2007). Hot Russian lesbian teen action! *Maxim Online.* Retrieved July 12, 2007, from http://www.maximonline.com/entertainment/reviews.aspx?p_id=10852

Phillips, K. (1993, January/February). How *Seventeen* undermines young women. *Media Awareness.* Retrieved August 9, 2005, from http://www.media-awareness.ca/english/resources/articles/gender_portrayal/seventeen.cfm

Photo galleries of pre-teen girls. (n.d.). Retrieved June 22, 2006, from http://www.mini-models.com

Pimp. (n.d.). Retrieved October 22, 2006, from http://en.wikipedia.org/wiki/pimp

Plans for dolls based on Pussycat Dolls canned: Hasbro decided the dolls were "inappropriate" for the company to market. (2006, May 24). *MSNBC.* Retrieved August 19, 2006, from http://www.msnbc.msn.com/id/12959770/

Playboy. (n.d.). Retrieved March 17, 2006, from http://www.playboy.com

Plot summary for the documentary *Living Dolls: The making of a child beauty queen.* (2001). Retrieved May 8, 2005, from http://www.imdb.com/title/tt0285298

Plot summary for the movie *Barbarella.* (n.d.). Retrieved June 10, 2006, from http://imdb.com/find?s=all&q=barbarella

Plot summary for the television show *Undressed* (2002). Retrieved June 10, 2006, from http://www.imdb.com/title/tt0190106

Plot summary for the television show *V.I.P.* (1998). Retrieved June 10, 2006, from http://www.imdb.com/title/tt0134269/

Pollet, A., & Hurwitz, P. (2003, Jan. 12). Strip till you drop. *The Nation.* Retrieved September 22, 2006, from http://www.thenation.com/doc/20040112/pollet/3

Popkin, H. A. S. (2006, March 5). "It's hard out here" for a good Oscar song. *MSNBC.* Retrieved August 19, 2006, from http://www.msnbc.msn.com/id/11593167/page/2/

Porn mag sales going limp. (2003, Nov. 11). *Wired.* Retrieved September 22, 2006, from http://www.wired.com/news/business/0,1367,61165,00.html

Product description for *The Real World* hook-ups. (2003). Retrieved August 8, 2006, from http://www.amazon.com/Real-World-Hook-Ups-MTV/dp/B0000CABJN

Prosser, A. (1998, August 15). New reader rifs on political correctness. Retrieved May 8, 2006, from http://www.likesbooks.com/readrif3.html

Pussycat Dolls. (n.d.). Retrieved July 15, 2007, from http://en.wikipedia.org/wiki/Pussycat_Dolls

Quart, A. (2003). *Branded: The buying and selling of teenagers.* Perseus Publishing.

Quotes from Polly Tix in Washington. (n.d.). Retrieved September 4, 2005, http://www.imdb.com/title/tt0023348/quotes

Racism is to be expected from Don Imus. (2007, April 9). Retrieved April 16, 2007, from http://www.fair.org/index.php?page=3082

Ransford, M. (1997, Feb. 17). Professor says beauty pageants aren't for kids. Ball State University NewsCenter. Retrieved August 19, 2006, from http://www.bsu.edu/news/article/0,1370,-1019-260,00.html

Razdan, A. (2004, April 22). The chick lit challenge. *Utne Magazine.* Retrieved August 9, 2005, from http://www.chicklit.us/News.htm

Real Sex. (2003). HBO [Television Broadcast.]

Real World (n.d.). Retrieved August 8, 2006, from http://en.wikipedia.org/wiki/The_Real_World

Red Ninja. (n.d.). Retrieved June 22, 2006, from http://en.wikipedia.org/wiki/Red_Ninja:_End_Of_Honor

Reid, S. (2007, April 13). Hip-hop on the defensive after Imus incident; Sharpton calls for "dialogue" with MCs. Retrieved April 17, 2007, from http://www.mtv.com/news/articles/1557094/20070413/index.jhtml

Reitman, J. (2006, June 1). Sex & scandal at Duke. *RollingStone.* Retrieved August 8, 2006, from http://www.rollingstone.com/news/story/10464110/sex__scandal_at_duke/4

Reynolds, S. (1996). *The sex revolts.* Harvard University Press.

Riley, S. (n.d.). Too few animated women break the Disney mold. Media Awareness Network. Retrieved September 22, 2006, from http://www.media-awareness.ca/english/resources/articles/gender_portrayal/break_mold.cfm

Rimer, S. (2007, April 1). For girls, it's be yourself, and be perfect, too. *New York Times.* Retrieved July 6, 2007, from http://www.nytimes.com/2007/04/01/education/01girls.html?ex=1333080000&en=f6763bfc6a421fb6&ei=5088&partner=rssnyt&emc=rss

Risky Business description (n.d.). Retrieved July 14, 2007, from http://www.cduniverse.com/productinfo.asp?pid=1261901

Rob Zicari. (n.d.) Retrieved June 22, 2006, from http://en.wikipedia.org/wiki/Rob_Zicari#Obscenity_prosecution.

Ronai, C. R., & Ellis, C. (1989). Turn-ons for money: Interactional strategies of the table dancer. *Journal of Contemporary Ethnography* 18:271-298.

Rosenberg, M. (2007, May 12). The naked truth: Beard not hurting sports. *FOX Sports.* Retrieved May 27, 2007, from http://msn.foxsports.com/other/story/6796300

Rushkoff, D. (2001). *Merchants of cool* [video]. WGBH Educational Foundation

Ruth Handler—Barbie's mom. (n.d.). *Goodbye Magazine.* Retrieved September 22, 2006, from http://www.goodbyemag.com/apr02/handler.html

Ryan, T. (1999, May 17). Fo' real?. *Star-Bulletin*. Retrieved May 8, 2006, from http://star-bulletin.com/1999/05/17/features/story1.html

St. James, I. (2006). *Bunny tales: Behind closed doors at the playboy mansion*. Philadelphia, PA: Running Press Books.

Salerno, S. (2005). *Sham: How the self help movement made America helpless*. New York: Three Rivers Press.

Samuels, A. P. (2003, March 10). Pushing hot buttons and wings. *St. Petersburg Times*, p. 1A. Retrieved June 12, 2006, from http://irreverent-antisocial-intellectual.blog spot.com/2006/06/things-that-are-pissing-me-off-today.html

Santich, K. (2004, March 15). Sweating to the oddities. *Orlando Sentinel*.

Sauer, A. (2004). *Girls Gone Wild*: Milking it. Retrieved August 19, 2006, from http://www.brandchannel.com/features_profile.asp?pr_id=178

Scaramouch (2006, November 23). Top ten lady liplocks: YouTube edition. Retrieved February 4, 2007, from http://www.yesbutnobutyes.com/archives/2006/11/top_ten_lady_li.html

Schabe, P. (2000). The great whoredom. Retrieved July 14, 2007, from http://www.popmatters.com/tv/reviews/w/who-wants-to-marry-a-millionaire.html

Schneider, J. (2004, March 8). Chick-lit: Decrying women novelists—Can't say I blame you! Retrieved September 22, 2006, from http://www.cosmoetica.com/B135-JAS2.htm.

Schools race to restrict MySpace. (2005, October) *Curriculum Review*. Retrieved July 12, 2007, from http://www.highbeam.com/doc/1G1-137755310.html

Schwyer, H. (2006, May 17). Thinking about women, sports, and hazing. Retrieved August 8, 2006, from http://hugoboy.typepad.com/hugo_schwyzer/2006/05/theres_been_a_f.html.

Scott, D. A. (2003). *Behind the g-string*. Jefferson, NC: McFarland & Company.

Sex buying into sexy: The sexing up of tweens. (2005, January 9). *CBC Marketplace*. Retrieved August 19, 2006, from http://www.cbc.ca/consumers/market/files/money/sexy/marketing.html

Sex and relationships in the media. (n.d.). Retrieved August 19, 2006, from http://www.mediaawareness.ca/english/issues/stereotyping/women_and_girls/women_sex.cfm

Sex sells: Marketing and age compression. (2005, January 9). *CBC Marketplace*. Retrieved August 19, 2006, from http://www.cbc.ca/consumers/market/files/money/sexy/

Sexual abuse prevention. (2005). Retrieved May 8, 2006, from http://loveourchildren usa.org/

Sexualization of girls is linked to common mental health problems in girls and women—Eating disorders. (2007, February 19). *Women's Health*. Retrieved March 3, 2007, from http://www.medicalnewstoday.com/medicalnews.php?newsid=63367

Shallit, W. (2000). *Return to modesty*. New York: Free Press.

Shapira, I. (2006, September 27). Teens' T-shirts make educators squirm: Suggestive messages challenge dress codes. *Washington Post*, p. 01. Retrieved August 19, 2006, from http://www.washingtonpost.com/wp-dyn/content/article/2006/09/26/AR 2006092601489.html

Shaw, R. (2005). How male fantasies now define female "empowerment." Retrieved March 8, 2006, from http://www.beyondchron.org/news/index.php?itemid=1338

Shellenbarger, S. (2006, March 17). Helicopter parents now hover at the office. *The Wall Street Journal Online*. Retrieved July 12, 2007, from http://www.career journal.com/columnists/workfamily/20060317-workfamily.html

Shen, F. (2002, February 17). Barbie, Bratz and age compression. *The Washington Post*. Retrieved August 1, 2005, from http://george.loper.org/trends/2002/Feb/73.html.

Shenfeld, H. (2007, March). Rules of attraction. *MSNBC*. Retrieved April 4, 2007, from http://www.msnbc.msn.com/id/17407419/

Shirley Temple. (2005). Retrieved February 11, 2007, from http://www.bbc.co.uk/dna/h2g2/A3682316

Short story submissions. (2006). Retrieved August 8, 2006, from http://www.eroticauthorsassociation.com/html/circletcall.html

Showbiz moms and dads. (2004). Retrieved April 23, 2004, from http://www.fansofrealitytv.com/forums/showthread.php?t=28058

Silverman, V. (2005, April 11). Retrieved August 19, 2006, from http://www.mindfully.org/Health/2005/Breast-Implant-FDA-Hearing11apr05.htm

Simple Life 4 to feature Paris and Nicole as "surrogate mothers" (2005, September 29). Retrieved September 22, 2006, from http://www.realitytvworld.com/index/articles/story.php?s=1004835

Skipper, J. K., & McCaghy, C. (1970). Stripteasers: The anatomy and career contingencies of a deviant occupation. *Social Problems* 17:391–405.

Slack, D. (2005, March 3). Milton Academy cites more sex cases: Parents to be told of a third episode. *Boston Globe*. Retrieved August 22, 2006, from http://news.bostonherald.com/forums/index.php?board=5;action=display;threadid=11749

Slade, J. W. (2000). *Pornography in America: A reference handbook*. Santa Barbara, CA: ABC-Clio Inc.

Smith, N. (2004, May 24). Show-stealer Madonna on tour. *BBC*. Retrieved July 15, 2007, from http://news.bbc.co.uk/1/hi/entertainment/music/3704915.stm

Smith, S. J. (2002). College-aged viewers love them, advertisers are leery of them, but reality dating shows are undeniably hot. *Young Money*. Retrieved August 1, 2005, from http://www.youngmoney.com/entertainment/television/030716_02

So you'd like to ... Comic book movie heroines wear boots! (n.d.). Retrieved August 19, 2006, from http://www.amazon.com/exec/obidos/tg/guides/guide-display/-/EKR6E77R9QY5/102-0324139-5348953

Spain, W. (2007, February 13). *Playboy* profit slumps almost 20%. *Market Watch*. Retrieved February 13, 2007, from http://www.marketwatch.com/news/story/playboy-profit-slumps-magazines-tv/story.aspx?guid=%7BA555332A-C6D9-4C34-8DC9-425B3768B40F%7D

Spousal rape laws: 20 years later from victim policy pipeline. (2004.) National Center for Victims of Crime. Retrieved August 19, 2006, from http://www.ncvc.org/ncvc/main.aspx?dbName=DocumentViewer&DocumentID=32701

Springen, K. (2006, April 27). Gender equality: Young women are catching up with their male counterparts when it comes to alcohol—often to disastrous effect. *Newsweek*. Retrieved August 19, 2006, from http://www.msnbc.msn.com/id/12468058/site/newsweek/

Stanley, A. (2004, January 16). Women having sex, hoping men tune in. *New York Times*. Retrieved July 19, 2007, from http://query.nytimes.com/gst/fullpage.html?res=9B01E1D71130F935A25752C0A9629C8B63

Steffans, K. (2005). *Confessions of a video vixen*. New York: Amistad.

Stein, R. (2005, March 27). Pharmacists' rights at front of new debate because of beliefs: Some refuse to fill birth control prescriptions. *Washington Post*, p. A01. Retrieved August 1, 2005, from http://www.washingtonpost.com/ac2/wp-dyn/A5490-2005Mar27?language=printer

Steve Kardian gives advice to *Inside Edition* on dangers of foam parties. (n.d.). Women's Self Defense Institute. Retrieved November 9, 2006, from http://www.rapeescape.com/foam.htm

Stratton-Coulter, D. (2006, August 19). Are underage foam parties good, clean fun? *The Gazette* (Colorado Springs). Retrieved November 9, 2006, from http://www.findarticles.com/p/articles/mi_qn4191/is_20060819/ai_n16674933

Stubbs, D. (1999, June 14). Gender equity: *Sports Illustrated* swimsuit issue. Canadian

Association for the Advancement of Women and Sport and Physical Activity. Retrieved August 8, 2006, from http://www.caaws.ca/e/gender_equity/article. cfm?id=225, 1999.

Suicide girls. (n.d.). Retrieved August 19, 2006, from http://en.wikipedia.org/wiki/Suicide Girls

Summers, V. J. (2007, May 16). Sorority dumps 23 "ugly" sisters. *WOAI*. Retrieved August 19, 2006, from http://www.woai.com/news/local/story.aspx?content_id= 795b26f8-456c-4ca1-98e3-2513127408f8

Sweney, M. (2006). The rise and rise of YouTube. *Media Guardian*. Retrieved November 3, 2006, from http://technology.guardian.co.uk/news/story/0,,1834036,00.html

Swift, E.M. (2005, June 6). Danica Patrick, fourth at Indy, was still a big winner. *Sports Illustrated*, p. 102 (23). Retrieved July 18, 2005, from http://dynamic.si.cnn.com/ si_online/covers/issues/2005/0606.html

Sybian for women. (2007). Retrieved July 13, 2007, from http://www.sybian.com/

Sydney Bristow. (2006). Retrieved August 8, 2006, from http://www.alias-tv.com/sydney.html

Taglines for Pretty Woman. (1990). Retrieved July 16, 2007, from http://imdb.com/ title/tt0100405/taglines

Tam, K. (2005, August 9). More curves hit pages of women's magazines. MSNBC. Retrieved July 13, 2007, from http://www.msnbc.msn.com/id/8886240/

Taormino, T. (2000, October 31). Pucker up: Organizing jizz joints. *Village Voice*. Retrieved August 8, 2006, from http://www.villagevoice.com/issues/0043/ taormino.php

Taylor, C. (2004, August 25). Review of the book *How to make love like a porn star*. Salon. Retrieved September 22, 2006, from http://dir.salon.com/story/books/review/ 2004/08/25/jenna/index_np.html

Teen breast implants. (2005). Retrieved July 12, 2007, from http://www.aboardcertified plasticsurgeonresource.com/breast_implants/teen.html

Things that are pissing me off today. (2006, June 12). Retrieved August 8, 2006, from http://irreverent-antisocial-intellectual.blogspot.com/2006/06/.html

Tiara girls. (2006). Retrieved August 8, 2006, from http://www.mtv.com/ontv/dyn/ tiara_girls/series.jhtml

Tomb Raider. (n.d.). Retrieved June 22, 2006, from http://en.wikipedia.org/wiki/ Tomb_Raider

Top ten reasons I hate lesbian porn. (2005, February 13). Retrieved August 8, 2006, from http://monkeyfilter.com/link.php/7336

Traister, R. (2004, June 18). Bridezilla bites back! *Salon*. Retrieved September 22, 2006, from http://dir.salon.com/story/mwt/feature/2004/06/18/bridezilla/index.html

Twenge, J. M. (2006). *Generation me: Why today's young Americans are more confident, assertive, entitled and more miserable than ever before*. New York: Simon & Schuster.

Ulibas, J. P. (2004, July 6). The weird and wild world of Ken Russell: An interesting retort to *Pretty Woman*. Retrieved July 14, 2007, from http://www.imdb.com/title/ tt0103253/usercomments

Ultimate Coyote Ugly search. (n.d.). Retrieved December 10, 2006, from http:// www.cmt.com/shows/dyn/ultimate_coyote_ugly_search/series.jhtml

Ultimate superheroes, villains, and vixens. (2005). *Bravo* [Television broadcast].

Uncensored video chat (2007, July 12). Retrieved July 12, 2007, from http://incredible-cam.com

Upper School dress code. (n.d.). Retrieved July 14, 2007, from http://www.savcds. org/admissions/admissions_faq.html

Vemartin (2005). Review of the movie *Leaving Las Vegas*. Retrieved August 19, 2006, from http://search.reviews.ebay.com/Leaving-Las-Vegas.

Vernon, P. (2005, July 10). Skank chic. *The Observer.* Retrieved September 29, 2005, from http://www.thefashionspot.com/forums/f49/skank-chic-28713.html

Wang, A. L. (2006, May 23). Teen blog watch is on. *Chicago Tribune.* Retrieved August 19, 2006, from http://www.chicagotribune.com/news/local/nearwest/chi-0605230128 may23,1,3081331.story?coll=chi-newslocalnearwest-hed&ctrack=1&cset=true

Warn, S. (2003). VMA's Madonna-Britney-Christina kiss: Progress or publicity stunt? Retrieved July 14, 2006, from http://www.afterellen.com/TV/vmakiss.html

Webb, C. (n.d.). Hookers for heaven. Retrieved July 20, 2007, from http://www.free-thinkerscs.com/articles/hookers.html

Weisstuch, L. (2005, January 12). Sexism in rap sparks black magazine to say, "Enough!" *The Christian Science Monitor.* Retrieved April 17, 2007, from http://www.csmonitor.com/2005/0112/p11s01-almp.html

Weitz, K. (2007). I prefer underage girls. *The Sun.* Retrieved July 15, 2007, from http://www.thesun.co.uk/article/0,,2003061831,00.html

We keep our site clean! (n.d.). Retrieved May 26, 2006, from http://www.child supermodels.com

Welcome to Pimpfants. (n.d.). Retrieved July 14, 2007, from http://www.pimpfants.com/about_us.asp

Welcome to the original coed party site! (n.d.). Retrieved July 12, 2007, from http://nebraskacoeds.com

What are the dangers of anal sex? (2007). Retrieved July 16, 2007, from http://www.soc.ucsb.edu/sexinfo/?article=faq&refid=125

What not to wear to an interview. (2006). *Career Builders.* Retrieved December 3, 2006, from http://www.careerbuilder.com/JobSeeker/careerbytes/CBArticle.aspx?article ID=462

When metal ruled the world. (2003). *VH1.* [Television broadcast.]

Why sports participation for girls and women: The foundation position. (2000, August 14). Retrieved August 7, 2005, from http://www.womenssportsfoundation.org/cgi-bin/iowa/issues/body/article.html?record=577

Williams, P. (2006, February 3). MySpace, Facebook attract online predators. *MSNBC.* Retrieved August 19, 2006, from http://www.msnbc.msn.com/id/11165576/

Williams, S. (2006). Dressing the part. WGHB Educational Foundation. Retrieved January 3, 2007, from http://www.pbs.org/wgbh/amex/eleanor/sfeature/fashion_1.html

Winfrey, O. (2003, May 27). The Glenbrook North hazing incident. *The Oprah Winfrey Show.* Retrieved March 10, 2005, from http://www.oprah.com/tows/past-shows/200305/tows_past_20030527_b.jhtml

Winfrey, O. (2006a, April 24). Healing mothers, healing daughters. *The Oprah Winfrey Show.* Retrieved December 8, 2006, from http://www.oprah.com/tows/slide/200604/20060424/slide_20060424_284_102.jhtml

Winfrey, O. (2006b, April 10). Smart women on "stupid girls." *The Oprah Winfrey Show.* Retrieved December 8, 2006, from http://www.oprah.com/tows/slide/200604/20060410/slide_20060410_350_105.jhtml

Winfrey, O. (2007, April 16). After Imus: Now what? *The Oprah Winfrey Show.* Retrieved April 17, 2007, from http://www.oprah.com/tows/pastshows/200704/tows_past_20070416.jhtml

Wolf, N. (2003, October 20). The porn myth. *New York Metro.* Retrieved August 19, 2006, from http://newyorkmetro.com/nymetro/news/trends/n_9437/index.html

Women in sports. (n.d.). Retrieved July 14, 2007, from http://www.sports-wired.com/women/

Women's erotic wrestling. (n.d.). Retrieved October 4, 2002, from http://www.wextremew.com

Wong, G. (2005, May 20). Ka-ching! Wedding price tag nears $30K. *CNN*. Retrieved September 22, 2006, from http://money.cnn.com/2005/05/20/pf/weddings/

Yaeger, D., & Pressler, M. (2007). *It's not about the truth: The untold story of the Duke lacrosse rape case and the lives it shattered.* New York: Simon & Schuster/Threshold.

Young, C. (2006, May 28). The great Girls Gone Wild scare: Is oral sex really the latest teen? *Chicago Sun-Times*. Retrieved August 19, 2006, from http://www.findarticles.com/p/articles/mi_qn4155/is_20060528/ai_n16435205

Youngblood, M. (2006, June 6). Mixed media: Images of female athletes. Retrieved August 8, 2006, from http://www.womenssportsfoundation.org/cgi-bin/iowa/issues/media/article.html?record=1097

You think I'm kidding about the dress code? (2006, August 28). MSNBC. Retrieved October 12, 2006, from http://www.msnbc.msn.com/id/14549938/from/RS.3/

Zeynep, T. (2004, August 24). Beach volleyball. Retrieved August 8, 2006, from http://www.underthesamesun.org/content/2004/08/beach_volleybal.html

Zillmann, D., & Bryant, J. (1988). Effects of prolonged consumption of pornography on family values. *Journal of Family Issues, 9,* 518–544.

INDEX